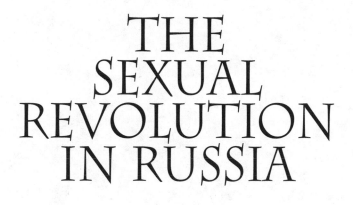

# THE SEXUAL REVOLUTION IN RUSSIA

# THE
# SEXUAL
# REVOLUTION
# IN RUSSIA

*From the Age of the Czars to Today*

# IGOR S. KON

*Translated by James Riordan*

THE FREE PRESS

NEW YORK   LONDON   TORONTO   SYDNEY   TOKYO   SINGAPORE

The Free Press
A Division of Simon & Schuster, Inc.
866 Third Avenue, New York, N. Y. 10022

Printed in the United States

printing number
1   2   3   4   5   6   7   8   9   10

**Library of Congress Cataloging-in-Publication Data**

Kon, Igor Semyonovich.
     The Sexual revolution in Russia: from the age of the czars
  to today/by Igor S. Kon: translated by James Riordan.
          p.   cm.
     Translated from the Russian.
     Includes index.
     ISBN 0–02–917541–0
     1. Sex customs—Russia (Federation)   2. Sex customs—Soviet Union.
3. Communism and sex—Soviet Union.   4. Russia (Federation)—Social
life and customs.   5. Soviet Union—Social life and customs.
I. Title.
HQ18.R9K66   1995
306.7'0947—dc20                                              94—49589
                                                                  CIP

# CONTENTS

# THE
# SEXUAL
# REVOLUTION
# IN RUSSIA

*Introduction*

# SEXUALITY AND REVOLUTION

I n 1986, at the beginning of perestroika, during one of the first Ameri-
can-Soviet television debates, a woman from Leningrad answered a
question from an American with the words, "We have no sex here."
The words immediately took on legendary status, vividly reflecting the
long-standing and official antisexuality stance of the Soviet regime. For several decades Soviet society hypocritically pretended to be absolutely asexual and even sexless, and from the early 1930s, the ruling Communist
Party systematically and ruthlessly eradicated everything related to sexuality, whether it was sex research, sex education, erotic art, or erotic literature. Repressive sexophobia was an integral part of maintaining totalitarian
control over individuality.

Was this crusade successful? The leaders of the failed 1991 coup
solemnly pledged to suppress "the cult of sex and violence" that had pur-
portedly arisen in Gorbachev's Soviet Union. Had the country really
changed since 1985, or simply, had the arcane become mundane? Are we
witnessing a belated sexual revolution, like that of the 1960s in the West,
or is the present situation a manifestation of social and cultural anarchy?
And how is the sexual behavior of yesterday and today related to traditional patterns of Russian eros? Was the sexophobia of the Bolsheviks a
denial of pre-Revolutionary sexual values or a continuation of them?

These are not rhetorical questions. Russian sexual life is still something
of a mystery. For Soviet scholars, the subject was absolutely taboo until
1991, and Western researchers had no access to the primary sources. Now
the situation has begun to change. The first two scholarly historical monographs, by Eve Levin[1] and Laura Engelstein[2] and a number of important
papers (by Laurie Bernstein, Wendy Goldman, Sheila Fitzpatrick, Simon
Karlinsky, Eric Naiman, Alexander Poznansky, Susan Gross Solomon,
Richard Stites, Elizabeth Wood, to name but a few) have been published,
and more are in preparation. Yet all this research is historical. The current
Russian sexual scene is described mainly by journalists, who do not offer
any serious historical or sociological analysis.[3] The first collection of professional papers by Russian and British scholars, *Sex and Russian Society*,

published in 1993,[4] covers such topics as sexuality and culture, patterns of birth control, sex in the movies, homosexuals and lesbians, beauty contests, young people's sexual behavior, and the state of Soviet medical sexology but makes no pretense to generalization.

So this book is a first, very preliminary attempt to provide an overview of the evolution and present state of Russian sexual culture as a whole, from a historical and sociological point of view. It is not about exotic "Soviet/Russian sex" but rather about the grandiose Soviet social experiment in shaping a new personality type.

The development of new sexual values, scripts, policies, and behaviors is related to all other aspects of social change. Sexual revolution is an integral part, and if you will, a mirror of social revolution. As Friedrich Engels justly noted, "the question of 'free love' comes to the fore in any large-scale revolutionary movement. For some it is revolutionary progress, liberation from the old traditional bonds that have ceased to be necessary; for others the eagerly accepted tenet is a convenient cover for all manner of free and easy relations between men and women."[5]

October 1917 was not an exception to this rule. The Bolshevik revolution was one of the most radical revolutions in history. It promised to change the entire structure of social life, to abolish all forms of inequality, to jump from the prehistory to the genuine history of humanity, and to transform not only society but human nature itself. The creation of a new socialist personality—rational, collectivistic, disciplined, and socially oriented—was the main goal of this thoroughgoing transformation.

Yet one of the obstacles to this glorious transformation was sexuality—irrational, individualistic, capricious, and spontaneous.

The history of the Soviet regime was one of sexual repression. Only the means of legitimation and phraseology of this suppression were changeable.

In the 1920s, sexuality had to be suppressed in the name of the higher interests of the working class and Socialist revolution. In the 1930s self-discipline was advocated not in the name of the proletariat but for the sake of the Soviet state and Communist Party. In the 1950s state-administrative control was gradually transformed into moral-administrative regulations, this time for the sake of stability of marriage and the family.

But with all these ideological differences, the practical message regarding sex remained the same: DON'T DO IT! The Communist image of sexuality was always negative and the need for strict external social control was always emphasized. The elimination of sexuality was beyond the abilities of the Soviet regime. But the net result of this sexophobia was a practical liquidation of all sorts of erotic culture and the prohibition of sexual discourse, whether in the area of sex research, erotic art, or medical information. All sexual activity, even marital sexual activity, was considered indecent and unmentionable, a subject only for the degenerate underground.

Painful and problematic aspects of sexual life, such as birth control, abortion, prostitution, marital infidelity, sexual promiscuity, homosexuality, sexually transmitted diseases, and so on, certainly did not disappear because of this conspiracy of silence. And a lot of new problems emerged. Enforced silence strengthened traditional hypocrisy, which, in turn, was easily transformed into cynicism. The lack of serious discussion about sex differences produced a fantastically sexist everyday consciousness as well as a host of misunderstandings and mutual recriminations between men and women. The absence of scientific sex education resulted in widespread sexual ignorance. There is also a growing generation gap in sexual values, attitudes, and behavior. And like confrontation of the country's economic and social problems, and those of ethnic and national identity, resolution of these burning issues was postponed for many decades.

As soon as the grip of the repressive regime was weakened, the beast began to break its chains. Sexual freedom became one of the most important aspects and symbols of social liberation. But just as the privatization of state property without preliminary accumulation of capital is common robbery—the Russian government simply gave former state property to its own corrupt officials, plant managers, and common criminals, without any compensation for law-abiding citizens—the liberalization of sexual morality without parallel development of an erotic culture produced a host of unpleasant and potentially dangerous phenomena.

In Russia now, there is a torrent of pornography and primitive erotica in the open market, but no sex education in the schools; and in a national public opinion survey conducted in 1992, only 13% of the respondents said that their parents had ever told them anything about sex. The most widespread means of birth control is induced abortion, the rate of which is higher than anywhere else in the world. The estimated average lifetime rate of five abortions per woman in 1982 was 6.5 times the rate of abortion in the United States and almost 13 times the British rate. In 1992, only 22% of fertile women used methods of controlled contraception, and fewer than 3% used modern hormonal contraceptives. In 1988, there were 166 induced abortions for every 100 live births in Russia; the number rose to 225 in 1992. Since 1988, the incidence of sexually transmitted diseases has risen rapidly, especially among minors; the incidence of syphilis in Russia in the last year has grown 3.5 times. The incidence of sexual violence is growing all across the country. Prostitution, the existence of which had been hypocritically denied, became one of the most prestigious occupations for women. The number of new marriages in Russia decreased by 20.3% from 1990 to 1992, while the number of divorces increased by 15%. Means of prevention of sexually transmitted disease, including AIDS, are grossly inadequate.

But what stands behind this terrible picture? Are these negative trends the continuation of the Communist past, as a natural outcome of repressive sexophobia? Or are they simply manifestations of the general social and economic disintegration of the country? Is the current situation a catastrophe, a challenge, or both? How are Soviet/Russian experiences related to similar problems in Western societies? What can we expect in the near and distant future?

To answer these questions—even to think about them in a meaningful way—we must begin with an historical prelude, going back to the time before the Communist regime was established.

Here, however, we face the problem of finding reliable data—notoriously difficult to come by in the area of sexuality. The problem is greatly complicated by the systematic Soviet policy of clamping down on sexuality. Until recently, data from pre-Revolutionary Russian sexual and erotic history were either officially classified or kept under lock and key, with even serious scholars denied easy access. Further, after the 1920s, a period rich in sociological studies and informative literature, Soviet data on sexuality became unreliable—if they existed at all. Thus, to present as realistic and detailed a portrait of Russian and Soviet sexual culture as possible, I have drawn from a wide variety of sources.

The first source is literary and scientific data taken from different disciplines—history, ethnography, demography, sociology, medical sexology, criminology, epidemiology, philosophy, literary criticism, history of the arts, and so on. These data are fragmentary, elusive, and of uneven quality. For example, Russian ethnography and anthropology have much more to tell us about sexual behavior and values than the much more conservative and underdeveloped science of social history. Journalistic reports are sometimes more informative and impressive than unreliable and often falsified official statistics. Among Russian researchers whose work was important to my own, I must mention my former student, the pioneer of Soviet empirical sex research, Professor Sergei Golod; the founding father of Russian historical demography, Professor Anatoly Vishnevsky; and, for information on abortion and contraception, Dr. Andrei Popov and Dr. Larissa Remennick (the latter now living in Israel).

A second major source is recent public opinion polls. Before 1990 nobody would have dared to ask the Soviet people about their sexual attitudes in a large-scale survey. But since 1990, the former All-Union, now Russian, Center for Public Opinion Research has surveyed the general population several times about their attitudes to sex education, erotica and pornography, marital values, love, premarital and extramarital sex, promiscuity, homosexuality, and even, in 1993, their sexual practices. As the center has been occupied by more pressing political issues, the results of these polls have never been published or analyzed in depth. Professor Urie Levada, the director of the center, kindly gave me the data and permission to use them in this book, and I am highly appreciative.

A third source is the first-ever Russian questionnaire on adolescent sexuality. This survey of 1,600 teenagers in Moscow and St. Petersburg was conducted in 1993 by Professor Vladimir Shapiro and Dr. Valery Chervyakov of the Institute of Sociology of the Russian Academy of Sciences; I am the scientific adviser of this project, which is now being continued involving different and larger samples, thanks to a grant given by the John D. and Catherine T. MacArthur Foundation. With these data, we can, for the first time in Russian history, assess some real shifts in adolescents' current sexual behavior and values. These data have been corroborated and supplemented, especially in the areas of rape and sexual abuse, by a study being conducted in St. Petersburg by a former student of mine, Dr. Igor Lunin; I am acting as the scientific adviser on this project as well.

Finally, in this book I also draw upon my personal history. To insert personal stories into a more or less scientific text is a risky business. Our memories are subjective, selective, egocentric, and often self-exalting. Yet the fact of the matter is that since the mid-1960s, I have been the organizer of or a participant in virtually all Soviet undertakings concerned with the study of gender and sexuality, as well as functioning as the most important conduit of information about Western research and ideas on these subjects for my country. Thus, my memory, for all its shortcomings, is perhaps a better source of information about Soviet sex research than any journalistic report—I can truly offer the "inside story."

But to make this claim credible, I must share something of myself and my career.

I came to study sexual issues to some extent against my will. Having been brought up in a puritanical atmosphere, with the usual sexual inhibitions, I had no intention of infringing upon societal taboos. My own personal questions had been fully satisfied in the 1950s when I came to read Theodore Van de Welde's 1928 classic, *The Ideal Marriage*. And in terms of scientific and philosophical theory and research, sexuality did not seem to me to be a worthy subject.

I received my first doctorates in 1950, in modern history and in philosophy, writing on, respectively, John Milton's political ideas and Nikolai Chernyshevsky's ethical theory. In 1959, I received a doctor of science degree for a book on the history of twentieth-century Western philosophy of history. In the early 1960s, I became one of the founding fathers of the new Soviet sciences of sociology and social psychology, publishing several books on the history of Western sociology, personality, and the self. In 1979, having become interested in the sociology and psychology of adolescence, I published the first Soviet textbook on adolescence in 50 years. When ideological pressures made continued studies in sociology impossible, I moved to the Institute of Ethnography and there initiated an historically comparative study of the anthropology of childhood.

My involvement in these diverse issues triggered my interest in the study of sex, gender, and sexuality. Back in the early 1960s, while researching my book *Positivism in Sociology*, I had read Alfred Kinsey's reports and some similar works, which I found very interesting. Having found something important, I was moved to share it with others. In 1966, I published my first article on these topics. My book *Sociology of Personality* (1967) contained a few pages on the sexual revolution and individual psychosexual development. My article "Sex, Society, and Culture," published in *Inostrannaya literatura* [*Journal of Foreign Literature*] (1970) was the first and, for many years, the only Soviet attempt to discuss these problems more or less seriously.

Despite my interest in these subjects, they were very much on the periphery of my primary work; if someone had told me that I would become "the leading Soviet [later Russian] sexologist," I would have laughed. However, it happened. My books *Introduction to Sexology* (1988) and *Tasting the Forbidden Fruit* (1992) are the only nonmedical books on sexuality available in Russia. And although I am not happy about it, I am involved in all public debates about sex research and education.

But to return to the matter at hand: what can the Western reader hope to gain from reading this book?

First, if my assumptions about sexuality as a reflection and model of social evolutionary and revolutionary processes are correct, the book may help readers to understand the nature and internal contradictions of the present Russian anti-Communist revolution. Its hopes and dangers, progressive and reactionary trends are more visible in debates over sexuality than many other issues.

Second, the history of Soviet sexophobia and its practical consequences may be instructive for Western conservatives. The Soviet case shows what can happen when the state tries to conceal or block so important a sphere of social and private life. The view through this lens may offer a valuable opportunity for reflection on such issues as abortion, contraception, and sex education in schools.

Third, the book contains specific information about prevalent aspects of contemporary Russian sexual and nonsexual culture—rules of etiquette, ideas of love, attitudes toward the body, and the images of masculinity and femininity. Thus it may be of some practical value for our expanding personal and business contacts.

I have tried to avoid technical detail and excessive references that are often designed more to demonstrate the author's erudition than to assist the reader. With only a few exceptions, the notes at the end of the book indicate only sources of direct quotation and fundamental research on which I rely and in which the professional reader will find further information.

*Part I*

# THE HISTORICAL PRELUDE

*Chapter One*

# SEX IN "HOLY RUSSIA"

*. . . "Sex . . . what's that? What we were always doing, or something new?"*

—Mikhail Zhvanetsky

As most historians must acknowledge, ideological stereotypes and insufficient knowledge strongly hinder the emergence of the truth. This is certainly the case with sexuality. Even in the West, it is only recently that a scientific history of sexuality has begun to emerge, given powerful intellectual impetus by Michel Foucault in 1976 and by the founding in 1990 of *The Journal of the History of Sexuality*.

Certain adherents of present-day "Russian social patriotism," as the fascists and national chauvinists coyly term themselves, claim that ancient, "primordial" Russia was a realm of utter spirituality in which "dirty sex" did not exist until, like drunkenness, it was imported by wicked foreigners, especially the Jews. But the historical record shows otherwise. Back in the seventeenth century, the Western European diplomat Adam Olearius noted with some astonishment that Russians frequently "talk of voluptuous disport, shameful vices, perversions, and love affairs concerning themselves and others; they tell all sorts of risqué stories, and the person who uses the foulest language and tells the most disgusting jokes accompanied by vulgar gestures is the one they regard as the best and most respected in the community."[1]

We have only a poor awareness of Russian sexual-erotic culture not because it did not exist but because first the czarist and subsequently the Soviet censor forbade publication of relevant sources and research. Some

early research studies of Russian proverbs and folktales were either published privately or published only abroad.[2] In post-perestroika Russia, the
first attempts to survey the history and offer an interpretation of "Russian
sex" began only in 1991.[3] It is hardly surprising, then, that knowledge of
Russian sexuality, despite the existence of no less rich primary sources
(chronicles, memoirs by foreign travelers, ethnographic descriptions, etc.)
than in the West, remains exceedingly fragmentary, and its interpretation
superficial.

Thus, some commentators "patriotically" aver that Ancient Rus had no
culture of sex or erotica, while others, equally "patriotic," claim that Russian erotica not only existed but was no different from erotica in Western
Europe. In my view, both these positions are erroneous.

The scientific, authoritative history of Russian sexuality is still to be
written, and it will be a very difficult task. One must take into account
particular *stages of historical* development: the basically prosexual nature of
ancient Slav paganism, the antisexual values of early Christianity, their
gradual adaptations to historical and cultural realities, the subsequent secularization of sexuality in the transition from feudal to capitalist society
and from a rural to an urban way of life, and so on. Nor can one ignore
the enormous *geographical and regional differences* between central Russia
and the provinces, the north and the south, the towns and the villages.
Even more important are *social class and cultural differences* between feudal
nobility, rural gentry, clergy, peasantry, industrial workers, small business-
men and the petite bourgeoisie, and the intelligentsia. Important differences between *religious, moral, and cultural values*, everyday *social norms
and attitudes*, and *practical sexual behaviors* are omnipresent. Finally, the
*institutional and symbolic contexts* of these phenomena should not be over-
looked: marriage and family relationships, basic elements of gender stratification, traits of a community lifestyle, moral values, normative standards
of reproductive behavior, specific modes of gender socialization, forms of
social control over personality, and so on. All these contexts are interrelated but different.

Until such sociologically sophisticated comparative historical research
is done, any generalizations about the cultural specificity of the Russian
eros will inevitably remain unreliable and speculative. Nevertheless, I shall
offer three hypothetical suggestions.

First, the contrast between the official "high" culture, sanctified by the
church and antisexual by its very nature, and the "low," everyday culture of
the common people, in which sexuality was accorded a positive value, was
considerably greater in medieval Russia than in the West.

Second, refined and elegant erotic art came into being and gained acceptance much later in Russia than in the West. And it is only through the medium of erotic art that sexuality can be included in "high" culture at all.

Third, the development of civilized forms of everyday social life (what the German sociologist Norbert Elias calls "the civilizing process") was in early modern Russia more closely associated with the state than with civil society. Because new rules of propriety were often introduced by the political authorities, there was more pressure toward the uniformity of everyday conduct than toward individualization and diversification; and without established and reasonably diverse subcultures there can be no basis for normative pluralism, one manifestation of which is sexual tolerance. Sexual dissidence was seen as a form of political opposition.

These three factors are interconnected historically and functionally. According to the great Russian historian Vasily Klyuchevsky, the most constant, fundamental trait of Russian history was its extensivity: "The history of Russia is the history of a country in the process of constant colonization. The area of this colonization expanded together with the territory of the Russian state."[4]

Because of this ongoing territorial expansion, the process of Christianization of Russia, stretching over several centuries and all the while involving new nationalities and peoples, was in many ways inadequate and superficial. In popular beliefs, ceremonies, and customs, Christian norms not only coexisted with pagan norms but frequently incorporated them.[5]

Paganism was a particularly strong influence in matters of love and sex. As late as the first half of the nineteenth century, Russian peasants continued to rely on "spells" in regard to love: the St. Petersburg historian Boris Mironov made a quantitative analysis of 372 spells popular among the peasants and found that for every 6 love spells with a Christian attribute, there were 25 pagan and 2 that combined both—that is, 82% of all love spells were either directly pagan or had pagan elements.[6]

The Russian Orthodox Church was incapable of vanquishing the innumerable and immensely varied vestiges of paganism, so it had either to incorporate them or turn a blind eye to them. Therefore, it sometimes appears more "realistic" and tolerant than Roman Catholicism, on, for example, such issues as the celibacy of the clergy. At the same time, the concessions the church made to ineradicable "naturalistic" habits of peasant life and conceptions of human nature were balanced and even overcompensated for by an intensified spiritualism and otherworldly asceticism in church doctrine itself, thus encouraging the idea of a near fanatical spirituality as unique to Russian culture. The contradiction between the "high" culture's supreme spirituality and utter disregard for the life of the body and the "low" culture's insistence on the inescapable reality of natural life runs like a thread through the entire history of Russian culture.

Russian Orthodox believers, like all Christians, believed that sex and everything associated with it was the handiwork of Satan, although there was some ambiguity about its relation to procreation. In medieval iconography, Adam and Eve were typically depicted without sexual attributes in Paradise, before the Fall; symbols of masculinity and femininity appear only after the Fall. In Russian icon painting, the most important symbol of sexual desire was large, pendulous breasts. An adulterous male was sometimes depicted with large breasts, as was the Serpent-tempter. Later, the woman was usually portrayed as a dangerous source of temptation; one folktale showed woman as capable of tempting and outwitting even the devil. A good, decent-living woman had to be absolutely asexual.

High value was placed on chastity (the Russian word *tselomudrie* means literally "intact wisdom") and retention of virginity, even within marriage. For instance, according to his "vita," Saint Dmitri Donskoi, an entirely historical figure, and his wife, the Princess Avdotia, managed without carnal relations—which did not, however, prevent them from producing several children.

Within Russian canon law, as within every Christian culture, sexuality was officially sanctioned only when there had been a lawful church wedding and when sexual relations were employed exclusively "for the sake of begetting progeny" and not "for succumbing to weakness." Even then, sexual intimacy was regarded as a profanity, which literally had to be washed away. A man who had not washed himself below the waist after the sexual act did not dare to enter a church or kiss sacred relics, and a menstruating woman was not supposed to have sexual relations with her husband, or go to church, or receive communion. There were prohibitions and penances prescribed for nocturnal emissions and erotic dreams, for failure to refrain from sexual congress on certain days (Fridays, Saturdays, Sundays, church festivals, and fast days), for indulging in incorrect sexual positions or with the wrong partner, married or unmarried (of course, the penalties varied immensely).

The only "correct" sexual position was what has since been called the "missionary" position, with the woman lying on her back and the man on top. This position was called "on the horse" (*na kone*), and it emphasized the domination of man over woman in bed, as in everyday life. The "woman on top" position, by contrast, was regarded, as in the West, as "a great sin" and a challenge "to the image of God," and was punished, according to most penitential codes, by a penance of between three and ten years, with innumerable daily prostrations. Entry from behind was also forbidden, inasmuch it was considered "cattle-like" or to resemble homosexual contacts. No distinction was made between vaginal and anal entry from behind, both being sins worthy of 600 prostrations, or even worse, excommunication. Church authorities took into consideration specific circumstances: how frequently the sinful position was adopted, who had initiated it, and whether the wife had participated willingly or under duress. Young couples under the age of 30 were normally treated leniently, but older couples suffered harsher penalties.

Nongenital caresses, like deep kissing, were also considered sinful, yet they were punished relatively lightly: by 12 days of fasting. (One Russian penitential calls this "Tatar" kissing, although it was well known in Rus long before the Tatar-Mongol invasion.) Were the husband to put his finger, hand, foot, or an item of clothing into his wife's vagina, the punishment would be three weeks of fasting. Fellatio and cunnilingus were more serious sins meriting from two to three years of fasting, virtually the same penalty as for adultery or incest.

The concept of "sodomy" in Ancient Rus[7] was even vaguer than it was in the West, designating both homosexual relations and heterosexual anal intercourse, as well as any deviations from "normal" sexual roles and partners—for example, intercourse in the "woman-on-top" position. The most serious sin in this respect was "male lechery" (*muzhebludie*) or "male fornication" (*muzhelozhstvo*), when coitus with the "wrong" sexual partner was compounded by the "wrong" sexual position (anal penetration). Rus was more tolerant toward this "vice" than the West; church punishment for it varied between one and seven years—i.e., within the same parameters set for heterosexual transgressions. The punishment depended on the sinner's age, his marital status, how often he had indulged in it, and the extent of his own active involvement. The penalties for juveniles and young men were more lenient than for married men. If no anal penetration had taken place, reference was no longer made to "male fornication" but to masturbation (the Greek *malakia* or the Russian *rukobludie*, meaning "hand abuse").

Lesbianism was usually categorized as a form of masturbation. In the twelfth century in Novgorod, Bishop Nifont regarded sexual contact between two juvenile girls as a lesser sin than heterosexual "lechery," especially if maidenhood remained intact. The Orthodox Church was very concerned about homosexuality spreading in the monasteries, yet it was fairly tolerant of its practice in everyday life.

Almost all foreign travelers and diplomats in Russia during the fifteenth through seventeenth centuries remarked on the widespread occurrence of homosexuality in all social milieus, and the surprisingly tolerant—by European standards—attitude toward it. The English poet George Turberville, who visited Moscow as part of a diplomatic mission in 1568, was struck more forcibly by the frank homosexuality of Russian peasants than he was by Ivan the Terrible's executions.[8]

As the Croatian Catholic priest Jurai Krizhanitch, who lived in Russia from 1659 to 1677, wrote, "here in Russia they simply joke about that disgusting crime, and nothing is more publicly talked about in light-hearted banter: some laud it as a sin, others rebuke the rest, still others dare people to sin; all that remains is for someone to commit the crime in full public view."[9]

This probably came less from conscious tolerance than from indifference and a naturalistic acceptance of the "facts of life." The same trend existed in the early Middle Ages in Western Europe; it was only much later that the persecution and bonfires of the Inquisition flared up. Whatever the case, homosexuality was neither mentioned nor punished in any Russian legislation from the time of Yaroslav the Wise to Peter the Great. It was only in 1706 that punishment for "unnatural lechery" first appeared in Peter the Great's military code, which was composed on the Swedish model. Yet ten years later, Peter, himself not adverse to bisexual relations, watered down the punishment, replacing burning at the stake with lifelong exile—and that only for military personnel, not the civilian population.

Marital fidelity was the principal family virtue, especially for women. In Ancient Rus, a man was branded an adulterer if he had children from an extramarital liaison, whereas the wife stood so accused for any such affair, whether or not children were the result. Motherhood was glorified and romanticized in lore and literature, since the birth and upbringing of children constituted the social and spiritual raison d'être of marriage, which took place early, and at the will of parents, not of the young marriage partners. A major reason for early marriage was to preserve chastity. Since parents were held responsible for premarital sex or loss of virginity by their children, it was not uncommon for parents to pledge and marry their children in their early teens—although both new spouses might then return to their own homes until they came of age.

The Orthodox Church punished sexual violence and rape severely, standing implacably against the idea of dismissing rape as merely a form of lechery or adultery, as was the practice in some other countries; in Russia, a woman's "honor" was taken more seriously. The Russian Orthodox

Church, as was the case in medieval Christianity generally, played an important positive role in mollifying and civilizing sexual mores and relations between men and women.

Medieval Rus society had strict norms and regulations regarding sexuality. But we must ask whether these norms and regulations were enforced, and how their observance changed over time.

Whatever the picture painted by lore and literature, in reality, peasant customs were contradictory and ambivalent. On the one hand, the village community prized virginity highly, sometimes extending the demand from the bride to the bridegroom as well. If the bride (the literal meaning of the Russian word for bride, *nevesta*, is *nevedomaya*, "unknown person") was found not to be intact on her wedding night—and it was practically impossible to hide anything like this from the village censor—the marriage could be annulled. On the other hand, in Russia, as in many other countries of Europe, there were also customs and norms in which one can trace the vestiges of group or trial marriage. The institutionalized forms of group social life among the young—*posidelki, posedki* (sitting together), *besedki* (talking together), *vecherki* (evening gatherings), *igrishcha* (group games), *vecherniytsl* (the Ukrainian "evening assemblies")—not only permitted but in fact required a certain liberty of behavior and speech, to the point where a *devushka* (maiden) who put up too much resistance drew attention to herself and licentious jokes, and might even be excluded from the assembly.[10]

In the Ukraine in the nineteenth century, there was the custom of *podnochovyvanie* (spending the night together), when a young man, and sometimes even two or three young men, would remain with the maiden until morning. Although they were supposed to be preserving her virginity, in practice, that depended on their individual attitudes. What was strictly forbidden was the maiden's liaison with a young man from another village. *Podnochovyvanie* is unknown in Russian villages; any sexual intimacy that might occur would be kept a secret, although friends of the young pair would frequently know about it.[11]

At the turn of the twentieth century, in the Russian north one could still find the custom of *skakaniya*, or "galloping," which took place on the eve of the wedding ceremony in the groom's house; all the young guests would stand in a circle, resting their arms on one another's shoulders and galloping, kicking their legs up high, the maidens lifting up their skirts, and all of them singing blatantly erotic songs. This group carousing would end with them all sleeping side by side. There was also the custom of *yarovukha* (from Yarilo, the pagan god of fertility), a gathering of young people at the bride's home for a party, after which they would remain to sleep side by side, with every liberty save the final intimacy being permitted.[12]

Some Russian peasant communities were relatively tolerant of premarital sex and liaisons. One nineteenth-century folklorist cited a whole list of common statements from Vologda province: "Before he marries, a bachelor has two or three children from different mothers," "Of ten marriages, only one involves a pure maiden." "In most parts of the province," he noted, "no one pays strict attention to a maiden's chastity. Having a child may get her married quicker—it means she won't be infertile, and infertility is always ascribed to the wife."[13] But generally, "illegitimate" births were rare, making up, in the late nineteenth century, only some 2% of all births in European Russia overall.[14]

There were other clashes of normative canon and social reality. For instance, substantial dispute surrounds the subject of Russian carnivals. In medieval Western Europe, carnivals served as a sort of bridge between "high" and "low" culture. Carnival, as described by the eminent Russian scholar Mikhail Bakhtin, is "not a spectacle seen by the people; they live in it and everyone participates because its very idea embraces all the people. While carnival lasts, there is no other life outside it. During carnival time life is subject only to its laws, that is, the laws of its own freedom."[15]

In Russia, as the linguists Yuri Lotman and Boris Uspensky show,[16] there was a greater measure of reservation and social control. Distinguished persons, especially clerics, did not take part in the dances and games of the jesters (*skomorokhi*), treating them merely as humorous entertainment. In pre-Petrine Rus it was considered sinful to provoke laughter (*smekhotvorenie*—"laughter making") or excessive laughter to the point of tears (*smekh do slyoz*). There were similar inhibitions about giving oneself up to playful merriment.     Foreigners noted with some astonishment that dancing at a ball staged by a Russian nobleman was merely performed as a spectacle, and, like any art, a matter of labor: those who danced were working and did not make merry; merriment was the preserve of the spectators, who were too important to dance themselves. In the words of a Polish writer in the early seventeenth century, "Russian nobles laughed at Western dances, considering it improper for an honorable man to dance. . . . An honorable man, they said, should sit in his seat and only enjoy the jester's frolics, but not himself be a jester for the amusement of another: it is not good form!"[17]

Of course, these inhibitions applied only to "official" behavior, and we do not find them among the peasants. All the same, this haughtiness and extreme concern for preserving "face" are fairly typical.

When Ivan the Terrible forced his boyars to don masks and other attire that was incompatible with their notions of dignity, it was a deliberate attempt to humiliate them, and it often involved blasphemy, followed by bloody reprisals. There were elements of blasphemy too in the entertainment elements put on by Peter the Great among his cronies, although he also introduced the custom of perfectly respectable court balls and masquerades.

How did Russian sexual behavior and erotic values fare over the course of time?

Over the centuries, Russian life, grounded on the importance of family and village order, remained stable. Early marriage for economic and social motives was encouraged by the authorities, and undertaken by nearly everyone.[18]

But if marriage was the norm, marrying for love was not. Neither church nor society nor the village community considered love a necessary or sufficient condition for marriage. This was true even among the educated gentry.

The prominent eighteenth-century thinker Andrei Bolotov writes that in the search for a bride he was desirous of finding a maiden who "might not be a beauty, but at the very least the sort of person whom I could love and who could love me."[19] The wife he found, who was barely more than a young girl, did not excite his tender imagination: "No matter how I tried, no matter how much I wanted to find in her person something captivating that I could seize on, I was unable to find anything of the sort: her great youth was the cause of it all . . . I was content with that, at least I found nothing abhorrent and disgusting in her."[20]

Women had even less opportunity for choice. The eighteenth-century poet Gavriil Derzhavin, having secured permission for marriage from his future wife's mother, decided "to get to know her thoughts on the matter, thinking it insufficient to rely only on the mother's consent." When he met the maiden, Derzhavin asked whether she was aware of his intentions. "'My Mummy told me,'" she replied. "'What does she think?' 'It depends on her.' 'But if it were you, could I hope for your assent?' 'You are not unattractive,' whispered the beauty, blushing."[21]

Could one expect passionate love from such marriages? Only in exceptional circumstances. The same Bolotov describes relations with his wife:

I, having fallen in love with her from the very first day [we have seen that this was not true], loved her with sincere husbandly love. But no matter how I tried to get close to her, however much I sought and employed all

my wiles to amuse her, to cheer her up and to win her over to me as inti-
mately as I could, my success was very small. . . . I could not gain from her
the slightest mutual affection or the same sort of love and affability . . .
which young wives normally show both in public and to their husbands in
private. No, I never had that satisfaction in my life![22]

Nevertheless, Bolotov felt he ought to be "content with [his] marriage
and grateful to God."[23]
Although in the nineteenth century this attitude began to change somewhat among the nobility, marriage for love was a luxury unknown among
the peasantry. Individual attraction was possible and desirable, but not
essential. People operated on the principle that "If you can get used to one
another, you will love one another."

In the nineteenth century, village children knew far more about the
physiology of sex than did later generations of urban youngsters. After all,
they lived in close contact with nature and were not shocked by the spectacle of animals mating; they also usually had a good view of everything their
parents did. The naturalistic philosophy of sexuality ill fitted the ideas of
love and romance. "Peasants see conception and birth by analogy with animals and plants, and that the latter exist for precisely that, to bear fruit,"
wrote the priest F. Gilyarovsky about village life in the 1850s—1870s.[24] It
was a philosophy for life that did not change in the next 50 years.

The birthrate, like that of infant mortality, was high—both, it was considered, as the result of God's will. People could not afford to be soft-
hearted or romantic about this. Here Bolotov, like Michel de Montaigne
three centuries before, very calmly recounts the death of his child:

Smallpox . . . has carried off our first-born to the immense grief of his
mother. As for myself, although I granted him a few teardrops, I endured
this event with deliberate steadfastness: philosophy greatly helped me in
this, and the hope . . . that shortly we would have more children, for my
wife is pregnant once more, and that aided us in swiftly forgetting the misfortune, if one may call it a misfortune.[25]

A man's functional attitude toward his "old woman," who was needed
for work and for the birth and raising of children, was evident in the very
rhythm of marital sexuality. The intensity of sexual life in rural Russia, as in
preindustrial Western Europe, was closely dependent upon the calendar of
religious fasts and festivals, which also set the pace for agricultural work.
Ethnographer Olga Semyonova-Tyan-Shanskaya, who studied the lives of
peasants in Ryazan province, remarked that the sexual activity of husband

and wife depended on whether the man was hungry or full: "With a full belly in autumn, especially after a bottle or two, Ivan was always intemperate. But a hungry Ivan did not live with his wife in the true sense during work time."[26] The nineteenth-century writer Gleb Uspensky, who was a close observer of peasant life, noted "the existence in peasant life of a desire to maintain the woman for as many workdays as possible—and a desire by the man to keep his 'old woman' fit during harvesting, so that she was not in labor or pot-bellied"[27]—and the sequence of religious fasts and festivals banning or encouraging sexual activity made it easier to meet this task.

The peasants constituted the largest class in Russian society and were the most traditional; yet new trends in sexual morality and conduct—and reactions to the same—came into being in the towns rather than in the countryside.

The most general trend in the establishment of bourgeois society was increasing pluralization and individualization of lifestyles—and a concomitant change in the ways and means of social control over sexuality.[28] In the towns and cities, the hitherto uniform norms of religious morality began to stratify, giving way to specific codes associated with a particular class or social group.

First to be emancipated, naturally, were the nobility and gentry—although even earlier, some had not considered themselves particularly bound by religious restrictions. Indeed, it had always been considered very much the natural order of things for the young noble's son to find his first sexual partner in a peasant girl. Landowners had long abused their dependents, sexually as well as otherwise; the abolition of serfdom in 1861 altered little in this respect, except that now the noble had to pay for sexual services.

For the peasantry, the rise in social mobility was a major factor in undermining regular family life. Millions of male peasants participated in seasonal work in the city, while their wives remained in the village community, a circumstance that wreaked havoc on regular sexual relations in marriage. A man might remain in the city for three to five years, leaving his wife behind. He was free to satisfy his sexual demands in one way or another on the side, while she, depending on her inclinations, either abstained from sex in his absence or sought relief in extramarital affairs. But such affairs could have repercussions if carried out in full view of fellow villagers. If the husband found out, he could beat his unfaithful wife to death with the full backing of his neighbors. In the late nineteenth century, it was still possible to see a naked woman tied to a cart, tarred and feathered, and pulled through the streets by her husband as punishment for infidelity. One such case was described by Maxim Gorky in his short story "Vyvod."

The customs of town factory workers, by contrast, were much freer, if no less cruel, than those in the village communities. Overcrowding and poverty, exacerbated by drunkenness, left little opportunity for a happy and stable marital life, and rape, prostitution, and disease were rampant.

In the words of the celebrated Russian jurist Anatoly Koni, "urban living is related to premature sexual development of youths and the artificial perversion of their minds, under the influence of the stupid examples of their companions, a peculiar spiritedness and widespread prostitution, as well as harmful diversions that are mostly unavailable to village youth."[29] "Sexual depravity," venereal disease, and child prostitution are all mentioned in descriptions of town life at the end of the nineteenth and beginning of the twentieth centuries, and often appear in stark and negative contrast to the imagined "purity" and "chastity" of the traditional peasant lifestyle.

*Chapter Two*

# THE RUSSIAN EROS

*There is something dark and tormented, obscure and often deformed*
*in Russian love. We have not had genuine romanticism in love.*

—Nikolai Berdyaev

As we have seen, the history of sexuality in Russia is complex and contradictory. The development of Russian erotic art—the visual and literary representation of the Russian eros—was even more so. In Russia the contrast between the naturalistic physicality of "low" culture and the idealistic incorporeality of "high" culture was particularly acute, running through the entire history of literature and the arts. These two poles formed two different cultural traditions that sometimes intersected but never coincided.

The pervasive influence of 'low culture' can be seen, for example, in the extreme refinement of Russian obscenities (*mat*), which even today are a matter of national pride and are reinforced by the use by all nationalities in the former Soviet Union of predominantly Russian swear words. Foul language was not only in common use everywhere in everyday life but permeated the whole of Russian folklore.[1] Collections of Russian folk songs and folktales by such celebrated figures as Afanasiev and Kirsha Danilov could be published only in uncut versions abroad. Nor is it merely a matter of lexis.

Russian so-called erotic tales do not simply describe sexual actions naturalistically and in detail; rather, they sympathetically tell of polygamous heroes and their sexual misdemeanors, such as the possession of a sleeping beauty without her permission, or the dishonoring—i.e., rape—of a maiden in revenge for her refusal to marry the hero. Such actions are represented in the popular consciousness as natural, just, and even heroic. The roots of these subjects go deep into pre-Christian times. Peasant children, nonetheless, continued to be brought up on them even as late as the nineteenth century. The popular folk ditties (*chastushki*), sung by both boys and girls, remain even today exceedingly frank and obscene.

Similarly, primitive Russian folk prints—*lubok*—depicted very free and frank scenes.[2] Although strict clerical censorship was introduced in 1679, and several government decrees on the subject were issued during the eighteenth century, they had scant effect. Sometimes the relatively decorous pictures were accompanied by less than decorous texts. One of them, dating back to the eighteenth century, tells us that three "young wives" played a trick on a bald-headed old man, telling him he should rub "woman's cream" on his pate to restore his hair. In response, the fellow takes out his other "bald pate" and says he had been rubbing it in "woman's cream" for over 40 years without its sprouting any hair!

At the other pole—the officially sanctioned Christian art—in contrast, one finds only the absolutely unworldly.

Western religious art, from the late Middle Ages on, presents a view of the entire human body, with only the sexual organs covered; even the latter are sometimes displayed, though naturally without any hint of eroticism.[3] On Russian icons, by contrast, only the face is alive, with the body fully covered or outlined in an emaciated, ascetic form. Russian Orthodox icon painting is much stricter and more ascetic than Western religious art.[4]

Secular painting also appeared in Russia much later and under more stringent control than in the West. Whereas Italian painters were portraying the naked body in secular settings in the Renaissance, Russian artists gained that right only in the late eighteenth century. And attitudes toward the body and nudity are major factors in sexual culture.

The emergence of an open, aristocratic sexual-erotic literature and art in Russia dates from the mid—eighteenth century, under the direct influence of the libertine culture of France, where this tradition had a long history. The imperial court of Catherine the Great led the way, and Gatchina Palace, presented by Catherine to her lover Grigory Orlov, was filled with exceedingly sensual frescoes and specially ornamented furniture.[5]

French novels of varying degrees of license—and in Russia, everything European and particularly French appeared licentious—penetrated into country estates of the Russian gentry. Young noblemen whose fathers owned excellent domestic libraries eagerly read anything that made any reference to the erotic. Alexander Pushkin talks about this in *Eugene Onegin*:

> Heartfelt desire torments us early.
> Oh, beguiling deception,
> It's not nature that teaches us love,
> But Stael and Chateaubriand.[6]

Young gentlemen of Pushkin's time could enjoy not only Denis Diderot's *Immodest Treasures* and the writings of the French "libertines" but also the bawdy verses of Ivan Barkov, famous as Russia's first erotic poet. Barkov (1732–68), who was expelled from the academy and whose works were too scandalous to be published and instead circulated in manuscript for years, died in complete obscurity. A mass Russian readership was able to discover Barkov for the first time only in 1991. Yet he was held in high regard by Pushkin: "Barkov is one of the most eminent personages in the Russian language; his poetry will in the not-so-distant future attain huge importance. . . . I do not doubt that the first books that will be published uncensored will be Barkov's complete poetic works."[7] Pushkin even dedicated to him the poem "Barkov's Shadow," which is just as outrageous as the work of Barkov himself.

Barkov's poetry is indeed blatantly bawdy; it is by no means erotic in the Western European sense. As literary critic Alexander Ilyushin writes:

> The intention is not so much to enflame lecherous lust, nor to provoke amorous temptation and languor. We descend not into a rosy haze (it is there, but in trifling little doses), but into the smoky, bawdy atmosphere of tavern curses, where folk view carnal copulations without a crafty, playful wink, yet noisily cursing and blinding, which destroys any illusion of intimacy. There is no place here for bon viveurs seduced by the secrets of passion: it is sheer "effing" and "blinding". . . . An erotomane would probably remain indifferent to it all. . . . For we are confronted not with eroticism (when there is nothing more than genitals it can hardly be genuinely erotic) but sheer mischief-making that has long awaited its renaming as hooliganism—at a time when that word simply did not exist.[8]

Yet Barkov provides frank parody as well as smut. He parodied and mocked everything—morality, decency, literary genres, his contemporaries, and his own predecessors. In the preface to his poem "A Maiden's Toy"—a good title for such bawdiness—Barkov referred to "noble nature" that endows people with genitals. All the same, notes Ilyushin, Barkov's sexuality is "nowhere near to the grandeur of Mother Nature; it is rather unadornedly unnatural. He gives full rein to the deformed grotesque where . . . women do not meet men, but are instead only independently working sexual organs."[9] He throws in incest, violence, bestiality, rape. A dragoon rapes an old woman, a clerk rapes a Frenchman, a monk rapes a nun; a grandson screws his elderly grandmother to death; an old sage finds himself in Hell and copulates with Charon, Cerberus, Pluto, and the Furies; previously on earth he had succeeded in doing so with beasts and birds as well as women.

This attitude makes a general mockery of eroticism. Given the circumstances of a rigid clerical and secular censorship, obscenity was a direct challenge to authority. The Russian poet-democrat Nikolai Ogaryov was not the first to remark on the kinship of political and erotic poetry. In the preface to his Russian "secret literature" collection, which he published in London, he wrote, "Obscenity and the poetry of civil aspirations . . . are more closely connected than it would seem. In essence, they are branches of the same tree, and you will find a political slap in the face in every indecent epigram. . . . everywhere the same foe of civil liberty is chastised."[10]

Barkov laid the foundation for the whole tradition of Russian bawdy poetry, which has continued unabated ever since. The most gifted and tragic figure involved in it was the youthful Alexander Polezhayev, whom Nikolai I handed over to the army for his obscene and indecent autobiographical poem "Sashka" (1825); he died shortly thereafter.

Alexander Pushkin and Mikhail Lermontov both gave bawdy verses their due. The complete text of Pushkin's poem "Gavriiliada" was published, with a foreword and commentary by poet Valery Bryusov, only in 1918 with a print run of 555 copies. The main obstacle to a pre-Revolutionary edition of the work was not so much its eroticism as the anticlerical, blasphemous nature of the poem.[11]

A lot of bawdy verse was anonymous and passed from hand to hand in manuscript form. The Barkov-ascribed poems "Luka Mudishchev," which was written no earlier than the second half of the 1830s, and "Prov Fomich," composed in the last third of the nineteenth century, for example, were widely distributed.

No matter what the literary worth and faults of this kind of poetry were, it existed at the periphery of "high" literature. More often than not these verses were the collective products of young men locked up in the closed educational institutions and striving through sardonic writing to play out and discharge their fairly primitive and utterly irreverent sexual fantasies and feelings. These works successfully fulfilled their function and later provided a similar solace to the generations of youngsters that followed, yet no one took them seriously.

More important was the fact that the Russian censor and literary critic did not generally see any difference between pornography and eroticism. In the latter part of the eighteenth century, the authorities warned young gentlemen, not to mention gentlewomen, against reading both frivolous French novels and the highly moralistic works of the British sentimentalists. Samuel Richardson's *Pamela*, for example, was considered indecent, and in 1806 the journal *Avrora* warned its readers of the "harmful intrusions" in sensual scenes in Jean-Jacques Rousseau's *New Eloise*. In 1823, *Vestnik Yevropy* praised Sir Walter Scott for having no "seductive" episodes in his work. During the 1820s romanticism in art came under virulent attack for "sensuousness."[12] In 1865, the magazine *Sovremennaya letopis* exposed "eroticism," which it had taken to extremes, "in the most cynical expression" by the highly moral and eminently decent Russian playwright, Alexander Ostrovsky, in his plays *The Pupil* and *Thunderstorm*. In his play *In a Smart Place*, Ostrovsky, in the words of his critic, "Stopped short of the very pillars of Hercules beyond which begins the realm of the Marquis de Sade and his confreres."

None of this prudery was exclusively Russian; after all, even in France (which had the reputation in Russia of being the land of eroticism and perversion), both *Madame Bovary* and *Les Fleurs du mal* were in 1857 formally condemned by the court. The author of *Madame Bovary* was finally exonerated, since "the offensive passages," "while fully meriting censure, occupy a very small part by contrast with the overall size of the novel," and Gustave Flaubert himself "declares his respect for morality and for everything that pertains to religious morals." Charles Baudelaire, on the other hand, was condemned for "coarse realism that is offensive to human decency," and six poems from *Les Fleurs du mal* were banned.[13] So we ought not be particularly surprised at the reactions to such things in Russia, which had, at any rate, less hypocrisy than Victorian England.

Nevertheless, the emergence of erotic culture in Russia was more tortuous than in the West, where erotic art, or what passed for such, had only one major enemy—the church. In Russia, this enemy was especially strong, resting not only on the authority of religion but also on state power. Yet the internal contradictions of Russian eros were more important than both external censorship and conservative public opinion.

Russian classical literature of the nineteenth century created exceptionally vivid and profound images of romantic love. Yet literature in Russia, as nowhere else, also had the firm imprint of what Freud called the internal contradiction of male sexuality: the conflict between affectionate and sensual love. Women in classical Russian literature are either images of "divine loveliness" or perfect bitches. There is no middle way. Yet both extremes are merely forms of the male imagination.

Such contradictory feelings in everyday life did not apparently trouble aristocrats of Pushkin's generation. In Pushkin's verses, Anna Kern is a "momentary vision," "a genius of pure beauty," yet in a personal letter to a friend the poet casually mentions how he had recently, "with God's help, . . . her."[14] The artistic synthesis was much more problematic.

Coarse sensuality was unacceptable to classic Russian literature. Ivan Turgenev's young women cannot be lusted after; it is hard to imagine them in bed. To use the words of writer Alexander Herzen, carnal "love for sex" usually stands in opposition to a purely spiritual "love for the person" or a serene "love for wedlock," founded on marital fidelity.

Pushkin's Tatiana, who as a maiden plucks up courage to declare her love to Onegin, is no longer mistress of her own fate once she has married: "I am pledged to another; I shall be true to him forever." Another Pushkin heroine, Masha, from *Dubrovksy*, acts in precisely the same way.

This heightened poetic attitude toward women, peculiar to Russian classical literature, was all very well, but it both reflected and engendered inevitable disappointment and dramas. As James H. Billington, the thoughtful American historian, writes:

> The passion for ideas and the development of psychological complexes about certain names and concepts, though generally characteristic of European romanticism, were carried to extremes in Russia. . . . There was an unhealthy compulsion about some of the Russian attachment to classical antiquity and an element of sublimated sexuality in the creative activity of the period. The prodigious and original careers of Bakunin and Gogol both seem to have been developed partially as a compensation for sexual impotence. There is, in general, little room for women in the egocentric world of Russian romanticism. Lonely brooding was relieved primarily by exclusively masculine companionship in the lodge or circle. From Skovoroda to Bakunin there are strong hints of homosexuality, though apparently of the sublimated, Platonic variety. This passion appears closer to the surface in Ivanov's predilection for painting naked boys, and finds philosophic expression in the fashionable belief that spiritual perfection required androgyny, or a return to the original union of male and female characteristics. Ivanov in his preliminary sketches of the all-important head of Christ in his "Appearance" used as many feminine as masculine models.[15]

The ideal woman of Russian literature in the first part of the last century was either an innocent maiden or an overweening mother, but never a lover. Says Billington, the aristocratic intellectual was "always the egocentric lover; he embraced both women and ideas with a mixture of passion and fantasy that made a sustained relationship almost impossible."[16]

All of this, of course, was not exclusively Russian and was often mentioned in Western European literature both before and after Freud. But in the West this normative image was largely supported by the conservatives, while in Russia democrats were also among the main opponents of eroticism.

The radical democrats played an important part in nineteenth century Russian culture. In their origins and upbringing, they were a world apart from the nobility. Gentlemen of Pushkin's time received a good secular education from childhood; even while remaining deeply religious people, they invariably distanced themselves from official hypocrisy. This was much more difficult for the next generation of Russian intellectuals, who had been educated in seminaries and/or were themselves from ecclesiastical backgrounds. While breaking with some principles of their former lives, they were unable to overcome others. Transplanted into an alien social milieu, many of them suffered acute shyness and tried to repress the desires of their own flesh, the more so because, like other people, not everything was "orthodox" in their sexuality by a long shot.

There was, of course, nothing exceptional in masturbation or in homoeroticism, or in the gap between sensual and tender attraction. Such experiences were typical of many young men in the nineteenth century, in the West as well. But the unsuccessful inner battle, instead of helping young and ambitious Russian radicals to develop sexual tolerance, turned into a principled moralistic-aesthetic condemnation and renunciation of any sensuality as something repulsive and unworthy.

For instance, Vissarion Belinsky, the leading literary critic of his day, was totally unable either to restrain or accept his own sensuality.[17] And because of this, he was extremely disapproving of any manifestations of sensuality in literature—for example, in the poetry of Alexander Polezhayev. Reasoning from the standpoint of an imagined "innocent young boy," who had to be protected from seduction in every way possible, he denounces Boccaccio in passing; he calls Paul de Kock's novel a "squalid and ignoble work." Similarly, the critic Dmitri Pisarev condemned Heinrich Heine for "his simple view of women."

It ought to be emphasized that the suspicious-circumspect attitude to sensuality among the men of the 1860s and the revolutionary terrorist organization *Narodnaya Volya* (People's Will) followers was not simply a manifestation of personal psychosexual problems and difficulties but also a very clear-cut ideology. While the conservative-religious critic censured eroticism for contradicting religious dogmas, the revolutionary populists simply could not make it fit the normative canon of a person called upon to give up all his energy for the struggle to liberate the working classes. In comparison with this grand social design, everything else paled into insignificance. Even the subtle, intimate lyrics of Afanasy Fet, Yakov Polonsky, or Konstantin Sluchevsky seemed vulgar to the radical populist critics of the latter part of the nineteenth century, such as Grigory Novopolin, who could see no difference at all between erotica and pornography.

The views of Russian feminists of the time were quite similar. Although their opposition to ecclesiastical marriage and demands for full equality with men, including sexual equality, frequently led to their being accused of propagating subversive "communist theories of free love," on all important sexual issues their views coincided with the more puritanical English and American feminists.[18] In doing away with the sexual double standard, they called not for women to acquire the sexual freedom of "the stronger sex" but for elevating men to the higher spiritual plane occupied by women.

In other words, the sociopolitical and moral maximalism of Russian democratic thought was turning into a militant foe of the very quotidian, emotional, and psychophysiological realities out of which normal human life was essentially taking shape. Any artist or writer who attempted to deal with these realities came under a withering attack from both right and left simultaneously, a situation that seriously hampered the emergence in Russia of lofty, refined erotic art and corresponding language—without which sexuality and all talk of it inevitably appear base and sullied.

We must certainly not simplify the picture. Although Russian academic painting of the early part of the nineteenth century did not portray erotic scenes, without Karl Bryullov, Alexander Ivanov, and Fyodor Bruni, the history of representation of the nude would be incomplete. Alexander Venetsianov created wonderful images of ballerinas, women bathing, and bacchante.

Like their Western European counterparts, Russian artists for many years were forced to use the strategy that the historian Peter Gay has called "the doctrine of distance": "This doctrine, an impressive exemplar of a cultural defense mechanism at work, holds that the more generalized and idealized the presentation of the human body in art, the more draped in elevated associations, the less likely it is to shock its viewers. In practice this meant abstracting the nude from contemporary and intimate experience by lending it the alien glamour that titles or poses drawn from history, mythology, religion, or the exotic could provide."[19]

Until the last decade of the nineteenth century, eroticism was considered an important aspect of private life, but its significance in the culture was debased or vulgarized. In the 1890s the situation changed radically and "the sexual issue" suddenly became a central ideological symbol of the epoch.

This spiritual revolution had deep roots. The gradual weakening of state control and the power of the censor as the modernization of Russia advanced brought to the surface many hitherto clandestine tendencies. As Billington notes, the new sensualism and preoccupation with sexuality was a natural "reaction against the long dominant moralism and ascetic puritanism" of the time, and it was "directed as much against the official religious morality as against the hypocritical premises of the democrats of the 1860s."[20] A natural stage in the development of Russian romantic culture itself, which was no longer limited by normative ethical and aesthetic structures, the new sensualism was in fact but one aspect of the new philosophy of individualism that was powerfully coming to the fore.

The publication of Tolstoy's *The Kreutzer Sonata* in 1891 provided an impetus for people to appreciate the general crises in marriage and sexuality.[21] In *The Kreutzer Sonata*, Tolstoy set out to condemn carnal love and to show that "the incorrectness and therefore poverty of sexual relations come from the view common to people in our world that sexual relations are a subject for enjoyment, satisfaction."[22]

The main character, Pozdnyshev, is panic-stricken about sexuality, his own or anyone else's, no matter how ennobling it might be: "Theory has it that love is something ideal, elevated, yet in practice it is something loathsome and swinish about which it is loathsome and shameful to talk and think."[23] This point of view, in tandem with pathological jealousy, makes Pozdnyshev incapable of enjoying any mutual understanding with his wife and ultimately brings him to kill her. Yet this tragedy, in Tolstoy's opinion, had its roots not in the character's personal qualities but in the very nature of marriage, which is based on "animal" feelings.

After the book came out, some of its democratic critics endeavored to distance Tolstoy from Pozdnyshev. Yet in the later afterword to the story, Tolstoy openly identifies with his character and makes clear his views: "Attaining the aim of uniting in or outside marriage with the object of one's love, however poeticized it may be, is an aim unworthy of human beings."[24] More intolerant than St. Paul, Tolstoy went on to say, "A Christian's ideal is love for God and one's neighbors, renunciation of oneself for service to God and one's neighbors; carnal love, marriage, is service to one-self and is therefore, at any rate, a hindrance to serving God and people; so from a Christian standpoint it is falling from grace and a sin."[25]

*The Kreutzer Sonata* was banned by the czarist censor as too frank in its discussion of the physical side of marriage and potentially explosive; it was only after Sofia Tolstaya received a personal audience with Alexander III that the Czar reluctantly permitted the publication of the story in Tolstoy's collected works. Nonetheless, the work was immensely popular, being read in manuscript form in private homes in Russia and provoking heated debates everywhere.[26]

Russian writers from Anton Chekhov to A. K. Sheller-Mikhailov reacted strongly to the book, many of them penning answers to Tolstoy's work or expanding on his theme.[27] All those taking part in the argument agreed that society and the institution of marriage were undergoing an acute moral crisis, but they disagreed on the reason for the crisis and the ways to resolve it.

Philosophers also became involved in the argument over the nature of sex and the meaning of love. Some, such as Vladimir Solovyov, expressed views similar to Tolstoy's idealism,[28] while others, like Vasily Rozanov, joined the fray by defending carnal love in no uncertain terms: "We are born to love. And as long as we do not fulfill our love, we shall languish in this world. And as long as we have not fulfilled our love, we shall be punished in the other world."[29]

Rozanov was attacked from all sides; he was called an erotomaniac, an apostle of vulgarity. Yet the philosopher Nikolai Berdyaev sprang to his defense:

> Rozanov is laughed at and morally condemned, yet the service this man has rendered is immense and will be appreciated only later. He is the first to break the hypocritical silence with unprecedented boldness; he has loudly and with inimitable talent said what everyone has felt, yet kept hidden inside; he has exposed the universal torment. . . . Rozanov has with the frankness and sincerity of a genius proclaimed for all to hear that sex is the most important issue in life, a fundamentally vital question, no less crucial than social, legal, educational and other generally recognized sanctioned issues, that this question goes much deeper than family types and at root is related to religion, since all religions took shape and developed through sex because sex is after all a matter of life and death.[30]

The Russian philosophy of love and sexuality at this time was, however, more metaphysical than phenomenological. Although they rehabilitated an abstract eros, philosophers were still suspicious about real, everyday, earthy enjoyment. Abstract philosophical formulations enabled them to avoid any tormenting personal self-revelation. As Laura Engelstein justly remarks, "the open-mindedness of the philosophers was limited by the other-worldly quality of their ruminations."[31]

There was more immediacy in turn-of-the-century (Silver Age) Russian literature and painting than in philosophy, although the same issues were essentially being debated. Poets from Konstantin Balmont and Vyacheslav Ivanov to Valery Bryusov wrote of the importance of eros, which they called sacred; said Balmont, "Love has no human face. All it has is the face of God and the face of the Devil."[32]

The symbolist poets proclaimed the cult of Eros as the supreme principle of human existence. The cold and sober-minded Valery Bryusov wrote in the journal *Vesy* in 1904:

> Passion is that lush color for which our body exists, like a seed, for which it crumbles to dust, dies, withers away, unconcerned about its own death. The value of passion does not depend on us and we can do nothing to change it. Our time, which has illuminated passion, has for the first time enabled artists to portray it, without being ashamed of their work, with a faith in what they are doing. Chastity is wisdom in passion, an awareness of the sanctity of passion. The one who sins is he who has a simple-minded attitude toward passionate feeling.[33]

Vyacheslav Ivanov echoes Bryusov: "All human and worldly activity may be reduced to Eros . . . Ethics and esthetics no longer exist—both are reduced to eroticism, and any audacity born of Eros is sacred. Only hedonism is shameful."[34]

Although there was much about these expressions that was rhetorical, feeling and sensuality at last enjoyed civil rights in Russian poetry—in the works of Alexei Apukhtin, Konstantin Balmont, Nikolai Minsky, Mirra Lokhvitskaya, and many others.

In the early twentieth century, Russian erotic prose also made its first appearance. It is enough to mention Leonid Andreyev ("In the Fog" and "Abyss," published in 1902), Mikhail Artsybashev (*Sanin*, published in 1907), Fyodor Sologub ("The Little Demon," published in 1905), Nikolai Oliger's "The Dacha Corner" and "In the Rest Hours" (1907), Yevdokiya Nagrorodskaya's "The Wrath of Dionysius" (1910), and Anastasiya Verbit-skaya's "The Keys to Happiness" (1910–13).

There was a real explosion of eroticism and sensuality in Russian painting, which convincingly demonstrated Alexander Golovin's maxim that no costume existed that could compare with the beauty of the nude human body. We can mention in this regard the canvases of Mikhail Vrubel, Valentin Serov's "Ida Rubinstein," Mikhail Zichi's witty, frankly sexual caricatures, Zinaida Serebryakova's and Natalia Goncharova's opulent beauties, Konstantin Somov's elegant marquis and marquesses and love scenes, Lev Bakst's daring drawings on folkloric themes, Kuzma Petrov-Vodkin's exquisite naked boys, Mikhail Larionov's enticing "Prostitutes."

Nikolai Kalmakov signed his paintings of images of Leda, Salome, and odalisques with initials in the form of a stylized phallus. In his decorations for the Temple of Venus scene in the St. Petersburg production of *Salome*, the female genitals were so blatantly portrayed that the decor had to be removed right after the dress rehearsal.

Nikolai Feofilaktov was known as "the Moscow Beardsley." He enjoyed portraying half-dressed women, and he achieved particular notoriety with his album of *66 Sketches* in 1909. The poets Andrei Bely and Valery Bryusov held him in high regard; the latter decorated his Moscow apartment with Feofilaktov's sketches.

This erotic art was far from being always "pleasant." Sexual violence was often depicted and even romanticized. As in poetry, where Bryusov and Sologub were fond of necrophilia, so the painting of the Silver Age artists widely depicted themes of death, suicide, demonism, corpses, and skeletons. V. N. Masyutin's engravings, such as those in the *Sin* album of 1909, are full of fantastic, hideous shapes and images of various monsters.[35]

Such "sex secrets" as androgyny, hermaphroditism, homosexuality, and bisexuality fascinated people in the early years of the century. The publication of *Sex and Character* (1903) by the young Austrian philosopher Otto Weininger gave a strong impetus to discussion of such problems. Between 1909 and 1914, the book came out in at least five different Russian translations, with a total print run of over 30,000 copies.[36]

Uncommon forms of sexuality that had previously been concealed were openly admitted, discussed, and even deliberately flaunted in the early twentieth century by many members of the artistic elite. The poet and writer Mikhail Kuzmin openly appeared in public with what his detractors liked to call his "little darlings." The peasant poet Nikolai Klyuev, a one-time member of the Khlyst sect, also did not hide his homoerotic inclinations. Internationally famous impresario Sergei Diaghilev founded—together with his cousin, friend, and probably lover, Dmitri Filosofov—the magazine *Mir iskusstva* (*World of Art*) and later, the famous New Russian ballet. He enjoyed enormous notoriety and often provoked scandal. According to the reminiscences of Sergei Makovsky, Diaghilev would flaunt himself like a dandy "when the occasion demanded and paraded for all the world to see, ignoring à la Oscar Wilde the 'prejudices' of proprietous society and never disguising his unusual tastes to the disgust of hypocritical well-wishers."[37] Diaghilev's ballets were festivals of the human body. Never had the male body been revealed and demonstrated so fully, erotically, and un-self-consciously as in the dance of Mikhail Fokine and Vaclav Nijinsky. Russia also had a few well-known bisexuals as well as famous female couples, among them feminist writer Anna Yevreinova and her lifelong friend Maria Fyodorova, and the poet Poliksena Solovyova and Natalia Manaseina, who left her scholarly husband to live with Solovyova.

Kuzmin's work was of particular importance to the emergence of an original Russian literature of homoeroticism. In his autobiographical novel *Wings*, first published in 1906, the main character is an 18-year-old peasant boy, Vanya Smurov, who finds it hard to comprehend the nature of his intellectual and emotional attraction to Shtrup, an educated half-Englishman. When he discovers Shtrup's sexual affair with the lackey Fyodor, Vanya is shocked: revulsion mingles with jealousy. But Shtrup explains to the youth that a man is given a body not just for procreation, but that it is wonderful in itself, that "there are ligaments and muscles in the human body which cannot be seen without quivering," and that same-sex love was understood and valued by the ancient Greeks. At the end of the story, Vanya accepts his destiny and goes off with Shtrup:

> "One more effort and you will grow wings; I can see them already."
>
> "Maybe, yet it is too difficult when they grow," retorted Vanya with a smile."[38]

*Wings* provoked a tempestuous debate, with some social democratic critics finding the story "repulsive" and reflecting the degradation of high society, while others praised its artistry.[39]

Kuzmin's romanticizing of male-male love was joined by Lidia Zinovieva-Annibal's book, *Thirty-Three Freaks*, which was published in 1907 and was the first frank depiction of lesbian relationships. In this melodramatic novel, the actress Vera disrupts the wedding of a young woman with whom she is in love. The abandoned groom kills himself, and the two women begin living together. Their idyll does not last long; Vera's friend needs male society and finally leaves Vera, who also commits suicide.

It must be emphasized that Russian erotic literature was very varied in both its artistic quality and the tasks it set itself. Simultaneous with the emergence of the lofty avant-garde art that so shocked the public, eroticism of all sorts began to find a prominent place in commercial mass culture. Newspapers began to feature illustrated advertisements whose frankness would have been unthinkable a few years back ("How to quench your sexual thirst" and "Any woman can have an ideal bust" were two of these), and photographs of naked beauties began to feature in the advertisements.

Most of Russian society at the beginning of the twentieth century was not yet ready for a differentiated perception of these variegated phenomena. To many intellectuals, they formed a single picture of a terrifying "sexual Bacchanalia." People dealt with their sense of moral panic by finger pointing, name calling, and demanding tougher laws and stricter censorship.

Sexuality and eroticism became generalized political symbols through which people expressed their own general moral-political views. Conservative authors seeking to safeguard public morality maintained that "obsession with sex" undermined the foundations of the family and morality and that it was engendered by the revolutionary movement and godlessness. The social democrats, on the other hand, considered the obsession with sex part of an ideological reaction to the defeat of the revolution of 1905, a consequence of intellectuals' disillusionment with social issues and withdrawal into their own private lives.

Of course, both sides were right. Society could not be democratized without a critical review of patriarchal morality, including methods for social control over sexuality; and demands for "sexual liberalization" were an integral part of the social renovation program that preceded the 1905 revolution. At the same time, the defeat of the revolution, which undermined people's interest in politics, encouraged them to seek compensation in their private lives and first and foremost in sex.

For the extreme right, sexophobia merged with judophobia and misogyny. The reactionary, anti-Semitic Black Hundred press claimed that Jews were the owners of all Russian brothels as well as the drinking dens, thereby seeking to bring about not only the moral dissipation of Russians, but reductions in their numbers and even their physical extinction.

The populist and social-democratic critics, on the other hand, railed against "erotic individualism" and pornography as products of dissolute bourgeois culture, the means through which the bourgeoisie was trying to infect the naturally spiritually healthy working class. For them, such literary advocates of eroticism as Kuzmin and Zinovieva-Annibal were simply "degenerates cultivated on poor aristocratic soil," "degenerates perverted through indolence," and "parasites sucking the people's blood and craving their flesh."[40] The logic of both left and right was, as we see, one and the same: sexuality was a dangerous weapon of the class—or national—enemy, through which this enemy was undermining, with some success, the spiritual and physical health of "our side." So both right and left warned the public to be on guard.

It is true that many of the popular works of erotic literature were artistically mediocre at best, and often startlingly crude. As the celebrated lawyer and writer Anatoly Koni said in 1908, "This is not literature at all, but some masturbating verbiage."[41]

At the same time, any book that touched upon the "sex issue" in one way or another was bound to offend someone and therefore was instantly treated as scandalous. A primitive understanding of literature as a means of education led to books being assessed on sociopedagogical rather than artistic criteria, on whether they were suitable as examples for imitation by all and everyone. Since sexuality, even the most common, seemed problematic, the criticism was particularly carping, with the authors being accused of every mortal sin.[42]

After reading the first few pages of Alexander Kuprin's novel, *The Pit*, Tolstoy told the pianist A. B. Goldenweizer, "I know he appears to be exposing [the depravity of lust in a brothel]. Yet in describing it he seems to revel in it. And from a man with an artistic flair, that cannot be concealed."[43] The literary critic Kornei Chukovsky was likewise derogatory about the book: "If Kuprin was truly disgusted by this ancient structure, he could have communicated his disgust to the reader. But . . . he seems to revel in it all, enjoying all the detail . . . so that we too are affected by his appetite."[44]

Educators and doctors pontificated in even more primitive tones on the harmful effects of erotic literature on young people. Izrail Kankarovich, a pediatrician, speaking in 1910 at the first nationwide congress on combating prostitution, said directly that boys who read Jules Verne dream of journeys and sometimes run away from home; tales of crimes create criminals; and erotic art excites sexual instincts and perverts people.[45]

The new Russian eroticism—and here was its liberating significance—consistently and boldly rehabilitated sensuality. All the same, expression of those feelings was often very problematical. For example, Artybashev's *Sanin*, published in 1907, the most discussed novel of the period, intersperses sexuality with violence and death. In the space of a fairly short book there are three suicides and one failed attempt at suicide. Sex itself appears coarse and joyless: the man takes the woman by force, degrades her, and she is happy to endure it, following which they both feel guilt and shame.[46]

The simplified story lines easily lent themselves to further simplification and parody. "Russian pornography," wrote Kornei Chukovsky in 1908, is not simply pornography, like the French or German, it is a pornography with a notion. Artsybashev is not merely describing Sanin's voluptuous doings, but summoning everyone to come and join in. . . . People should enjoy love without fear and prohibition he says, and this word *should* is a vestige of former intellectual habits, a vestige of a former moral code which is disappearing before our very eyes.[47]

Yet this was *not* pornography. Artybashev was affirming not so much hedonism as the individual's right always to be himself and not to set limits to his desires. In the stuffy little provincial town where the book's action takes place, there is nothing for a person to do but engage in sex. In the final scene of the novel Sanin abandons the town and walks toward the rising sun, as if hinting to the reader that his real life is ahead of him. This "new person," an individualist and cynic, is not particularly sympathetic, but he is strong and, given the circumstances of capitalist development and Stolypin reform, the future was likely to be with him.

But was it really?

The art and literature of the Silver Age indisputably shows that Russian culture was moving toward creation of high eroticism and doing so fairly successfully and originally. Costs and errors in the process were inevitable and to be expected. In that sense, Russia was no different from the West. Yet, Russian erotic art, in greater measure than Western, was what one might term "elitist," nonorganic, existing only on the upper surface of the culture. Both right and left perceived it as something sick, decadent, a product of the crisis in public life, something alien to Russian classical traditions, amoral and aesthetically repulsive. Its first feeble shoots never had time to take firm root in social life and were swept away by the revolutionary storm of 1917.

*Chapter Three*

# THE "SEX QUESTION" ON THE EVE OF THE OCTOBER REVOLUTION

*The question about sex and love is at the very center of our whole
religious-philosophical and religious-social world-view.*

—Nikolai Berdyayev

The "sex question" that occupied a prime place in Russian social thought at the end of the nineteenth century could essentially be broken down into two parts: the problem of women's equality and the problem of sexuality per se. Here I will concentrate exclusively on the second aspect.

Since Russia had begun bourgeois development later than the West, Russian thinkers—the radical social democrats as well as the conservative Slavophiles—were highly sensitive to the negative aspects of urbanization and industrialization and pondered how Russia might avoid the high potential costs involved.

The American historian Laura Engelstein notes:

In Russia, as in Europe, the intrusion of the capitalist marketplace, the emergence of commercial culture, and the institutional consolidation of professional expertise generated a contest over the authority to regulate sexual conduct, to determine the boundaries of individual autonomy, and to demarcate public from private life. But the local context in Russia was different. Not only political expression but access to political power was severely restricted in the tsarist empire, even for those who stood at the top of the formal social hierarchy and enjoyed the privileges of Westernized culture. The transition from administrative to legal principles of governance occurred more hesitantly than it had in continental states. Urbanization and industrialization took forms that diverged in various degrees from the experience of Western countries, where the modern socioeconomic revolution was already well under way. . . . Just as the critique of capitalism preceded the full appearance of capitalism itself on the Russian scene, so Victorian notions of sexual respectability and danger were questioned before they had a chance to take root. None of the interrelated protagonists of the Victorian sexual drama made a wholly successful transition to the Russian stage: neither the self-disciplined bourgeois male, nor his erotically unresponsive, homebound wife, nor the sexually undisciplined working-class male, nor the diseased and promiscuous prostitute.[1]

In Russia, as in Western Europe, sexuality was not discussed on its own terms but in the context of such health-related problems as abortion, prostitution, and venereal disease, as well as childrearing and the commercialization of culture.

In medieval Russia, the only official justification for sexual life was to produce children. Thus any attempt to prevent conception was as sinful as abortion or infanticide; no distinction was made between any of them, the generic name given being murder (*dushegubstvo*, literally, "destroying the soul"). On occasion, attempts to prevent conception with the aid of herbs or charms were punished even more severely than abortion, as not only an attempt on the life of an unborn child but also as evidence of "paganism" and anti-Christian sorcery.[2] Nevertheless, Russian folk medicine employed a number of methods, often primitive and dangerous, to destroy the fetus or cause an artificial abortion.[3] The church, naturally, did not approve of these practices. In the nineteenth century, doctors and intellectuals joined in the condemnation.[4]

But moralizing did not diminish the objective need for family planning and birth control. From 1897 to 1912, the number of abortions in St. Petersburg grew tenfold, despite the fact that under Russian law, artificially induced abortion ("illegal miscarriage") was a criminal offense. A person guilty of abortion was to be punished by deprivation of all property rights and social rank, and exile to a settlement in a remote part of Siberia. Although this penalty was severe, in point of fact, the law was only rarely applied and juries usually rendered verdicts of "not guilty."[5]

An obvious way of avoiding the dilemma of abortion was development of reliable methods of contraception. Many doctors, however, not to mention moralists, were as adamantly opposed to contraception as they were to abortion. In 1893, A. G. Boryakovsky wrote in *Vrach* (*The Doctor*) that "methods preventing conception, the so-called 'preservatives' [i.e., condoms] are acquiring ever-increasing popularity. Papers even print advertisements; they are always in abundance and placed in the most obvious place in drugstores, pharmacies, and instrument and rubber shops." In Boryakovsky's view, however, condoms, like coitus interruptus, were so harmful to health that "it would be better to refrain from sex totally than to augment grief by disease."[6]

Disputes among the experts—doctors and jurists—on the subject of abortion and contraception continued for many years, with various arguments being advanced. Those who directed attention largely to the medical facet of the matter (for instance, the lack of hygiene and the clumsy methods that led to women aborting themselves using knitting needles, quills, sticks, etc.) were prepared to decriminalize abortions in order to make them less dangerous. Others, taking the opposite point of view, cited reasons of morality and considered abortion as a generally inadmissible practice.

In 1911 and 1913, respectively, the Fourth Congress of the Society of Russian Midwives and Gynecologists and the Twelfth Congress of the Pirogov Society, Russia's most influential and progressive medical organization, finally adopted a liberal stance in recommending the government decriminalize abortions performed by doctors. In February 1914, after a heated debate, the Tenth General Assembly of the Russian Group of the International Union of Criminologists recommended decriminalization of abortion as well.

The Pirogov Congress had also spoken of contraception as the only real alternative to induced abortion: "Measures preventing pregnancy are the only practical means . . . already acting as a considerable restraint on the production of an illegal miscarriage and promising to do much more to eradicate this evil in the future. We should do all we can to improve and extend these measures."[7]

Legislation on sex crimes and prostitution also underwent major revision at the end of the century. Like their European models, the Russian criminal codes of 1813 and 1845 refer to all sexual crimes in religious and moral terms: "shameful crimes," "offenses to decent morality," "perverted behavior," "unnatural vices." Even the New Criminal Code of 1903 brought together all sexual crimes under the rubric of "obscenity" (*nepotrebsto*). But "sin," "vice," and "crime" are not the same thing; they require different definitions and different means of social control.

Making the law more efficient required a clearer understanding of what exactly was to be protected and by what means. Protection of the individual from sexual harassment and abuse is not the same as safeguarding the population's health or morals. The overall trend in states governed by law was to cut down the number of bans on actions that did not pose a direct public danger or that by their very essence did not lend themselves to administrative control. As Engelstein notes, by the nineteenth century most "European states had relinquished much of the burden of initiative and regulation to society itself, while restricting the notion of police to encompass only the limited, technical agency by which the state enforced the laws."[8]

Although czarist Russia was not yet truly a law-governed state, and protection of individual rights occupied a very modest place in its legislation, it was nonetheless developing in the same direction as most other European states, as was convincingly demonstrated in the disputes on such issues as prostitution, venereal disease, and homosexuality.

As in Western Europe, prostitution had existed in Russia since antiquity.[9] Catherine II, influenced by European models, brought it under police supervision and opened the first hospital for the treatment of women with venereal disease. From the 1840s, the police in a number of cities began to issue official permits for the opening of legal "comfort houses," which offered medical supervision; according to the criminal legislation of 1845, "obscene conduct" (a euphemism for prostitution) was punished only when the "shameless and corrupting actions" took place in public places. This engendered a certain moral and legal paradox—the de facto legalization of conduct that was at the same time being roundly condemned. On the other hand, it created maximum opportunities for police and medical supervision.

By the 1890s, Russia had an estimated 1,262 comfort houses and 1,232 secret dens, more than 15,000 "comfort house" prostitutes and more than 20,000 individual prostitutes.[10] Scholars reckoned that the number of prostitutes per capita in St. Petersburg in the early twentieth century was approximately the same as in other European capitals, such as London, Paris, Vienna, and Berlin.

As elsewhere, male public opinion looked upon the brothel system quite tolerantly. One did not speak about brothels in female company, but many young gentlemen started their sexual life there. Frequently boys were taken there for that very purpose by their older brothers or friends.[11]

Under the law, prostitutes were supposed to register with the police and undergo routine medical examinations, but of course not all did so. Furthermore, this medical and police supervision was expensive, open to abuse, and rather ineffective hygienically. According to an investigation in 1889, roughly 60% of "loose women" suffered from the "evil disease," as venereal disease was known. The prevalence of prostitution and the venereal disease that accompanied it provoked heated debates. One faction argued that prostitution was due to social causes such as poverty and thus could be dealt with only by dealing with social factors, while the opposition maintained that prostitution and venereal disease were consequences of the decline in public morals as a result of the country's urbanization and Westernization. A third faction contended that prostitution was due to the fact that some women who possessed heightened sexual desires had an innate "predilection for vice." Fundamentally, the issue was in deadlock. The Russian government could take money for all sorts of antisocial activities, like selling vodka, but to legalize and to tax prostitution looked too immoral. On the other side, public opinion was highly skeptical and suspicious about police administrative control over prostitution, even for the sake of public health. And last but not least, Russian literature and public opinion were prone to see the "fallen woman" not as a guilty person but as helpless victim of social and moral injustice (Katyusha Maslova in Tostoy's *Resurrection*, Dostoyevsky's Sonechka Marmeladova, and so on).

At the last quarter of the nineteenth century, Russian physicians and educators were also very concerned about the "secret vice" of boys' masturbation, which they condemned unequivocally.[12] Given to politicizing every conceivable issue, many of them reckoned that both masturbation and adolescent sexuality were signs of the decadence of the wealthy classes, whose easy life inclined them to every possible excess, but were largely absent from the lives of the common people. However, as they became acquainted with the habits of the working class, they soon lost their illusions. After 1905, educators found pathology in working-class sexuality, owing not to suppressed desire but to a disorderly, promiscuous family life, precocious childhood sex, and adult sexual indulgence.

Interest in the sexual behavior of schoolboys and university students, and especially the spreading of venereal disease among young people, led the Pirogov Society to conduct a number of "sex censuses" in universities in Kharkov, Moscow, Yuriev, and, somewhat later, Tomsk. The largest survey was in Moscow, where the Student Medical Society of Moscow University, under the guidance of Mikhail Chlenov, distributed a substantial questionnaire among students, receiving 2,150 replies. There were questions on a wide range of issues, from personality and living conditions to health, recreation, family background, marriage and extramarital sexual life, and masturbation and "other sexual follies," and about venereal disease.[13]

The results were extremely informative. The respondents were young men, mostly between the ages of 19 and 21, mainly urban dwellers, and, as university students, well-educated. Two-thirds of those surveyed assessed the style of their family upbringing as religious-moral. "Early sexual feeling" was noted—though not defined—by 92%, who associated it with the influence of pornographic books, "street education," the conduct of friends, and the like. Family sex education was sparse, consisting mostly of moral instructions and admonitions about the danger of venereal disease and the psychological problems resulting from masturbation. Only one in eight had received any explanation of sexual processes—and these fortunate few had overwhelmingly (62%) received their information only from friends. As many as 96% had read books "on the sex question"; 63% had read popular medical books (it must be remembered that the survey was conducted by the Student Medical Society, and that 30% of the respondents were medical students). Before entering university 25% had been attracted to pornography; 16% read pornographic literature during their student terms.

In terms of sexual activities, some 67% had had sexual affairs before coming to university, while 23% had deliberately avoided them. Some 57.1% said they were frustrated because of sexual abstinence. Only 7% of the students were married; of these nearly two-thirds had sex with their wives more than four times a month, 51% had irregular intercourse, 3% did not have sex with their wives at all, and 9% were having extramarital affairs. Some 57% took precautions against conception: 25% used withdrawal, and 16% condoms.

Of those who had started their sexual lives before coming to university, half had done so before the age of 17. For 41% the first partner had been a prostitute, for 35% a servant, and for 10% a married woman. As a rule, intercourse occurred while they were sober (82%) and not in company (73%). All the same, the sex life of students was irregular, and intercourse was rare—once a month for 14%, even less for 40%—and haphazard. In 47% of the cases, students went to prostitutes for sex. As many as 79% took measures against infection and conception. The moral values and personal behavior of the students were often in flagrant contradiction: two-thirds of those surveyed were opposed in principle to extramarital relations.

The question of masturbation, as might be expected, was a painful one, as everywhere at the time. Some 60% owned up to having done it, while

14% said they were engaging in it now; the peak ages for the practice were 15–16. To a more detailed question about masturbation frequency, only 38% replied. Some 59% had discovered masturbation for themselves, and 42% through someone else. The great bulk of students were trying to stop this "harmful habit" on moral grounds and out of fear of the consequences. But not all of them were succeeding. Most students complained of "energy loss" from masturbation, but they feared even worse. One student even called masturbation "a spontaneous manifestation of our nervous age, the cause of a degeneration, perhaps, more serious than syphilis."

Of the students surveyed, roughly a quarter had suffered from venereal disease, mostly gonorrhea, a few from a mild form of chancre and syphilis. More often than not the students had caught the disease in their first year or even before entering university; the primary source (from 70 to 83%) was a prostitute. In addenda to the questionnaires, some students suggested that the university should assign a doctor to a special post responsible for venereal disease.

In drawing conclusion from this "census," Chlenov suggested that it revealed serious social problems that gave rise to concern for the material welfare of students; he suggested earlier marriages, self-education groups, increased respect for women, special legislation on prostitution, and combating pornography by cultural rather than prohibitive means. By European standards of the time, these proposals were thoroughly progressive.

Some researchers attempted to correlate the political atmosphere on the eve of and after the revolution of 1905 with students' sexual attitudes. In fact, the Tomsk survey was conducted in 1910 by Yakov Falevich, a 22-year-old student, who attempted to explain how political work by students influenced their attitudes toward sex and their own sexual experience. But neither the researchers nor the students were proposing "sexual freedom"; on the contrary, they were appealing for restraint. Half the Tomsk students who had taken part in revolutionary activities said it had changed their feelings: 80% noted the beneficial impact of revolution on their sexuality, while another 13% said they had experienced a decline in their sexual needs.[14] This was not at all the experience of the student revolution of the 1960s, which took place under slogans of sexual freedom.

Another subject of fervent debate at the turn of the century was homosexuality. By the end of the eighteenth century, with the growth of civilization and extended contact with Europe instead of its former indifference, genteel society began to feel uneasy about it.[15] Among the common people, it was concentrated primarily in certain religious sects like the Khlysty, whose rituals included definite homosexual, bisexual, and sadomasochistic elements. And among the aristocracy, homosexuality tended to cause scandal mostly for the nepotism and corruption it fostered, notably in various government ministries, college, and the military, as powerful people settled their accounts with their young protégés by making high appointments that in no way corresponded to their abilities.[16] As in the West, homosexuality was most widespread and visible in closed educational institutions—the Page corps, cadet corps, the Junker colleges, the School of Jurisprudence, and so on. Since it was a mass phenomenon, boys were quite accepting of it, even lighthearted, dedicating to it a host of bawdy, jesting verses. This theme occupies an important place in Lermontov's Junker verses ("To Tizenhausen," "Ode to a Latrine"), first published in 1879 in the Geneva collection *Eros russe* (*Russian erotica not for ladies*). Attempts by school or corps administrators to put a stop to such "indecent conduct" came to nothing.[17]

Until 1832, when the new criminal code was promulgated, homosexuality, except for the military, was a religious and moral issue but not a legal one. In 1832, *muzhelozhstvo* (buggery)-anal contact between men—was outlawed, with punishment set at loss of all civil and property rights and exile to Siberia for 4 to 5 years; rape or the perversion of a minor was punished by forced labor for between 10 and 20 years. Lesbianism was not mentioned. This legislation remained in force until 1903, when a new, more lenient criminal code was adopted: *muzhelozhstvo* was now punished by imprisonment for not fewer than three months, with aggravated circumstances resulting in imprisonment for a period between three and eight years.[18] The well-known lawyer Vladimir Nabokov (father of the writer) proposed decriminalizing homosexuality in 1902, yet the proposal was seen as too radical for the time.

Still, this legislation was rarely enforced—only ten people were prosecuted for homosexuality in 1894. And at least in regard to the privileged classes, homosexuality was no hindrance to either personal liberty or public careers. Although most Russian doctors, like their European counterparts, considered homosexuality a "perversion of the sexual feeling" and debated the possibility of treating it, many other people simply turned a blind eye to it. A few members of the royal family even followed a blatantly homosexual lifestyle—for example, Nicholas II's uncle, the Grand Duke Sergei Alexandrovich. Nor did intellectuals generally suffer persecution for their proclivities. The poet Alexei Apukhtin led an openly homosexual life; he was a classmate and friend of Peter Tchaikovsky at the School of Jurisprudence, which had gained a reputation for such traditions. Students even had a humorous anthem, which asserted that sex with one's companions was more pleasant than with women. So the legend of the composer's suicide as the sentence of a court of honor made up of his former classmates is patently absurd. Even if a scandal had in fact blown up over Tchaikovsky's sexual preference, it would have posed no real danger to him.

Thus, at the beginning of the twentieth century, Russia, like other European countries, was beginning to confront the broader social context of sexuality. As elsewhere, rigid normative uniformity and moralization were gradually giving way to a rational secular understanding. Russian medical personnel, lawyers, and sociologists had a good grasp of West European literature on sex and sexuality and came to similar conclusions as their Western counterparts. However, as in Western Europe, sexuality provoked many irrational fears, and its examination primarily in relation to dangerous and adverse phenomena (venereal disease, abortion, prostitution, crime) did not alter the cautious and fastidious attitude toward it that many had inherited from the past.

# Part II

# THE SOVIET SEXUAL EXPERIMENT

## Chapter Four

# FREEDOM FOR WHAT?

*What does liberation mean? If I free someone in the desert and he
cannot go anywhere, what is his freedom worth? Freedom exists only
for someone who wants to go somewhere. Liberating someone in the
desert means arousing a thirst in him and showing him the way to a
well. Only then do his actions take on meaning.*

—Antoine de Saint-Exupéry

How did people's sexual behavior and sexual values change under the
impact of the October Revolution, and were these changes a consequence of deliberate Bolshevik policy or of spontaneous development?
As we have discussed, the process of sexual change is always complex
and contradictory, and this was certainly the case in Russia under the Soviets.[1] Although the available data are fragmentary, inconsistent, and somewhat unreliable, and await the analysis of professional historians, for our
purposes we may delineate four major stages:

1917–1930: The disintegration of the traditional family structure;
the social emancipation of women; the weakening of the institution of marriage and the sexual morality based on it; normative
uncertainty in regard to sexuality.
1930–1956: Official attempts at strengthening institutions of marriage and the family by command-administrative methods;
establishment of totalitarian control over the individual; denial
and repression of sexuality; elimination of sexual culture.

1956–1986: The replacement of totalitarianism by authoritarianism; gradual expansion of the sphere of individual freedom; transition from police-administrative methods to moral-administrative methods for protecting marriage and the family; the shift from a policy of denying and repressing sexuality to one of regulation and domestication; the medicalization and pedagogization of sexuality.

1987–1994: Weakening of state and Party social control; the downfall of the Soviet regime; sex comes out of the closet; anomie and moral panic; commercialization, trivialization, and "Westernization" of sexuality.

Originally, some aspects of the Bolshevik sexual policy were not repressive but daring and progressive—involving the social, political, and thus sexual emancipation of women. All gender and sexual issues were deliberately formulated in social, rather than medical or biological, terms, which meant that understanding of the interaction of these phenomena was shared by more than a small group of narrowly focused professionals. Concentration of power in state hands enabled the authorities not only to proclaim their ideas but to carry them out in practice. Soviet demographic and medical politics were closely linked to progressive practices in Western Europe, particularly in Germany. The regime could draw on an excellent intellectual tradition in pre-Revolutionary social medicine, exemplified by the work of such brilliant scholars as A. P. Dobroslavin, F. F. Erisman and G. V. Khlopin. And the field was headed by an educated and courageous health commissar, Nikolai Semashko.

However, the authorities soon found themselves overwhelmed by the sheer magnitude of difficulties involved in attempting the simultaneous economic, educational, and cultural modernization of the country.

Before the revolution Marxists had no definite policy in regard to sexuality. The "sex issue" was for them mainly economic and sociopolitical and essentially boiled down to the problem of emancipating women and overcoming gender inequality. Sexuality was mentioned only in passing, especially in relation to the family.

In contrast to the Soviets, who sought to eliminate sexuality even as they pretended to ignore it, the founders of Marxism were no canting hypocrites. Marx had stressed that "the love passion . . . cannot be constructed a priori inasmuch as its evolution constitutes a real development taking place in the sensual world and among real individuals."[2] According to him, the measure of historical individualization of gender relationships "reveals the extent to which man's natural behavior has become human . . . , the extent to which he in his individual existence is at the same time a social being."[3]

Although Marx was dedicated to his social cause, he was also capable of experiencing and expressing genuine passion, as this letter to his wife testifies:

> Whoever of my innumerable slanderers and backbiting foes has ever accused me of fitting the part of the first lover in some second-rate theatrical production? Yet such is the case. . . . My love for you is such that, should you be far from me, my love would grow to what it really is— gigantic proportions; it contains all of my spiritual energy and all the power of my feelings. Once again I feel myself human in the full sense of the word, for I sense an immense passion. After all, the versatility which is forced upon us by present-day education and upbringing, and the skepticism which obliges us to doubt all subjective and objective impressions, only exists to make us petty, feeble, peevish, and irresolute. What makes man human again in the full sense of the word, however, is love for his beloved woman, for you, my dear, and not love for a Feuerbachian "person," for a Moleschott "metabolism," or for the proletariat.[4]

But the question of sexuality occupied little of Marx's time, while he conducted his personal affairs on the very principles of bourgeois morality that he rejected philosophically.

The happy-go-lucky bachelor Engels was much more sympathetic and tolerant than his powerful friend. Engels sharply mocked "the false Philistine timidity" of nineteenth-century German socialists: in reading their works, he said, "you'd think people had no sexual organs at all."[5] His book *The Origin of the Family, Private Property, and the State* (1884) contains a fine essay of the historical sociology of love and sexual morality, which he considered a product of property relations.

Engels regarded bourgeois marriage based on private property and the enslavement of women as a historically transitory institution, although he was cautious about the future:

> All that we can presuppose today about forms of relations between the sexes after the impending destruction of capitalist production is primarily of a negative character; it is defined in most cases by what will be removed. But what will replace it? That will be determined when there is a new gen-

eration: a generation of men who will never in their lives have to purchase women for money or for other social means of power, and a generation of women who will never have to give themselves to men for any other inducement other than genuine love, nor will they have to reject intimacy with a beloved man out of fear of economic consequences. When these people appear they will cast to the four winds the idea of behaving according to existing conventions; they will know themselves how to act, and they themselves will work out their own social views according to each person's separate will—and nothing more.[6]

While Engels's views of ideal male-female relations was quite progressive and perhaps even radical in 1884, the same could not be said of his views on homosexuality. In his *Origin of the Family*, he treats ancient Greek pederasty as a "degradation" and as a manifestation of "indifference" (!?) to the sex of a loved person caused by insufficient individualization of feelings of love. And in a letter to Marx in June 1869, he vulgarly pokes fun at Karl Ulrich's defense of homosexuality.

Lenin's views on sexuality, as on other issues, were far more primitive than those of Marx and Engels, for two reasons. Despite his intellectual pretensions, Lenin was not a philosopher but a politician, and he was a man cast in a rigid puritanical mold, subject to a host of unconscious complexes. Both on the "women's issue" and in regard to the family, he saw mainly the social and political aspects, ignoring psychology and emotion. And for Lenin, individual pleasure was invariably considered suspect.

Clara Zetkin reported that in his widely known conversation with her, Lenin said,

The feelings of the individual change swiftly in an epoch when powerful states are crumbling, when the old relations based on domination are withering on the bough, when an entire social world is starting to perish. In these circumstances, the whipped-up frenzy for variety and enjoyment easily acquires unrestrained power. The forms of marriage and communion between the sexes in bourgeois society no longer satisfy people. In the area of marriage and sexual relations, the revolution is nigh, in keeping with the proletarian revolution."[7]

But that "in keeping with the proletarian revolution" is relative, since the danger of individualism lurks within sexual freedom. Lenin found the principle of "free love" suspect, since it could be abused (as if there exists any freedom that cannot be abused!). Thus, all Lenin's words on this issues, although frequently quite reasonable, tended to reflect his conservative views, as if he were afraid of what people would do without strict social supervision.

There were good grounds for caution. The Bolshevik revolution had destroyed or undermined traditional norms and regulators of sexual conduct—church weddings, religious morality, established gender social roles, even the very concept of love. The revolution had proclaimed that everything was beginning anew, on an empty plane. Unfortunately, that plane was too empty—the revolution posited nothing with which to replace the old beliefs and norms. As on other questions of social life, the Bolshevik philosophy on gender and sexuality was as primitive as that of a caveman's club:

1. All problems that have long perturbed humanity are caused by private property and human exploitation.
2. The socialist revolution can and must abolish them.
3. This may be accomplished swiftly and radically, without counting the cost, and initially relying on the power of the proletarian dictatorship.
4. Class interests and social control are more important than individual freedoms.

Initially, the problems with these views in relation to matters of gender and sexuality were not readily apparent. Soviet legislation and social policy on issues of marriage and procreation in the 1920s were the most daringly progressive in the world.[8] As early as 1918, women were accorded full equal rights with men in all social and private areas, including marriage and family relations. Women had the right to choose their surname, place of residence, and social status. Their involvement in productive labor was supposed to ensure them economic independence of men. If they became pregnant, they were entitled to paid holidays. To relieve women of onerous "domestic servitude," the state began to set up a system of crèches, nurseries, and communal food supplies. Medical service for mothers and children was expanded and improved and became entirely free.

Unfortunately, the realities of life that confronted the Bolsheviks immediately after the revolution were much more difficult than they had anticipated. Many of the splendid beginnings of equality were impossible to carry forward in the midst of economic ruin, poverty, and lack of culture; these plans had to be put on the back burner for a time. And the costs associated with the subsequent breakdown in marriage and family patterns—unwanted pregnancies, fatherless children, prostitution, the spread of venereal disease—were great and provoked mounting concern. The Bolsheviks had to do what was necessary, rather than what was desirable. But these necessary measures often had boomerang effects that only aggravated the original difficulties.

The liberation of women from the bonds of church-based marriage made them more vulnerable to sexual exploitation. The massive involvement of women in the labor force proved to be detrimental to family life and the education of children. The legalization of induced abortion produced a drastic decline in the birthrate. Added to this were material shortages and poor housing conditions.

Insofar as the attempt to improve social conditions proved to be a failure, the state had to return to more and more restrictive social policies. The aim of changing social conditions, adapting them to the needs of individual human beings, which was the essence of the original Marxist theory of alienation, was gradually reformulated as the task of adapting human behaviors, needs, and even feelings to the extant poor and inhuman social conditions. *Volens nolens*, Soviet society had to be totalitarian. Social control had taken the place of individual freedom. And while open resistance to these pressures was or seemed impossible, it was easy to conclude that it was easier to transform human nature than to transform social structures.

Yet this was only another dangerous illusion.

Ultimately, the Bolsheviks had two alternative strategies in regard to sexuality: acceptance or suppression.

The first, more liberal, viewpoint was formulated by Alexandra Kollontay in her 1923 sensation-making article, "Make Way for Winged Eros!":

> During the years of tense civil war and battle against the country's collapse, there was neither the time nor the spiritual energy for the "joys and torments" of love . . . Dominating the situation for a time was the uncomplicated voice of nature—the biological instinct to reproduce, based on the attraction of two sexual individuals. Men and women easily—more easily than hitherto, more simply than before—came together and drew apart. They came together without great spiritual emotions and they drew apart without tears and pain. . . . Prostitution, it is true, disappeared, but there was an obvious increase in free communion of the sexes, made without mutual pledges, in which the motive force was the naked instinct for reproduction, stripped of the torments of love. This frightened a few. But in fact relations between the sexes in those years could not have developed in any other way. . . . The class of warriors, at a time when the invitation to revolution incessantly range out above laboring humanity, could not succumb to the power of winged Eros. . . .
> But now the picture is changing. . . . Men and women today are not

only "coming together," not only are tying a transient bond for alleviating the sexual instinct, as mostly happened during the revolution years, but they are beginning once more to experience "romantic love, " recognizing once more all the torments of love, the whole inspiration of happiness and mutual love.[9]

Kollontay by no means dismissed or denounced the serious nature of love relationships. On the contrary, she opposed "sexual fetishism" and "hedonism," contemptuously labeling the casual relations of the civil war period as merely manifestations of the sex instinct unworthy of a Bolshevik. Even this thoroughly moral viewpoint, however, provoked numerous attacks on her.

The second, more rigid, and dogmatic stance on sexuality was taken by Aron Zalkind, the author of the popular books *Youth and Revolution* (1924), *Sexual Fetishism: A Review of Sex Questions* (1925), and *The Sex Issue in Soviet Social Conditions* (1926). Zalkind admitted the existence of a biological sexual drive in human beings and the harm of "sexual self-corking." At the same time, however, he proposed wholesale subordination of sexuality to the proletariat's class interests. What follows is a summary of his "Twelve Sexual Commandments for the Revolutionary Proletariat":

Sexual life is permissible only in so far as it encourages the growth of collective feelings, class organization, creative endeavor in work and military activity. . . . Because the proletariat and the laboring masses economically allied to it comprise the main bulk of the proletariat, *revolutionary expedience is thereby the best biological expedience*, the greatest biological blessing. . . .

Here is the proletarian approach to the sexual question:

1. *Sex life should not develop too early* among proletarians. . . .
2. *There should be sexual abstention before marriage, and marriage should take place only in a state of complete social and biological maturity (i.e., between the ages of 20 and 25).* . . .
3. *Sex should only be the ultimate completion of a deep all-round sympathy with and attachment to the object of sexual love.*

    Purely physical involvement is impermissible. . . . Sexual involvement with a class enemy, moral enemy, or object unworthy of one's love is just as repulsive as the sexual involvement of a human being with a crocodile or orangutan. . . .
4. *The sex act must only be the last link in the chain of deep-seated and complex feelings connecting the lovers at a given moment.* . . .
5. *The sex act must not be repeated frequently.* . . .

6. *One should not change one's sexual partner often. Less sexual variety is needed. . . .*
7. *Love must be monogamous, monandrous (one wife, one husband). . . .*
8. *During every sexual act one must always remember the possibility of giving birth to a child and generally think of one's progeny. . . .*
9. *Sexual choice must be based on class, on revolutionary-proletarian expedience. Love relationships must not involve elements of flirtation, frivolity, coquettishness and suchlike methods of sexual conquest.*

    Sexual life is rightly viewed by the class as a social rather than a narrowly personal function; this is why social, class virtues must attract and predominate in one's love life, and not specific physiological-sexual allurements, which are predominantly either a vestige of our precultural development or a result of the putrid effect of exploitative conditions of life. . . .
10. *One must not be jealous. . . .*
11. *One must not engage in sexual perversions. . . .*
12. *In the interests of revolutionary expedience, the class has the right to interfere in the sexual life of its members. The sexual must be subordinate in everything to the class, in no way hampering it, and serving it in all it does. . . .*

    *Hence, all those elements of sexual life that harm the establishment of a healthy revolutionary new generation, which rob class energy, let class joys rot, or spoil intra-class relations, must be mercilessly swept away from class practice.*[10]

Today all this reads like farce, but in 1924 it was utterly serious revolutionary stuff. Apart from the vulgar sociology of "class" formulations, it was these premises, as we shall show later, that determined the attitude of the Bolshevik Party and the Soviet state toward sexuality right up to the last days of its inhuman regime.

Of course, Lenin did not read the Zalkind commandments, since they were promulgated after his death; if he had, he would have laughed them to scorn.[11] He could not bear stupidities of vulgar sociologisms, emphasizing that "relations between the sexes are not simply an expression of a game between social economics and physical needs."[12] And yet, in their inner intentions, their emphasis on social control, the Zalkind Commandments were much closer to Lenin's views on sexuality than the uncontrollable "Winged Eros," which put the accent on individual freedom—much less the notion of "free love."

Like many intellectuals, Lenin was nauseated by the reduction of sexuality and love to "the simple satisfaction of sexual need." In his conversation with Clara Zetkin, he roundly criticized the widespread view among young people that under socialism it would be just as simple to satisfy the sexual drive as to drink a glass of water.

Of course, Lenin argued, "you have to quench your thirst. But would a normal person in normal circumstances lie down in the dirt of the street to drink out of a puddle? Or even from a glass whose rim was dirty from the lips of dozens of people? The social aspect is far more important. Drinking water is really an individual act. But two people take part in love, and a third, new life comes into being. Here we have social interest and a duty to society."[13]

These words are eminently sensible. Lenin was opposed to asceticism and hypocrisy, yet he was also annoyed that expenditure of sexual energy diverted young people from the revolutionary struggle: "The revolution requires from the masses and from the individual concerted energy and concentration of resources. It will not stand orgiastic states like those common to d'Annunzio's decadent heroes and heroines. Lack of restraint in sexual life is bourgeois: it is a sign of decadence. The proletariat is the rising class. It has no need of intoxication for stupefaction or excitement."[14]

Lenin was skeptical of and even frankly hostile to all theories touting the absolute importance of sexuality, above all Freudian theory. He felt that all such theories flowed from personal requirement, "from an aspiration to justify one's own abnormal or excessive sexual life in the face of bourgeois morality and to seek toleration for oneself."[15]

But whence does society draw its ideas of what is normal and abnormal? Why is sexual toleration bad? Such questions apparently did not even enter the head of the leader of the proletarian revolution. For him, individuals were social agents, representatives of different social classes, elements of "productive forces," but never free, spontaneous human subjects.

Ethical and aesthetic standards as seen in early mass Soviet literature were equally contradictory.

Bolshevism abolished, on the one hand, God, ecclesiastical marriage, and absolute moral values, and, on the other, the individual's right to personal self-determination and love that might stand higher than all social duties. Now Bolshevism was helpless in the face of ethical relativism. Hence it produced either a mechanistic biologization of sexuality or the equally old and equally mechanistic subordination of individual desires to class group norms.

Soviet mass literature of the early 1920s is full of complaints about "sexual Bacchanalias" and "moral disorientation."[16] One such article published in 1920 said, "The old rotten foundations of the family and marriage are crumbling and moving towards complete destruction with every passing day. Yet there are no guidelines on creating healthy and beautiful new relations. An unimaginable Bacchanalia is in full flood. Free love is perceived by the best people as free perversion."[17]

"We have no love, just sexual relations," declares the main character in *Without Bird Cherry*, a sensationalist novel by Panteleimon Romanov published in 1926. Tania Aristarkhova, the heroine of another sensationalist book, *The Moon on the Right Hand, or Unusual Love*, by Sergei I. Malashkin (1926), had already had 22 lovers by the start of the story; she takes part in orgies, drinks heavily and takes drugs, yet subsequently overcomes the harmful impact of the NEP (New Economic Policy) and acquires moral purity in the bosom of the Party.

In Alexandra Kollontay's popular short story, "Love of Worker Bees" (1923), we read,

> You are most surprised about my going with men whenever they take my fancy without waiting to fall in love with them? Well, you see, to "fall in love" you have to have plenty of leisure time; I've read a lot of novels and I know how much time and energy it takes to be in love. And I don't have time. Our region is currently such an important zone. . . . Anyway, when in all these past years did we ever have plenty of leisure? Always in a hurry, always our heads full of something different.[18]

Soviet poetry and prose of the 1920s contain many coarse, primitive, naturalistic sexual scenes and symbols. It could hardly have been otherwise: the writers, coming to literature straight from the wooden plow or from the workbench, had no knowledge of erotic subtleties; they described what they themselves felt and saw in real life. This shocked Party intellectuals, but how else was the Party to react to such things when it held all private life to be public? It simply had no idea.

Whatever a young man or woman did, he or she would, in American scholar Sheila Fitzpatrick's perceptive comment, fall into the sin of *meshchanstvo* (vulgarity, petit bourgeois morals). If the youngster were to live like his parents, he would fall into the "bourgeois marriage" trap; and if he were to become a sexual revolutionary, he would fall under the shadow of bourgeois-bohemian irresponsibility, "Yeseninism" (after the great Russian lyric poet Sergei Yesenin, who had romanticized the culture of the tavern), or "Yenchmenism" (after the young philosopher and "free love" advocate, Emmanuil Yenchmen, who was "exposed" by Party ideologue Nikolai Bukharin in 1923). And these were not purely academic issues.

The disintegration of marriage and family also had very serious social consequences. From 1912 to the 1920s, the number of divorces per thousand people increased sevenfold.[19] Ecclesiastical marriage lost its moral and legal significance, and many people didn't take civilly sanctioned marriages seriously. Some convinced Communists believed the institution of marriage was altogether unnecessary. The parents of a friend of mine, who had lived together happily and faithfully for more than 50 years—their entire lives—registered their marriage only in the mid-1980s, simultaneous with the marriage of a grandson (who has since had two divorces). And they did so only for practical reasons, such as the wife's being allowed to take advantage of her Party veteran husband's privileges at a special polyclinic, which would have been illegal had they not married.

But not all de facto marriages were so stable. As might be expected, women suffered the most. There was even a joke: in sexual relationships, the third correlate of liberty and equality was not fraternity but maternity.[20]

Under the circumstances, the authorities had to do something. One such unpleasant but necessary measure was the legalization of induced abortion.

Back in 1913, in a commentary on the results of the Twelfth Pirogov Congress, Lenin had supported the demand "for an urgent revocation of all laws prosecuting abortion or the distribution of medical knowledge about preventive measures, etc." He saw in that the safeguarding "of the basic democratic rights of all male and female citizens."[21]

Ideologically, the Soviet state was oriented from the start on a pronatal policy, favoring a high birthrate, and it did all it could to protect the life and health of mother and child. Nevertheless, in 1920, the Soviet government was the first in Europe to legalize abortion. Given the undeniable fact of impending economic ruin, the real choice was not between abortion or promotion of a high birthrate, but between legal and relatively safe abortion and illegal and dangerous abortion—in Moscow in the 1920s, the risk of dying of infection as a result of an abortion was 60 to 120 times higher than the risk of death while giving birth.[22] In such a situation, social considerations outweighed moral principles, such as the concern for preserving the life of the fetus, on which midwives and gynecologists had been insisting both before and after the adoption of the law.

Legalization of abortion was a risky decision, yet it seemed to be the right one. Although the number of induced abortions sharply rose after their legalization—according to some figures, they tripled; if we are to credit the local medical statistics, in 1924 abortions amounted to half the total number of live births in Leningrad, and to 43% in one Moscow clinic[23]—the number of nonhospital abortions sharply fell. So the articulated goal had been achieved.

But the number of abortions continued to grow. As many as 102,709 legal induced abortions were carried out in Russian hospitals in 1926.[24] Moscow and Leningrad accounted for 39% of that figure, while regional and district centers amounted to 30%, and small towns 16%. Women in the countryside, who constituted as many as 83% of the female population, accounted for as few of 15% of all abortions.

Does that mean that life was easier, more stable, less desperate in the countryside? By no means. A study of 1,087 peasant women from 21 villages in Smolensk province showed that despite almost half trying to take some sort of contraceptive precautions (467 practiced coitus interruptus and 22 used the syringe method), every fourth woman had to resort to induced abortion, which was the second-most widespread method of birth control.

The experts—midwives, gynecologists, and social hygienists—were seriously worried by the situation. Interestingly enough, however, women as subjects of free sexual choice were largely absent from these professional discussions and disputes.

The disputes mainly involved the "correct" relationship between a woman's family role—i.e., as mother—and her extrafamilial social role—i.e., as worker. Was it more important for the state to safeguard the woman's health as a mother, a procreator of the human race, or as a worker realizing herself in social life? Because this issue was discussed practically without the participation of women, the "experts" were prepared to resolve this in the same way for all women, without reckoning with the fact that different women might have different priorities.

Another concern was the rise in the incidence of venereal disease and prostitution. According to a survey of patients carried out in 1925 at the Second Moscow Venerealogical Clinic, as many as 45% of the men and 81% of the women had no knowledge whatsoever of the nature of and treatment for sexually transmitted disease. What is more, the source of between 54% and 88% of all cases could be traced back to prostitution.[25]

The emergence of a host of problems, old and new, directly or indirectly linked to sexuality, stimulated extensive new social research into sex and sexuality. As we know, Russia already had some experience in this field; at this time, there were numerous questionnaires on sexual behavior—more than in other countries.[26] In fact, no period of Soviet sexual history is so richly documented as the 1920s.

At first glance, all the data gathered testify to profound, revolutionary, and rather negative changes. Premarital and extramarital sex was very common among young workers and students.[27] According to Russian sociologist Sergei Golod's estimates, aggregating the results of several large-scale surveys in the 1920s, between 85 and 95% of men and 48 and 62% of women engaged in premarital sex.[28] On average, men commenced their sexual lives between the ages of 16 and 18, and approximately a quarter of those who had had sexual experience by the time of the survey had lost their virginity before their sixteenth birthday. Women began their sexual lives later than men, but the gap was steadily diminishing. Women named "love" (49%), "attraction" (30%), and "curiosity" (20%) as the main reason for entering upon an affair and starting their sexual lives; men named "sexual need" (54%), "attraction" (28%), and "curiosity" (19%).

The high incidence of extramarital affairs came as no surprise. According to S. Golosovker's statistics (1925), about half of the women students in Kazan approved of them as a matter of principle, while a third actually engaged in them. Among the male metal workers and engineers in M. Barash's Moscow survey (1925), half had had extramarital affairs. In Z. Gurevich and F. Grosser's study of Kharkov (1930), men gave as their reasons "separation from their wife" (38%), "attraction" (25%), and "dissatisfaction with family life" (14%), while women named "separation from their husband" (38%), "dissatisfaction with family life" (21%), and "sexual dissatisfaction with their husband" (17%).

A high number of sexual affairs, along with low sexual culture, and the practical difficulties in acquiring any contraceptives, which were in permanently short supply or too expensive, forced young people to make do. Among 2,300 students in Odessa surveyed by D. Lass (1928), 308 employed condoms, 265 resorted to coitus interruptus, and 51 used chemical means, but none of this saved them from unwanted pregnancies and abortions.

The researchers, who as social workers were very concerned about the number of unwanted pregnancies and abortions and felt that these issues should by no means be swept under the rug as the "natural results of revolution," emphasized the negative, problematic aspects of the situation. But were these facts, seen in their historical context, really so novel and sensational?

As Sergei Golod justly remarks, the empirical material demonstrates the destruction of traditional norms and values rather than the emergence of new ones. The "sexual freedom" brought by the October Revolution was merely "freedom from," not "freedom for." People felt themselves free from certain former norms and constrictions, but they still did not know what to do with that freedom, or where to go with it. And without the positive dimension, a "negative" freedom is incomplete.

According to Sheila Fitzpatrick, who analyzed statistics on the sexual behavior of Soviet students in the 1920s, "the reported behavior of Soviet students provides more evidence of the persistence of traditional sexual patterns—including male machismo and prudent female chastity—than of liberating sexual revolution."[29]

Although students in Moscow and Odessa were frequently skeptical about the ideas of family, marriage, and love, the proportion of them who were married was considerably higher than among Moscow students surveyed by Chlenov in pre-Revolutionary 1904.

Neither was their level of sexual activity so terribly high in a comparative context. Some 10% of male students in Odessa were still virgins, another 10% had had previous sexual experience but were apparently not sexually active during the survey period, while 50% said they had sex only "haphazardly." Only 29% of those surveyed—somewhat less than the number of married students—had sex once a week or more. It is not surprising that three-quarters of the young people in the survey considered themselves deprived and dissatisfied, complaining that exhausting work and poor food were making them sexually impotent. As many as 41% of Odessa students revealed that they were suffering from impotence, whether "complete" (135 replies) or "relative" (603 replies). Student youth had neither the strength, nor the money, nor the time, nor appropriate living conditions for the sexual orgies so picturesquely attributed to them in the literature of the New Economic Policy period.

Encounters with prostitutes were far from universal either. Among Moscow University students surveyed by Chlenov in 1904, almost 42% of male students had begun their sex lives with prostitutes, and 36% with a housemaid. Of the Moscow students questioned by I. Gelman (1923), only 28% started with a prostitute, and none had any maids at all in their families; the corresponding figures from young Omsk men questioned by V. Klyachkin (1925) were 20% and 14%, while those for Odessa men (1928) were 14% and 9%. Initial sexual experience was now being acquired not with women hired for the purpose but with girlfriends from their own social milieu (38% in Batkis's figures [1925], 26% in Klyachkin's).

The inner psychological freedom of students was also less than might have been expected. Like pre-Revolutionary youngsters, they had particularly serious "hang-ups" about masturbation. Most Odessa and Omsk students experienced fear and revulsion when thinking about it: "As far as I am concerned, I think it has had an adverse effect on my memory, which has markedly deteriorated"; "As a result of ten years of daily masturbation, I feel I've become a monster." Between 43% and 49% of those surveyed maintained they had never masturbated, either in the past or the present. (Only 27% had given such an answer in the Chlenov 1904 study.) Apparently, this can be attributed primarily to the differences in student social origins, as those from a worker or peasant background had not yet realized that masturbation was not as dreadful as it was made out to be.)

Only rarely were students prepared to admit to homosexual experience. Gelman and Klyachkin each discovered only two such cases, Lass only three. Youths from worker and especially peasant backgrounds were more forthcoming about sexual contacts with animals than they were about them with other men—8% of peasant students at both Odessa and Omsk universities owned up to experience with bestiality.

All the surveys clearly reflected different experiences for men and women. While men were concerned with sexual inhibitions, impotence, and masturbation, women were much more worried about sexual permissiveness. If we take the results of the four surveys in the aggregate, we find that 55% of the women revealed they were virgins and 37% were married or had been married; only 13% of the unmarried women were sexually active. Although only a third of female students were virgins upon marriage, most of them had lost their virginity with their future spouses rather than through casual sexual encounters. Is this the stuff of "sexual Bacchanalia"?

Young people's views on sexuality were often more radical than their own sexual behavior. Many of them were skeptical about marriage and the family, saying they did not believe in romantic love, and every tenth male student was in favor of "free love." Yet their own life experiences tell a different story. For example, only 44% of male students in Odessa said they believed in the existence of love, yet 63% said they had experienced it!

In short, Sheila Fitzpatrick noted,

> the liberating effects of revolution can be seen in the students' unquestioning acceptance of unregistered marriage, divorce, and abortion. But on other questions they were clearly conservative—unliberated by either modern Western standards or those of the pre revolutionary Russian intelligentsia. . . .
>
> In fact, the surveys suggest that the last thing which the students could be accused of was a carefree attitude to sex, whatever rules of behavior they adopted. Many responded to the questionnaires as if they were being consulted on public policy. The consensus of the men was that sex was a serious matter and the problems it created were beyond the power of indi-

viduals to solve. The government should open free brothels, or oblige female students to satisfy the men's sexual needs, or forbid men with children to desert their wives, or make marriage viable by raising student stipends.[30]

Whatever the solution, general opinion was that "the sexual question in student conditions is extraordinarily complicated, and it must be decided at governmental level."[31]

The Soviet government stood ready to take on this responsibility.

*Chapter Five*

# SEXOPHOBIA IN ACTION

*It was not merely that the sex instinct created a world of its own that was outside the Party's control and which therefore had to be destroyed if possible. What was more important was that sexual privation induced hysteria, which was desirable because it could be transformed into war-fever and leader-worship. . . . For how could the fear, the hatred, and the lunatic credulity which the Party needed in its members be kept at the right pitch, except by bottling up some powerful instinct and using it as a driving force? The sex impulse was dangerous to the Party, and the Party had turned it to account.*

—George Orwell

It is usually thought that the Bolshevik crusade against sex began in the 1930s, as part of the general process of Stalinist tightening of the screws on and suppression of the individual—and there is an element of truth in that contention. During the 1920s the USSR had allowed the existence of erotic art, sociological surveys, and biological-medical sex research. However, all of this, and particularly the "decadent" erotic art that was clearly at odds with "proletarian culture," existed and developed despite the efforts of rather than with the endorsement of the Party. It was simply that, given the times, the Party was unable to ban them and had to confine itself to half-measures.

Nevertheless, it did combat them when it could. For example, in July 1924, a joint circular was issued by Glavlit (the censor's office) and Glavrepertkom (the Main Committee for Control over Repertoires and Performance), giving the following evaluation of the fox-trot, shimmy, and other popular Western dances that Russian young people had begun to copy: "As products of Western European restaurant culture, these dances are oriented on the very basest instincts. In their niggardly, monotonous movements they are essentially a 'salon' imitation of the sex act and all manner of physiological perversion. . . . Within the working atmosphere of the Soviet Republic's attempts to reconstruct life and sweep away rotten petit-bourgeois decadence, dancing should be quite different—exhilarating, joyful, ennobling."[1]

This was only the opening salvo. The entire history of Soviet culture, from start to finish, consists of out-and-out campaigns and mandates in which sexophobia plays a leading part.

Furious attacks against erotica were an attempt to neutralize the "demoralizing" influence of the New Economic Policy (NEP). As the American historian Eric Naiman has noted, the highly publicized tales of "sexual depravity" of the mid-twenties—Pateleimon Romanov's *Without Bird Cherry*, Lev Gumilev's *Dog Alley*, Sergei Malashkin's *The Moon on the Right Hand*, Nikolai Borisov's *Vera*—"when read today, seem didactic, moralizing tracts. But in 1926 and 1927 they were attacked as immoral and slanderous."[2]

The rising incidence of sexual crimes was also used for this purpose. For example, the 1926 gang rape in Chubarov Alley of a young woman by 26 drunken Leningrad youths, half of them Komsomol members, returning from a funeral, was deliberately made into a political sensation. The number of assailants was given in some newspapers as 40, and in the course of the trial Leningrad newspapers received a huge number of letters and petitions—over 54,000 signatures—demanding the death penalty.[3] The word *chubarovshchina* came to signify not only sexual depravity, but a general "lack of ideological discipline."

Bans were slapped on not only more or less straightforward, blatant eroticism but on practically everything associated with sexuality or that might be construed as hinting at it—and what, with proper effort, cannot be construed in that spirit?

Here are some extracts taken literally at random from the notebooks of the famous Soviet satirist Ilya Ilf, from the period 1925–37:

> Kicked out for sexual excess. . . .
> Dialogue in a Soviet film: Love is the most awful vice: "Do you fly?" "I do."
> "Far?" "Far." "To Tashkent?" "Yes, to Tashkent." That means he has loved her for a long time, that she loves him, that they even got married, perhaps even had children. Sheer allegory."[4]

In their 1932 satirical short story "Savanarylo"—the title is an allusion to the fanatical Florentine monk of the Renaissance, Savonarola, who destroyed works of art; in Russian, his name is made up of two words, savan, meaning "shroud," and rylo, "snout"—Ilf and his coauthor, Yevgeny Petrov, tell of an editor locking the door and bawling out an artist for his advertising poster:

| | |
|---|---|
| EDITOR: | "What the hell is this?" |
| ARTIST: | "A waitress." |
| EDITOR (pointing): | "No, this here! This!" |
| ARTIST: | "A sweater." |
| EDITOR (checking on the locked door): | "Don't you play games with me. You tell me what's under the sweater." |
| ARTIST: | "Breasts." |
| EDITOR: | "So it's a good thing I noticed right away. The breasts have to be eliminated." |
| ARTIST: | "I don't get it. Why?" |
| EDITOR (timidly): | "They're big. I would even say huge, comrade, huge." |
| ARTIST: | "They're not huge at all. She has a small, classical bosom. Aphrodite-like. Just like Canova's 'Venus at Rest' . . . or think of the famous German work of Professor Anderfakt, 'Bruste und Buste,' where he proves with numbers that a modern woman's breasts are much bigger than those in antiquity. . . . But I drew these from antiquity." |
| EDITOR: | "Well, what does being bigger make it? You mustn't let yourself drift in that direction. Breasts have to be organized. Don't forget, women and children will see that poster—even grown men." |
| ARTIST: | "You must be kidding. After all, my waitress is fully clothed. And her breasts are quite small. In terms of real size, they work out at no more than size 33." |
| EDITOR: | "So we need a boy's size, about 28. Anyway, cut the cackle. You know what I mean. Breasts are indecent."[5] |

All this seems too grotesque to be anything but satire, yet I remember an occasion as late as the 1950s, when the chiefs of the Leningrad publishing house Lenizdat refused to allow the use of a picture of Venus de Milo as an illustration on a brochure on aesthetics; they called it pornographic. The affair was kicked upstairs to the regional party secretary in charge of propaganda, who turned out to be reasonably intelligent and defended the honor of Venus de Milo; he was an exception, however, since as a rule, Leningrad Party secretaries, even when measured against the overall gray background, were distinguished by their dimwittedness and intolerance. And he hardly would have given his approval had the statue been made by a contemporary Soviet sculptor.

In 1936, when Dmitri Shostakovich was being "worked over," one accusation made about his opera *Lady Macbeth of Mtsensk* was that the music naturalistically depicted the creaking of bedsprings.

Accusations of eroticism and "unhealthy sexual interests"—by definition, Soviet men and women had and could have no healthy sexual interests!—were employed in just about every ideological campaign and attempt at vilification. Stalin's foremost ideologist and cultural aide-de-camp, Andrei Zhdanov, spoke contemptuously in 1946 of the greatest of all twentieth century Russian woman poets, Anna Akhmatova, as "half-nun and half-whore." During the 1960s, Nikita Krushchev was sent into paroxysms of rage at the sight of a nude female body in Robert Falk's paintings.

Art was merely the earliest victim of Bolshevik sexophobia. In the late 1920s and early 1930s, the antisex crusade was all-pervasive. When Wilhelm Reich, the influential German protégé of Freud and admirer of Marx, visited Moscow in 1929, hoping to find there a Mecca of sexual freedom, he was surprised and shocked by its new "bourgeois moralistic attitudes."[6] One repressive measure followed another.

The first measure was an official restoration of criminal penalties and reinforcement of persecution for male homosexuality. The initiative for revocation of the antihomosexual legislation, following the February 1917 Revolution, had come not from the Bolsheviks but from the Cadets (Constitutional Democrats) and the anarchists. Nonetheless, once the old criminal code had been repealed after the October Revolution, Article 516 also ceased to be valid. The Russian Federation criminal codes for 1922 and 1926 did not mention homosexuality, although the corresponding laws remained in force in some places where homosexuality was traditionally the most prevalent—in the Islamic republics of Azerbaijan, Turkmenia, and Uzbekistan, as well as in Christian Georgia.

Soviet medical and legal experts were very proud of the progressive nature of their legislation. At the Congress of the World League for Sexual Reform, held in Copenhagen in 1928, Soviet legislation was cited to representatives of other countries as an example of progressivism. In 1930, medical expert Mark Sereisky wrote in *The Great Soviet Encyclopedia*: "Soviet legislation does not recognize so-called crimes against morality. Our laws proceed from the principle of protection of society and therefore countenance punishment only in those instances when juveniles and minors are the objects of homosexual interest."[7]

The official stance of Soviet medicine and law in the 1920s, as reflected in Sereisky's encyclopedia article, was that homosexuality was not a crime but a disease that was difficult, perhaps even impossible, to cure:

> While recognizing the incorrectness of homosexual development, society does not and cannot blame those who bear such traits. . . . In emphasizing the significance of sources that give rise to such an anomaly, our society combines prophylactic and other therapeutic measures with all the necessary conditions for making the conflicts that afflict homosexuals as painless as possible and for resolving their typical estrangement from society within the collective.[8]

Sereisky pinned indefinite hopes for a future "radical cure" for all homosexuals on the possibility of transplanting testicles from heterosexual to homosexual men, as had been suggested by the German biologist E. Steinach.

During the 1920s, the status of Soviet homosexuals was relatively tolerable. Some homosexuals—Mikhail Kuzmin, Nikolai Klyuev, and Sophia Parnok, among others—played major roles in Soviet culture, although the opportunity for an open, philosophical, and artistic discussion of the theme, which had opened up at the start of the century, was gradually whittled away.[9] On December 17, 1933, however, the government announced the change in law, which would be compulsory in all the republics in March 1934: accordingly, *muzhelozhstvo* (buggery) once more became a criminal offense. An item to that effect was inserted in the criminal codes of all the Soviet republics. According to Article 121 of the Russian Federation Criminal Code, *muzhelozhstvo*, sexual relations between men, was punishable by deprivation of freedom for a term of up to five years, and, in cases involving physical force or the threat thereof, or exploitation of the victim's dependent status, or in relation to a minor, a term of up to eight years.

In January 1936, Nikolai Krylenko, people's commissar for justice, announced that homosexuality was a product of the decadence of the exploiting classes who knew no better; in a socialist society founded on healthy principles there was no place for such people. Homosexuality was, therefore, directly tied to counterrevolution.[10]

Subsequently, Soviet lawyers and medical authorities and specialists described homosexuality primarily as a manifestation of the "moral decadence of the bourgeoisie," reiterating verbatim the arguments of German fascists.

Typical in this respect was the anonymous article on the subject of homosexuality in the second edition of *The Great Soviet Encyclopedia*, published in 1952. References to possible biological sources of homosexuality, which had hitherto been used for humanistic purposes as reasons to decriminalize homosexuality, were now rejected:

> The origin of H. is linked to everyday social conditions; for the overwhelming majority of people indulging in H., these perversions stop as soon as the person finds himself in a favorable social environment. . . . In Soviet society, with its healthy mores, H. as a sexual perversion is considered shameful and criminal. Soviet criminal legislation regards H. punishable with the exception of those instances where H. is a manifestation of marked psychic disorder. . . . H. is practically unpunished by law in bourgeois countries, where it represents an expression of the moral degradation of the ruling classes.[11]

The precise number of victims of Article 121 is unknown. According to calculations made by St. Petersburg gay activist Sergei Shcherbakov, an average of a thousand men a year fell victim to the law. The first official information on the subject was released only after perestroika had begun and refers to 1987, when 831 men were found guilty under Article 121. The number of victims must have been far larger in previous years.

Article 121 was not aimed solely at homosexuals. The authorities frequently employed it also for dealing with dissidents and for prolonging labor camp sentences. Sometimes the KGB was directly involved in the prosecution, as, for example, was the case in the early 1980s, when the well-known Leningrad archaeologist Lev Klein was charged; his trial was orchestrated from start to finish by the local KGB in gross violation of all procedural norms. Typically, the purpose of such actions was to intimidate the intelligentsia and keep them from pressing for freedoms and reforms.

Application of the law was selective. If eminent cultural figures kept their noses clean, they enjoyed a kind of immunity, with the authorities often turning a blind eye to their homosexual proclivities. But they had only to fall afoul of an influential bigwig for the law to go into high gear. This was the scenario that destroyed the life of the great Armenian filmmaker Sergei Paradzhanov; the responsible prosecutor on the staff of the Kiev procurator's office still boasts of his handiwork to this day.[12] As late as the latter part of the 1980s, the Chief Director of the Leningrad Yuny Zritel Theater, Zinovy Korogodsky, was arraigned before a court, fired from his post, and deprived of all his honorary titles (and the accusations against him have had nothing to do with minors). Such examples are legion.

Once the antihomosexual legislation was again in place, some of those who had formerly been tolerant backed away from that cause. Maxim Gorky, for instance, had apparently overcome a certain amount of earlier homophobia[13] when in 1926 he published a sympathetic foreword to the Russian translation of Stefan Zweig's story "Confused Feelings": "Zweig is the first person in literature to depict the torments of same-sex love, and the magic of his talent confronts the reader with yet another harrowing human drama."[14] Yet in May 1934, Gorky wrote an article that was published in both *Pravda* and *Izvestiya*, called "Proletarian Humanism," in which he welcomed the new repressive legislation, even maintaining that tolerance of homosexuality was a reason for the triumph of German fascism: "Annihilate homosexuality, and fascism will disappear!"[15]

Soviet sexophobia was not confined to antihomosexual legislation. In October 1935, the USSR law "On Responsibility for Preparing, Keeping, and Advertising Pornographic Publications, Representations, and Other Objects and for Trading in Them" was passed. The vague and inexact formulation of this law enabled the authorities to institute criminal proceedings and imprison people on the most ridiculous of charges.

Artificially induced abortion was forbidden and became criminally punishable in June 1936. The authorities had been preparing for this for some time. From the late 1920s the birthrate had been steadily declining: the number of births per thousand people had fallen from 45 in 1927 to 31.1 in 1935.[16] There were many reasons for this, but what stood out was the simultaneous decline of the birth rate and the increasing rate of abortion in many areas—Bryansk, Moscow, Leningrad, part of the Ukraine, the Northern Caucasus, to name several. The number of abortions per thousand women in Leningrad had risen six-fold between 1924 and 1928; there were 21 abortions per 100 live births in 1924, and 138 in 1928. There were twice as many abortions as births in Moscow during the 1930s. When the number of illegal abortions is added to the calculation, the seriousness of the problem is evident.

In legalizing abortion in the 1920s, the authorities conceded the futility of trying to repress the practice of abortion; at the same time, however, they attempted to stimulate the birthrate by proffering material assistance to mothers and children. During the 1930s, however, it became clear that the birthrate was declining not because of poverty—the better-off urban families were producing fewer children than the poor ones—but because working women with more education simply did not want to give birth to many children. However, the regime was profoundly indifferent to the wishes of women.

"Demographic" arguments began to dominate disputes over abortion, in sharp contrast to the "health" arguments of the 1920s: the state needed new workers (and soldiers, too). To women who protested the abortion ban—and there were many—Justice Commissar Nikolai Krylenko answered that it was a gross error to regard "freedom of abortion" as a woman's civil right. The people's commissar of justice naturally kept silent on Lenin's more positive view of the subject. Another top Party official explained that motherhood was both a biological and a social—i.e., state—function.

In prohibiting abortion, the authorities considered only the primitively and imperfectly understood interests of the state, rather than women's health; the abortion ban was not balanced by the promotion of more humane, effective, and civilized forms of contraception, as Russian medics had proposed back in 1913.

The Soviet regime did not, of course, succeed in bringing about any substantial rise in the birthrate by such repressive measures. Following a short-lived upsurge, the birthrate was once more on the decline by 1938, and by 1940, it was back to the 1935, pre-abortion ban level. Nevertheless, the repressive antiabortion legislation remained on the statute books for the next 20 years.

Attitudes toward scientific research also altered. During the 1920s the Soviet Union had seen many investigations into sex problems, both biomedical and social. I have already mentioned sexual surveys, but there was much else besides. The eminent Russian ethnographers Vladimir Bogoraz-Tan and Lev Shternberg were pioneers in the study of ritual transvestism and sex change among the tribes of Siberia and the Far North. The classical scholar Olga Friedenberg (cousin to Boris Pasternak) studied and published on sexual and gender symbolism in ancient Greek and Latin literature. Mikhail Bakhtin, in between sentences of exile, had elaborated his conception of medieval culture and bodily canon (his classic book on Rabelais came out in 1965 yet had been written long before World War II). In the 1920s, virtually all the major works of Freud were translated into Russian, although attitudes toward Freud varied considerably. The Soviet Union had been officially represented in the World League for Sexual Reform, and the 1931 congress was even scheduled to take place in Moscow (the major item on the agenda was "Marxism and the Sex Question"), although the meeting did not actually take place there and had to transfer to Brno in 1932. At the same time, the eminent Soviet psychologists Lev Vygotsky and Pavel Blonsky were writing extensively about adolescent and juvenile sexuality.

All this research was deemed first unnecessary, then dangerous, and was finally prohibited in the 1930s. Some scholars vanished into the Gulags, and their books were either destroyed or disappeared into the so-called *spetskhrany* (special divisions of the libraries, which did not issue books for people to take home to read; one could study them only in a special reading room if expressly granted permission by the KGB, or later, by various Party bodies), their work cast into oblivion since it could not be mentioned in the press. Other scholars simply kept silent or shifted into less controversial areas of study.

Sex education, of which little enough had existed, now gave way utterly to "moral education." The reasoning behind this came from none other than the most eminent of all Soviet educational theorists, Anton Makarenko. Makarenko started with some thoroughly just criticism of the physiologization of sex education, which reduces all problems to the "secret of procreation." Sex education, in Makarenko's view, should be part of a general moral upbringing, the goal of which was to teach the child to love. Yet from these laudable premises Makarenko drew the ludicrous conclusion that sexuality was a very simple matter, requiring no explanation at all:

> Since the very creation of the world, there has not been a single recorded incident of young people getting married without enough knowledge about the "secret of procreation," and as we well know always in the same single version, without any marked deviations. The secret of procreation would seem to be the only area where no dispute, no heresy, no blank spots can be observed.[17]

In raising his own sexological ignorance and naïveté to the level of pedagogic principle, Makarenko regarded special efforts for the sexual enlightenment of children and adolescents as unnecessary and harmful:

> Discussions on the "sex" issue with children can add nothing to the knowledge that will come in good time without prompting. But they do debase the problem of love: they deprive it of that restraint without which love may be termed perversion. To uncover the secret, even in the most intelligent way, is to reinforce the physiological aspect of love, to encourage sexual curiosity, rather than sexual feelings, making sex trite and overly accessible.[18]

This sounds fine and moral, but in practice it is nothing more than the traditional fig leaf of silence, leaving adolescents isolated with their sexual problems and fears.

The medical authorities, like the Party ideologues, tried to convince Soviet youth that sexual activity was dangerous not only because of the possibility of disease and pregnancy but also because of the waste of energy involved. Sexual energy, if retained, collected, and directed into socially productive activities, could produce positive results both for the individual and for the state.

In 1926, Professor Ivan Aryamov, a leading expert on adolescence and sexuality, even used Alexander Pushkin as an example to claim that "a man's creative work is directly proportional to the energetic activity of his sex glands when this energy is not accompanied by the external expulsion of sexual products."[19]

This theory of sublimation, of course, had distinct political implications.[20]

What were the real reasons for Soviet sexophobia, which was unprecedented in the twentieth century and led to a situation wherein sexuality became literally unmentionable over one-sixth of the globe? What were its social functions?

First and foremost, as Orwell put it so pithily, to ensure absolute control over the personality, a totalitarian regime endeavors to deindividualize it, to destroy its independence and emotional world. What poses a danger to totalitarianism is not so much elementary physiological sex as individual passionate love. The link between sexophobia and deindividualization was well recognized by such Russian Soviet writers as Mikhail Bulgakov, Yevgeny Zamyatin, and Andrei Platonov.

In Zamyatin's novel We (written in 1920 but first published in the USSR only in 1988), people are turned into faceless "numbers." They sing daily "Odes to the Benefactor," read a handbook entitled "Stanzas on Sexual Hygiene," and mate according to pink tags that the "numerator," an authority, distributes. Individual love is considered a crime against the Union State, and the extermination of fantasy, which offers the possibility of going beyond the borders of the present reality, is seen as a means to liberate humans both from love and from historical memory. This "extermination of fantasy" is clearly a symbol of spiritual castration.

Platonov's short story "Antisexus" (written in 1926, although it first saw the light of day in 1989), tells of the invention of a new device that eliminates irrational, unregulated, disorderly sex. "Unregulated sex is unregulated soul—unprofitable, tormented, and procreating suffering—which cannot be tolerated in the age of universal scientific reorganization of labor." The new device removes erotic feelings from human relations, enabling each person to regulate his or her pleasures rationally

> and thereby attain the optimal degree of spiritual harmony—i.e., to prevent the organism becoming over-exhausted and to raise the tone of vitality. Our slogan is that while our client is carrying out the sexual functions, his spiritual and physiological fate must lie totally in his own hands placed upon the right switches. And we have managed that.[21]

At first glance, "Antisexus" seems a parody of the mechanistic experiments in sexology that were very popular in the 1920s, and not only in the USSR. But in fact, the story is a satire on the entire totalitarian social structure, and for that reason could not be published in Stalin's time.

Sexophobia helped to confirm the fanatical cult of the state and the leader and assisted in the maintenance of state social control. As Orwell's character puts it in *1984*,

> When you are in love, you're using up energy; and afterwards you feel happy and don't give a damn for anything. They can't bear you to feel like that, they want you to be bursting with energy all the time. All this marching up and down and cheering and waving flags is simply sex gone sour. If you're happy inside yourself, why should you get excited about Big Brother and the Three-Year Plans and the Two-Minute Hate and all the rest of their bloody rot?[22]

Sexualization of the leader and his conversion into a powerful phallic symbol really did take place in Soviet psychology and mythology. The Russian philosopher Yuri Borev's book *Staliniada* provides examples of folk ditties testifying to Stalin's sexual potency and polygamous exploits:

> Oh, Snowball tree, snowball tree,
> Many wives did Stalin see.

Borev remarks that he heard this *chastushka* in 1936 from a housemaid in the neighborhood, and being an idealistic young boy, he said, "Dasha, where did you get the idea that Stalin had many wives? It's not true." Back came the reply, "That's what folks say in the village, and they be knowing all." Borev also includes short stories about Stalin's orgies with bacchanalian figures all around and a big walrus phallus hanging from the ceiling, and about Stalin, like the dragon in so many myths, taking young maidens.[23]

Sexophobia in the USSR also performed quite specific "applied" political functions. The authorities frequently used accusations of sexual perversion, decadence, and the keeping or distributing of pornography for dealing with political opponents and dissidents. Such accusations were usually utterly trumped up, and even if they could be convincingly disproved, which happened extremely rarely, the reputation of the accused would remain sullied. The KGB and its predecessors thoroughly enjoyed such games, the more so since not a few outright sadists served in their ranks.

The secret police subjected the wife of Pyotr Postyshev, the executed Party Central Committee secretary, to such a kangaroo court-cum-sideshow. The woman was "dragged into a big office where six or seven young men with jockey whips in their hands waited. She was made to strip naked and run around a big desk in the center of the room. As she ran, the young men, who were the age of her sons, urged her on with the whips, whooping encouragement. She was then invited to lie on the desk and display 'in every detail' how she 'lay underneath Postyshev . . . '."[24]

But although sexophobia was the official policy of Stalinist times, it was also in a certain sense a "people's policy." One should not go too far in rationalizing it, or reducing it to the personal traits of the Great Leader of the Peoples and his lieutenants. As a result of industrialization and collectivization, as well as political repression, the social composition of leading state and Party personnel was rapidly changing in the early 1930s: yesterday's peasants were replacing intellectuals and people from the working class everywhere. This "cultural revolution," in concert with mass repressions against professionals, was accompanied by a general upsurge in anti-intellectualism. Unsophisticated former peasants found the "antisex" arguments far more convincing than had the previous ruling elites insofar as the arguments dovetailed with their officially ridiculed and disgraced, though never totally forgotten, fundamental religious convictions and taboos. In the eyes of the new elites, sex really was dirty, and any discussion of it was indecent. These rising new Party members could hardly renounce sex itself, nor had they any intention of doing so, but it was very easy for them to expunge it from the culture—and that they did with relish and sincerity.

The middle 1930s saw a gradual, deep, and radical change in official language. Whereas the sexophobia of the 1920s had been reinforced by arguments about "class interests" and by mechanistic theories about the possibility and necessity of channeling individual "sexual energy" into more exalted social goals, the authorities now propagated a strict morality camouflaged as concern for shoring up marriage and the family.

Bourgeois and peasant families that owned private property were not dependent on the state, so the Bolsheviks tried to destroy or at least weaken them through the process of socialization of everyday life and especially the education of children. As the American historian Richard Stites notes, in the 1920s, this policy of "defamilization " of everyday life had been motivated by the noble mission of "rescuing housewives from the slavery of kitchen life," kitchen life being "the strongest symbol of a nuclear family."[25] But the state's provision of food and preschool education turned out to be much less effective than domestic family provision. "Student communes," which had been widespread in the 1920s, were also short-lived, one of the difficulties being that "the open-door policy interfered with sexual activity."[26]

The Soviet return to the ideals of stable marriage and family life in the 1930s seemed a retreat from the original ideology of the Revolution, and many Western scholars trumpeted noisily about it. Yet the appeal for the stabilization of marriage and the resurrection of "family" ideology was merely a manifestation of the growing conservatism of Soviet society. Having no private property, the "new Soviet family"—all income and living arrangements of which depended exclusively on the state—not only could not be independent of the state but was itself becoming an effective instrument of social control over the individual. To fulfill that mission, the "strong family" had to be an administratively controlled and regulated union.

In 1936, the procedures for dissolution of marriage became more complicated. This change was in certain ways quite reasonable, inasmuch as previously divorce had been practically unregulated—one spouse could dissolve the marriage by a simple declaration at the registry office, without even informing the other. But actually, the increasing difficulty of obtaining a divorce was just one more way in which the state could legally intrude into the life of the individual. After 1944, divorce could be effected only through the courts, which was relatively expensive (although much less so than in the United States) and time-consuming. The court could delay the granting of a divorce considerably, and in some cases could even refuse to grant one. The degree of the judges' liberalism depended upon the instructions given by the Supreme Court. During one period of time, they tried to prevent the granting of any divorces at all, whereas at other times, they acted more liberal.

Promulgation of the policy of strengthening marriage and family stability at any cost was invariably accompanied by attacks on "anarchic" sexuality. People whose inhibitions or lack of education deprived them of the words to articulate and express intricate erotic experiences were now convinced that only perverts and decadents talked freely about sex. Healthy sex was simple, "natural," and unpremeditated, so what was there to talk about? Thus, sexual intolerance, behind which often lurked personal sexual anxieties and alarm, became an essential aspect of global social intolerance.

Generally suspicious attitudes toward sexuality were particularly apparent in regard to Freudianism. In the early 1920s, Soviet intellectuals were quite taken with Freud and his ideas, yet by the end of the decade Freudianism was subject to ideological devastation; and in the 1930s, it became more or less a term of abuse in the mass consciousness, associated with perversion.

I shall never forget an incident that took place in the liberal 1960s when I was asked to address officials of the Leningrad law enforcement agencies on the subject of psychoanalysis. The audience was entirely university-trained; and I was given a good, attentive hearing and was quite pleased with myself. Afterward, a police investigator sought me out for advice: he was investigating a complaint from some local residents that a student group in the next apartment was "engaging in Freudianism." "But what are they reading?" I asked. Nothing, as it turned out; they were simply engaging in group sex. . . . The "criticisms" of Freud in most medical and psychological publications were entirely at the same level of distortion.[27]

If sexophobia had been only part of the official ideology, it would not have been so terrible. As time went on, the bans would certainly have lost their resilience, especially after Stalin's death; people would have steadily ceased to countenance them, and it would even have become fashionable to violate them. However, it was not only Party ideology that operated against eroticism, but rather the entirety of everyday experience.

One of the greatest tragedies of Russian society throughout history has been its shortage of what in English is called "privacy." Sovietologists often maintain that the Russian language does not even have a word for it, since the value itself is evidently absent from the Russian mind. However, it is not merely a matter of lexis.

The French language does not have a word for "privacy" either; one has to talk of "la vie privée," which causes certain difficulties in Russian translation: one may say chastnaya zhizn (private life) or lichnaya zhizn. By the first term we mean everything that is not social or public; by the second, we mean only personal, individual life. All the same, nobody believes that the French are less developed in regard to individuality than the English-speaking peoples.

There are material reasons for "the lack of a clear concept of privacy in the Soviet mentality of the past."[28] The historical lack of concern for the autonomy of personal life and intimacy may be attributed to the existence of serfdom and the village community. Serfs were not the masters of their own bodies, all of which belonged to the feudal landlord—not excepting their sexuality and its manifestations. In turn, the feudal lord was not supposed to feel embarrassed before his peasants and could do in front of them what he could never do in the presence of his equals.

The peasant community itself did not typically permit much privacy. Everyone knew everything about everyone else, and all behavior was fairly rigidly controlled. The individual's vulnerability to outside interference was exacerbated by crowded living conditions both in the countryside and in the cities.

The Soviet government inherited these problems; it did not resolve them, and in fact, in certain respects it made them even worse. Above all, the poor living conditions hampered sexual intimacy. Millions of people were forced to live for years—and many throughout their entire lives—in hostels or communal apartments, where several families shared one flat. Adult married children frequently lived in a single room with their parents. How can one talk of sexual intimacy when everything is in view and within earshot?

To the question "What hampered your sexual life in the USSR?" asked of 140 Soviet émigrés in the 1970s by writer Mark Popovsky, 126 mentioned the lack of an apartment, 122 the lack of a separate bedroom, and 93 the "excessive attention" of apartment neighbors.[29]

Naturally, the situation was even worse for people attempting to engage in pre- or extramarital sex. The question of "Where?" was always the most difficult for Soviet lovers to answer. As a Moscow sculptor told Mark Popovsky, "We are born in the hallway, we make love in the hallway, and we die in the hallway."[30]

Legally as well as practically, it was impossible to rent a room in a hotel with someone of the opposite sex to whom one was not married; even if this had been simple to do, there was always a dreadful shortage of rooms. One had no right at all to rent a hotel room in one's hometown, and away from home, one had to wage war with the administrators to take a guest to one's room, even in the daytime for a short period of time. Hotels stationed numerous women on each floor for one purpose only: to keep watch over the morals of their charges, making raids on them and subsequently sending reports to their places of employment. The police likewise kept an eye on parks and gardens—though the Russian climate was often cold enough to put off even the most ardent lovers. People used every means possible: booking separate cubicles in the bathhouses for 45 minutes, using rooms vacated for a time by friends, turning holiday homes and health facilities into brothels, and so on.

Workers and students living in dormitories—i.e., the majority of young people—were utterly shorn of any legal sexual rights. The administrators enforced a rigid sexual segregation. I well remember being shown a nine-story dormitory belonging to a local, almost exclusively female college of education in the Far Eastern town of Ussuriysk in the early 1980s. I was told how cadets from the neighboring military academy made their way inside: a bold youth, risking life and limb, would climb up to the top floor by way of a decrepit old drain pipe. "But we've now set watch," I was informed. When I said that the lad perhaps deserved more respect than Romeo and that it might be simpler just to open the doors, the deputy rector thought I was joking.

I also remember a Party meeting of the Leningrad University Faculty of Philosophy in the 1950s, where we had to sit through a discussion of the "personal case" of a 30-year-old student: being drunk, he had brought a prostitute into the dormitory and was having his evil way with her in the corridor right outside the room next door. Naturally, the poor fellow was reprimanded, but among themselves the teachers asked what else he could have done. Abstaining from sex until he finished his studies was impractical at his age, perhaps even harmful. He couldn't get into a hotel; it was too cold in the park, and in any case, one had to keep an eye out for the police. The only way for him to avoid violating the norms of Soviet law and Communist morality was to masturbate. But one could hardly say that publicly.

The harsh living conditions naturally did not arise from some deliberate policy. When Nikita Khrushchev came to power in 1954, housing construction accelerated and many people finally became the possessors of the separate apartments of which their parents and grandparents had only dreamed. Nor can the authorities be blamed for sex segregation in the hostels and dormitories; similar regulations existed until only recently in American and Western European colleges and universities; they even served as fuel for the student rebellions in 1968.

Segregation by sex in school dormitories was one thing; administrative meddling in one's personal life was quite another. Yet that was what the Soviet state and Communist Party had been doing systematically. Restrictive passport and residency permit systems were introduced in 1932. A person could live only where he or she was officially registered, and the police found it easy to control any moving around. Furthermore, the neighbors also kept an eye on people's movements. Listening in on private conversations and collecting denunciations and gossip were favorite pastimes of the KGB and police, and were widely used for blackmail and as a tool in dealing with anyone they did not like. Every Soviet citizen felt him- or herself to be in the public view during both the Stalin and later years; and few dared protest about it.

The Party was no better than the KGB. It officially and openly declared that a Communist should not keep secrets from the Party organization, and it unceremoniously interfered in the holy of holies of one's intimate life. Divorce made a person "politically unreliable," and while Brezhnev was in power, it was a cause for being banned from foreign travel. If such a person tried to travel anyway, he would have the notice "Reasons for divorce are known to the Party organization" inscribed in his references—which meant that they were accepted as valid. Bachelors were considered even less trustworthy: the man could well be a womanizer, or, even worse, a homosexual!

Reports from jealous or divorced wives were studied avidly at Party meetings, with Party members eagerly pouring over the details. A joke made the rounds on the ways that women of different countries held on to their husbands: the German by being a good housewife, the Spaniard by being passionate, the Frenchwoman by her elegance and refined caresses—and the Russian by the Party committee. Another joke had the Party committee receiving a wife's complaint that her husband was not performing his marital duties. "Why is that?" he was asked. "Firstly, comrades, " he said, "I am impotent." "No," broke in the Party secretary, "firstly, you are a Communist!"

Did this hypocritical and repressive morality help to reinforce the family and promote "healthy sex"? Of course not. People sought ways to circumvent the regulations. Despite official control and vigilance, group sex flourished openly in the youth hostels and dormitories. All too common was what went on in the vacation homes and outdoor recreation centers: once out of sight of parents or spouses, many young people (and the not so young) caroused as if there were no tomorrow, fulfilling and overfulfilling the plan, making up for what was out of reach in everyday life. There was, of course, a joke about this as well: A foreign tourist returning home from a visit to the Soviet Union was asked whether the Soviets have any brothels. "Yes, they have," replied the tourist. "But for some reason they call them holiday homes."

World War II caused serious dislocation of marital and family relationships and sexual morality. It tore millions of people from their homes and families and gave rise to innumerable temporary liaisons and children born out of wedlock. The deaths of millions of men at the front made some women widows, and deprived others, still young, of the chance to find a husband and start a family. According to estimates made by the demographer I. P. Ilina, as many as 78.7% of Soviet women between the ages of 25 and 29, and 81.8% of the 30- to 34-year-olds were married in 1939; and according to the 1959 census, the corresponding figures were only 54.9% and 48.3%, respectively.[31] A change of such magnitude was bound to leave its imprint on the sexual behavior and moral principles of an entire generation.

The Gulag system had a continuously negative effect on the family as well. Many millions of people were incarcerated in Stalin's camps and prisons. Not only were they torn from their families and deprived of normal sexual lives for years at a time; they also had to put up with terrible cruelty—including the sexual abuse (same-sex rape)—of the camps. How did that affect their subsequent sexual lives, and what experience did they pass on to their children, to their nearest and dearest?

As can clearly be seen from this brief resume, a plethora of issues confronted Soviet society in the late 1940s and early 1950s, yet nobody dared give thought to them, much less address them directly. Everything connected with sex, directly or indirectly, was, in the words of a Russian Jewish song, "unseemly, unhygienic, and unsympathetic."

*Chapter Six*

# FROM SUPPRESSION TO DOMESTICATION

*Our firm is called upon to destroy human sexual savagery and to raise human nature to a higher culture of tranquillity and to an even, steady, and planned tempo of development. . . . We have converted sexual feelings from elemental grossness into a noble mechanism and given the world moral conduct.*

— Andrei Platonov, "Antisexus"

The Stalinist sexual policy was consistently repressive, based on the suppression and negation of sex. Was it successful? Yes and no.

It was certainly successful in terms of the suppression of sexual culture and adequate understanding of sexuality in the public consciousness. All knowledge and civilized notions about that sphere of life was eradicated in the USSR root and branch. Generations of Soviet people were brought up in an atmosphere of sexual ignorance and the anxieties and fears that usually accompany such ignorance. Until the 1960s, sex was practically unmentionable; not a shred of public information was available about it. The USSR had no scientific literature of its own, and foreign books did not reach even the special-custody libraries; it was even dangerous for scholarly libraries to order them.[1]

Virtually all sexological literature remained in special-custody sections until 1987. Chief librarians were even more "vigilant" than the censor. The writer Mark Popovsky recalls that the Lenin State Library had refused him the works of Freud, despite his medical training and reputation as a writer. And that was Freud![2] Even the insufferably boring Soviet books on sexopathology, which were written in pidgin language and could be found only in the special libraries, were refused even to medical doctors unless they could produce a special letter from a superior testifying that "Comrade So-and-So" was actually engaged in sexopathology studies and not simply satisfying morbid curiosity.[3]

While doing away with sexual culture, Stalin and his successors were unable, nonetheless, to destroy sexuality or even fully subordinate it to their control. There are no objective data at all on the sexual behavior of the Soviet people for the 35 years from 1930 to 1965; all that exists are scattered and exceedingly subjective personal reminiscences. Yet as soon as life became slightly freer, it was clear that both the value orientations and the sexual conduct of Soviet youth were moving in the same direction as those of their counterparts in the West. There were even people eager to study these processes.

The first such enthusiast was my Leningrad University postgraduate student, Sergei Golod. When in the early 1960s—under the influence of Kinsey's book—he first expressed a desire to study the sexual behavior of contemporary Soviet young people, I told him at once that the subject was dangerous and "nondissertationable" under the present conditions; all the same, I gave him permission to try. His were truly Herculean labors. The questionnaires had to be cleared with the Party regional committee, which found fault with everything. For example, a question on the number of sexual partners was removed when the sectional chief of the committee asked, "What does that mean? Personally, I'm living with my wife." (The Leningrad intelligentsia knew full well that he was also "personally living with" a number of ballet dancers from the Kirov Theater.) Beyond difficulties with getting Committee approval, Golod found that the surveys themselves were difficult to organize. People were afraid to answer even the most innocent questions, and the researcher was immediately suspected of being a "sexual pervert."

When Golod's dissertation, which took twice the time usually allotted for completion, was presented for defense in 1969, an ominous call came from the Party regional committee: "Who had dared to write about such things?!" The defense had to be set aside. We went to work on the manuscript, removed all the pro-sex quotations from Alexandra Kollontay, and rescheduled the defense to take place in Moscow, at the Institute for Applied Social Research of the USSR Academy of Sciences, where I headed a department—and where the atmosphere was more congenial than at Leningrad University. This time, however, the Komsomol Central Committee demanded to see the dissertation; the first secretary, Yevgeny Tyazhelnikov, called Golod's work "an ideological diversion against Soviet youth"; if the defense was not canceled, he warned, he would complain to the Party Central Committee.

There was nothing particularly seditious about the dissertation. It simply mentioned that Soviet youth, like young people everywhere, were engaging in premarital sexual affairs without getting overwrought about it; indeed, the dissertation had already received quite a few complimentary comments from sociologists, physicians, and lawyers. But the sociological institute was already under enough fire from the Party without adding Golod's work as additional provocation. On the scheduled defense day, therefore, it was announced that the defense had been postponed because of the candidate's illness—even though he was alive and well and sitting in the auditorium. We did not return to the issue again. Golod shortly defended another dissertation, on working women (i.e., women in industry), who, as everyone knows, have no time for sex anyway. . . . The Leningrad Regional Party Committee made sure that the new dissertation contained no statistics from the former work. Golod assembled further material on youth sexual conduct at his own risk and responsibility, in his spare time.

In 1965, Golod surveyed 500 students from ten Leningrad colleges and 205 young white-collar workers; in 1969–70, he followed this up with a survey of 120 Leningrad blue- and white-collar workers; in 1972 another 500 Leningrad students; in 1974 as many as 334 young industrial workers; and in 1978, within a project on student lifestyles, some 3,700 students from 18 Russian colleges, asking questions on their motivation for making sexual advances and for engaging in sexual affairs. In 1978 and 1981, he surveyed 250 married couples, and in 1989 another 250 professionals.

Golod's figures, published in a series of books and articles,[4] comprise the only sociological documents on the sexual behavior and attitude of Soviet youth in the 1960s and 1970s (other similar investigations have used much smaller samples and did not always employ sound methodology). Although when judged on strict professional criteria, Golod's samples and questionnaires have not always been compatible, and some of his conclusions are debatable, the overall trends in development are sufficiently clear-cut to warrant serious attention; the more so when they are supplemented by other sociological, demographic, and medical statistics.

While I shall talk of this in greater detail in the third part of this book, I must note here that the overall trends in sexual behavior within Soviet society were, in the main, the same as in the West.

First, we see a global process of change and breakdown in the traditional systems of relations between the sexes and of gender stratification. In all areas of social and private life, relations between men and women are becoming more democratic and equal, while the stereotypes of masculinity and femininity are less diametrically opposed than they used to be. These changes allow for the development of individuality, which is no longer stuck in the Procrustean bed of traditional sex-role stereotypes (a strong, aggressive male and a gentle, passive female), yet at the same time engender a wide range of social and psychological problems and conflicts.

Second, the composition, structure, and social functions of the family are changing.[5] As a result of the decline in the birthrate and the trend toward "nuclearization," the family is becoming smaller, especially in towns and cities. Overall rates of fertility for the USSR dropped from 2.8 children per woman in 1958–59 to 2.45 (2.1 in the Russian Federation) in 1988.

As some traditional socioeconomic functions of the family whither away or begin to acquire new meaning, family relationships become more intimate and take on deeper psychological overtones; increasingly greater value is accorded to psychological closeness and intimacy between family members, and spouses in particular. The enhanced autonomy and significance of each member of the family parallels enhanced individual choice in marriage. Marriage based on free choice, which is usually represented as being founded on love, is more intimate, yet simultaneously more fragile than traditional marriage motivated by economic considerations. Hence the rise in the rate of divorce: the average annual number of divorces per thousand married couples in the Russian Federation increased from 6.5 in 1958–59 to 17.5 in 1978–79.[6] People have even begun to conceive of marriage as perhaps being temporary, similar to the concept of "serial monogamy" in the Unites States; young Soviet wives refer to marriage half-ironically as "a run for a husband." There is also a marked growth in the number of "singles," people who for one reason or another do not enter into a registered marriage. The number of Soviet men between the ages of 25 and 29 who did not marry grew by 14% between 1959 and 1970, and by 45% in the 30–39 age bracket.[7]

Shifts in marriage and family relationships reflect the general trends toward individualization of social life. In the former patriarchal society, the idea of a separate individual was unthinkable; no one could conceive of himself apart from the social group. Today, more and more people have begun to sense that the individual is at the center of his or her own world; any social role and societal identity seem only aspects of the personality, while the quintessence of the personality is the self. External social control correspondingly yields to self-control. The values of self-expression and self-realization acquire increasing meaning. "Sentimental education" today signifies not only and not so much an ability to control one's feelings and to subordinate them to the mind, but the ability to express and articulate them adequately, to listen to one's heart, and so on.

Such changes in social structure and culture are bound to manifest themselves within sexual erotic values and behavior. We may identify a few general trends:

- Earlier sexual maturation and awakening of erotic feelings among adolescents
- Earlier onset of sexual life
- Social and moral acceptance of premarital sexuality and cohabitation
- Weakening of the sexual "double standard"—i.e., of the varying norms and rules of sexual conduct for men and women
- Enhanced significance of sexual satisfaction as a factor in making and sustaining a happy marriage
- Resexualization of women, whom Victorian morality regarded as generally asexual
- Narrowing of the prohibited sphere within culture and an increase in public interest in the erotic
- Rise in toleration of the unusual, diverse, and deviant forms of sexuality, particularly homosexuality
- A growing gap between the generations in terms of sexual principles, values, and behavior—much of what was absolutely unacceptable to parents is now regarded as normal and natural by their children.

These trends have been common to the Soviet Union and the West. But whereas in the West they have been openly discussed, and frequently over-exposed, over the course of several decades, thereby enabling the public consciousness to internalize and digest their potential consequences gradually (although conservative circles have been incapable of so doing), in the Soviet Union, everything was swept under the carpet. While people's behavior and values, particularly those of young people, have been changing, official society has pretended that nothing has been happening. Unmistakable symptoms of profound, long-term, and irreversible transformations have been treated as isolated incidents, or extraordinary events engendered by the malicious influence of the "decadent West," necessitating administrative discipline.

The contradictory and harrowing process of liberalization of Soviet society, which commenced immediately after Stalin's death in 1953, was primarily a process of the disintegration of Communist power and ideology. This disintegration began with the Party hierarchy, whose behavior was increasingly at odds with its own propaganda.

Although they officially advocated asexuality, high-level Party functionaries drew on the state purse to maintain innumerable lovers on the side, were eager viewers of Western pornographic movies, and sometimes hosted actual orgies. Back in Khrushchev's time, a scandal erupted over the USSR culture minister, the well-known Party ideologist Georgi Alexandrov, who, along with other high-ranking apparatchiks, organized an entire harem of young actresses. When Alexandrov lost his post, a joke went the rounds that he was scripting his memoirs under the title *My Sexual Life in Art* (a play on Konstantin Stanislavsky's *My Life in Art*). Similarly, the gossip about Brezhnev was that during his time as Party secretary to the Central Committee of the Communist Party of Kazakhstan, he mortally offended local Party personnel by taking several mistresses from Moldavia with him to that erstwhile Islamic republic. The Youth Organization Committee attached to the Komsomol Central Committee under Brezhnev, headed by Gennady Yanayev, a future vice president of the country under Gorbachev and then chairman of the State Emergency Committee during the failed August 1991 coup, was regarded as being the citadel of all manner of corruption, including sexual, in the 1970s. Many fascinating escapades took place behind the tall fences of government dachas. As the bard Alexander Galich put it:

> And night after night
> Behind locked doors,
> The big bosses lapped up
> Porno films of whores.

And so on down the line: the little bosses imitated the big bosses, and so did the underground moneybags—the future pioneers of the Russian "market economy." At state expense, the authorities built and maintained cozy, luxurious bathhouses, saunas, hotels, and hunting lodges in which local and visiting bigwigs could savor the joys of life—including, of course, sex—free of charge. This was but a tiny part of the larger corruption. In the meantime, young people—"golden," "silver," or base-metal youth—determined not to lag behind their elders, were conducting their own, unadvertised, but also thinly veiled, non-Communist lifestyle, complete with drinking, screwing, making pornographic films, and so on. One only had to avoid discussing it openly.

Cant was a compulsory norm of Soviet life—or perhaps not so much common cant as the double-think described by Orwell: the ability to possess two different, mutually exclusive judgments on one and the same question. In essence, double-think was necessary to survival. The person who sincerely believed in official ideology was doomed because life was ruled by very different laws; sooner or later, the naive lover of the truth had to "wise up" or find herself in a prison or a psychiatric ward. And because consistent cynics are very rare, the person who believed in nothing was also doomed; sooner or later she would let the cat out of the bag or fall prey to neuroses. It was simplest of all to believe sincerely in the official rules of the game in public, and just as sincerely—and without a twinge of conscience—to violate the rules in one's personal life.[8]

But let us return to sexuality. . . .

The key achievement of the 1960s and 1970s was the birth of medical sexology—which, in the USSR, went by the name "sexopathology." The name itself is symptomatic of the times, suggesting that "normal " sexuality is problem-free, that all is as clear as day—and that anyone who has a problem should see a doctor. It was not a matter of words alone.

That the study of sexual problems in the postwar USSR started in medicine was perfectly natural; the same thing had happened in the nineteenth and early twentieth centuries in Europe and in pre-Revolutionary Russia. But the Stalinist terror eradicated everything that had gone before, and scholars had to start from scratch.

The hiatus in research is patently obvious in the statistics of the relevant publications. According to the calculations of Leningrad researchers Andrei Masevich and Lev Shcheglov, Russian books on sexopathology kept in the Leningrad Public Library may be divided by year of publication, as in Table 6.1.

**Table 6.1**

| | |
|---|---|
| Before 1917 | 126 |
| 1917–1936 | 52 |
| 1937–1960 | 5 |
| 1961–1969 | 14 |
| 1970–1980 | 61 |
| 1981–1984 | 35 |

One can trace the same kind of changes in the number of books for a general audience published on the subject of sexual hygiene.

It was enormously difficult to set the new discipline of sexology on its feet. Like everything novel in the USSR, it had to be set up not by will of the Party and the medical establishment but in spite of them, through the efforts of dedicated individuals. Apart from the general adverse societal attitude toward sexuality, there was also hostility from members of the old-line medical disciplines, which slowed development in the field. Urologists were the most obstructive; most were convinced that if they knew that the penis and prostate were functioning properly, everything else was superfluous.

The first countrywide seminar on training physicians as sexopathologists was held in 1963 under the leadership of Professor N. V. Ivanov in the city of Gorky (Nizhny Novgorod). Gorky was also the venue for the two seminars held subsequently, in 1964 and 1966. The third was held in 1967 in Moscow, at the Sexopathology Department of the Moscow Psychiatric Research Institute of the Russian Health Ministry. In 1973, this department gained the status of an All-union scientific method center, specializing in sexopathological issues and coordinating the activity of sexopathologists throughout the country.

The publication of several small-circulation collections followed in the wake of the seminars: *Urgent Issues in Sexopathology* (1967), *Questions in Sexopathology* (1969), and *Problems in Contemporary Sexopathology* (1972). The quality of the proceedings was uneven, yet the seminars did enable experts from various branches of medicine to exchange their data and clinical experience, and the publications made appropriate references available.

Initially a monodisciplinary approach predominated in Soviet sexopathology: urologists set the tone, and to a lesser extent, gynecologists and endocrinologists. Subsequently, however—from the moment that Professor Georgi Vasilchenko, a neuropathologist, took charge of the all-union center in 1973—the picture began to change. Vasilchenko's opinion was that sexopathology should not take the team specialty approach, wherein the urologist treats his pathology, the psychiatrist his and the endocrinologist his, with the sexopathologist operating only to direct traffic; no, said Vasilchenko, sexopathology had to be an independent clinical discipline employing an interdisciplinary approach.

It was in this spirit that the first Soviet sexopathology handbooks for doctors were written under Vasilchenko's editorship and largely by himself—*General Sexopathology* (1977) and *Special Topics in Sexopathology* (two volumes, 1983), as well as *The Reference Book of Sexopathology* (1990). In accordance with his philosophy, said Vasilchenko, the training of sexopathologists should be multidisciplinary, too. There was no doubt that this approach carried the risk of dilettantism and of potential conflict between members of the various disciplines. But with the "system method," for the first time, doctors were oriented toward seeing sexuality as a whole, rather than solely in its separate parts and dimensions.

On a volunteer basis—i.e., without any financial backing—Professor Abram Svyadoshch set up the first sexological center attached to the city health department in Leningrad. His 1974 book *Female Sexopathology* enjoyed three editions and became a genuine mass audience best-seller. In fact, there is a story that when burglars broke into the apartment of a wealthy man, they carried off only one book from the whole library along with the usual valuables—*Female Sexopathology* by Abram Svyadoshch.

The Leningrad psychiatrists Professor Dmitri Isayev and Dr. Victor Kagan began studying the formation of gender identity and problems in juvenile and adolescent sexuality in the late 1970s. In 1986, they published the first Soviet guide for doctors on the subject—*The Psycho-Hygiene of Sex among Children* (the title *Child Sexology* would have been considered too brazen for that time).

In the Ukraine, urologists and neurologists under Professor Ivan Yunda established their own school, with a urological orientation, within the Sexopathology Center of the Kiev Research Institute of Urology. And there were attempts to set up yet another center, in Rostov.

To Western scholars, Soviet sexopathology may seem odd in some ways. With rare exception, Soviet authors had only a poor knowledge—and in some cases, no knowledge at all—of contemporary foreign scientific literature. In part, this was due to its absence from libraries; in Moscow and Leningrad, libraries had very little, while those in the provinces had absolutely none at all. In addition, Soviet ignorance of foreign sexology was due, in part, to ignorance of foreign languages. But there was also an unwillingness to read, based on the pervasive ideological principle that everything Soviet was better than anything Western. Nor was this attitude merely the result of pressure from above. Ignorance is a great encouragement to a good opinion of oneself: one can develop original concepts without worrying about whether they meet independent scientific criteria. How wonderful it is to be the first discoverer! For an interdisciplinary subject such as sexology, this attitude was particularly ruinous. And unfortunately, some young Russian sexopathologists of today are no better in this respect than members of the older generation, even though their working conditions are much more favorable.

In contrast to their Western colleagues, many Soviet sexopathologists have taken scant account of psychological factors in sexual behavior.

Explanatory theories are often based on outmoded biological models or an admixture of "worldly wisdom" and a large dollop of moralizing. For example, Victor Nagayev's 1987 dissertation, which allowed him to become a doctor of medical sciences in psychiatry, defines deviant sexual behavior as everything that "deviates from moral norms."[9] Examined from this perspective, any pre- or extramarital affair can be deemed deviant and pathological.

Too narrow a definition of what is "normal" gives rise to an authoritarian attitude and sexual intolerance among doctors, a striving to "cure" what should not properly be treated. These attitudes were part and parcel of Soviet "repressive psychiatry," which allowed the KGB to lock political dissidents away in psychiatric units.

Insufficient psychological knowledge is especially dangerous in sexology. According to Soviet medical statistics, the great bulk—up to 70–75%—of "patients" (most Russian doctors stubbornly continue to refer to them as patients rather than clients) come to the sexopathologist's office with problems of a psychological rather than an organic nature. Yet it is with psychological questions that the doctors are the most ill-prepared to deal. Psychoanalysis was banned to all intents and purposes under Soviet rule. Psychology had been taught only poorly in medical academies, and any discussion of sex and sexuality was totally absent in the psychology department.

The psycho-endocrinologist Professor Aron Belkin, a pioneer of Soviet research into transsexualism, even carried out sex-change operations without conducting any psychological testing or employing any other sort of psychological expertise—not because he didn't want to do it; the country simply had no literate psychologists or approved tests to aid him. It was generally considered that whereas one must study assiduously for a career in biology or medicine, virtually anyone could become a psychologist or sociologist because so little training was involved.

Sexopathology had been an outcast in Soviet medicine. The first sexopathological centers came into being in 1963; in 1973, the USSR Health Ministry officially inaugurated the state sexopatholgical service in cities with over a million inhabitants. This was little enough. But the training in sexopathology was carried out as part of medical education in psychiatry—only in an unsystematic way, through short-term courses. The few positions for sexopathologists were frequently filled by psychiatrists who had taken no special sexological training. Sometimes the resolution of all sexopathological problems was put in the hands of the family consulting bureaus, a patently absurd situation.

Through the long-term efforts of Professor Vasilchenko and his colleagues, who worked hard to deal with the Soviet bureaucracy, the USSR health minister launched a new policy in May 1988, setting up specialized medical-psychological family advice clinics in cities with over a quarter of a million residents; the purpose of the clinics was the early identification and treatment of sexual disorders and sexual disharmonies within marriage (sex outside marriage continued to be ignored as if it did not exist). The staff of the new departments consisted of a sexopathologist, a medical psychologist, a nurse, a laboratory assistant, and an orderly.

In order to train sexopathologists, the authorities finally established special chairs in three medical institutes set up to administer continuing education courses—the Leningrad (now St. Petersburg), Kharkov (now the Ukrainian Institute), and the Central (Moscow). The decision to establish these faculties was momentous. All the same, the program was late by at least 20 years and once again inadequate. Professional training of sexopathologists was, of course, necessary, but it did not obviate the delicate and complicated task of teaching sexology to all medical students. There are still no programs or textbooks for this course, however, and the demise of the Soviet Union and the breakdown of its economy make any such endeavors incredibly difficult.

The establishment of sexopathology as a discipline was an attempt to bring sexuality under medical control. But the medicalization of sexuality is impossible without its simultaneous establishment as a pedagogic subject; treatment is inseparable from enlightenment. And here the legacy of Stalinism has been even more onerous.

The 30-year conspiracy of silence naturally resulted in a monstrous sexual ignorance. Soviet children and adolescents were not given even elementary sexual information. The situation was particularly woeful in intellectual families, where the parents tried to keep absolutely everything from their children; workers and peasants looked at these things more simply: what the eye does not see, the heart does not grieve.

One of the respondents to Mark Popovsky's survey, a theatrical producer from Leningrad, the son of an engineer and a doctor, relates,

Once, when I was eight and in the first form, a playmate who was my age delivered the astounding news that grown-ups, on going to bed, "stick their willies into each other and make children." The news just about knocked me off my feet, yet I was still a bit doubtful. "Well, OK," I said. "But what if the man feels like a pee at the same time; what happens then?"

My chum explained that that was precisely how children were born. This making of children seemed unaesthetic and even disgusting to me. "Is that really what they all do?" I asked. "Well, your mum and dad and my mum and dad don't do that, but all the rest do," he said.[10]

Grown-ups, of course, knew what to put where. Yet for many, that was where their knowledge ended. In the 1950s and 1960s some progressive Soviet education experts, doctors, and psychologists began to talk of the need for some sort of sex education for adolescents; and in 1961, a newspaper article by the psychologist Artur Petrovsky entitled "Educational Taboo" stirred up much discussion. Other articles began to appear in its wake.

These initial forays into the subject of sex education were by no means radical but rather conservative. Sex education was conceptualized primarily as moral education; the idea of a special course in sexual enlightenment invoked a dreadful panic among most progressive educators, who often declared it to be totally unnecessary. No one even dared contemplate the idea of acquainting adolescents with the fundamentals of contraception. In school textbooks on human anatomy and physiology, there was no description of the human sexual system; rabbits, rather than humans, were the species used in discussions of reproduction. The portrayal of male or female sexual organs was considered pornographic. When Vasilchenko showed his Psychiatry Institute colleagues the school textbooks he had brought back from Denmark, they accused him of being obsessed with pornography.

Two popular little books were translated into Russian during the 1960s: *Questions on Sex* (1960 and 1962) and *A New Book on Wedlock* (1969), both by Rudolf Neubert, a physician hygienist from East Germany. They became immediate best-sellers. These books had been deliberately selected by the authorities for the Soviet reader as the least "offensive" and most moralistic. All the same, even the elementary material they contained appeared threatening to all too many.

In his foreword to *A New Book on Wedlock*, Professor Victor Kolbanovsky, an eminent psychologist, clearly set out the paramount task facing Soviet sex education—to safeguard young people from sexuality:

In order to release the pressure of the central nervous system from impulses coming from the sexual sphere, one must divert the attention of the younger generation, who are largely pupils and students, toward attention to the various phenomena of reality. Work in scientific clubs, at centers for young naturalists and technologists, doing sports and outdoor recreation, testing their creative endeavor in poetry, literature, and various forms of art, as well as in social activities, so engrosses and diverts attention from sexual problems, that adolescents, young men and women, are able to deal with them easily.

A classical Victorian approach of the late nineteenth century!

And what sort of adolescents do we have here?! It turned out that Kolbanovsky thought even adult married couples should engage as little as possible in sex:

> In regard to marital relations, we have to say that the enormous work and public commitment by men and women, along with their concern for bringing up children and constantly satisfying their mounting cultural needs, divert their attention from intensive sexual feelings to a considerable extent, and sexual intimacy stops being a habit. The spouses' spiritual interests begin to prevail, particularly if they have an interest in creative activity.[11]

One might well conclude that Kolbanovsky was hostile, not friendly, to sex education! All one had to do was make do without sex. . . .

The department on Ethical-Esthetic Problems in Sex Education, set up with the USSR Academy of Pedagogical Sciences, engaged mainly in doleful and banal moralization, and indeed, with Doctor of Medical Sciences Lidiya Bogdanovich in the lead, in frightening adolescents with the terrible consequences of masturbation, such as impotence, memory loss, and so forth. (Incidentally, the pedagogical textbook published in 1940, which I studied during the war and which removed this great burden from my mind, went on to say that adolescent masturbation was not dreadful at all; in the postwar era, however, it had once more become dangerous.)

Life nonetheless followed its own sweet course. For some reason, adolescents were not inclined to use sports or studies in naturalism to drown their sexuality, and young married couples continued to complain about their lack of sexual education, with the backing of a few brave doctors.

The growing social need for sex education became clear in the very first Soviet public opinion survey, conducted by the daily *Komsomolskaya pravda* under the direction of the future progressive sociologist Boris Grushin and the future editor-in-chief of the reactionary Communist-cum-Black Hundred, anti-Semitic, and sexophobic newspaper *Sovetskaya Rossiya*, Valentin Chikin (in the early 1960s, his real feelings were not as obvious as they would be later). The results of the survey were printed in the magazine *Molodaya gvardiya* (1964, nos. 6 and 7). Young people were bitterly complaining about their sexual ignorance and asking for professional help!

Interestingly enough, the very first shoots of sexual enlightenment (or, rather, talk about it) immediately provoked a rabid fury from neo-Bolshevik, nationalist-fascist forces in the Party and Komsomol. The neo-Bolshevik and militarist 2in russ*Code of Morals* (1965), written by Valery Skurlatov, an official at the Moscow City Komsomol Committee, had this to say:

> We must conduct a protracted campaign for the ancestral, moral, and physiological value of a maiden's honor, against the crime of premarital affairs. . . . We must not stop short even of employing ancient peasant customs: the tarring of gates, displaying the bed sheets after the first conjugal night, punishing those who go about with foreigners, branding and sterilizing them. . . . We must not embark on so-called sex education, nor excite interest in the problems of sex. Sex is an intimate affair where everything should be decided by ourselves. We must suppress interest in sex problems by encouraging interest in romance and revolution. . . . We must sublimate sex in creative endeavor.[12]

For the start of the Brezhnev era Skurlatov's program was too extreme, so it was quietly condemned by Soviet officialdom. Subsequently, however, Skurlatov had a brilliant career among Russian nationalists.

It has always been dangerous to advocate or engage in sexual education in the USSR. In 1973, Professor Svyadoshch initiated the country's first professional advice bureau on issues of "Marriage and the Family" in Leningrad. The city authorities gave it the go-ahead, yet prohibited every type of advertisement for this service. When they registered their marriage, young couples were invited to attend a two-lecture cycle for a nominal fee. The first lecture was on questions of family economics and ethics, and the second was on sex. However, when Svyadoshch told the first advisory council of the organization that he intended to talk to young couples about the principal sexual positions, the objections came thick and fast: how could he mention "such things" to innocent girls? "Pardon me, " said Svyadoshch, "but where have you seen innocent girls lately? And even if our bride has come straight to the Wedding Palace from a nunnery and has not heard anything at all, she'll still have to take up some position on the nuptial couch, won't she? So why not teach her beforehand?" "But if we do that," a council member objected, "we could be accused of propagating perversion and pornography."

The speaker was not some reactionary Party functionary but a liberal professor of psychotherapy, later a founder of the department of sexology at the Leningrad institute for continuing education for doctors. He realized what he was saying; he was just too scared. Can anybody blame him, taking into account Soviet history?

If it was difficult enough to deal with the issue of sexual enlightenment of adults, it was a thousand times harder to do anything for adolescents. Disputes about whether Russians needed sex education, and if so, exactly what this should involve, lasted a good quarter of a century. Only in 1983 was a two-part course on preparation for marriage and family life formally introduced into Russian schools: "Hygienic and Sexual Education" (12 hours), taught to adolescents at the age of 15, within a course on human anatomy and physiology, and "The Ethics and Psychology of Family Life," a 34-hour course for 16- to 17-year-olds. The course also included some elements of sexual education. All the same, the program existed on paper only.

First and foremost, nobody had concerned him- or herself hitherto with training the teachers, which proved fairly difficult to do. In general, Russian teachers are poorly trained, and to force schoolmistresses, many of whom have unsettled private lives themselves, to use such "shocking" words as "sexual organs" or "masturbation" proved altogether impossible.

The teaching aids, written by the physiologist Antonina Khripkova, vice president of the USSR Academy of Pedagogical Sciences, and the endocrinologist Dmitri Kolesov, head of the Institute for Age Physiology, were *Girl—Adolescent—Young Woman* (1981) and *Boy—Adolescent—Youth* (1982). The printing for the first book was 400,000 copies and for the second book, one million copies. The books were miserable failures—ridiculous mixtures of physiological information and primitive moralizing dressed up as hygienic prescriptions. Here are a few extracts selected at random:

- "Sexual attraction is a specific relationship between members of one sex and members of the other sex."
- "Bashfulness (but not affectedness) is attractive in a woman but unacceptable in a man . . . bashfulness in a certain situation may be viewed as a manifestation of sexual weakness of the man."
- "If a woman constantly covers her face, as in some Eastern countries, that is what makes her attractive to men, and vice versa; no one pays attention to naked legs. If a woman goes about with an uncovered face, yet wears a long dress, shortening it above the knee will serve as an object of heightened interest for the male sex, etc."
- "The fact that some women smoke shows that they are poor mothers, whatever they were in the past; only previously, this would have manifested itself in another way."[13]

- "Sexual maturity is the male's ability not only to produce a child, but also to ensure the best conditions for the mother to bring forth and bring up the child, for its physical and spiritual development."
- "Length of hair is naturally a matter of taste. All the same, a desire by members of the male sex to wear their hair in a way that approximates a traditionally female hair-style is bound to produce bewilderment."
- "You should dress a boy, adolescent, or youth so that his clothing does not draw attention to himself, but is light, warm, and comfortable."[14]

Armed with such maxims, teachers could scarcely teach old-age pensioners about sex; they would have had a disastrous effect on the sardonic young people of the time. Educational aids for schoolchildren were naturally even more conservative.

The following information was available in a teacher's guide written by Ivan and Leonid Yunda for the course in the "Ethics and Psychology of Family Life" at the Ukrainian colleges, a text officially endorsed by the Ukrainian Ministry for Higher and Secondary Specialized education (1990):

The wide variety of sexual positions described in specialized literature is largely a result of vulgarization and refinement. . . . If after the end of the sexual act you have a desire to experience something unusual, this is a sure sign of sexual satisfaction. It is better to halt and take a rest.

. . . Sexual abstinence up to the ages of 25–30 is both harmless and very useful, and in the premarital period—i.e., between 18 and 26—it is even necessary.

. . . Regularly engaging in repeated sexual acts is not recommended even given the desire and opportunity to do so.

. . . Masturbation . . . is an utterly unnatural method of satisfying the sexual urge. . . . As applied to demographic indices within our country the most correct definition of onanism is "an unnatural and depraved means of sexual activity."[15]

This program is essentially no different from Zalkind's "Twelve Commandments" of 70 years earlier.

Naturally, there were other, quite professional publications, such as *Sex Education and the Psycho-Hygiene of Sex among Children* (Leningrad: Meditsina, 1979 and 1980) by Dmitri Isayev and Victor Kagan, and Kagan's popular brochures, but as they were printed in editions of 15,000 copies at most, their existence did not alter the overall picture.

On the whole, Soviet pedagogy coped badly with the task of sex education and sexual enlightenment, and when in the late 1980s Gennady Yagodin, chairman of the USSR State Committee on Education, actually announced replacement of the "Ethics and Psychology of Family Life" course, nobody was particularly sorry, even though nothing took its place.

Sex education in Russia was a failure nearly before it was begun as a result of the prevailing reactionary ideology, as well as the lack of professionalism and interdisciplinary contacts. My own experience may illustrate how difficult it was to do anything in this situation.

My shift from the sociology of sexual behavior to theoretical and methodological problems of sexology came about during the preparation of the third edition of *The Great Soviet Encyclopedia* (*GSE*), for which I was a scientific adviser, in the 1970s.

Volume 46 of the first *GSE* edition, published in 1940, contained a very conservative article on "Sexual Life," in which the accent was on how to avoid "unhealthy interest" and to attain " a sensible transfer of sexual interest to the sphere of labor and cultural interests"; at the same time, the article informed readers that there was no such thing as a "sex issue" in the Soviet Union.

By the time the second *GSE* edition came out in 1955, the country apparently had neither a sex issue nor a "sexual life"—that edition of the encyclopedia had no article at all on the subject.

It was decided to restore the subject for the third edition being published in the 1970s, yet when in my role as consultant I received a whole sheaf of articles on sex, I was horrified. The main article on "Sex," written by an eminent geneticist, had nothing to do with either the social or even the human aspect of the subject; it all boiled down to the genetics of sex, with the focus largely on the silkworm. The article did not mention either endocrinology or evolutionary biology, let alone the social sciences. The traditional moralizing dominated the other articles. To save the situation, the editors asked me, together with Professor Vasilchenko, to write a fairly extensive article on "Sexual Life" and another one on "Sexology."

In 1976 I gave a course on adolescent sexuality in the Bekhterev Psycho-Neurological Institute. As a result, the Polish sexologist Kazimerz Imielinski asked me to supply a chapter for the collective work *Cultural Sexology*. The Kossuth Hungarian Communist Party publishers, who had translated all my books, commissioned me to write an original book on *Culture and Sexology*. The book came out in 1981; a revised German version, *Introduction to Sexology*, was published in 1985 and immediately sold out in both German states.

At first I did not take my work on sexology particularly seriously, considering it as purely popular, as it actually was when one considered the genre. But in 1979 at the initiative of the American sociologist John Gagnon and the West German sexologist Gunter Schmidt, I was invited to the Prague session of the International Academy of Sex Research, the most prestigious international association in that area of knowledge, and through an oversight of the Party overseers (after all, it was only Czechoslovakia!), I was allowed to attend despite my pessimistic expectations to the contrary. Then I came to realize that some of my ideas were not so trivial after all but of interest to fellow professionals. Naturally, that made it all the more urgent for me to publish a Russian version of my book.

All the Soviet reviewers of the manuscript—and altogether there were more than 40, because of the multidisciplinary nature of the book—were asking sympathetically, "But why is this being published only abroad? It is of interest to us too and needed even more here than it is there!" Thus, after the manuscript had passed through Glavlit unhindered, I thought it might be worthwhile to publish it in Russian, since no one seemed to object. For a sociologist of my age and experience, this was, of course, an unpardonable stupidity.

In early 1979, I proposed my much-read and foreign-published manuscript to the *Meditsina* publishers. My application was turned down at once as being "inappropriate to the publisher's profile." After that, the heads of the Ethnography Institute, who appreciated the importance of my work, tried to press it upon *Nauka*, the official press of the Academy of Sciences. The project had the backing of the eminent physiologists and members of the Soviet Academy of Sciences Yevgeny Kreps and Pavel Simonov; it would bear the stamp of both the Ethnography Institute and the Institute of Higher Nervous Activity and Neurophysiology. But despite the positive decision by the editorial board of the USSR Academy of Sciences and the huge number of positive reactions, *Nauka* did not publish the book.

I wrote a very unusual and defiant (by Soviet standards) letter on January 1, 1984, to the academician Julian Bromley, director of the Ethnography Institute, saying that I was stopping all work on the book and requesting his permission to consign my manuscript to the institute archives. At the same time, however, my manuscript was being circulated ever more widely by the literary and scientific underground.

My first theoretical sexological article was published in 1981 in *Voprosy filosofii* under the deliberately obscure title "At the Junction of Sciences" to obviate creating an undesired and dangerous sensation. A majority of members of the editorial board had turned down an initial version. One academician had said that there was nothing new or theoretically worthwhile to write about either gender or sex; all was obvious. About the article's discussion of the philogenetic sources of the phallic cult—I had used data on apes making a ritual display of an erect penis—it was said the material would have been fine for a section on satire or humor, but the periodical sadly had no such section. However, not one of the editors returned the manuscript of the article to the board, despite the rule to that effect. Instead, they took copies of the manuscript home for the enlightenment of their friends and relatives. One professor, a member of the editorial board, told me that after she had shown my rejected manuscript to her husband, a colonel in the military, and her son, a university student, she had a sort of family quarrel; the angry men could not understand why she had voted against publication, and she had no rational explanation. At the second, extended meeting of the editorial board, my article was accepted but I had to remove information about the indecent monkeys, as well as another section.

Incidentally, there was absolutely no scandal after publication. The editor-in-chief had a telephone call from the Party Central Committee, but it was not a reprimand; they simply asked him to send all available copies of the journal for their own co-workers.

I then found myself invited to attend various scholarly and quasi-scholarly seminars. Everyone wanted to learn about sexuality, yet dared not call a spade a spade. In one biology institute of the Academy of Sciences, my report was entitled "The Biologo-Evolutionary Aspects of Complex Forms of Behavior." I don't even remember the name of my lecture to the All-Union School of Biomedical Cybernetics; the scholarly words were too numerous. At a seminar for the Union of Cinematographicists, my lecture was called "The Role of Marxist-Leninist Philosophy in the Development of Science Fiction"! And nobody realized not simply how ridiculous it all was, but how humiliating, as if I were showing them dirty photographs under plain brown wrappers. . . .

I endeavored to appeal to higher Party bodies about my book, as did a number of my colleagues. The Party apparatchiks, however, even those who were sympathetic to the situation and wanted my book to be published, were afraid they would be accused of having "morbid sexual interests."

After the situation with my sexology book had turned into an obvious public scandal, the manuscript was sent to the ethics section of the Philosophy Institute of the Academy of Sciences. It was firmly expected that the manuscript would ultimately be rejected, since all discussion of sexual life was considered dubious from the standpoint of official "Communist morals." But the ruse misfired.

The Philosophy Institute gave my book a good official report over four signatures, recommending it for publication and emphasizing that "there is no other author in the country [who can] write on this theme." However, as a matter of the usual "playing it safe," the referees (perfectly worthy, respectable souls) raised the question of the book's intended audience. If it was intended for specialists only, it could be published in toto. But since the book was of real interest to everyone, and since Kon was so eminently readable an author, the "uneducated reader" might misconstrue this or that. For example, "the thesis on the brain's bisexuality could ill serve sexual education in the fight against sexual perversion."

I had a good long laugh when I read the report. If one followed this logic, astronomers would have to classify as secret the fact of the earth's rotation to prevent tipsy citizens from using it to justify their instability. One ought also to keep silent on the fact that we are all mortal: not only is it a gloomy thought, but doctors might stop treating patients altogether! Nonetheless, the publishers at the USSR Academy of Sciences chose to seize precisely on the viewpoint of the imaginary "uneducated reader," and the manuscript was returned to me.

After that I gave up all hope of a Soviet edition. By chance, however, the late medical academician Victor Zhdanov happened to hear of my story. He wrote a letter to the new head of *Meditsina*. The publishers agreed to review the previous decision. The philosophical review that *Nauka* had deemed negative turned out to be absolutely positive for *Meditsina*. The manuscript was once more reviewed by Vasilchenko and again received his backing. I restored the "sexopathology" section—and my Russian-language *Introduction to Sexology* at last saw the light of day in 1988. A year earlier, its shortened Estonian version had also come out.

Initially the publishers wanted to restrict the book to a small print run of 5,000 to 10,000 copies, without doing any preliminary advertising, and to sell exclusively to a "closed" market—so as to avoid perverting innocent Soviet readers. Then commercial considerations forced them to increase the print run to 200,000 copies. Yet not a single copy was sold in a bookstore in the normal fashion; the entire print run was distributed among medical and scientific institutions according to special lists. Subsequently, they printed another 100,000 and then in 1989 another 250,000, for a total of 550,000 copies in print. Yet the average reader could read the book only by buying a copy at the black market price from a secondhand book dealer. In spite of this, the book became extremely popular, and I am now known in the mass media mainly as a professor of sexology, without anyone knowing exactly what the term means.

As I said in the Introduction, I have found myself working in a field that is not my own. But since not a single Soviet gynecologist had ever heard of the Gräfenberg spot, someone had to tell them about it. Russian oncologists, of course, know how important it is for women to undergo breast self-examination for early detection of breast cancer, yet for some reason they had not provided information on how this is done, so I felt obliged to provide a simple picture in my new book, *Tasting the Forbidden Fruit* (1992). Similarly, I found myself explaining to Russian boys and their parents that it is necessary to wash the glans penis under the foreskin. I find it mortally offensive to spend the remnants of my life doing such things, but since the country lacks appropriate professionals, one is obliged to provide at least elementary literacy if one can. . . .

Western scholars justly poke fun of the policies of "medicalization" and "pedagogization" of sexuality as just another naive attempt to manipulate human beings and their feelings. But in the case of the Soviet Union, as had been the case earlier in the United States and Europe, this policy was a necessary stage in the transition from barbarism to civilization. No matter how ridiculous and conservative the arguments of Soviet medics and educational scholars of the recent past now seem, they deserve respect for at least raising the issues. It is not so important to know whether their conservatism was sincere or feigned, and whether it was the result of ignorance, hypocrisy, or doublethink; by contrast to previous utter rejection of sexuality, this was a step forward.

The reformist strategy in sexuality, however, was just as much a failure as the Khrushchev and Kosygin reforms in economics. The Stalinist legacy was too somber and resistant to change. Attempts to "cultivate" Soviet sex were too slow and indecisive. The "medicalization" of sexuality in the mid-1980s managed to take only the first timid steps, while "pedagogization" remained generally at the level of appeals alone. Besides, the "reformers" themselves had but a poor understanding of what they wanted. Sexuality remained an enemy for them, a dangerous wild beast that had to be bridled. But real education, as opposed to primitive circus-style taming, requires love and affection for the creature, who becomes in a certain sense a partner in the process. With humans, a repressive-prohibitive strategy does not work at all.

Recognition of the very fact of the existence of sex and sexuality was exceedingly important. Like recognition of the inefficiency of centralized economic planning, it made absolute normative bans relative and problematical, depriving them of legitimacy. The emperor, as in Hans Christian Andersen's story, turned out to be naked. Yet nobody knew what to do about this moral-repressive system. With the relaxing of external control it inevitably was doomed to disintegrate in the most dramatic way.

And that is precisely what happened after 1987.

*Chapter Seven*

# THE BEAST
# HAS BROKEN LOOSE

*Oh, how quickly time flew,*
*Racing down the line.*
*He who doesn't booze or screw*
*Is wasting his time.*
　　　　　　　　—Modern Russian *chastushka*

lthough a properly analytical history of the final phase of Soviet history has yet to be written, it is clear that Gorbachev's perestroika did not signal a change in the Communist Party's official attitude toward sexuality; it remained just as hostile and suspicious as before. Even in the initial period of the new rule, when intellectuals still clung to the illusion of reform from above, the authorities had no thought-out sexual policy apart from the usual "ban and plan."

Liberal scholars did their best to convince the Party leadership that the ostrichlike policy of rejecting and suppressing sexuality was fallacious and produced only a boomerang effect, that the country urgently needed another, more realistic and tolerant strategy aimed not at "saving" people, including adolescents, from sex but at teaching them to control sensibly this important area of their personal and public lives; they pointed to the need for social research into young people's sexual behavior, and the like. However, as in other aspects of life, Soviet liberalism, pinning its hopes on enlightened absolutism, was shooting at the moon.[1]

In the summer of 1987, the Party Central Committee and the USSR

Council of Ministers brought out an ambitious draft resolution on health development over the next ten years. For the first time, a document on health spoke bluntly of the need for promoting contraception and reducing the incidence of abortion; I will discuss these issues later. Yet this bold (for the Soviet Union) directive neglected, as always, the subject of sex education—without which all the other parts of the plan were impossible. I therefore sent a letter to *Pravda*, which published it on August 26, 1987:

> It is hardly necessary to demonstrate how important sexuality is to the cause of public health. Sexual well-being is a condition of people's psychological health; it is one of the three main factors determining the stability and happiness of married life; it is an important factor in childbirth and the upbringing of children. Our level of sexual culture, however, is extremely low. These issues have been omitted from the draft.

My proposal to supplement the draft with an indication of the need for sexual education and the preparation of young people for family life was accepted and was indeed included in the final text of the document. Yet absolutely nothing was done in practice.

The Health Ministry, which now had to acknowledge the problem of adolescent pregnancies and abortions, had already begun to appreciate the need for sex education. Instruction, however, was not within its purview but rather that of the State Committee on Education, whose chairman was Gennady Yagodin, a highly intelligent and progressive statesman but one who wanted nothing to do with such a "squalid" matter. When confronted with the subject by teachers, parents, or the press, he would usually reply, "Yes, sex education for teenagers is a very important and necessary business. But can such a complicated task be accomplished through a single school course? Of course not. We must all deal with it together." "Dealing with it together," of course, meant that no one in particular was responsible. The only consequence of Yagodin's activity in this field was to do away with the course on the ethics and psychology of family life introduced in the period of stagnation. And one could hardly call that an achievement. If this logic were to be followed, one might just as well replace courses in all other school subjects and even do away with schools altogether, because life itself is the best, and in a certain sense the only, real educator of young people.

In coming to realize they could expect no help from the state and could rely only on themselves, doctors and educational experts began in the late 1980s and early 1990s to set up voluntary public organizations and projects associated with sex education.

The first group to come into being was the Association for Health and the Family, which received assistance from the Health Ministry, the Soviet Children's Fund, and the Soviet Women's Committee. In 1990 one of the Moscow district sanitary education centers was transformed into the country's first Center for Shaping Adolescent Sexual Culture, with the goal of providing confidential counseling and lectures for schoolchildren. For two years, until it was closed by Moscow medical bureaucrats, the small staff of the center managed to meet the needs of some six thousand teenagers annually. In 1991, the Association for Combating AIDS, the *Ogonyok*—Anti-AIDS charitable fund, the Association for the Prevention of Sexually Transmitted Diseases, the Russian Family Planning Association, and the sexological association Health and Culture were established.

By contrast with what had gone before, progress since 1985 has been enormous, yet in comparison with what the country—or even the city of Moscow alone—really needs, these changes were just a drop in the ocean. As in other spheres of life, true progress can come only with the application of more money and qualified personnel.

In an atmosphere of general social crisis, the downfall of liberal reforms naturally opens the way to revolution, which, given the paucity and undeveloped state of organized structures, immediately grows into anarchy. So it has been in the Soviet economy, politics, and international relations. The sexual revolution has followed the same path.

As soon as the chains of censorship began to rust, Soviet sex burst them asunder and presented itself to the world in all its primitiveness, all its nakedness and ugliness.

Although Gorbachev's perestroika came to grief, glasnost did change the sociopsychological climate in the country radically. The external framework and forms of social control disintegrated. At the same time, the public, especially young people, had long since grown tired of hypocrisy. All that had been secret now became open, and people began to shout the previously unmentionable from the rooftops. Moreover, attitudes toward sex became, just as during the years of "student revolution" in the West, a paramount symbol of the new, liberal, pro-Western, anti-Soviet, individualist, and hedonistic mentality that the Communist Party had long repressed and persecuted. Sexual symbols and values, which earlier had been peripheral to the ideological nucleus of culture, now became a sort of watershed dividing "right" and "left," as well as the generations. Sexuality quickly began to polarize and politicize. This created a host of very acute political, moral, and aesthetic problems that society was just as ill-equipped to understand—let alone resolve—as had been the universally damned state power.

The first more or less open discussion of this "forbidden theme" in the mass media began in early 1987 with my interviews in the popular weekly *Argumenty i fakty* and on the boldest and most popular television program, *Vzglyad*. The impetus for the interviews came from the editors and producers, respectively. My words were highly circumspect, meant more to raise the issue of the proper place of sexuality than to delve deeply into it. All the same, the word was out and it evoked a stream of vituperative letters from members of the older generation.

"I do not respect today's young people, nor do I share their views or convictions," wrote G. Shibanov, in a typical letter. "They should do more work, toil harder, and that would leave them no time to worry about sex or leisure. That all comes from being fat and lazy."

Younger people, meanwhile, complained of my lack of specificity and evasiveness: "At a time of burgeoning democracy and openness you could have dealt with the problem in a more concrete and serious way, indicating more precisely what the problem is and what needs to be done, rather than giving airy-fairy formulations typical of ten years ago."

Having decided to move from mere words to deeds, in the spring of 1989 the weekly *Semya* (*Family*) brought out, with my introduction, the first volume of the illustrated French *Encyclopedia of Sexual Life*, which had originally been published in 1973 and was intended for children ages seven to nine. This highly discreet book, translated into many European languages and containing nothing but elementary anatomical-physiological information, was gratefully received by Soviet parents who had not known how to answer their children's time-honored questions. And yet, the celebrated writer and Russian national chauvinist Valentin Rasputin devoted the best part of a speech at the First Congress of USSR People's Deputies to this blameless book. In Rasputin's view, "Such pictures are shameful, even for a grown man to see, let alone a child."

Even before they had come into being, sexual culture and sex education at once became the object of cynical political intrigue; the Communist and ultra-right forces used them to suffuse the atmosphere with moral panic. As the British sociologist Jeffrey Weeks points out, the sociopsychological mechanisms of moral panic are well enough known:

> The definition of a threat in a particular event (a youthful "riot," a sexual scandal); the stereotyping of the main characters in the mass media as a particular species of monsters (the prostitute as "fallen woman," the pedophile as "child molester"); a spiraling escalation of the perceived

threat, leading to the taking up of absolutist positions and the manning of the moral barricades; the emergence of an imaginary solution in tougher laws, moral isolation, a symbolic court action; followed by the subsidence of the anxiety, with its victims left to endure the new proscriptions, social climate, or legal penalties. In sexual matters the effects of such a flurry can be devastating, especially when it touches . . . on public fears.[2]

That was the case with the Soviet Union. People accustomed to total prohibition were unexpectedly confronted by the naked body and frank, erotic scenes on television and cinema screens. Moscow, and then other towns and cities, became the venue of beauty contests whose winners received expensive gifts and prestigious jobs as models abroad; meanwhile, to the minds of puritanically trained Soviet people, an actor's or model's presentation of even a half-naked body differed little from prostitution, and indeed the new frankness really was closely tied in with the commercialization of sex.

Video clubs, both legal and illegal, began to open their doors to young and old alike, allowing them to view erotic and even openly pornographic pirated films. Prostitution, which hitherto had been coyly veiled and passed over in silence, now came out into the open an even began to flaunt itself. The youth press started—initially in the form of criticism, and then with relish—to write about group sex, rape, and child abuse. Homosexuals and lesbians became visible and audible; many people had never even suspected or imagined so much as their existence, or if they had, they viewed them as the devil incarnate. Yet now, all of a sudden, they were hearing that gays were also human beings whose civil rights should be recognized. Boys and girls began to kiss openly and embrace in the streets and in the subway. There was good reason for the older generation to take fright and generally be aghast.

This sexual-erotic boom caught both the Soviet public and the government unawares. Owing to the absence of pertinent sociological research and the unreliability of official statistics, nobody then could say with any certainty what was actually new and what had always existed and had now merely come to the surface. What is more, whether they liked it or not, Soviet people had become accustomed to thinking one thing, saying another, and doing yet a third. That had been a condition of survival, and no one was shocked to find that had been the case with more than just sex. Now there was an obvious crumbling of all supports.

The appearance of the new and the unknown invariably causes fear, particularly among people unused to change. Conformist Soviet society, accustomed to uniformity and rigid external control, was without any elaborated individual, internal, differentiated, and hierarchical moral-aesthetic compass. Indeed, it had practically no need of them, since the Party—the self-proclaimed "mind, honor, and conscience of the epoch"—had made decisions for everyone down to the last person. Thus, in the absence of any generally meaningful norms and rules of behavior, society found itself in a state of moral shock and anomie.[3]

According to an old Soviet joke, there are four varieties of human society:

1. The society in which everything that is not banned is permitted;
2. That in which everything that is not permitted is banned;
3. That in which even what is banned is permitted; and
4. That in which even what is permitted is banned.

From the October Revolution until 1987, the Soviet Union had patently been in the fourth category, but now, suddenly, without any preparation, it had moved into the third category. There were good grounds for trepidation.

Sexual freedom and eroticism were firmly associated in the Soviet mass psyche with the violence and crime that were becoming more common with every passing day. The underground passages and subway stations became crowded with purveyors of primitive erotica and quasi pornography, which appeared even more squalid for being badly printed on poor-quality paper. The lack of control over this bazaar amazed and shocked even foreigners accustomed to seeing such things sold freely back home—although abroad, pornography was not sold on every street corner, and did not stand out starkly naked but was lost among a host of other, more attractive commodities absent from impoverished Russia. On the half-empty shelves of the markets of Moscow and Leningrad these pitiful sheets, which would have gone largely unnoticed in the West, stood out in their nudity and obscenity. The older generation looked on in helpless horror as teenagers leafed through the scandal sheets.

The long-ignored problem of differentiation between "decent" eroticism and "squalid" pornography, between sexual freedom and the exploitation of sex for commercial purposes, became uncommonly acute and urgent. At the same time, there was no apparatus for a discussion of these pressing issues.

Out of habit the authorities initially took repressive measures. Their particular victims in the mid-1980s were the owners of video equipment, which was at that time accessible only to the very well-off. Artistically and sexually illiterate investigators, prosecutors, and judges, relying on equally ignorant "expertise" from often inappropriate witnesses (gynecologists and sexopathologists, schoolteachers, Party functionaries, and their ilk), launched a vicious campaign of intimidation against video culture, condemning numerous classics of world cinema as pornographic or propagating a cult of violence and cruelty; they even included films that had been shown on Soviet screens or at the Moscow Film Festival, such as Fellini's *Satyricon, Amarcord, Casanova*, and *La Dolce Vita.*

In a 1989 retrospective analysis of criminal cases examined by courts in the Ukraine, Uzbekistan, Kirghizia, and Lithuania, as well as several Russian territories, the USSR prosecutor's office established that some 60% of those condemned in these campaigns had been prosecuted without any legal grounds.[4] According to the art experts, nine-tenths of the films adjudged by the courts to be pornographic or likely to encourage violence and cruelty did not belong in that category at all. To obviate such cases in the future, the prosecutor general decreed that "on the subject of the investigation and nature of tasks to be resolved, expert opinion on video films shall be taken only from art critics and [shall] entail the compulsory participation of a specialist in cinematography with appropriate education in and experience of the work." (One has to ask, however, whether the country has many such experts and whether their judgment is irreproachable.)

To ease the burden thus placed on them, a group of Moscow cinematographers formulated a whole series of formal and constructive criteria to distinguish erotica from pornography. As is well understood, however, such a distinction works only at a philosophical level, and in certain restricted cases. The rest is a matter of taste and aesthetic (and, partly, sexual) culture. After all, at one time, Edouard Manet's *Déjeuner sur l'herbe* was considered to be highly improper because it features a naked woman in the company of two fully clothed men. And even as the authorities of some Soviet cities banned masterpieces of Italian or Japanese cinematography, either on their own initiative or at the demand of a conservative public, their children were busy looking at cheap American films that contained less nudity but incomparably more violence. (Most foreigners find the American public's toleration of violence and intolerance of nudity beyond their ken.)

The situation in regard to evaluation of literary work was no better. In the late 1980s, a Moscow court almost sentenced a young man for photocopying Vladimir Nabokov's *Lolita.* It was officially concluded that Nabokov's book was pornographic for the simple reason that sexopathologists use the term "Lolita syndrome" in their work. The court completely ignored the contrary conclusion of three very well-known—and very different—writers: Andrei Voznesensky, Fazil Iskander, and Vladimir

Soloukhin. The young man was saved from incarceration only by the testimony of the academician Dmitri Likhachov, the doyen of Russian literary
criticism and a man much respected by all.

After a series of scandalous setbacks, the public prosecutor and police
became more circumspect. Yet then the public started to heap abuse on
them for inaction.

Not surprisingly, it was the Communist Party press that set the tone.
This is what the *Pravda* journalist Nikolai Volynsky had to say in his article
"The Price of Strawberries" (October 11, 1989):

> Scholars, particularly foreign scholars, have noted a very dangerous trend:
> the portrayal of pornographic scenes or what often passes for "erotica"
> invariably leads to impotence in both males and females. . . .
> And if pornography continues to develop here at such a tempestuous rate,
> we will soon have to resort to the services of new doctors—specialists in
> the artificial insemination of women. . . .
>
> We should have to give serious thought, I feel, to the establishment of
> police vice squads. . . . "Who would take such a job?" I am asked. "Where
> would we find such people?" Where there's a will, there's a way. The job
> should suit at least some of the 18 million bureaucrats we have. They do
> have some experience with prohibitive activity. And if their efforts have
> been essentially anti-social in many spheres, now they have a chance to do
> some public good.

Imagine entrusting people who managed to ruin the economy with the job
of controlling culture! Yet it was not a joke. That is what the Party had
been doing throughout its history and aspired to do for all time. Its cadres
simply had no other skills but to prohibit and ban. That is why the Party
peddled the "antipornographic" line so ruthlessly even as its authority
diminished.

The entire final year of Mikhail Gorbachev's stewardship, right up to the
August 1991 coup, passed under that banner. The presidential commission
headed by the Culture Minister Nikolai Gubenko contained not a single
sexological expert, but rather the usual blend of Party functionaries,
churchmen, and conservative writers. In fact, the experts, particularly the
Sexology Association Board, publicly warned that repressive-restraining
measures in regard to third-rate low erotica could produce positive results
only if combined with a positive program for promotion of real sexual culture and enlightenment. But the opinion of scholars was, as always, totally
ignored. The Resolution of the USSR Supreme Soviet of April 12, 1991, on
"Urgent Measures to Halt the Propaganda of Pornography and the Cult of

Violence and Cruelty" merely listed repressive and censorious measures, and contained no positive program at all. The people's deputies were scheduled to gather to hear the report on the implementation of their resolution in late 1991, but other events overtook them. . . .

In whipping up a moral panic in the country, the Communist Party pursued very clear, though always unacknowledged, political goals:

- Diverting of popular attention from pressing political issues and blunting of public awareness of the government's economic failures.
- Deflecting of blame from the Party for the weakening and destruction of both morals and the family.
- Cementing the developing alliance between Party and conservative religious and national chauvinist organizations, including blatantly fascist groups.
- Directing popular fury and frenzy against the glasnost that was so hated by the Party apparatchiks, by branding the democratic mass media as part of a Jewish-Masonic conspiracy bent on corrupting the morals of young people, destroying traditional popular values, and so forth.
- Restoring lost Party control over young people.

Reactionary pundits invariably portrayed young people not as subjects of social activity but as the eternal objects of education, lost sheep vulnerable to any stupefying influence (though never any sensible one), from which they had to be saved, by force, if necessary, against their own will. Tellingly, the ideologists of Russian national chauvinism, the writers Valentin Rasputin, Vasily Belov, and Yuri Bondarev, were just as virulently opposed to all other elements of the youth subculture, such as rock music, as they were to sex.

In their complaints about the general availability of erotica, Party officials were patently nostalgic for their own "personal keyhole" through which they could view what others could not. What the privileged observers found attractive was not so much the variety and quality of what they consumed—after all, any Western sex shop had much more of both—as the sense of being part of the elite: I can, while others cannot. And now, all of a sudden, what only the ruling elite and its lackeys had been able to enjoy at closed viewing sessions was becoming accessible to all. The end of the world was nigh!

It seemed the authorities surely could not lose by playing on the public's sexual fears. But they did lose, just as they experienced defeat in all other Party-inspired propaganda campaigns. This was convincingly demonstrated by the results of the survey carried out in late February 1991 by the All-Union Public Opinion Study Center (VCIOM), at the very height of the antipornography campaign.

In response to the question "What would you say about the present state of public morality?" only 31% of those surveyed agreed that there had been "a sharp fall in moral values," and most of them were elderly people, women, factory and office managers, old-age pensioners, Party members, and military personnel. Yet some 35% felt that "What had hitherto been concealed had now come to the surface," while 21% believed that "people's morals were changing and each generation has its own moral standards"; 13% had difficulty answering at all. In other words, people were concerned about the moral state of society but were not inclined to count that as the exclusive consequence of glasnost.

Even less were most Soviet people prepared to connect the suggested "decline in morals" primarily with the spread of pornography and erotica, as the chauvinistic press was doing. A mere 11% (13% of women, 8.5% of men) so stated in answer to the question "What do you mainly have in mind when you think of the decline in public morality?" People were mainly concerned not with pornography but with the overall rise in violence and cruelty, people's indifference to those around them, the diminishing discipline in the labor force, and much else besides. Furthermore, persons under 30 and the more educated were by no means inclined to identify erotica with pornography, maintaining that the two were different.

The public was certainly disturbed about the uncontrolled distribution of sexual-erotic material, especially among children and teenagers. As many as 76% of those surveyed, including the better educated, agreed with the proposal to set an age limit on this issue. A mere 8% opposed the idea. On the other hand, only 29% (largely the elderly, old-age pensioners, the poorly educated, Party members, and military personnel) agreed that the authorities "should ban the showing of films and distribution of publications with an erotic content." Some 42% were against; only 8% of the under-25 supported the proposition.

Generally variances in the ages and social status of the respondents made for substantial differences in opinion. For example, 40% resolutely condemned "the appearance of nude scenes on film and television screens"; yet among those over 60, a full 60% subscribed to this view, whereas of those in the below-30 age range, only 12–15% were in accord. As few as 28% agreed that "free discussion of sexual problems in the mass-circulation newspapers and magazines" exerted only an adverse influence on public morality; among them, however, were once again predominantly the elderly and old-age pensioners, as well as subscribers to the military daily *Krasnaya zvezda* (*Red Star*). The remainder of respondents thought differently.

In short, it was largely old-age pensioners, military personnel, and Party members (and often these categories overlap) who supported the "anti-erotic" clamor of the Party and the chauvinist press.

The survey also confirmed the catastrophic state of sexual education in the country as a whole. A mere 13% answered in the affirmative to the question "Did your parents ever talk to you about sexual education?"; 87% answered negatively. Young boys were particularly ill-served: while parents had spoken to 15% of the girls, they had done so with only 10% of the boys. Again, the social and age differences spring to the eye here: some 27–28% of those under 25 replied affirmatively, while only 5% of those over 55 had had any parental guidance. Urban parents talked about sex with their children more frequently than did rural parents.

The respondents are bringing up their own offspring differently, or intend to do so. As many as 51% (6% more women than men) replied affirmatively to the question "Have you spoken or do you intend to speak to your children about sexual education?"; 48% answered negatively. Yet the preponderance of affirmative answers may be put down primarily to young people, falling from 83% in the 20–24 age group who are speaking merely of their intentions, to 23–24% among those over 55, who describe their actual experience.

Perhaps, then, the public really does not want sex education, as chauvinistic leaders assert?

In late 1989 a representative USSR public opinion survey was conducted; answers to the question "What channels for obtaining information on sexual issues do you consider most acceptable and effective?" were as follows[5]:

| | |
|---|---|
| a special course in schools and colleges | 45.6% |
| special popular literature | 42.5% |
| special popular films or television programs | 28.7% |
| consultations with medical specialists | 22.2% |
| talks with parents | 21.4% |
| discussion of sexual problems with peers | 5.3% |
| other means | 0.7% |
| there is no need to enlighten young people on sex | 3.0% |
| difficult to say | 6.2% |

Evidently, the great bulk of the public supports the notion of systematic, professionally managed sex education. According to a Russian survey in 1991, as many as 60% (61% of women, 58% of men) were in favor of sex education in schools, for children aged 11–12; 21% were against. What strikes one once again is the age disparity: over 80% in the under-25 answered affirmatively, whereas only 38% of the over-60 were in favor.

The failure of the August 1991 coup—whose leaders were preparing to combat "the cult of sex and violence" with tanks and armored personnel carriers—temporarily depressed the social pressure over erotica. Other issues came to the fore. Life became freer but more austere. All the same, unresolved problems did not become any simpler because of the greater freedom.

There are several sex shops (selling erotic magazines, videos and books, fancy lingerie, condoms, etc.) now in Moscow; the first was opened by the president of the Sexological Association, Sergei Ogarkov. Yet the country is still awaiting organized sexual education of any sort as well as allocation of funds with which to carry out research. Nobody now stands in the way of safe-sex propaganda, yet what is the point of lauding the use of condoms when the great majority of people, including sexually active teenagers, cannot afford to purchase them? And for all the new openness, the level of sexual culture remains low—an absolute majority of Russians have never even heard of lubricants.

Russian-language translations of a few popular Western books on sexology have been published since 1989, but the best books remain out of reach because there is no hard currency to purchase copyright and the publication itself is too expensive. The censorship is gone, but libraries have no money to subscribe to foreign journals, and interlibrary exchange, even within the country, has come to grief. Nor are funds available for foreign travel or even correspondence.

Even the old and well-established academic research centers in Russia are completely ruined. Individual scholars can survive only if they can obtain some foreign grants or are doing something commercial (one of my former students, now full professor and father of three, is selling books on the street). So what to expect from sexology?

Private practice provides doctors with a decent means of existence, but there are no sexological clinics and no journals. Each may invent his or her own bicycle, which people are indeed doing, trying, in the best Soviet tradition, to convince themselves and others that they really are the very best in the world.

Yet without professional education and fundamental open-ended research, there can be neither proper medical and psychological assistance nor effective sexual education.

The situation with regard to erotic art at first glance seems better. (I speak not as an art critic—my personal tastes in this area are too traditional and conservative for me to venture any independent judgments— but only as a sociologist.) In a certain sense, erotic art is more important than sexology. Sexology as a science mainly describes and analyzes already existing forms of sexual behavior and sexual values, frequently simplifying and distorting. Erotic art, on the other hand, if genuine, does not so much reflect everyday sexual life as create new forms. It creates the language of erotic communication, elucidates the hidden motives of human behavior, and suggests all imaginable situations, even the forbidden. It delights, inspires, perplexes, and contradicts, and is often difficult to understand, especially for those who aspire to provide uniform and socially acceptable conclusions.

Stalinism destroyed Russian erotic art, or rather, drove it deep underground and made Western art inaccessible. During the 1960s and particularly the 1970s, Russian erotic culture began slowly to revive. In the fine arts—painting and sculpture—erotic motifs and subjects are patently apparent in the work of Mikhail Shemyakin, Yevgeny Zelenin, Vladimir Makarenko, Boris Messerer, Ernst Neizvestny, and Vadim Sidur. In ballet the choreographic miniatures of Leonid Yakobson based on the Rodin sculptural triptych *The Kiss, The Eternal Spring,* and *The Eternal Idol* were real sensations, as was his staging of Khachaturian's *Spartacus* at the Kirov Theater in Leningrad. In poetry, the verses of Andrei Voznesensky and Yevgeny Yevtushenko stirred up considerable interest and sometimes scandal. Some erotic literature—the more open, or more intricate in form— could not break through the censorship net and had to be published either abroad or in *samizdat.* In some instances the hindrance was the naturalistic, frank language; in others, the complicated artistic form; and in yet others, the noncanonical sexual content. More often than not it was a combination of all three.

The weakening of censorship bans and ideological control opened up new possibilities to Russians. With a delay of decades they finally saw uncensored many outstanding works of Western cinematography that had previously been inaccessible. For example, Bertolucci's *The Conformist* was shown in a version a third of its original length, having had everything about the hero's childhood and youth cut out.

The journal of translations, *Inostrannaya literatura* (*Journal of Foreign Literature*) acquainted its readers with James Joyce's *Ulysses,* Vladimir

Nabokov's *Lolita*, D. H. Lawrence's *Lady Chatterley's Lover*, Henry Miller's *Tropic of Cancer*, Jean Genet's *A Thief's Diary*, Truman Capote's *Other Voices, Other Rooms*, and so on.

Since 1992, it has been legal to publish erotic literature in Russia. The first swallow, after a special issue of the *Literary Review* (1991, no. 11), was the collection entitled *Three Centuries of the Poetry of Russian Eros*. The Serebryany Bor company is publishing an excellent series, called *Inter-eros*, with good, professional commentaries. The first volume was devoted to the Russian "Silver Age" and included works by Marina Tsvetaeva, Mikhail Kuzmin, Aleksei Remizov, Georgi Ivanov, Fyodor Sologub, and Vladislav Khodasevich. The second volume was devoted to works from eighteenth-century England and includes Russian translations of John Cleland's *Fanny Hill* and William Congreve's *The Way of the World*. Also in 1993, an anonymous author, writing under the pseudonym "Vassily Ivanov-Petrov-Sidorov," published a collection entitled *A Russian Decameron*, which included Alexander Afanasiev's erotic tales, some sexual *chastushki*, and frivolous poetry by Alexander and Vassily Pushkin, Mikhail Lermontov, Alexei Tolstoy, and others. A collection of Russian children's erotic folklore by first-rate professional folklorists is in preparation. An excellent collection of Russian translations of the old Chinese erotic treatises was published in l992, as was a Russian translation of the Indian *Kamasutra*.

Many books that were previously banned have been published, both those by émigrés and those by home-based authors, such as Vasily Aksyonov, Venedikt Yerofeyev, Victor Yerofeyev, Yuri Aleshkovsky, Eduard Limonov, and Valeriya Narbikova. Special festivals of foreign erotic films began to be held, and Russian erotic cinema, theater, and photography began to appear.

Initially all of this caused anxiety and alarm. Thus, in order to open the first exhibition of erotic books and painting from the private collection of Leonid Bessmertnykh in Moscow, it was necessary to set up a respectable commission of experts to assure the district authorities that nothing indecorous would be displayed. Persons under the age of 18 were denied entry. Nonetheless, a man dressed in the uniform of the fascist Pamyat "national-patriotic" society hurled a smoke bomb into the hall, and under the smoke screen, stole several exhibits (the campaign for "moral purity" is often accompanied by hooliganism and criminality, and not only in Russia). Subsequent exhibitions, however, went off without a hitch—and without needing expert testimony in advance.

All the same, much remains problematic and in dispute.

The body, including the buttocks and private parts, is now being rehabilitated and is often publicly displayed. Sometimes this is aesthetically motivated. Audiences in St.Petersburg, like those in New York and London, found the naked dance sequence in the 1993 Maryinksi (formerly Kirov) Theater production of Sergei Prokofiev's opera *The Fiery Angel*, which was staged by the British director David Freeman, morally acceptable. Similarly, few people object to seeing naked male bodies in Roman Viktiuk's theater. And Russians are gradually becoming accustomed to seeing nude and seminude bodies on television and in the movies.

Some of the older generation are offended by this nudity, which is sometimes merely a display of bad taste. But as a reaction to previously disembodied imagery, it has latent psychotherapeutic potential. Men and women are rediscovering, accepting, and beginning to enjoy their own bodies. In the big cities, the first "body" shops, featuring cosmetics, hygiene products, clothing, and the like, have opened. Fashionable new clothing designs are extensively advertised. The TV shows extremely beautiful international exhibitions of haute couture—not as an advertisement but for the enlightenment of individual tastes. True, all these new things are outrageously expensive but at least they are available. The message is: Yes, you have a body and you should care about it. The old asceticism is over!

An integral part of this cultural revolution is the growing interest in erotica. For many decades the word "erotica" itself was employed by Soviet propaganda exclusively in a negative sense—i.e., erotica was equated with decadence and squalor. Yet when people were asked in the VCIOM 1992 survey whether erotica was good or bad, 42% of the men and 25% of the women in the Slav regions (Russia and Ukraine) selected "good" as a response (in the Baltic states of the former USSR, the numbers were 57% and 32%, respectively). The proportion of positive answers sharply increased among the younger and better-educated respondents. Russia took second place among the former Soviet republics in the reading of erotic literature, after Estonia, where 38% of the indigenous population read erotic literature, as compared with 22% of respondents in Russia.

The level of mass, commercial, erotic art is, as in the West, extremely low. That is particularly apparent in the cinema. Partly in compensation for the long period of forced hypocrisy and sexlessness, and partly out of money-making considerations—to bring in the viewers—Russian cinema directors order their actors to undress today at the drop of a hat, without rhyme or reason, men as well as women.

Lynne Attwood, the British writer on Soviet cinema, who has viewed dozens of recent Soviet films, begins her article on "Sex and the Cinema" in the following vein:

An article in the first edition of the new Soviet film journal *Kinoglaz* (*Cine-Eye*) notes with amusement that East European buyers at a recent Soviet film market were amazed by the number of genitals, particularly men's, on the Soviet screen. This was not the part of the male anatomy which struck me most in the films I saw at the 17th Moscow film festival in July 1991. It was the male bottom, which appeared on screen with astonishing frequency—naked, and always in vigorous motion. This, it turned out, was the favored way of depicting the sex act, a virtually obligatory feature of Soviet films in the era of perestroika.[6]

Some of the new films are quite good, and by Soviet standards, even innovative. But if we view them as an expression of group fantasy in post-Soviet society, they are bound to give cause for alarm. The major themes of this cinema, according to Attwood, center on nudity, sexual violence against women as compensation to men for their social powerlessness, prostitution, sex as a relief from boredom (although it also appears to be boring), and sexual orgies. The films feature strong and very macho men, and women with sex appeal. Sex frequently accompanies murder, suicide, and drug abuse. Moral indifference often shifts to sexual apathy; and all is viewed through male eyes, even when the film is made by a woman director.

Some of these films have an avowedly sociocritical character and portray a deviant subculture in which a similar ideology really does predominate. Yet their common philosophy remains traditionally sexist and often antifeminist. As Lynne Attwood concludes, "experimentation with new images and genres is generally to be applauded. However, the proliferation of images of sexual violence against women is a disturbing new development and not one which is likely to further the cause of women's equality."[7]

The literary critics note analogous trends in contemporary Russian erotic literature. Scribes of Russian erotica write a lot about sex, but it turns out to be largely banal, routine, joyless, and, very often, cruel. Writers do not so much share with their readers emotional-erotic joys as they scrupulously dissect the physiology of the sex act and catalog its various methods, paying special attention to what is morally and aesthetically unacceptable to most people.

It goes without saying that that is the author's right. Artistic literature, particularly postmodernist, does not pretend to be a school for morals nor a textbook on how to become happy. Much writing is cruel because is it experimental. Yet how does one relate word and deed, joining the one to the other? In the West, intellectuals—and only intellectuals, since the rest of the public does not read highbrow books—have long learned to appreciate the conventional nature of any cultural contents without taking intellectual and artistic experiments too seriously. In Russia, however, things have always been different; the writer has long been seen as a teacher of life, and the Soviet state virtually made a rule of this. This has created enormous problems, depriving the artist of the right to make aesthetic experiments. So what happens if people do wish to follow where the writer is floundering in his or her own imagination?

At a round-table discussion entitled "Literature and Erotica," organized by the editors of *Inostrannaya literatura*, the writer Victor Yerofeyev, celebrated for his sharp, paradoxical perceptions, voiced his doubts on this issue. In the West, he said,

> culture is culture, and life is life. And nobody was shocked, for example, by Nietzsche writing, "Give the falling man a shove." Yet Rozanov said what a swine he was to propose this! From the Russian viewpoint, Rozanov was right. Yet in the European tradition this was included in some sort of net, and "the shove" was understood as a certain cultural challenge or provocation. Of course, no one rushed out to actually give a falling man a shove. . . . The trouble with us is that we suffer each problem as something personal, vital. And for us, each problem turns into something painfully existentialist, a sort of mixture of life and culture.[8]

Soviet attitudes to art have always been normativistic: What should one do and how should one act? When *Little Vera* (a first-class film, in my view, which, in spite of the excellent "bedroom" scenes, contains nothing specifically erotic) hit the screens as the first Soviet "erotic" film, I received a phone call from *Uchitelskaya gazeta* (*Teachers Newspaper*), saying that the paper was receiving many letters with roughly the following content: "I've been living with my wife for thirty years, and have never come across such a sexual position. Why is the cinema advertising sexual perversion?" How should the newspaper reply to such letters? I had seen *Little Vera* at its first showing in the Union of Cinematographers Club, but could not recall the "position" referred to. When I asked what position it was, the woman at the other end of the telephone gasped, then muttered, "the woman on top." "So what?" I replied. "Splendid. That's a perfectly normal position. But your paper is not going to open up a dispute on the issue. We'll soon have published a book from Poland with the appropriate pictures, so recommend the book to your readers."

Why do I mention this conversation? The Soviet-trained schoolteacher is convinced that everything has to be uniform; if he or she does not know "that position," it must be a perversion. And if the author of a film is right, the viewer should follow the example.

In the given instance, it was easy to provide an answer. But what if Victor Yerofeyev or Valeriya Narbikova portray in the novels both bestiality and violent sex and much else besides? Certainly Russian life is not more chaste than literature; in fact, just the opposite is true. As Victor Yerofeyev went on to say,

> We are scared of uttering certain words, yet all around us women are being raped, perversion and cruelty are flourishing about which the West has no inkling. . . . Any erotic pornographic works portray the land of sugarplums in comparison with Russian actuality. . . . Our literature may be put to shame by any daily police record.

What the West mainly talks or jokes about, Yerofeyev believes, Russia does in a serious fashion, following every dangerous example seen in erotic literature, from rape to bestiality to pederasty. And then the society calls literature to account for it. The bold literary experimenter and mystificator then begins to take fright:

> I really do find a situation where we give full reign to erotica frightening, and this is what is happening. What will come of it? Goodness knows. Will it bring liberation to the Russian people or will it bring yet another element of universal permissiveness to the criminal mind, that is enabling us to do barefacedly what we used to do on the sly? I am naturally against bans. I think we have learned our lesson, that bans are evil, that we possess no moral right whatsoever to prohibit something. Yet, clearly, we are faced with a dilemma which we shall have to deal with in the near future.[9]

If the Russian sexual situation has confused even such a radical as Yerofeyev, is it any wonder that the ideologists of Russian conservatism are panic-stricken?

The situation is reminiscent of the arguments used by Russian intellectuals after the failed 1905 revolution in the celebrated *Vekhi* collection. After all, it was one thing to quote Chernyshevsky's ideological proclamation, "Call Rus to the ax!"; it was quite another to witness roughhewn axes being wielded on landowners' estates and the culture that went with them. Playing at revolution, whether political or sexual, is more attractive to refined intellectuals than the rude reality of revolutionary practice. Yet then there inevitably arises also the very "Russian" question, quite alien to "Western" left-wing radical thinkers, of responsibilities for one's own ideas. I personally found quite shocking the political play making of the elderly Jean-Paul Sartre with youthful terrorists. And when I heard that one of the leaders of the Pol Pot regime—Thieu-Samfan, if I'm not mistaken—had written a dissertation in Paris, setting out a program of social and cultural genocide that was later implemented in Kampuchea, I was desperate to discover what his official Parisian advisers subsequently thought of it and whether they later had any twinges of conscience.

Of course, sexual games, even the most exotic, are more harmless than political games. Even so, if your wonderful erotic imagination, expressed on a piece of paper, can excite a real sex maniac to carry out a crime, you must give extremely careful thought to whether it is worth circulating your fantasies beyond your circle of close friends.

I am convinced that the beast is not as terrible as it is made out to be. Russia is not a zoo, and our teenagers, like their Western European and North American counterparts, would not try out on themselves all that used to be prohibited, no matter what films they might have watched. Their sense of humor and ability to understand the rules of the game are no worse than anyone else's. So let the erotic writers experiment; if they turn out to be too unintelligible or tiresome, they simply will not be read. People will not become sadists or rapists from reading bad erotic literature; and the scum that presently covers the surface of Russian society has appeared not because the dam has burst, but because the stream had long been sullied and left uncleaned. Given time, all will pass.

It is nevertheless a shame that the Russian sexual revolution, like the socioeconomic transformations that it accompanies, has to take place in such unfavorable conditions, and that we so frequently take smut rather than culture from the West. Weeds are always sturdier and grow through their own efforts, while cultural shoots have to be carefully cultivated; they have their own growing seasons and their preferred soil, and if you miss the season. . . .

And the present Russian government, like the former Soviet government, knows only the language of repression. Openly fascist newspapers and leaflets are sold in Moscow without hindrance, and their publishers and editors are important political figures. But the editor of the erotic newspaper *Yeshcho* was still imprisoned for the whole year, awaiting trial for distributing pornography. I don't like this newspaper and believe that at least some of its materials are really in very bad taste. But what is one to think about the authorities who free killers and arrest journalists?

*Part III*

# THE SUM
# AND
# THE REMAINDER

*Chapter Eight*

# SEXLESS SEXISM

*Women have long hair but short minds.*

—Russian proverb

S exuality is connected with gender in almost everything. We cannot understand the social structure of any human society, its culture, its education, or its usual course of personality development without studying sex differences, gender differentiation, cultural stereotypes of masculinity and femininity, sex-role socialization, and the way girls and boys are reared.

How does the former Soviet Union stand with respect to these issues? It is a paradox, a riddle, an enigma. There have been other antisexual cultures in human history, and more than a few in which it was considered improper to talk about sexuality. But who could conceive of a society that keeps silent about and thereby completely ignores sex differences themselves? Such a case would seem impossible. Yet that was precisely what happened in the USSR.

To judge by scholarly dictionaries and reference books, the Soviet people had neither sexuality nor gender. The five-volume *Filosofskaya entsiklopediya (Encyclopedia of Philosophy)* (1960–70) contained not a single article on sex or issues derived from sex; it only mentions in passing "sex selection," and touches on "the woman question" and the medieval "female mystique." A painstaking search through the extensive *Filosofsky entsiklopedichesky slovar (Philosophical Encyclopedic Dictionary)* (1983) for any mention of sex is equally disappointing, while the *Demografiche\sky ensiklopedichesky slovar (Demographic Encyclopedic Dictionary)* (1985) contains only a single reference, an entry entitled "The sex structure of labor resources."

The *Biologichesky entsiklopedichesky slovar* (*Biological Encyclopedic Dictionary*) (1986) would appear to be a big improvement on the previous books; it contains entries on "sex," "sexual reproduction," "sexual maturity," "sex dimorphism," "sexual cycle," "sex hormones," "sex organs," "sexual reflexes," and "sex chromosomes." But the entries are entirely biological in nature and written as though human beings differ in no way from other animals.[1]

One would think that psychology texts would reflect more of the realities of daily life than volumes of philosophical reference, but the same situation prevails in them. Thus, one of the best Soviet books on developmental psychology from the 1960s, Lidiya Bozhovich's *Personality and Its Formation in Childhood* (1968), examines the development of the child's personality from preschool age to the end of secondary school, yet the children under discussion are neither boys nor girls, nor do they grow into men or women. They are simply children—first infants, then preschoolers, then junior and finally secondary school students. They study, engage in social activities, attain a world outlook and even self-awareness. But they have no sex; their gender identity in no way affects them and is reflected in their psyches not at all.

The *Kratky psikhologichesky slovar* (*Concise Dictionary of Psychology*) (1985) has nothing on gender, sex, or sex differences. The textbook *Obshchaya psikhologiya* (*General Psychology*) (1977), which was edited by A. V. Petrovsky for use by students at teacher training colleges, looks at all manner of psychological qualities and relationships but makes no mention of gender/sex differences. The study aid *Vozrastnaya i pedagogicheskaya psikhologiya* (*Developmental and Educational Psychology*) (1983) gives the first reference to sex differences while in a discussion of "the anatomical and physiological readjustment of the adolescent organism" during puberty; that chapter also contains a paragraph on "the characteristics of relationships between boys and girls" (evidently preschool and junior high school students do not have to grapple with these problems).

Yes, there were exceptions. *Chelovek kak predmet poznaniya* (*The Human Being as an Object of Cognition*) (1969), written by the eminent Leningrad psychologist Boris Ananiev, contained a chapter on "Sex Dimorphism and Human Psychophysiological Evolution," but the author was referring more to psychophysiology than to psychology. A few Soviet psychologists and educators identified some behavioral and motivational differences between boys and girls; for example, Vladimir Venger and Valeria Mukhina found certain empirical sex differences when studying children's games and artistic creations. But all this was done on a haphazard and tangential basis.

Sociologists discussed the dynamics of division of labor by gender—the way men and women interact at work and in the family—yet this was interpreted within the framework of everyday consciousness without bringing to bear any scientific theory. The degree of women's emancipation was in most cases evaluated by analyzing the extent to which women had become involved in traditional male occupations, while men were assessed on the extent to which they helped women in the home.

In the field of theoretical biology, Vigen Geodakyan had been working since 1965 on an original general theory, based on cybernetics, that considers sex dimorphism as a specialization according to two major aspects of evolution: the preservation and change of genetic information. In his view, the first, conservative function is always performed by the female, the second, innovative function by the male.[2] Geodakyan's theory is not ideological speculation but is based on solid research data. Unfortunately, it was never debated sufficiently seriously by biologists, and many Soviet psychologists accepted a simplified version of it as proof of the innate and unchangeable nature of all sex differences.

Geodakyan objected, for example, to a simplified interpretation of male-female equality as their "sameness" and "interchangeability" in all spheres of human activity. He wrote: *"The idea of the social sameness and interchangeability of the sexes must be replaced by that of their complementarity. And that requires a knowledge of the fundamentals of biology."*[3] In the meantime, however, the Leningrad psychologist Vladimir Bagrunov, lumping together laboratory experiments on rats with observations of chess players, boldly made the following statement:

> With boys, whether at home in the family or in preschool, primary, or secondary education, in vocational guidance or industrial training, at work or at play, we must always take into account their natural inclinations and not hinder their natural development. . . . With girls, the formation and mastery of the necessary qualities will be more successful if societal institutions create favorable conditions—constant supervision, various kinds of reward—for them that take into account the higher degree of trainability and educability of women.[4]

Put into simple language, what Bagrunov is saying is that interaction between men and women, always and everywhere, in all areas of activity, is like the interaction of rider and horse. A boy should be given more independence, whereas a girl should be disciplined and taught to perform. One would think this was a matter of at least some debate, but no one raised any doubts about the methodology of Bagrunov's research, and the academic board of Leningrad University's Psychology Faculty awarded him his doctorate without missing a beat.

Very few Soviet psychologists read Western scholarly literature on gender difference, even though it was available in Soviet libraries and, unlike that on sexuality, had never been banned. The first Russian reference book to include such basic international terms as "sex/gender," "sex roles," "sex identity," and "sex differentiation" (all introduced in articles written by me) was *Psikhologia: Slovar* (*Psychology: A Dictionary*), edited by A. V. Petrovsky and M. G. Yaroshevsky and published in 1990.

As the British author Lynne Attwood has put it in her book *The New Soviet Man and Woman: Sex-Role Socialization in the USSR* (1990), "Psychologists in general have shown little interest in developing an understanding of the extent to which these sex differences are biologically or culturally constructed, and the process by which their development takes place. The existence of sex differences is generally taken as a given; the main concern has been to determine what influence these [differences] have on other psychological problems."[5] Soviet educational literature of the late 1970s and early 1980s, she found, was no more scientific: "It offers little more than a description of psychological sex differences, with the implicit suggestion that these are biologically determined. Yet just in case social influences start to interfere, a programme is recommended, designed to nurture these differences and thus produce healthy, dichotomized male and female personalities."[6]

The normative sexlessness had very important long-term cultural implications and consequences, including the complete disregard of the human body and its manifestations.

It is very fashionable now in Russia to complain that the Communists destroyed or at least undermined traditional Russian spirituality. The "resurrection of spirituality" and the turning of Russia into a "Realm of the Spirit" became popular slogans in the late 1980s, wielded by both conservatives and liberals, such as the poet Andrei Voznesensky. The term also has strong religious, nationalistic, and anti-Western connotations.

Yet for all its popularity, the notion of spiritual values is usually defined in a negative way—as being concerned with the "nonmaterial" and the "nonutilitarian." In an ironic play performed by the Leningrad actor Vadim Zhuk in 1987, the answer to the question "What constitutes spiritual values?" was roughly as follows: "Tania bought some wonderful shoes abroad, but they are too small for her. She can't wear them and is reluctant to sell them. She has therefore put them on her sideboard next to her crystal so that she and her friends can admire them. Now that shows spiritual values."

Yet for all the complaints about lack of spirituality, if we carefully exam ine the normative image of the "Soviet person"—which lives on in Russian public consciousness—we find that he lacked body even more than spirit. And the bodilessness of his existence was directly related to the sexophobia of Soviet culture.

Attitudes to the body are of paramount importance in the values of any culture. As the great Russian scholar Mikhail Bakhtin once put it, the body is a social construct, not simply a physical, natural phenomenon. Writing in the 1920s, Bakhtin not only defined the essence of the bodily canon as a general normative orientation of culture, but he traced its historical development in the Middle Ages and the Renaissance.[7]

We have seen that the watershed in traditional Russian culture between the spirit and the flesh, and between the bodily "top" and "bottom," was exceptionally high and impenetrable. This manifested itself both in painting and in dress. The body, particularly the female body, was wrapped about in a thousand veils through which it was hard to divine its contours. Whereas the West emphasized the female waist, for example, Russian traditional dress concealed it. Male attire was more liberal in that respect. During the Soviet era these traditional, symbolic, unconscious, and often conditional bans—let us recall that mixed bathhouses and ancient habits of naked bathing continued to exist in Russia until the beginning of the twentieth century—were intensified by mass poverty, rigid police surveillance, and sanctimonious verbal taboos.

Soviet philosophy pretended to be Marxist and materialist. Yet the human being that it reified was absolutely nonmaterial and largely disembodied. The five-volume *Philosophical Encyclopedia* (1960–70) contains no article on "The Body" per se, and even the occasional mention of "the body," "corporeal substance," and "corporeality" is confined almost entirely to historical-philosophical articles devoted to Plato, Thomas Aquinas, Leibnitz, and idealist philosophical anthropology. *The Philosophical Encyclopedic Dictionary* (1983) is just as noncorporeal in its orientation. This was, of course, not a matter of being coy. Simply put, a person deprived of individuality and reduced (philosophers presumed, and quite sincerely, that it was a matter of being "elevated") to his or her "social essence" had no need of a corporeal body at all; it would only get in the way. The first Soviet philosophical book on the subject of the body was published only in 1988.[8]

The situation was no better in Soviet psychology. Neither the psychological dictionaries nor the psychology textbooks contained any mention of the body as a general concept. When in the early 1970s I became interested in the problem of adolescent self-awareness, in which body image and appearance play an important part, I discovered that in the USSR only psychiatrists had studied the body, and that only because of the distorted body image common in some cases of schizophrenia. This lack of concern with the body was perfectly logical on the whole. If only sexopathologists study—and in a sense socially construct!—sexuality, then it must be psychiatrists, physicians who are charged with the care of those suffering mental illnesses, should study—and socially construct!—the body. Normal, healthy people do not feel their body, have no reason to be aware of it, and have no interest in it.

This ideological, cultural, and scientific neglect of the body was reflected in certain verbal conventions. Although there was little privacy in everyday life, educated, middle-class Soviet citizens were typically ashamed to mention elementary body functions in conversation, especially with persons of the opposite sex. There is an old joke about a Soviet diplomat at a party in England who needed to use the toilet and asked his hostess its location. "Very simple," the good lady replied. "Go down the hallway, turn right, then left, and you will see a sign 'Gentlemen'—but pay no attention and go straight in." The point of the story is that no gentleman would ask a lady a question of this sort. Such were the rules of good etiquette.

Imagine my amazement when on my first visit to Cornell University in 1988 I was taken by a young secretary from one lecture hall to another and on the way was shown the men's room. She asked me whether I needed to use it. I replied automatically—and untruthfully—that I did not, thank you. Then when we arrived in another building, a young professor excused herself for a moment, saying, "I'm just running to the ladies' room." In the Soviet Union, such a conversation between people of the opposite sex would be improper, at least among members of the older generation. When a young man and woman go to the theater, for instance, they go their separate ways to the rest rooms, with both trying to do so as discreetly as possible. Natural bodily functions would seem not to exist. This is not so much a matter of modesty, which remains rather undeveloped because of perennial overcrowding, but of the particular rules of verbal etiquette.

Excessive taboos and an inability to talk in a matter-of-fact way about natural bodily functions create a host of psychological problems when it comes to sex. Despite a long and rich folk tradition of vulgar or "foul" language, the everyday Russian vocabulary for the sexual and the erotic is exceedingly impoverished.

Many years ago, I asked a group of young men, former students of one of my own former students, to record anonymously all the words they used to designate quality of sexual experience, and then, separately, to designate female sexual reactions. All the men in question had served in the armed forces, where Soviet men usually complete their sexual education; some had had contact with deviant subcultures as well. Thus, there was every reason to expect they would have a good sexual vocabulary. They were asked in strictest confidence, they knew why I needed the information (there could be no question of real scientific investigation of such a theme), and their relations with their former professor were also fairly cordial and trustworthy. All the same, the task was virtually beyond them. First of all, they were terribly embarrassed about putting such "indecent" words down on paper. And even when they overcame their embarrassment, their sexual-erotic vocabulary turned out to be appallingly poor.

"Foul language," in spite of its extensively rich nature, focuses only on the most superficial, physiologically technical level of sexual interaction, and is totally inadequate for expressing complex emotional experiences. Nor is the problem that most people have no knowledge of medical-biological terminology, for that terminology is unsuitable for expressing complicated experience because of its sterile, clinical nature. For true expression of erotic experience, we need religious-philosophical or artistic metaphors. Without them—and where are they to be found if the country has no erotic culture?—people are doomed to silence or to the use of words that markedly humiliate, impoverish, and physiologize their sexual experience. Additionally, vulgar "men's language," which often refers to women as sexual objects, is frequently offensive to women. As a result, even married couples find themselves in terrible straits because they possess no acceptable words to express their specific desires or explain their problems, even to each other. Doctors trained as sexopathologists encountered this problem as soon as the first sexological consultation clinics came into existence.[9]

The desire to mask, to conceal, and, if possible, to eliminate the body also extended to clothing. In the 1920s the official Party and Komsomol dress style was typically "unisex," the identical cheerless form of attire for men and women. As society became more prosperous and varied, "the State's hatred of the feminine," in the caustic expression of the writer Mark Popovsky, softened somewhat. Yet when gender-specific clothing was allowed, and even required, both the state and public opinion retained their antipathy to expressions of individuality.

At first glance it would appear that the authorities controlled and persecuted nudity most strictly of all. In the late 1950s shorts appeared for the first time in the country, but it took considerable courage for a person to wear them in public places, even in seaside resorts in the Crimea and Caucasus. Residents of these areas claimed that shorts offended their moral sensibilities. By order of the local authorities, men in shorts were not served in shops, cafeterias, post offices, or hairdressing establishments. If the police saw that the driver of a car was wearing shorts, they could stop him and demand an immediate change of dress. In Moscow and Leningrad, the wearing of shorts gradually became a privilege enjoyed only by foreigners; Soviet citizens won that right only later, in the late 1980s, and even then not everywhere. The police now will pay no attention to someone in shorts on the street, but should a student turn up for lectures in shorts, he might well be sent out of the class in shame.

For women, the situation may have been even worse. In some regions, like Siberia, not only shorts but even trousers were absolutely unsuitable and could easily provoke sexual harassment and aggression against the wearer. During the 1980s the rector of the Leningrad Institute of Culture(!) formally banned the wearing of jeans by women and beards for men. That illegal ban was ifted only after a strongly worded collective letter was published in *Komsomolskaya pravda*.

Women in dresses with low necklines and the traditional Russian sarafans (sleeveless cloaks) were persecuted just as vigorously. I recall a comic incident from my holiday in Gurzuf, in the Crimea, in 1970. A middle-aged woman, an art historian from Leningrad, had gone walking along the esplanade wearing a perfectly respectable sarafan. But it so happened that on that very day the local police had launched a routine campaign against slack public morals. The woman was stopped and fined one ruble (a purely symbolic sum); and when she asked for a receipt, the policeman naively wrote, "For denudation." The now priceless piece of paper went the rounds of the gleefully incredulous intelligentsia. Members of the local holiday house for artists simply crowded on to the esplanade, taking off not only what was permissible but even what was not. The police, however, had evidently quickly realized their mistake and turned their backs in embarrassment. The bold women who stood defiantly before the police in a state of seminudity were fined "For disturbing the peace"; the art historian's fine "For denudation" remained unique.

Nor was "denudation" the only such offense liable to persecution. During the 1970s the municipal authorities of many cities persecuted adolescent boys and young men for wearing long hair, and women for wearing blue jeans or trouser suits. In Leningrad the police and their assistants from "the people's law and order squads" would seize long-haired youngsters right on the street, abuse them in every way possible, forcibly cut their hair, and then photograph them and put their pictures, with their names and places of work or study, on display in the streets under the warning: "We'll cut off your hair without your permission!"

When I first set eyes on such posters in my hometown, I telephoned the first secretary of the Party district committee, and we had the following conversation:

"Galina Ivanovna, what you are doing is a criminal offense. The vigilantes who forcibly cut off young men's hair are no better than hooligans who cut off a girl's braids for sport. It's crude violence."

"But long hair isn't nice; and we get letters of thanks from teachers and parents."

"If you arranged public floggings for it, you'd get even more thanks. Did you know that Marx wore his hair long? So did Einstein and Gogol. Would you have shorn them, too?"

"They would have worn their hair differently today. Anyway, the vigilantes are only cutting the hair of teenagers."

"But do you think teenagers have no sense of dignity, that you can do what you like to them? You are a former Komsomol official working with schoolchildren. Have you no shame?"

She was adamant, however. The scandalous practice ceased only after *Literaturnaya gazeta* published a letter from a young woman whose boyfriend had been shorn and whose shoulder bag had been taken from him; the vigilantes claimed that the bag was a woman's and did not suit men. The USSR deputy prosecutor general explained that the vigilantes' actions constituted a criminal offense. Almost immediately the campaign in Leningrad quietly died, although such arbitrary actions continued in the countryside.

The negative attitudes toward "hippyish" appearances were an international phenomenon in the 1960s—and not even a new one. Harvard College had a special ordinance against long hair on men as early as 1649. Yet in the USSR the control lasted longer and was stricter and more brutal. Conservatives in the United States are very similar to Russian ones. But in the United States, students and their parents could appeal in some cases to the courts, and in the Soviet Union, nobody would accept such a complaint.

From such examples—the attacks on men wearing long hair and women wearing trousers or sleeveless blouses—one might think that the Party was committed to combating violations of sex-role stereotypes. However, although this was an important motive, there were others as well.

At the same time as they began to sport long hair—traditionally a sign of femininity—young Soviet men also began to wear mustaches and beards, traditional signs of masculinity that were also associated with the founders of Marxist-Leninism and the heroic Fidel Castro. However, the wearing of beards was fought no less vehemently than long hair, and not merely on a local level. When Brezhnev appointed the archconservative V. G. Lapin as head of Soviet television, Lapin immediately did two things: he disbanded the center for sociological research and he banned from television all long-haired and bearded intellectuals. The local authorities in the seaside resort of Sochi arrested, paraded on television, then expelled as *stilyagi* (dandies) young men with a predilection for colorful shirts.

So it was not so much the body or even sex as such that were persecuted as anything that was nonstandard or individualistic. The command-administrative methods of governing relied on the traditions of communal living, the major principles of which were conformity and uniformity; these notions profoundly permeated the public consciousness, including the public's ideas of fashion.

For Westerners, with the exception of teenagers, fashion is only a guide. It not only does not preclude individual variations but requires them. No one wants to look like everyone else. For Soviet citizens, on the other hand, fashion was a sort of compulsory uniform: everyone had to dress, talk, and act like everyone else; there was no other way. I don't believe that wearing a uniform is always a bad thing, despite the liberal stereotypes.[10] But when dressing for a situation of uncertainty, when there are no "correct" or "incorrect" answers, a person oriented toward uniformity is completely at a loss.[11]

Of course, this orientation to uniformity goes beyond clothing. In Russia, people are accustomed to everything being regulated by bans. Once a ban is lifted, they can do the previously forbidden. And if they *can* do it, they *must* do it. As a result, people begin to do much that does not suit them, that they should not do, and even some things that they do not actually like to do. Of course, this preoccupation with conformity will pass in time, but how much aesthetic, moral, and even political cost it entails in the meantime!

In everyday life, Russians are not particularly coy and are not inclined to false modesty. On any public beach you can see men changing into their bathing suits under a towel if there is a shortage of changing rooms or too long a line for them. No one thinks that indecent. In Cuba, that situation would be absolutely impossible; in the United States, only a child could get away with it. And yet when it comes to the fine arts, the situation changes markedly.

Mark Popovsky tells the following story: in the 1960s a writer from Moscow invited a peasant fellow notorious for his lechery and attitude of machismo up from the country and took him to an art gallery. The man seemed to turn to stone before a painting by the nineteenth-century Russian artist Karl Bryullov: "Stopping before the painting, which portrayed a naked female figure, Vasily Fyodorovich suddenly blushed scarlet, covered his face with his bent arm, and turned away. Even his voice trembled in shock. 'I really didn't expect,' he muttered, 'such a respectable institution to show such shameful things.'"[12]

Village women in a short story by the conservative writer Vasily Belov show exactly the same sincere disgust at the Rubens painting *Union of Earth and Water*, a reproduction of which had been brought by chance to a local shop: "Naked women! How could they?!"[13] The picture was bought only for its frame.

A primitive perception of any nudity as "indecent" existed not only in the Russian countryside but in the more sophisticated cities as well. A hall in the Leningrad Political Education House on the Moika River (the former Yeliseyev mansion) used to have a vaulted ceiling with a lighthearted painting of naked putti gamboling and embracing. Nobody paid any special attention. Yet one day, following routine repairs to the building, I happened to glance up and notice that the little dears were now wearing shorts and Pioneer scarves. The ceiling had suddenly become indecorous: kissing putti was one thing, little Pioneers embracing was quite another. Evidently I was not the only one to have noticed; not long after, the scene was painted over completely.

Soviet leaders passed on their own hypocrisy to their Eastern European satellites. I was told the following story in Prague, in the early 1960s. The statue of a boy stood in the new Czech Children's House in Gradcany. The boy was naked and was as fully endowed as any other boy. Children passed the statue without a backward glance. Then one day, some party bigwig decided that a naked boy was indecent, and the statue was shorn of his male pride. Crowds of children subsequently began to gather around the statue, wondering whether it portrayed a boy or a girl. Ultimately, the statue had to be removed altogether.

Hypocritical attitudes toward the body also get in the way of children's aesthetic education. School teachers who take their small charges to the Hermitage Museum do all they can to block the children's view of the naked body in the paintings of Rubens and Giorgione. A band of 13-year-old Muscovites on a tour of ancient Greek art in the Pushkin Fine Arts Museum told their guide "how obscene it was to look at" Myron's *Discobo-*

*lus* and Polyclitus's *Doryphorus*. Before a Madonna and Child that features the Madonna with an exposed breast, teenagers usually begin to giggle and nudge one another.

A 1992 lecture to senior high schoolers at a Ryazan school showed a slide of Giovanni Bellini's *Woman with a Mirror*, which portrays a young woman sitting before a window and gazing at her hair with the aid of two mirrors. It is all quite decent—her naked breast is partially covered by her hand and a shawl is tied about her hips—but the entire school hall promptly burst into hysterical giggling and jeering. These teenagers are avid viewers of erotic and pornographic videos and films, yet the chaste and noble nudity of classical art embarrasses them—a direct consequence of their hypocritical upbringing and the prevailing societal sexophobia.

If discussion of biological sex is taboo, the social aspects of gender are inevitably underestimated.

My own theoretical interest in the problems of sex and gender differences arose by chance. For many years I had been working in Leningrad with an excellent typist named Nina Raskina, a well-educated woman with a good working knowledge of three European languages. Not only did she type my manuscripts, she also read them carefully and sometimes gave me the benefit of her critical opinion. When in the early 1970s I began to take an interest in adolescent psychology, she said, "Igor Semyonovich, what you write is very interesting, but it's all about boys. Where are the girls? They experience a good deal that is different." She was right, of course.

Starting from this criticism—after all, none of my colleagues had said anything of this sort to me—I began to ponder on it and to read the Western scientific literature. I soon found myself in a new and exciting world. Sex/gender turned out to be not a simple biological given but a complex and multifaceted social construct that required a multidisciplinary approach; and the social and psychological differences one observed between men and women, while both undeniable and important, were, at the same time, the result of historical development.

When I was asked to give a couple of lectures on the psychology of sexuality by Moscow University's Psychology Faculty in December 1980, I decided to devote the first of them not to issues of banned sexuality but to the notion of gender. A good-sized audience of undergraduates and postgraduates and a dozen or more celebrated professors assembled, and the lecture had to be broadcast to two additional lecture halls. I commenced with the declaration that Soviet psychology was sexless, which meant that it was neither psychology, since psychology cannot ignore one of the major dimensions of human existence, nor a science, since science studies reality, rather than simply playing with words.

I imagined that my statement would cause a scandal to erupt, but I was only asked politely whether I thought science could make generalizations without sex being taken into account. I replied that scholars have a perfect right to abstract themselves from anything they wish—sex, age, social environment, historical era, even the very fact of human existence. But if *all* researchers *always* ignored one of the most important aspects of the reality they were studying, they were no longer involved in a science but a game—for which the players, rather than the taxpayers, should pay. Nobody disputed that assertion; in fact, I received an urgent plea to provide an article for the next issue of *Voprosy psikhologii*.[14]

The article, "The Psychology of Sex Differences," came out in *Voprosy psikhologii*, no. 2, 1981. Despite the ambitious title, it was purely a survey piece, a modest attempt to set the subject in context; all the same, it was the first article in a Soviet professional publication to describe, complete with bibliography, how the problems of sex differences were being tackled in the West, and to define sex roles, sex identity, sex stereotyping, measurements of masculinity and femininity, psychological androgyny, and so on.[15]

Since that time, the situation has begun to improve. The 1980s saw an increase in both the amount and professionalism of research on gender issues. The psychiatrist Victor Kagan and the psychologists Igor Lunin, Tatyana Yuferova, and others began serious empirical psychological investigations into the emergence and development of gender self-awareness, sex-role socialization, and the images of masculinity and femininity among children and adolescents.[16] At the Institute of Ethnography (now the Institute of Ethnology and Anthropology of the Russian Academy of Sciences), interdisciplinary research into the comparative history of sex-role socialization, sex symbolism, images of masculinity and femininity, and gender stereotypes of speech behavior has been initiated.[17] The classic semiotic works of Vyacheslav V. Ivanov and Vladimir N. Toporov, dating back to the 1960s, provided an excellent methodological basis for such research.[18]

Yet the most important theoretical and political changes have been in sociology. Complaints that Soviet women occupy an underprivileged position both in the family and in public life were already widespread in the 1970s, though muffled by censorship and also by a general conviction that in spite of all difficulties, the Soviet Union was the most gender-egalitarian society in the world; if anything, the reasoning ran, Soviet society was perhaps too egalitarian. A small, dissident feminist group that had been

formed in Leningrad in the 1970s and had challenged this view was bru-
tally silenced by the KGB.[19]

The wave of social criticism in the late 1980s radically changed the
rather complacent general perspective. New feminist scholars, such as
Anastasya Posadskaya and Olga Voronina, as well as others, challenged the
assumption that the "women's question," like all other social problems, had
been fundamentally "solved" in the USSR. Now, women appeared not only
as an underprivileged social group but as one of the most exploited and
mistreated of them.[20]

But paradoxical though it may seem, the invariable natural result of the
official sexlessness of the USSR was sexism, the ideology that assumes that
all gender differences, including social inequality and male superiority, are
biological givens—natural, universal, and irreversible. In the absence of
social-scientific reflection on sex and gender, all the empirically observable
differences between men and women that confront us in our daily lives are
generally interpreted as being eternal and biologically predetermined.

One need not be a conservative to accept this line of reasoning. Yuri
Ryurikov, the popular Russian writer and publicist on love, family, and marriage, is generally an enlightened and liberal fellow. Yet although he admits
that "masculinity" and "femininity" are "by no means biological concepts,"
he, like Geodakyan, has no doubt that harmony between them is rooted in
the universal laws of biology; any retreat from them would signify "depar-
ture from the evolutionary mainstream" for the individual. Furthermore, the

> femininity which women are losing [the fact of such "loss" is apparently
> not in doubt to Ryurikov, though he gives no specific examples] is not dis-
> appearing. By some odd law of retention of psychological energy, it is shift-
> ing to men. Here the attributes which are the supreme attainment for
> women are turning into their antithesis for men: mildness becomes spine-
> lessness, attention to detail becomes pettiness, maternal caution becomes
> cowardice.[21]

Any educated social psychologist—and they do exist in Russia—knows
that these "attributes" and their interpretation depend above all on gender
stereotypes. But whereas that recognition requires thought and analysis, gar-
ish statements about the need for a traditional "mirrorlike" combination of
male and female roles within the family and society appear quite convincing
and readily understandable at first glance—the more so if they are anchored
by reference to prestigious though unread studies in genetics, which are
supposed to have established the truth of something similar somewhere.

The major sources and roots of Soviet sexism, like any other variety, are, of course, social.

An important slogan of the October Revolution of 1917 was the liberation of women and the establishment of full legal and social equality between the sexes. The Soviet regime revoked all forms of legal and political discrimination against women, attracting a host of women into industrial labor, education, and public activity. This was a serious and sincere attempt to put an end once and for all, at a single stroke, to gender inequality and the exploitation of women.

Like all other actions taken by the Bolsheviks, however, the program for gender equality was naive and unrealistic. First, they understood "gender equality," like other forms of social equality, in a purely mechanical way. Equality meant being absolutely identical, and its victory was an opportunity to destroy each and every social group and even natural difference between the sexes. The "liberation of women," like that of all other oppressed groups and minorities, was discussed mainly and even exclusively in socioeconomic and political terms. Make women equal in rights with men, give them an opportunity to develop themselves, and they will do and be the same and certainly no worse than men (no one considered the possibility of women doing and being something different—not better or worse, but precisely different—than men).

Oppressed groups typically start their liberation by acquiring the rights and privileges of their former oppressors and begin to live according to their oppressors' laws. Yet after that goal has been achieved, what usually happens is that the one-time oppressed find that certain elements of their new lifestyle are unacceptable or undesirable, and they begin to search for what does suit them. If that is the case for social, ethnic, and religious minorities, it should certainly be so for women. And in this case, we are discussing not simply an underprivileged social group but fully half of the human race, with its natural as well as sociocultural characteristics. One can criticize biological determinism and the "anatomy is destiny" formula as much as one likes, but it is naive to think that sexual dimorphism may not be manifest in culture and gender interrelationships.

What was typical of the Bolsheviks, and is indeed typical of any radical ideology, was an underestimation of the multiplicity and heterogeneity of the developmental processes at work, whether we are discussing individuals, groups, or entire societies. The Bolsheviks disastrously underestimated the objective and subjective difficulties with which even partial implementation of their program was associated. All historical, cultural, national, and religious factors of traditional gender stratification were ignored or viewed merely as "reactionary vestiges of the past," which could and must be removed by political means. Nor did they take into account that gender stratification may look and manifest itself differently in political, professional, and family life, so that positive shifts in one area of life may be accompanied by negative changes in another.

In the same way that the policy of forced "industrialization at any cost" contained within it the seeds of future ecological catastrophe, so the Bolshevik push for "emancipation of women" resulted in conflict with many basic elements of the traditional national life and culture. So even some evidently irrefutable achievements ultimately turned out to be Pyrrhic victories, having little in common with the original plans and provoking strong negative reactions.

Soviet propaganda has always boasted of the fact that for the first time in history, women were being drawn into the country's sociopolitical and cultural life. It is true that in 1987, Soviet women made up 51% of the labor force. Nine-tenths of women of working age were employed or studying. In terms of their educational standards, Soviet women were practically equal to men. The number of women with a university education was even higher than that of men, and in certain professions, such as teaching and medicine, women predominated absolutely.[22]

Was this real social equality? Alas, no. It was not so much an equalization as a feminization of the lower levels of the vocational hierarchy: women occupied the worst-paid and least prestigious jobs and were poorly represented on the higher rungs of the vocational ladder.

Let us take the situation in Soviet science as an example. In 1986, women made up 48% of all scientific employees in the country, 28% of the Ph.D.s, 13% of the doctors of sciences, and 0.6% of the members of the USSR Academy of Sciences, and held not a single place on the presidium of the academy.[23]

There is an old joke that says Soviet women can carry out any job, even the toughest—but only under male supervision. The joke is not far off the mark. Among men with a university education, every second one occupied some administrative post in the late 1980s, while only 7% of women with equal education did so. And among the heads of industrial plants a mere 9% were women.

With the transition to the market economy and the overall economic collapse, the social position of women has sharply deteriorated: entrepreneurs simply do not want to take on pregnant women, women who might become pregnant, or mothers with large families. Women have been the first victims of economic reform.

According to Alevtina Fedulova, president of the Union of Women of Russia, 73% of the unemployed in Russia are women.[24] And three million single women live only on their own salaries. Whereas earlier, women received about 70% of the salaries of men, now they typically receive only 40%. Both maternal and infant mortality rates are rising. Millions of families have lost access to nurseries and kindergartens because of closures and/or escalating prices.

It is no wonder that in the small, comparative international survey (March 1992) of 16 countries, from the United States and Germany to Singapore and India, Russians demonstrated the lowest levels of personal satisfaction with life; and they were the only nation to disagree strongly with the statement that "the opportunities for women in this society have improved a great deal over the past 20 years," men and women being almost equally pessimistic on this issue.[25]

The situation is the same in politics. When all policy was set by the Party bureaucracy, women were at least nominally represented at all levels of the political hierarchy with the exception of the Politburo (through the entire history of the Communist party only two women merited this honor—Yekaterina Furtseva, who, according to rumor, was Khrushchev's mistress, and Alexandra Biryukova, a Party functionary and deputy prime minister). During perestroika, even this formal representation came to grief. On the one hand, a few women have become genuine political figures—Nina Andreyeva and Galina Starovoitova, for example; on the other, the number of women deputies in the USSR Supreme Soviet fell from 33% in 1985 to 15.6% in 1989, and to only 5% in the regional and local soviets. In the December 1993 Russian elections the candidates of the gender-specific faction Women of Russia received 20 seats in the Duma because of its centrist and nonaggressive program, but there were few women candidates in the other parties and among the independent deputies.

Many Russians, women as well as men, are convinced that women are not suited for political and administrative positions, that their "natural place" is in the home. This view is sometimes shared even by young women, as quoted by Adrian Gaiges and Tatyana Suvorova:

A commodity expert, age 25: "A woman manager is no longer a woman."

An engineer, age 23: "There is no place for women in politics."

A medical student, age 21: "The country should be governed by men; they are smarter than women."

Only a minority of Russians prefer women as leaders and bosses. Many people believe that the idea of women in positions of leadership is contrary to the Russian historical tradition, but this is absolutely wrong. Historically, Russia has always had powerful women, even on the throne. Interestingly, Margaret Thatcher has always been one of the most popular of Western political figures with the Russians—precisely because of her reputation as the highly authoritarian "Iron Lady." When Ruslan Khasbulatov, ex-chairman of the Russian Supreme Soviet, made an offensive remark about Thatcher in 1993, the response was mass indignation. Nevertheless, in post-Soviet society, as in Soviet society before it, public life is dominated and governed by men. Women remain socially dependent.

No such simple statement can be made about family life because of the substantial national, ethnic, cultural, regional, and religious differences in the population. While Uzbek, Georgian, and Armenian families are traditionally patriarchal and paternalistic, the Russian traditional family always reflected a stronger female and maternal influence. On the whole, however, development in the Soviet Union, as in Western countries, has tended toward greater gender equality.[26] About 40% of all Soviet families in the 1970s were considered largely egalitarian.

Russian women, especially in the towns, were more socially and financially independent of their husband than at any time in the past. An indirect testimony to this is that in the 1970s and 1980s women initiated between 50 and 60% of all divorces in the USSR. Very often women bear the paramount responsibility for managing the family finances and for resolving the main issues of domestic life.[27]

A joke on the subject states that three women are talking about who makes the major decisions in the home. The first says, "My husband does, naturally." The second says, "How could I trust such a fool? I decide everything myself." The third says, "We don't have any problems on that score because we divide up power in our family. My husband is responsible for the major, overriding questions and I never interfere; but I decide all the personal, petty issues." "But how do you distinguish between the important and the petty questions?" she is asked. "Very simple. My husband deals with all the global issues, like the ecological crisis, events in Chile, and hunger in Africa. I am responsible for the personal things, like what to buy, where to go on holiday, which school the kids attend; my husband takes no interest in such things. So we never have any domestic rows on the subject."

The joke is not far short of the truth. In the late 1970s a group of television journalists went into the male enclave of a large factory, and they asked workers to show how much money they had with them. The men turned out their pockets, retrieving only three- and five-ruble notes in some embarrassment; very rarely did they have as much as a ten-ruble note. In the women's shop, however, the women produced ten- and even one-hundred notes. The point was that after work the women intended to make fairly large purchases in the shops or were holding the money for any unforeseen circumstances, because everything was in short supply.

It might seem this anecdote bears witness to women's power within the family. Should this enhanced responsibility be regarded as a privilege or as an additional burden? On the one hand, such responsibility is good for female self-respect. Russian wives and mothers are frequently strong, dominant, and self-assured. On the other, their household burden considerably exceeds that of men and is sometimes absolutely unbearable. The length of the working week was the same for women as for men in the 1980s. Yet women had to spend twice or thrice as much time on domestic affairs than men. See Table 8.1 for the findings of a sociological survey conducted in 1988 at factories in Moscow, where men and women were asked, "What kind of work do you personally do in the home?"[28]

**Table 8.1**

|                                       | Women (%) | Men (%) |
| ------------------------------------- | --------- | ------- |
| Looking after the children            | 79        | 20      |
| Doing the shopping                    | 74        | 32      |
| Cooking                               | 84        | 10      |
| Dish washing                          | 77        | 34      |
| Cleaning                              | 82        | 29      |
| Clothes washing and ironing           | 87        | 12      |
| Going to the laudromat or dry cleaner | 38        | 20      |
| Home repairss                         | 9         | 64      |

As we see, there can be no talk of real equality here.

Official statistics point in the same direction. In 1987, the nonworking time of an urban working woman was distributed as follows: housework, 51%, including shopping (12%) and direct household tasks (39%); child care 4%; leisure time, amusement, cultural recreation, 45%. For men the time was distributed rather differently: housework, 20%, including shopping (6%) and household tasks (14%); child care, 6%; and free time, 74%.[29] With the economic upheaval and social disruption of the last five years, leisure time has fallen substantially for both men and women; people take advantage of every opportunity to earn something on the side. And whatever the future political benefits of the dissolution of the Soviet Union, social justice and equality have not improved as a consequence.

It is not surprising that domestic compatibility—that is, "the fair distribution of household duties"—is a paramount factor in the degree of satisfaction with and stability of marriage; according to the sociologist Sergei
Golod, for married couples living together for more than ten years,
"domestic compatibility" is second only to "spiritual compatibility" (i.e.,
love, mutual respect) in importance; for younger couples, its importance
is somewhat less, yet nonetheless it is quite a large factor.[30] Mutual
recrimination and arguments about who is exploiting whom have been
typical features of Russian newspaper stories of domestic life for many
years.

Soviet policy on gender issues and sex-role stereotypes was remarkably
inconsistent. Before World War II, the authorities did all they could to
deny all gender differences. Although more was said with every passing
decade about the need to prepare women for future motherhood, the education of girls and boys was largely identical; based on traditionally male
patterns, it remained, to all intents and purposes, unchanged with the
passing of time. Female idols in the mass media were mannish—valiant
revolutionary women, heroic pilots, parachutists, and other women in traditionally male professions. School instruction was fully coeducational,
including physical education. Relations between boys and girls were usually simple and comradely, at least before puberty.

School education became sex-segregated in 1943, as part of a scheme
to improve military training for boys and men. The climate in schools
immediately changed radically. Relations between girls and boys, who
could now meet only at rare mixed parties under the watchful eyes of
teachers, lost their former comradely character, becoming instead eroti-
cized and sexualized.

During my last student and postgraduate years (1946–50), as an
unpaid Komsomol activist, I was able to observe the boys' schools becoming breeding grounds for all manner of foul language, while some head-
mistresses in the girls' schools hypocritically endeavored to turn their institutions into something like the pre-Revolutionary "finishing" schools for
noble young ladies by keeping out "those disgusting ragamuffin boys."
(Interestingly, it was precisely these schools that often had problems with
under-age prostitutes or senior students who had to quit school because of
pregnancy.) At school parties, the young fellows, trying to look nonchalant,
propped themselves up against the walls, while the girls danced with one
another; the boys came to life only when the party was coming to a close
or if someone managed to turn off the lights for a few moments. Komsomol organizations tried to counteract this segregation by arranging joint

activities, such as debates on moral themes, for both the boys' and girls' schools, but this did not always work out.

In 1954, soon after Stalin's death, separate-sex education, by demand of most teachers, parents, and the schoolchildren themselves, was revoked and Soviet schools again became coeducational. But the general educational emphasis on gender-specific training was very strong. As the Canadian educator Landon Pearson noted in her book *Children of Glasnost* (1990),

> My life experience has convinced me that some biologically based psychological distinctions between boys and girls are real and that they are just the same in the Soviet Union as they are in the West. But in Canada and the United States stereotypes of masculine and feminine behavior are crumbling even though legal and economic equality between the sexes has not yet been secured. In the Soviet Union, that process has been reversed.[31]

The problem of dual role expectations became more pressing with every decade. No matter how important the social-structural and educational factors of sex-role differentiation are in themselves, they cannot be understood without looking to profound, long-term shifts in the psychological stereotypes of masculinity and femininity—about which we may speak only conjecturally, and, to some extent, speculatively.

The problem of the "feminization of men" and "masculinization of women" first appeared in the pages of the Soviet popular press, starting with the weekly *Literaturnaya gazeta*, back in 1970, and the debate has not died down since. Women passionately and sorrowfully bemoan the shortage of "real men," while men complain about the dying breed of women who show female tenderness and affection.

Russians have never been the objects of professional, large-scale sociological surveys on masculine and feminine ideals. And journalistic questionnaires yield only very stereotypical, traditionally sexist pictures behind which stands a crying contradiction between the new system of gender roles and the traditional ideas of what qualities men and women should ideally possess so as to complement each other harmoniously (where exactly they are to complement each other—whether at work, in politics, or in the home—is rarely specified).

For example, in 1977 the popular weekly *Nedelya* ran a questionnaire on what qualities were the most desirable in men and women. Readers were asked to name a specific number of attributes, and they themselves supplied the list; yet the only one of the top five attributes common to both sexes was fidelity. All the rest differed. "Intelligence" took first place in the "male" set, while it came in last for the ideal female. "Femininity" came first in the list of attributes of the ideal woman, while "masculinity" took second place in the male ideal. Although virtually all Soviet women work, the "female" set of ideal traits contained not a single attribute that would be manifested predominantly in the sphere of work.[32] When discussing desirable female attributes, men automatically seemed to picture women as love objects, wives, or mothers, rather than as colleagues. Male-female relations were conceptualized as being mutually complementary, and apparently no one supported the idea of androgyny.

In themselves, the results of this survey were not surprising. Unless the context of work or the sociopolitical sphere is specifically emphasized, the issue of male-female traits will be viewed in the West, too, mainly in the context of care, love, sex, or the family. Yet why is it that in Russia arguments about this are so violent and explosive—on both sides? My view is that this is primarily a reaction to the breakdown in the Communist program for women's emancipation, which in practice turned out to be a nuisance for men and an extra yoke for women.

Reflection and research on gender issues, as a rule, begin—and often end—with women's problems. Yet, although it may seem paradoxical, the overall historical trend in Soviet society has been toward the demasculinization of men.[33] Despite many ethnic, religious, and historical variations, the traditional male lifestyle and archetypal male image always and everywhere emphasize such qualities as energy, initiative, independence, and self-direction. That does not mean that men in practice actually and always surpass women in these qualities—individual psychological attributes and their manifestation depend on a host of causes in addition to gender stereotypes. But these qualities are extremely important to any male self-esteem and self-image. If a man feels that his conduct and status do not correspond to sex-role expectations, his vanity receives a heavy blow that may have serious social and psychological consequences. Insofar as masculinity is closely associated with sexuality, male social helplessness is often linked also to sexual impotence and other psychosexual problems.

Could the Soviet man develop and demonstrate these traditional masculine values and virtues in his social and political life? The economic inefficiency of the Soviet system and the political despotism and bureaucratization of public affairs left little room for individual initiative and autonomy. Neither in his professional activity nor in public life could the average Soviet man shows these male traits. To be economically and socially successful, he had to be devious rather than bold, servile rather than proud, conformist rather than independent. These were the rules of the game, with rare exception; and people followed them *volens nolens*. At every moment in his life, from the cradle to the grave, the Soviet boy, adolescent, and adult man was likely to feel socially and sexually dependent and frustrated.

Who was to blame for his plight? The lack of social and economic freedom naturally did not depend on gender. But it was personified and intensified by the global feminization of all institutions and processes of socialization. This began in early childhood within the family. As a result of the high level of divorce and unplanned pregnancies, every fifth child in the USSR was brought up without a father or stepfather. In the mid-1980s some 13.5 million children were being raised in so-called single-mother families alone.[34] Yet even when the father was physically present, his influence and authority in the family and his role in bringing up the children were usually considerably less than that of the mother. A large series of sociological and educational studies in the 1970s and 1980s show that adolescents and senior high school students, irrespective of gender, were more frank with their mothers than with their fathers, and more often turned to mother for advice and reacted more sympathetically to her. As in the West, fathers had the advantage only in the informational sphere, when it came to views and advice on politics and sports.[35]

Thus, from the start, the boy is dependent on a loving but dominant mother. In the nursery and at school, most of the authority figures are women; male teachers are extremely rare. In official children's and youth organizations sponsored by adults, such as the Young Pioneers and the Komsomol, girls generally set the tone, making up, for example, three-quarters of school Komsomol secretaries. The junior and senior high school boys found kindred spirits only in informal street groups and gangs, where the power and the symbols of power were exclusively male. In Russia, as in the West, many such groups exhibit strong antifemale tendencies.[36]

When a young man marries, he is seldom the decision maker. His wife may be solicitous but is often very domineering, as his mother once was; she knows better than he how to plan the family budget and what they need for the home and family; and he ends up merely carrying out her instructions.

Finally, in public life, absolutely everything came under the control of the powerful, maternal Communist party, which knew better than anyone what was good for its members, and which stood ever-prepared to correct mistakes by force.

The Soviet style of gender socialization was utterly incompatible with either individual human dignity or with the traditional model of masculinity. How did the average male react?

The first possibility was psychological compensation and hypercompensation through idealization and imitation of the old, primitive image of a strong and aggressive male. The man who compensated in this way thus affirmed himself through drunkenness, fighting, cruelty, identification with aggressive male company, and social and sexual abuse. All these phenomena were present in the Soviet Union.

A second possibility was to combine humility and complaisance in public life with tyranny in the home and family with regard to the wife and children. That phenomenon was also fairly typical.

The third possibility was social passivity and learned helplessness, a flight from personal responsibility for oneself and one's actions into the careless, childish world of eternal boyhood. Not having learned in time to manage themselves and to overcome difficulties, many Soviet men fully renounced personal independence, compensating for it by a pervasive irresponsibility. Social responsibility was entrusted to the boss, family responsibility to the wife.

Such behavior would seem to contradict the traditional canon of strong masculinity, but in the circumstances of social and economic captivity, this strategy seemed psychologically sensible and justified. Why worry, why suffer humiliating disillusionment and frustration, if you can get someone else—women, in this instance—to do so instead?

Do women win from such deformation of the male character? Of course not. On the contrary, women lose just as much as men. Aggressive sexism as a means of compensation for enforced social futility gives rise to sexual violence. Very many Russian women patiently withstand vulgarity, drunkenness, and even bodily harm from their husbands, thinking life cannot be otherwise. Sometimes they even see in this crude behavior the manifestation of love; as was said in ancient Rus: "A man who doesn't beat his wife doesn't love her." Intelligent and educated women frequently sacrifice their own professional and public careers not only to sustain the family but also because they are afraid of outstripping and thereby offending their husbands. This is a particularly acute problem in socially and educationally unequal marriages where the wife's social status is higher than that of the husband—for example, a rural schoolmistress who marries a farm laborer. Humiliated male vanity overpowers any other feelings, so that even men who say they genuinely love their wives are sometimes cruel or abusive.

The situation is no better with husbands who calmly accept the wife's hegemony. In this case, though the wife's vanity does not suffer, she is nevertheless deprived of necessary psychological support. Her husband becomes merely a big child who has to be looked after as much as if not more so than her son (a growing son usually resists maternal guardianship).

Some women rebel against this sapping of male initiative by behaving rudely and aggressively; and, in behavior that is particularly unpleasant, may abuse their husband in the presence of the children, accusing him of being helpless, ineffectual, and the like. Later, they may try to appeal to their husband's fatherly authority, which they themselves have unwittingly undermined.

These cases of deformation of male or female character need not be fatal, of course; the outcome depends on the particular combination of qualities and sociopsychological compatibility of the couple. But gender conflict always existed in Russia—and on a mass scale.

As a result, opposition to the idea of gender equality has been mounting and widening since the 1970s. Men found it painful to lose their accustomed privileges and accept the uncertainty of their new social status. Women felt deceived because they are laboring under a double yoke, receiving support neither in the working world nor at home. As a consequence, a mighty wave of conservative backlash has arisen, with thousands dreaming of turning back the clock not only to pre-Soviet times but to pre-industrial and even pre-Petrine times—literally to those ancient days when the *Domostroi* rules for family living were introduced.[37] The ideal of the woman-mother is no longer simply being captured in appealing verse; it is aggressively counterposed to all other existing female roles.

In the early 1970s, when *Literaturnaya gazeta* began to discuss the problem of masculinity and femininity, it published an interview with Valentina Leontieva, the very popular announcer on Central Television; in the interview Leontieva had said that her work was the most important thing in her life. A furious male reader wrote in to say that although he had formerly admired Leontieva, he now realized that she was not really a woman at all and he announced that he would turn off his television whenever she came on the screen in the future. Nowadays such moods are much stronger and more openly expressed.

The ideas of American feminists, which are frequently portrayed in a distorted and caricatured form, are generally most unpopular in Russia, and not only among conservative men. The well-known and quite modern Russian writer Tatyana Tolstaya said to the American journalist Francine Du Plessix Gray, "But how can we understand your American feminists? The few I've talked to tell me they are fighting for the right to work in coal mines. My dear, Russian women are fighting *not* to work in coal mines."[38]

Feminism is often identified with aggressive lesbianism. The liberal and by no means ignorant St. Petersburg writer Daniil Granin asked Du Plessix Gray, "Isn't a feminist by very definition a woman who absolutely hates all men?"[39]

Here is how Efraim Sevela, formerly a Soviet writer and film producer, presently a prosperous citizen of the United States, describes American women in the mass-circulation newspaper *SPID-info*:

> America has experienced a women's liberation revolution. Feminists have managed to liberate themselves from men and, as a consequence, some of them have ended up on the street, and some have ended up with a vibrator in bed. They have now reached a crisis point: America is a land of female psychopaths. Women get into bed with men almost on the point of tears, scared of not achieving orgasm (nor will they after that 220 volt vibrator). So American women have become appendages of the machine in the literal sense. And American men abduct émigré women [Sevela's wife divorced him]. . . .
>
> . . . And American women are very practical: 72% of the country's wealth is in their hands. . . .
>
> . . . For an American woman the sex act is no problem. All she has to decide is whether she is curious enough to want to get into bed. This American expression "to make love" is exhaustive. A woman who is in a bad mood when she gets into bed with a man might well tell him it is his duty to "service" her. Further, American women always answer "fine" to the question "How are you?" saying they find it "impossible to cry on anyone's shoulder.[40]

Surely these reactionary views are not the whole story. Russian women are increasingly active in social and political matters. These activities are quite different. The Women of Russia political faction, whose leaders are mainly former Communist Party and Komsomol officials, emphasize family values, the importance of education for children, and so on—basic issues that are, incidentally, very important in the present desperate economic situation, and that male politicians often overlook or use only for political purposes. Yet new women role models are also emerging. There are popular independent businesswomen, such as Irina Khakamada, the Duma deputy—a woman who combines economic success with political activity, humor, and personal charm (which is very important for television). And the genuine feminist scholarship is emerging.

A promising Center for Gender Studies, under the direction of Anastasiya Posadskaya, has opened in the Russian Academy of Sciences. Another group of feminist scholars, among them Olga Voronina and Nina Yulina, is affiliated with the Institute of Philosophy.

At the Institute of Ethnology and Anthropology, a small group for ethnogender studies was formed to study, among other things, gender socialization processes and family and school violence. And it was only a few years ago that an excellent monograph by Natalya Pushkareva *Zhen-shchiny Drevney Rusi (Women of Ancient Rus)* (1989) provoked irritation among some members—all of them women—of the Slavic Department of the same institute; they didn't see then—nor do they see now—anything serious in the idea of women's studies, even in the area of history.

In St. Petersburg, a Center for Gender Problems was organized under Olga Lipovskaya in 1992. The center publishes a biannual bulletin *Vse lyudi—syostry (All People Are Sisters)*, which contains important information on women's issues, history, and the present state of the feminist movement, lesbian issues, and so on. The center also organizes and promotes regular lectures, seminars, and panel discussions. It has good contacts with the local Family Planning Association, the Juventa gynecological services, and other such organizations.

As Olga Lipovskaya has put it:

> For me, feminism is a way of life and a way of thought. Feminism holds an image of a world where neither myself, nor my daughters, nor my sisters or friends would be afraid to walk outside after dark lest they be raped. It is about equal rights in family duties and the equal responsibility of a father and mother for the education of children. It is freedom of choice for women and men: to create, to make money, to stay at home with the children or travel on business. . . .
>
> Feminism permits me to decide for myself—not the State, my husband, or the Church to decide for me—when I want to become a mother and when I don't, and whether I want to do so . . . at all. Feminism allows me to choose for myself how to look and what to wear. I want women to feel comfortable in their own bodies and in their dress. . . . In other words, feminism is a component of the general concept of democracy. It is a pity that few people in my country now understand this.[41]

Liposvskaya's ideas are really marginal, and at least as far as motherhood is concerned, unpopular and even defiant in today's Russia. But they are not rootless.

Of course, a return to the *Domostroi* rules is nothing more than another conservative utopia.[42] Family values are very important to the Russian people. But as in other countries, they are considered more important by women than men, and they are strongly correlated with educational background. In a hypothetical situation offering a choice between family and extrafamily activities and values, women with a university education are six times less likely to prefer family activities than women with only a secondary education.[43] And when the demographer V. A. Sysenko asked Moscow women in the late 1970s whether they would be willing to leave their job if their husband's salary was increased so that he alone would bring in what they now earned together, only 22% answered in the affirmative.[44] There is no way back in that direction.

The Soviet experiment is very educational on this issue, however. "Sexless sexism" is not a paradoxical metaphor but an exact description of a unique sociocultural stereotype. At one blow, the Soviet authorities tried to smash and transform the entire traditional system of gender stratification, to destroy all social and psychological correlates and consequences of sex difference and gender inequality. That attempt was utopian and unrealizable. The downfall of the revolutionary utopia, which had rejected everything old, produced the natural reaction—a longing for a conservative utopia, which in turn rejects all that is new. A culture of sexlessness has turned into one of rampant sexism.

It is also reflected in everyday life. According to one international comparative research project on gender relationships in West and East Germany, Poland, Russia, Hungary, and Sweden (a representative survey made from 1991 up to the end of 1992, asking more than 6,000 respondents), "life in Russia seems to be generally more gender-differentiated than in other countries." Russian men and women are more strongly oriented toward representatives of their own rather than the opposite gender. In answer to the question "What kind of life experiences have you had with men and women?" 77% of Russian men mentioned members of their own gender as their primary source of understanding, 74% as the primary source of practical support, and 57% as the primary source of psychological proximity. Among women, same-gender relationships were mentioned in these instances by 73%, 52%, and 62%, respectively. These data should not be interpreted in a "sexual" way, but rather as an indication that the social- psychological distance between Russian men and women is larger than in other countries.[45]

Yet it would be a grave mistake to regard the demise of the Soviet experiment only in ideological terms, to blame the Bolsheviks for everything, as is now being done in Russia. Sexism and gender inequality are global issues; they cannot be "solved" once and for all time. Simplistic, utopian ideas about gender are just as widespread among Western, especially American, left-wingers and feminists as is traditionalism among right-wingers. The failure of the Soviet experiment may be explained differently: by the country's technical backwardness; by the political features of a totalitarian state; by the national cultural legacy (for example, the hypothetical femininity of the Russian national character and culture). Before a final judgment is made, philosophers and scholars will have to give all this much more serious thought.

## Chapter Nine

# SEX, LOVE, AND MARRIAGE

*Love is an uncharted land to which we are all sailing,
each on his own ship, and each of us as captain, steering
the ship in his own way.*

Mikhail Prishvin

Judging by the literature, Russia is a very strange, even an exotic country. Some of its natives, having been educated under the Communist propagandists, claim that there is no sex. And according to some Western observers, neither do most Russians have any idea of romantic love.

In her book *Soviet Women* (1989), the American journalist Francine du Plessix Gray writes that she hardly heard of romantic love in all the time she was in the Soviet Union. Exhausted by the hard toil that was their lot in everyday life, women were not up to it. "I'm too tired to love!" one woman told her. Says Gray, "It confirmed my suspicion that love in the Soviet Union is a luxury, an accessory, but hardly a prerequisite for marriage or happiness as it is in Western Europe or the United States."[1]

To a Russian, Gray's statement sounds strange. Many years ago, when I first came across the American sociology of marriage and the family, I was much amused by the widespread view that romantic love was an exclusive achievement or invention of the people in the United States, or at least, in the West. Soviet literature of the time maintained that love did not exist in the United States, where people were always rushing about, thinking only of their work and their monetary ambitions; in any case, how could romantic love survive in the world of pecuniary calculation and the universal alienation it caused? The Soviet stereotype sounded just as convincing as the American—and was just as untrue.

"Love" and "friendship" have always been considered as important basic values and were considered the preconditions of a happy life in Soviet society.[2] However, for a more detailed and serious discussion of the subject, we must ask more precise questions:

- Is there a specifically Russian, as opposed to Western, idea of love?
- What is the place of love in the hierarchy of Russian family values?
- How is love related to sex and marriage, as far as attitudes and behavior go?

These are difficult questions.

Feelings of love exist fairly independently of social systems and material conditions of life. Recently the American anthropologists William R. Jankowiak and Edward F. Fisher, using a standard cross-cultural sample, were able to document the occurrence of romantic love in 88.5% of the cultures sampled, directly contradicting the popular idea that romantic love is essentially limited to or is the product of Western culture.[3] Their findings suggest that passionate romantic love constitutes a human universal, or at least a near universal.

Any definition of "Russian," "American," or " Japanese" sex, let alone love, presupposes some comparison, not always fully realized, and behind every generalization lies a host of age, gender, cultural, social, and—perhaps most important—individual differences and variations that no scientific experiment can reproduce. True, a given society or culture can admire or scorn a tender Werther or an artful Don Juan or a trophy-collecting Casanova, but they seem to be incapable of changing these very human types, which always and everywhere behave characteristically. At the same time, there is nothing more deceptive than "average" figures and statistically accurate "types."

The notion of romantic love was perfectly well known as early as the medieval era in Rus. The Novgorod birch bark letter of the late fourteenth century speaks movingly of passionate love—"What fire in my heart, and my body and my soul for you and your body and your person, let it set fire to your heart and your body and your soul for me, and for my body, and for my person."[4] In spite of the famous words of the nurse from Pushkin's *Eugene Onegin*, that "in our days we never heard about love," and the fact that romantic love between man and wife was neither an essential nor even a usual condition of marriage, love has always existed in Russia.[5] The very passion with which many Russian philosophers and writers, such as Nikolai Berdyaev, denied the existence of romantic love in Russia proves not so much its actual absence as the crying need for it. And all higher human needs are by definition insatiable.

The main character in Anton Chekhov's short story "Ariadna" (1895) says:

> We are not satisfied because we are idealists. We want the beings who give us birth and produce our children to be higher than us, higher than any-thing on earth. When we are young we romanticize and idolize those we fall in love with; love and happiness are synonyms. For us in Russia, love-less marriage is scorned, sensuality is mocked and induces revulsion, and those novels and stories where women are beautiful, poetic and elevated enjoy the most success. . . . But the trouble is that hardly do we marry or hit it off with a woman than, give or take a couple of years, we feel we've been disappointed, let down; we try with other women and again we find disillusion, again horror, and ultimately we convince ourselves that women are liars, petty, vain, unjust, uneducated, cruel—in a word, even immea-surably lower, not simply not higher, than us men.[6]

Under the influence of unsuccessful or simply mundane sexual experi-ence, the triumphant idealization of woman gives way to her aggressive abasement and vulgarization, but in both cases the individual is forfeited, distilled into the general stereotype of "woman the angel" or "woman the whore."

In the nineteenth century, this style of behavior was imposed on women, too. Irrespective of her own individual temperament, "a decent woman" could not display sensuality, but had to be embarrassed by it, even after marriage.

The arguments about hierarchy and ideal relationships among family values, individual love, and sensuality have never been an exclusively Russian phenomenon. What is interesting, however, is that these old dis-putes have been revitalized now, and that strong, all-consuming passionate love as well as irresponsible "sexual pleasure" are both under fire from con-servatives—all in the name of "family values."

The main character in The Gloomy Detective, a novel by the famous con-temporary Russian writer Viktor Astafiev, says the following:

> It is not the male and female of the species that copulate by nature's willing order to propagate the species, but human beings with human beings, united to help each other and the society in which they live and improve themselves, transfusing their blood from one heart to the other, and, together with their blood, all that is good in them. . . . Dynasties, societies,

empires would crumble to dust if the family began to disintegrate, if he and she lost their way and could not find one another . . . With the downfall of the family, harmony would cease, evil would begin to overcome good, the earth would open up beneath our feet in order to swallow up the rabble who call themselves people without any grounds for doing so.[7]

The Moscow philosopher Vyacheslav Shcherdakov continued Astafiev's argument:

Often people try to explain many disasters in love and the family by pointing out that we talk of the sexual aspect of life too little and too timidly. We hear calls to cast off all taboos and bans from these subjects. Those who advocate this forget that taboos and timidity conceal not ignorance and darkness, but profound moral feelings in danger of being trampled upon by invasions of educated cynicism. What is hidden from prying eyes are one's innermost thoughts, which are and must remain a secret. The family is founded on more than merely rational principles and sexual attraction.[8]

The eminent sociologist Yuri Davydov is even more severe:

Is it freedom from hypocrisy that hides behind the romantic cult of "passion"? No, it is not! We ought to be talking about lack of moral willpower. In life and literature nowadays, passion is often termed "sex" and loved ones "partners." The non-binding nature of relations between men and women has become so common you even find it among your literary advocates. Is this not testimony to the spiritual degradation of the individual? Of course it is! Morality cannot be a matter of fashion, and family values cannot be an object of commerce, of payment for pleasure![9]

Thus, from denunciation of the unbridled nature of sexual passion, Davydov moves on to debunking passionate love itself—in the name of the family—seeing in it, according to the etymology of the word "passion," primarily "suffering of the soul," "*the painful state of the spirit* related to *violation of any measure it might possess.*"[10] Conjugal love, by contrast, is based on a sense of duty, not passion. And for marital happiness we "need *genuine,* not feminized" men. Moreover, these men should possess both a male character and a male cast of mind "that does not shrink from responsibility for the consequences of decisions once made."[11]

This is a very telling statement. Everybody would agree that "love" and "sex" are not synonyms. But there are different types, or "colors," of love. And is social freedom always the equivalent of moral laxity? Are only men capable of responsibility, or are women capable of that too? And does this philosophy mean in practice that if you make a mistake and end up in an unhappy marriage, you should not ask for a divorce, even if you are desperately unhappy, that you must spread the contagion to those around you, especially your own children?

Clearly, we have squared the circle. In philosophy, as in politics, we stand once again before two alternative, incompatible ideologies, where compromise is necessary.

People on the street are more pragmatic and realistic about these matters than philosophers. Like people in other countries, Russians do believe that love, sex, and marriage are interrelated—but not identical. Public opinion polls paint a contradictory picture of the hierarchy of values.

Russians have always been and still are strongly promarriage and profamily. In 1979, the year of the last Soviet census, only 1.9% of men and 4% of women aged 45–49 had never been married.[12] In April 1992, a large-scale survey on the general subject of "culture" was conducted by the Russian Public Opinion Study Center (VCIOM). Some 3,500 people were interviewed in three large geographic areas: the Slav (comprising Russia and the Ukraine), the Baltic (drawing on subjects in Estonia and Lithuania), and Central Asia (drawing subjects from Uzbekistan and Tadzhikistan). The Slav area was surveyed without differentiating between national/ethnic affiliation, while in the other two areas, only members of indigenous nationalities were surveyed. The questionnaire included some questions relating directly to our subject: Are people happy in love and family life? What do they think of premarital and extramarital sex? How do they view eroticism and sex education?

The overwhelming majority of the sample agreed that stable marital and family relations are most essential for overall happiness. The respondents were presented with a wide choice of value judgments on what they considered the most important matters in life. As many as 58% of Russians agreed that "There is nothing more important to me than my family" (a sentiment second only to "The most important thing is to be an independent person," which was selected by 64%).

In response to the question "In which of the following situations do you feel yourself most free?" first place by far went to the response "At home with my family," which was chosen by 64% of the Russian respondents and even more in the Ukraine, Estonia, and Central Asia.

Most respondents (57% in Russia, 65% in the Ukraine, 48% of Estonians, 44% of Lithuanians, 49% of Uzbeks, and 62% of Tadzhiks) thought that the previous five years had brought a deterioration in family relations in most families; only 6% of Slavs surveyed felt they had improved.

This negative opinion is absolutely correct.

According to official statistics, in 1993, the birthrate in Russia had dropped 12% from 1991. More people now die than are born each year (*Izvestiya*, September 10, 1993). According to a recent statistical forecast, the population of Russia in the next ten years will be diminished by 11.2%, with the average life expectancy about 59.3 years (*Izvestiya*, December 22, 1994). In 1992, the number of new marriages had dropped from 1990 levels by 20.3% and the number of divorces had increased by 15%. According to recent research, in 1993 Russia had 49 divorces for every 100 marriages (*Izvestiya*, December 23, 1994). The proportion of single-parent families increased from 10% in 1989 to 17% in 1993. In 1991, 16% of children were born out of wedlock, and in 1992, more than 17% (*Sevodnya*, December 14, 1993).

All the same, satisfaction with one's own family life remains fairly high. As many as 56% of men and 42% of women in 1992 in Russia were more or less "satisfied with family life"; 14% and 24%, respectively, expressed their discontent, and 29% and 33%, respectively, found the questions difficult to answer.

Satisfaction with family life was closely correlated to responses to the question "Have you ever experienced real love in your life?" In the Slav area, 53% of men and 49% of women replied positively, while 26% and 18%, respectively, gave a negative answer, and 31% and 33%, respectively, found it hard to say. The proportion of positive responses was higher among the 24- to 54-year-olds, married persons, and those with a high level of education. Gender differences were more marked in the Central Asia area: 68% of men and 59% of women were satisfied with family life, while 57% of men and only 38% of women had experienced "real love."

A "happy marriage" and "happiness in love" by no means always coincided. Some 11% fewer men and 7% fewer women in Russia said they were "happy in love" than answered yes to the question "Are you happy in your family life?" Spouses often have a greater need for happiness in love than is normally to be expected in everyday family life.[13]

Most respondents answered the question "Is sex without love permissible?" in the negative. In the Russian Federation, only 15% approved of loveless sex, with 57% against. The most tolerant of the idea were Uzbeks (35%) and Estonians (25%); the least tolerant (9%) were Lithuanians and Tadzhiks. The proportion of positive responses from men in the Slav and

Baltic areas was three times higher than that from women there. The situation was reversed in Central Asia, where women approved of sex without love more frequently than did men (26% as against 18%).

Ideologically, romantic love is generally seen as a moral and emotional precondition both for marriage and for sexual intimacy.

In the public opinion polls, older respondents often put family duties above individual love when asked what should be done when they come into conflict. In surveys done in the 1970s and early 1980s, respondents were asked what a married man with children should do in the event of falling in love with another woman. Three possible answers were given: 1. He should stay with his family and children; 2. He should leave the family; and 3. He must make his own decision. Generally, the answers were rather traditional, putting family and children before and above the new love. But the answers strongly depended on gender (women being more profamily than men), marital status (married individuals differed from the unmarried and divorced), and social milieu (urbanites were more liberal than the rural population). The proportion of traditionalist profamily choices dropped from about two-thirds in rural Russia to 54–56% in cities such as Saratov, and only one-third in Leningrad.[14]

Younger people are quite ready to accept both sex and marriage without love. Young Russians seem to be less demanding and less selective in this than their American, Western European, and Japanese counterparts. In a comparative study of German and Russian college students conducted in 1990, Soviet students appeared less sure than young Germans about "the existence of the so-called great love." Positive answers to this question were given by 84% of Soviet students as opposed to 92% of East German and 86% of West German students. Only 33% of Russian students (53% of East German and 49% of West German students) said they themselves had already experienced "great love." And the Russian students have the highest numbers of sexual partners (4.3 on average). Whatever the official ideology, sex without love is widespread and considered morally acceptable.[15]

In a study conducted in 1992, a group of researchers headed by Susan Sprecher, using comparable samples of college students from the United States, Russia, and Japan, tried to assess their national "styles of love."[16] When they attempted to summarize the results, the researchers were struck by a singular observation: culture seems to have a less important, and less predictable, impact on young men's and women's attitudes and experiences in love than might have been anticipated.

The researchers asked the students, "Would you marry someone if he or she had all the other qualities you desired, but you were not in love?"

The only possible answers were yes or no. The authors had expected that only individualistic Americans would demand love as a prerequisite for marriage, and that both the Russians and the Japanese would be more practical in this regard. Yet both Americans and Japanese were romantic, and few of either group would consider marrying someone they did not love. Russian men were only slightly more "practical" than their counterparts in other countries: 30% of them were willing to marry such a partner. It was the Russian women who were most ready to "settle"; over 40% of them were willing to marry someone without love!

Why was this the case? Sprecher and her colleagues don't believe that the Russian women were considering social standing or wealth as they responded to this question, nor did they score higher than Russian men on the pragmatism scale; previous research had found women more attracted to the romantic love ideal than men. The women surveyed may have believed that as long as they were acquainted with the man, he had a good personality, was affectionate, and so on, they would come to love him in time even if they did not initially. And this, we have seen, is the traditional peasant attitude, which was expressed in the Russian proverb "*Sterpitsya— slyubitsya*," which means roughly, "Once you get accustomed, you will love each other."

In fact, motives for marrying were always multifarious; besides love, even supposing that everyone were to agree on a definition of the word, many other social and economic factors have to be taken into consideration. And this is true not only about marriage but also about first sexual contacts.

During the 1978–79 academic year, Sergei Golod asked students from 18 colleges and universities (a total of 3,721 people) why they thought contemporary young men and women had intimate relations.[17] The responses are reported in Table 9.1.

**Table 9.1**

|  | Men (%) (1829 surveyed) | Women (%) (1892 surveyed) |
|---|---|---|
| Mutual love | 28.8 | 46.1 |
| Intended marriage | 6.6 | 9.4 |
| Self-affirmation | 5.5 | 3.6 |
| Enjoyable pursuit | 20.2 | 11.4 |
| Desire for emotional contact | 10.6 | 7.7 |
| Desire to obtain pleasure | 18.1 | 9.2 |
| Extending sense of freedom or independence | 1.8 | 2.2 |
| Prestige, fashion | 4.1 | 4.8 |
| Curiosity | 4.9 | 5.6 |

It is patently obvious that in the minds of students, love and sexuality are sharply delineated from, rather than synonymous with, matrimonial intentions. Both love and sexuality are primarily associated with either emotional-communicational issues or with hedonistic-recreational ones. And there are important gender differences. Women feel that sexual intimacy should be primarily motivated by love. The males, on the other hand, express their preference for "pleasure" and "enjoyable pursuit." This value orientation was present as early as the 1970s, in spite of the official Communist ideological moralizing and hypocrisy. It was no surprise that in 1984, Soviet editors of Golod's book falsified the title of this table: instead of "Motives for entering intimate relationships," it was entitled "Motives for courtship."

Have these attitudes changed in recent years?

According to the VCIOM 1992 survey, the overall attitude toward premarital sex is generally tolerant, although it does vary from region to region. While 67% of Estonians believe it is all right to have sex before marriage, only 10% of Tadzhiks do (yet the corresponding figure for Uzbek fellow Muslims is 46%). Russians fall somewhere between the extremes on this issue: 37% think premarital sex is permissible and all right, whereas 41% do not. (In an analogous U.S. survey in 1989, 27% felt premarital sex was always wrong and 39% thought it was not wrong at all.[18])

Answers varied tremendously with gender and age. Half the men and only 28% of the women in the Slav area thought premarital sex was all right and permissible. (In the Baltic area, 61% of men and 46% of women felt it was acceptable. The picture is quite different in Central Asia: 32% of women and only 26% of men approved of premarital sex.)

In terms of age, the most tolerant on this issue were young Slavs and Balts—in the age group between 20 and 24, 61% and 91% of the men, respectively, approved of premarital sex. Older people took a diametrically opposed position on the issue.

In the Slav region, the people with the most liberal views on premarital sex were those with university education, those who had never been married, who lived in Moscow or St. Petersburg, or who were born in a big city. The link between urbanization and sexual permissiveness is less marked in the Baltic and Asiatic regions.

In the VCIOM 1993 survey, attitudes toward premarital sex became even more tolerant. Some 19% of men and 33% of women in Russia said that premarital sex is wrong, but 43% of men and 33% of women disagreed. Among the youngest respondents, only 15% believes premarital sex was wrong, while 56% disagreed, the numbers being 15% and 44%, respectively, for the college-educated.

But there is still a clear double standard in the answers: males are more permissive than females, and both sexes are more permissive toward males. In answering the question "What do you think about premarital sexual relations for young men?" 12% of men and 22% of women said it was wrong, but 25% and 13%, respectively, said premarital sex for young men was "not only permissible but useful, necessary"; in the youngest group, this stance was taken by more than 30% of respondents. Yet the same question asked about "young women" was answered differently: 19% of men and 30% of women were against premarital sex for young women, with only 11% and 6%, respectively, finding it permissible. Even younger and better- educated people, who were generally more liberal on sexual issues, were less tolerant of premarital sex for females than for males.

The attitudes toward premarital sex strongly depend on the respondents' background. In Golod's student survey (1978–79), premarital sex was approved by 58% of Leningraders, 50% of the regional centers' residents, 47% of the residents of other towns, 41% of the residents of urban-type settlements, and by only 35% of the rural population.

Marital fidelity is generally highly valued. In the VCIOM 1992 survey only 23% of Russians agreed that "It is permissible to have a lover as well as a husband/wife," while 50% were opposed. In other erstwhile Soviet republics, the proportion of positive responses to this question varies from 45% among Uzbeks to 14% among Tadzhiks. These two neighboring Muslim nations differ markedly from each other in almost everything.

Gender differences once again stand out. In the Slav area, 32% of men and only 18% of women approve of extramarital sex (the figures are 28% and 19%, respectively, in the Baltic area, while in Central Asia women were slightly more tolerant than men). Those most tolerant of extramarital sex in the Slav region were aged 24 to 40; in the Baltic they were younger—20–24—and in Central Asia, they were older—40- to 54-year-olds.

In the VCIOM 1993 survey, "People who often change sex partners" are censured by 42% of men and 57% of women; only 15% and 9%, respectively, were neutral on this question. Here too the double standard was present. Infidelity by a husband was condemned by 43% of men and 59% of women, and was accepted by 15% of men and 7% of women. A wife's infidelity, on the other hand, was condemned by 62% of men and 60% of women, and was morally acceptable to only 8% of men and women.

It is evident that sexual values and attitudes of contemporary Russians, like people elsewhere, are pluralistic and contradictory. The general trend is in the direction of liberalization, individualization, and autonomy with regard to sexuality, but there are important age, gender, educational, and regional, especially urban-rural, differences. The sexual double standard is still strong and pervasive in public consciousness.

And what about real sexual behavior? The direction of the shift is the same, but empirical data are scarce and much less reliable. Only a few researchers dare to ask questions about truly intimate personal behavior, and respondents are often unwilling to answer such questions, even anonymously. In the VCIOM 1993 survey, respondents were ready to discuss all sorts of moral issues, yet about 40% of the sample did not answer even the most general questions about their own sexual behavior. Respondents to a telephone survey conducted by D. D. Isayev in 1993 were more open: only 14% of men and 19% of women refused to answer personal questions. But because of methodological shortcomings, the results of different surveys are often unreliable and contradictory. So it is risky to make broad generalizations.[19]

Nevertheless, several general trends can be identified.

First, as we have seen, sexual initiation comes earlier than in previous generations. In the VCIOM 1993 survey, the average age for starting sex ("At what age did you first have sex?") was 19.5. However, when asked, "At what age do you think people should first have sex?" the respondents (among whom were far more elderly people than young), said 17.9 on average.

The average age for first sexual experience of 1,509 university students in Moscow, Leningrad, Gorky, and Riga (Latvia) in the spring of 1990 was 18.4 for men and 19.0 for women. Eighty percent of the sample and 95% of sexually experienced students had already had "petting" experience, with the age of initiation being 17.8 for men and 18.0 for women.[20] These figures are similar to those compiled by the Moscow epidemiologist Olga Loseva.[21] The men she interviewed in 1975–76 had begun their sex lives at age 19.2 and the women at 21.8; by 1983–84, the respective ages had dropped to 18.1 and 20.6. According to Isayev's telephone survey in 1993, the average age for first sexual intercourse was 18.4 (plus or minus 3.3 years) for men (42.1% did it before age 18 and 72.3% before age 20) and 20.1 years (plus or minus 3.5 years) for women (15.4% had their first intercourse before 18 and 43.4% before 20).

There is nothing sensational in this trend. In France, the average age of first sexual experience of men between 55 and 69 years old was 18.4 years and for young men between 18 and 24 years old, it was 17.1. For women, the respective figures are 21.3 and 17.9.[22] This shift seems to be international.

The first sexual experience is usually premarital. A marital union is no longer a precursor to sexual union but its continuation. When guests at a Russian wedding shout *gorko* (bitter), calling on the young couple to kiss and thereby make the vodka "sweet," no one expects any embarrassment from them or that something new and intimate is about to take place.

More and more frequently, not only sexual intimacy but also pregnancy precedes marriage—and sometimes pregnancy hastens marriage. In his analysis of the archives of the Leningrad Malyutka [Baby] Registry Office, Golod convincingly demonstrated a fairly stable growth in the number of premarital pregnancies: of the 239 young married couples who had registered the birth of their first-born child in December 1963, 69 (24%) had conceived the child three months before the marital union had been legally registered; in December 1968, there were 196 (23%) out of 852 couples in this situation; in December 1973, there were 240 (28%) out of 851 couples; in December 1978, there were 243 (38%) out of 643 couples; and in December 1984, there were 223 (49%) out of 448 couples. Similar results came from a study of registered births and marriages in another district of Leningrad.[23]

Premarital sex still has different meanings for men and women. According to Olga Loseva's data in the 1980s, every second woman, but only every sixth man, married the first sexual partner. As might be expected, men were generally more promiscuous and more sexually active than women. The number of sexual partners for men and women differed markedly: the average man had between 12 and 13 sexual partners, while the average woman had just over 4. For about one-third of men, their first sexual contact was short-lived, a few days at most; among women, that pattern was rare (only 4%), with three-quarters of them beginning their sexual life in a reasonably long-term relationship.

According to the VCIOM 1993 survey—more than 40% of respondents didn't answer the question, so the data are not statistically valid—3% of men and 4% of women never had had a sexual partner; 14% of men and 30% of women had had only one partner; 36% of men and 18% of women had had between two and five partners; 7% of men and 1% of women had had between six and ten partners; and 12% of men versus 2% of women had had more than ten partners over the course of a lifetime. At the time of the survey, 9% of men and 18% of women had had no sexual contacts; 5% of men and 2% of women had sex once a day; 21% of men and 17% of women had sex several times per week; 19% of men and 14% of women had sex several times per month; and 6% of men and 3% of women had sex once a month or less. The most sexually active group were those between the ages of 25 and 40.

Younger and more outspoken individuals admitted to having many more sexual partners but their sexual activities are polarized according to gender. Some 62.4% of St. Petersburg men (average age 35.4 years) and 84.6% of women (average age 37.3 years) questioned in 1993 by Isayev admitted fewer than 10 sexual partners during their lifetimes. Yet 11.1% of men and 3.7% of women have had more than 50 partners. In the year prior to the survey, 9.4% of men had had no sexual partners, 74.4% had had 1–2 partners, 7.7% had had 3–5 partners, and 8.6% had had more than 5 partners (3.5% among them had had more than 50 partners). For women, the respective figures were 9.1%, 79.4%, 8.2%, and 3.5%. As had been supposed, earlier sexual initiation is correlated, at least among men, with more extensive sexual life, greater number of partners, and riskier sexual behavior.

The level of sexual activity, mutual compatibility, and sexual satisfaction is an increasingly important aspect of marriage and family life. According to Golod's surveys in 1978 and 1981 (he investigated up to 250 married couples each time), sexual harmony invariably ranks third after spiritual and psychological compatibility among factors contributing to marital adaptation in spouses who have been married for up to 10 years, and after spiritual and domestic compatibility for those who have been together for between 10 and 15 years.[24]

Sexual pleasure and general satisfaction with the marriage are closely interrelated. Practically all couples expressing maximum satisfaction with the marriage said they were sexually compatible, while only 63% were sexually compatible among the dissatisfied. Golod's surveys in 1988 and 1989 confirmed this trend.

The propensity for and the number of extramarital liaisons also vary with levels of overall sexual satisfaction with marriage: 25% of wives professing "maximal satisfaction" had had extramarital liaisons, compared with 44% of wives with "satisfactory" marriages and 65% of wives with "unsatisfactory" marriages. At the same time, sexuality seems to be a relatively independent variable: one in ten wives is sexually dissatisfied even in a "maximally happy" marriage, while 30% of wives who are dissatisfied in their marriage are unhappy sexually as well.[25]

Not surprisingly, sexism and gender inequality manifest themselves in the marriage bed. The widespread disharmony of sexual-erotic needs and

desires between wives and husbands, which should be the subject of sexological study and open discussion, is often seen in Russia by the spouses
and those about them (social psychologists are the exception) as a manifestation of ineradicable sexual incompatibility, the only solution to which is
divorce. Even in the professional literature this problem is often discussed
not in terms of "process"—i.e., how the spouses adapt and grow accustomed to each other—but in "essential" terms—i.e. whether the spouses
and their individual traits are "compatible." These traits are too often considered inborn and unchangeable over time. Yet a married couple does not
simply consist of two different individuals sharing a bed, but instead constitutes a new entity.

The woman is almost always the one to suffer from poor sexual adaptation. In the survey of 600 healthy women carried out in the 1970s by
Zinaida Rozhanovskaya, 24.4% of the respondents reported that they
always experienced orgasm during sex, 33.2% often, 19% sometimes, 7%
extremely rarely, and 16.4% never. Failure to reach orgasm was surely due
at least partly to the women's own sexual inhibitions and ignorance. As
many as 35.5% of women who had some sexual education before losing
their virginity usually had orgasms, whereas only 23.8% of those who had
no foreknowledge did so; the rest began to experience orgasm only after
having given birth, sometimes a few years later, or only with another partner (the share of women who never experienced orgasm was the same in
both groups—a finding that Russian sexopathologists are inclined to
attribute to physiological reasons.)[26]

Sexological ignorance and the lack of a common language engender
many communication difficulties between spouses. Instead of discussing
their problems together or seeking professional help, each spouse runs off
to same-sex friends for advice or consolation.[27]

Professor Svyadoshch told me about a case in which a young woman
complained of lack of orgasm during intercourse with her husband. While
conducting a gynecological examination of the woman, Svyadoshch easily
found a sensitive, albeit somewhat uncommonly located, erogenous zone.
"All's fine," he said. "You have an excellent sexual response. Just come back
with your husband and I'll show him what to do." "Alas," said the woman,
"I can't do that. My husband thinks he knows everything. He tells me he
had no trouble with other women, so it must be me who's abnormal. I love
him, but I'm afraid we're heading for a divorce."

From her husband's standpoint, "all women have the same face"
(although we are discussing a very different part of the body here), and he
finds it impossible to accept her individuality. Quite a lot of husbands are

like that. Svyadoshch's files contain over a thousand clinical histories of virgin wives whose husbands have been unable to consummate the marriage.

Before the emergence of sexopathology in the Soviet Union, most women silently accepted their fate; many were not even aware they were being cheated. Gynecologists also were not concerned with pleasure. If a woman complained to her doctor of lack of sexual pleasure, the doctor would either not have understood her or would have given her a moral lecture on the subject of the serious business of marriage, on the need to be unselfish, on duty being more important than pleasure—or both. If the gynecologist were female, she might well have added something from her own woeful experience, concluding, "Never mind, my dear; we manage to get by somehow and raise lovely children!"

Now the situation is changing rapidly. Young women have come to learn that they "have the right to orgasm." But there is no point in shouting about "rights" or expecting someone to hand out the entitlement in question without making an effort at mutual understanding. To date, both sides are often obliged to make believe.

Sergei Libikh, chairman of the sexology department of the St. Petersburg Institute for Continuing Medical Studies, recounted an interesting case on this score: Within the framework of marriage counseling, sexopathologists asked a group of husbands about their intimate life—whether they practiced erotic caressing and what their wives enjoyed the most. When they put the same questions to the wives, the mismatch in the answers was sometimes quite striking. "Yes," said one woman, "my husband does such and such." "And how do you react to it?" "I don't." "And how would you like to be caressed?" Some women said they did not know. Others described very explicit actions. "So why don't you tell your husband?" they were asked. But how could the wife tell? The husband would demand to know where she had gotten the idea for the action, and it would come out that the woman had either experienced it with a more imaginative man or that she had discovered it for herself, through masturbation. Husbands detest both.

Disproportion also exists in the development of Russian sexopathology itself, and male sexuality receives the lion's share of attention.[28] At the first Soviet conference on sexopathology in Gorky in 1968, as many as 50 reports were devoted to male sexuality, a mere 10 to women's; at the Tambov conference in 1974, the ratio was 25 to 5; and at the 1981, 1984, and 1985 conferences, women were deemed worthy of only one paper. The proportion of women among the patients of sexopathologists ranges from 1 to 10% of the total, with three-quarters of them complaining of lack of sexual satisfaction. But although men are much more worried about sexuality than women, and therefore outnumber women patients drastically, husbands typically seek help only when their wives insist, rather than of their own volition. Herein also lies a source of quarrels and mutual recrimination.

Much of the new Russian erotic literature—domestic, translated, and émigré Russian—is aggressively sexist. The work of Mikhail Armalinsky, formerly of Leningrad and now residing in the United States, is particularly notorious in this respect. Women as individuals and even as bodies simply do not exist in his mind; the female body interests him only for its sexual orifice, which he depicts in his verses and prose; there can be no talk of a loving relationship with partners here:

> It goes without saying that fucking is masturbation for the male, but enriched by contact with a living opening, with sight and smell, with the fantasies of spiritual experience. Yes, dear feminists, the woman is indeed a wonderful apparatus for masturbation, a living pancake batter, but not man-made, like your vibrator; she is "God-made." Who is more human: the man who needs a woman for maximum satisfaction, or the woman who needs a vibrator for maximum satisfaction?[29]

This attitude is far from that expressed in Russian classical literature, but it bears a close relationship to daily quarrels about who should earn money, clean the apartment, or be a nursemaid to the children.

According to Olga Loseva, both husbands and wives are often uninformed about their partner's real sexual response and level of satisfaction. One-third of all couples questioned by Loseva in the 1980s referred to the monotony and uniformity of the sexual positions. Fifty-four percent of married couples used only two or three positions; only 16% had a more extended sexual repertoire. Seven percent of all wives reported never reaching orgasm, and 18% did so only "rarely."

Men are often emotionally insensitive to women when it comes to sex. Following are a few male voices from Gaiges and Suvorova's journalistic report of 1990:

Technician, age 21: "I'm interested only in my own satisfaction."
Doorman, age 22: "A woman must be beautiful and have a good figure—that's all that's necessary."
Industrial fitter, age 24: "Sex for me is purely animal."
Technician, age 21: "My only demand is that a woman doesn't give me a venereal disease."

Women complain that two-thirds of their partners short-change them when it comes to foreplay, while men complain that every fifth woman is passive during intercourse. Here are some women's voices:

> Television official, age 23: "I sometimes try to be a leader in our intimate duet but my husband always takes the reins in his own hands."
>
> Theater student, age 25: "Sometimes you have to sacrifice your pleasure for the man's satisfaction."
>
> Nurse, age 21: "I have a very sensitive clitoris but none of my partners suspects it. And I don't dare tell them about my desires myself; I feel uncomfortable. Sure, I'm used to being submissive. My mother always said, 'The affectionate calf can suckle from two cows.'"[30]

Sexual disillusionment in marriage is one of the causes of extramarital affairs. As in many other issues, there is a huge gap between moral attitudes and sexual behavior in this regard. Some 55.5% of men and 25.5% of women questioned by Olga Loseva acknowledged having extramarital sex. Men generally began this practice as early as in the first three years of marriage, women a little later—in the fourth or fifth year. About a third of married men who had been unfaithful had had one or two extramarital partners; another third had had three to five partners; and the others had had six or more. Women's behavior looks more moderate in this respect: four-fifths of unfaithful wives had had one or two lovers, and only 8% had had between three and five. Interestingly, adultery seems to be less rewarding than it is popularly believed to be, as people report that sexual technique and sexual satisfaction are more or less the same as in marriage.

According to Tatyana A. Gurko's study of 233 young couples in Moscow in 1989, 31% of husbands said they have had such liaisons and 11% believed that their wives also have had them. Wives' reports were more uniform: 18% admitted to their own liaisons and 16% to their husbands.[31]

According to Sergei Golod, who compared two similar samples of professional people in 1969 and 1989 (250 respondents each time), the number of extramarital affairs is growing, as is tolerance of extramarital sex—especially among women.[32] In 1989, 36% of professional women expressed tolerant attitudes toward extramarital affairs, with 33% neutral and 31% opposed. These numbers had not changed greatly since 1969. However, the number of women who reported that they themselves had

had extramarital sex had grown from 33% to 50% in the 20 years between the two surveys.

The same trend can be observed among men: in 1969, fewer than half of the married men surveyed acknowledged having had extramarital liaisons, a number that grew to more than three-quarters by 1989. Of course, one must also recognize the possibility that the change in response is due to people being less afraid to acknowledge such experiences and more accustomed to answering questions of this nature.

These statistics, while provocative, should not be taken as "the real picture." Owing to differences in number and quality of sample groups, to unvalidated and sometimes badly formulated questionnaires, and primitive statistical procedures, reliable qualitative analysis is impossible. The Russian Kinsey has not yet stepped forth, and we must remember that even Kinsey's original statistics were not beyond reproach. The methodology of even the best Western sex surveys is vulnerable to questions of accuracy,[33] and real Russian sex research has only just begun.

Despite the unreliability of statistical information, general shifts in Russian sexual values and behavior seem to be clear and going in the same direction as in the West: liberalization of sexual behavior, weakening of double standards, cultural acceptance and growing consumption of erotica. The leaders and agents of these shifts are also the same people as in the West: young, better-educated urban dwellers.

If we compare Russian and American sexual attitudes and behavior, we see both similarities and dissimilarities. As a social scientist—and as a human being—I worry about the desperate state of sex education in Russia. But when the Kinsey Institute in the fall of 1989 tested the basic knowledge of a statistically representative sample of 1,974 American adults, 55% of them failed, answering correctly only half—or fewer—of the questions. There were only 5 A students and only 58 received Bs. And no wonder. When questioned about the source of their sexual information when they were growing up, 42% mentioned "friends," 29% mentioned their mothers, 22% books, 17% "boyfriend or girlfriend," and only 14% sex education.[34] According to *The Janus Report on Sexual Behavior* (a recent study of 2,765 Americans between 1988 and 1992), 53% of men and 33% of women reported having learned about sex "from the streets," 25% of men and 40% of women from "home," and only 20% of men and 25% of women from school.[35] Is that really very much better than what we see in Russia?

The sexual double standard and general sexism are much stronger in Russia than in the United States. Although more than three-quarters of men and 91% of women in *The Janus Report* recognized that there is still a double standard regarding men's and women's roles, Americans are much more sensitive to these issues than are Russians, who often take gender inequality for granted, and either do not see the inequality or interpret it as a natural and unavoidable difference.

Americans have more egalitarian attitudes toward the premarital sexual experience of men and women than do Russians. Judging by *The Janus Report*, only 9% of U.S. men and 17% of American women had had no sexual experience before marriage, while 67% and 46%, respectively, had had "very much" or "much" premarital experience. The public attitudes regarding these experiences are less gender-specific than in Russia. In the United States, 56% of men and 52% of women surveyed thought the experience of premarital sex was very important or important for men; 46% of the men and 46% of the women considered premarital sexual experience to be equally important for women.

American and Russian men and women make much the same kind of complaints about their sexual partners, but American women seem to be more outspoken about sexual issues and there is much more publicity about the subject. Many Russian women, especially those of the older generation, simply don't know what sexual pleasure really is. After information about the Gräfenberg spot was published in *SPID-info* in 1992, the newspaper received letters of gratitude from many men and women, for whom the news proved a revelation.

It would be interesting to compare American and Russian women's orgasm experiences, but we should be careful with generalizations. And the survey's data are rather contradictory. According to the most recent and statistically most sophisticated U.S. national sexual survey, which I will call the Chicago survey, 3,432 Americans were interviewed; 75% of men but just 29% of women report always having an orgasm during sex .[36] Sexual satisfaction and dissatisfaction are based on certain cognitive criteria. The majority of Russian couples still dream about simultaneous orgasm, whereas almost two-thirds of the men and three-quarters of the women surveyed in *The Janus Report* "don't believe that simultaneous orgasm is a must for gratifying sex." But many American women report having to fake orgasm to please a man. . . .

Americans are exposed to much more erotica, are more interested in sexual experimentation (49% of the men and 36% of the women surveyed in *The Janus Report* agree that "a large variety of sex techniques is a must for maximum pleasure"), and are more ready to accept the realities of sexual life than their Russian counterparts. According to the Chicago survey, 41% of men and 16% of women purchased erotic materials in the past year.

In *The Janus Report*, 88% of men and 87% of women believed that oral sex is "very normal and all right." Ten percent of men and 18% of women selected oral sex as their "preferred way to achieve orgasm." And according to the Chicago survey, receiving oral sex is the third most appealing sexual practice in the United States. In another 1993 report, 74.6% of American men reported having performed and 78.8% having received oral sex.[37] The situation is similar in France, where three out of every four men and two out of every three women had experimented with fellatio.[38]

But what is behind the figures? Very often the gap between publicly professed moral convictions and private sexual behaviors in Russia is the same as in the United States. For example, in the VCIOM 1993 survey, group sex was strongly condemned by 67% of Russian men and 78% of women; only 9% of men and 4% of women believed it is acceptable, with a slightly higher percentage in the youngest group. However, according to Isayev's telephone survey, group sex was practiced by 16% of men and 6% of women. In *The Janus Report*, 43% of American men and 68% of American women thought group sex was "kinky"; only 17% and 8%, respectively, said it was all right and completely normal. But 14% of men and 8% of women indicated they had experienced group sex. Is this a big difference?

Adultery is strongly condemned and yet widespread in both countries. More than one-third of men and more than one-quarter of women in *The Janus Report* admit to having had at least one extramarital sexual experience.

The Chicago survey's figures are more conservative: only 24.5% of husbands and 15% of wives admitted to having had an affair, and 94% of married people said they were faithful in the past year. But some experts doubt the truthfulness of these responses. And it is difficult to reconcile the image of marital bliss—88% of U.S. spouses said they enjoyed great sexual pleasure—with a lot of sexological complaints: in the past year 15.8% of men and 33.4% of women lacked interest in sex, for 8.3% of men and 21.2% of women sex was not pleasurable, 8.3% of men and 24.1% of women were unable to experience orgasm, and so on.

Whatever the state of sexual information, Russian sexual values, attitudes, and behaviors are very similar to those of the Western world and are bound to the same problems and contradictions.

*Chapter Ten*

# ABORTION OR CONTRACEPTION?

*It is not so much public opinion as public officials that need educating.*

—Oscar Wilde

O ne of the most disturbing consequences of the lack of sexual culture in Soviet society was the public's astonishing ignorance about contraception—as a result of which, throughout the Soviet regime, induced abortion was, and remains today, the major method of birth control and family planning for the Russian people.

As we have seen, at the beginning of the century, Russian physicians called for the development of effective methods of contraception as the only alternative to abortion, with all its dangerous consequences, for family planning. Soviet physicians also understood this, and until the end of the 1920s the USSR was a leading advocate of the study of contraception and family planning. What then changed the situation so that by the 1950s, the USSR had become the world leader in abortions and unwanted pregnancies?[1]

Soviet policy was inconsistent on the issue. From 1920 to 1936, induced abortion was the main means of birth control. And although abortion was outlawed in 1936, women were given no compensatory help in family planning or contraception. At that time, few truly reliable, convenient, and safe means of contraception existed. The state of contraception was quite different, however, when the ban on abortion was finally removed in November 1955 because it had failed so miserably. By that time, barrier methods of contraception, such as diaphragms and condoms, had become widely available elsewhere in the world. Nonetheless, Soviet medicine had

nothing to offer other than induced abortion. To hide the woeful consequences of their policy from their own people and foreign observers, the
authorities simply ceased publishing statistical data on the subject.

As early as 1929, immediately following the publication of the manuals
*Abortion in 1925* and *Abortion in 1926*, all information on the subject was
classified as secret and held under the departmental monopoly of the USSR
Health Ministry. Of course, the statistics themselves would have been less
than helpful: statistics from Soviet ministries were not only inaccessible,
and thus invulnerable to objective criticism, but were usually unreliable as
well, having been gathered to further the interests of the department collecting them rather than to offer an objective portrait of the real state of
affairs. Research into the subject of abortion was never encouraged under
the Soviets, and the first official publication disclosing the number of abortions since 1929 came out only in September 1988.

Practically nothing is known about the contraceptive behavior of the
Soviet people from 1938 to the mid-1960s.[2] Official medical statistics made
no mention of the subject and no public surveys were undertaken. My personal recollection is that in the late 1940s and early 1950s young people
put their trust mainly in condoms. And if a Komsomol meeting took to
debating a "personal case" concerning someone's unplanned pregnancy (the
man responsible would be obliged to marry the woman in question; if he
refused, he could be formally reprimanded, which could have negative consequences for his career), there were likely to be jeers from the back
benches about the shoddy goods produced by the rubber industry!

Condoms appeared to go out of fashion with the next generation. In
1968, I brought back some condoms from Vienna for one of my students
as a sort of souvenir; they were special by Soviet standards. I remember my
student peering at them with curiosity and saying he would certainly give
them a try, though it would be the first time in his sexual experience. "But
what do you do to play it safe?" I asked naively. "Oh, that's not my concern," was his calm reply. "But what do the women do?" I asked. "It varies,"
he said. "And what if one gets pregnant?" The young man shrugged. Given
the typically cavalier attitude of most men, it is not surprising that induced
abortion has remained the principal form of birth control for so long.

According to Andrei Popov, Soviet family planning was distinguished
by the following general traits from its beginning up to 1988:

1. Although the right to family planning was formally proclaimed de
   jure in accordance with international conventions, it was never realized de facto.

2. Family planning services were inaccessible or nonexistent, owing to the lack of reliable information, the absence of specialized medical services and qualified personnel, and the unavailability of modern contraceptives.
3. The government prescribed reproductive behavior—from the formulation of the motives for human reproduction to the selection of reproductive goals and methods of birth control.
4. The only readily accessible method of family planning was (and, for the most part, continues to be) induced abortion.
5. Family planning behavior varies widely by region, according to the ethnographic, demographic, and socioeconomic realities within each region.[3]

Both the ideal and the actual number of children in Russian families have always varied with social strata, housing conditions, income, and other factors. In 1983, about 60% of newlywed Muscovites said they would like to have two children. In Leningrad, women wanted to have an average of 2.5 children, while men wanted 2.7.[4] In the 1990s, owing to the economic collapse of the country, both the desired number of children and the actual birthrate declined sharply. These days, many people simply cannot afford to have children.

The Soviet public, denied access to the necessary scientific information and the most modern contraceptives, was doomed to employ traditional and largely ineffectual methods of birth control. The picture from sample surveys taken in Moscow between 1965 and 1983 is shown Table 10.1.

The same doleful picture is painted by other surveys. Despite their generally high level of education, many women responding to one Moscow survey in 1976 could not assess the variety and quality of contraceptive methods available to them; half of the women could not even respond to the question of whether the local pharmacy stocked convenient and effective contraceptives. In a 1978 survey, respondents put mechanical methods in first place, calendar rhythm in second, and coitus interruptus in third. The researchers concluded that these results bore "witness to the public's low contraceptive culture, which is largely due to the lack of opportunity to use modern contraceptive methods."[9]

The demographer Y. Y. Babin came to the same conclusions from studying the contraceptive behavior of married couples in Moscow, Saratov, and Ufa in 1986; he surveyed approximately 1,000 cohabiting married couples with one or two children, with the wife being 35 years or younger. The method of contraception best known to Muscovites—an urban and pre-

Table 10.1
PERCENTAGE OF USERS OF SPECIFIC METHODS OF CONTRACEPTION
Moscow Sample Surveys, 1966–83[5]

| Method | Year of survey publication | | | |
|---|---|---|---|---|
| | 1965–66[6] | 1978[7] | 1982[7] | 1983[8] |
| Withdrawal | 32 | 34 | 14 | 25 |
| Rhythm (calendar) | — | 18 | 28 | 27 |
| Condom | 46 | 42 | 22 | 24 |
| Diaphragm | — | 1 | 1 | 1 |
| IUD | — | 8 | 11 | 10 |
| Oral | — | 4 | 4 | 2 |
| Spermicides | — | 1 | 3 | 3 |
| Rhythm (temperature) | — | — | 2 | — |
| Douche | — | 23 | 71 | 8 |
| Combinations | 12 | — | — | 12 |

Note: Columns do not add up to 100 because respondents were allowed to select two or more answers.

sumably more sophisticated and better-educated population than the average—was withdrawal. Between 11 and 60% of men and 20 and 75% of women were unable to answer questions about the quality of other contraceptives and were particularly badly informed about modern hormonal methods. Not surprisingly, men and women often differed in their assessment of the same methods: for example, 65% of men but only 45% of women thought the condom was inconvenient; the douche method was fine with 77% of the men but only 44% of the women.[10]

According to Golod's 1981 survey of 250 married couples, the calendar method took first place (used by 42% of men and 41% of women), and condoms came second with men (39% of men but only 18% of women) and induced abortion second with women (named by 34% of women but only 19% of men); third place went to withdrawal (named by 22% of men and 21% of women). Only 3.6% of women and 4.6% of men mentioned hormonal methods.[11]

The situation was even worse in the smaller towns, and, of course, in Russian villages and other Soviet republics. Since they had neither sufficient choice of contraceptives nor information about them, Soviet women were forced to resort most frequently to induced abortion, which appeared to them to be the least of all evils.

Very often women had abortions to terminate even first pregnancies. According to the demographer Mark Tolts, who examined the archives of Perm (population approximately one million) in 1981, the city had 272 recorded abortions, 140 extramarital births (births to unmarried mothers), and 271 births in the first months of marriage (the so-called shotgun weddings caused or hastened by pregnancy) for every thousand pregnancies of women who had not yet given birth.[12]

Most abortions were performed in hospitals, with or without the administration of a local anesthetic. Abortion was available on demand, but a woman was required to be examined and counseled by a doctor. Although doctors generally do not recommend abortion in the case of a first pregnancy, the ultimate decision belongs to the woman herself. A husband has no say in the matter, and sometimes he is not even informed. Conditions in the official state medical clinics are very uncomfortable; illegal abortions are performed in different places, often under highly unsanitary conditions.

Although abortion has long been accepted as the principal form of birth control, men and women have had different attitudes toward it. Women were not happy about it, but they were generally resigned to bearing the burden of family planning, and they were frank about the pain and humiliation abortion often entails. Here are some characteristic comments quoted by Adrian Gaiges and Tatyana Suvorova in a chapter entitled "The Way to Golgotha."[13]

> A biologist, age 27: "I was in my third month when I decided to have an abortion. It would have been better to have given birth! It was awful: neither Novocain nor a local anesthetic helped. I felt everything. . . . how they changed instruments, how they scraped. You sit there . . . and can do nothing. After the abortion, I lost 10 kilos."
>
> A student, age 19: "When I entered the operating room, I was scolded by the nurse: 'Where do you think you are, a disco? Go cut your nails!' I spent an hour in moral preparation."
>
> A model, age 23: "The operation was done without anesthetic. The atmosphere reminded me of a stable. The staff treated us women as though we were whores. The impression you get is that just going there is a punishment: you are punished for your behavior, for having sex. It's impossible to describe this experience to a male—you have to be a female to understand."

Some men, by contrast, remain emotionally distant, dismissive of the pain or humiliation that might be involved in abortion, and even hostile to the women:

An engineer, age 22, referring to the fact that his wife had had four
    abortions: "I often have to visit the dentist, yet I don't complain."
A laborer, age 26: "An abortion is a trifling operation."
A waiter, age 26: "These women are simply fools. They should have
    worried before the event."

Some men don't even know how many abortions their wives or girlfriends have had. They consider it none of their business. The result: more
hostility between the sexes. Said one female worker, "During the abortion I
began to feel hatred for my husband. He is absolutely indifferent to my suf-
ferings."

It was not so much a matter of the public's backwardness as the official
state policy that caused this situation. The authorities did all they could to
discredit new contraceptive methods and to prevent their introduction into
the country. They were particularly antagonistic to hormonal contraception.

Disputes over the relative advantages and disadvantages of the oral contraceptive raged in the 1960s; in the 1970s, the Health Ministry, basing its
policy on the views of ignorant gynecologists, took a rigidly conservative
line. By a ministry order of August 1, 1971, birth control pills were permitted only for medical purposes other than the averting of pregnancy (for
example, the treatment of endometriosis or hormonal disorders)—because,
according to the authors of the order, long-term use of the pill had a strong
carcinogenic side effect. A letter of instruction issued by the ministry in
1974 whipped up even greater fears: the birth control pill, the letter said,
had been proved to be contraindicated for women suffering from as many
as ten different illnesses. When these numbers were added to those of
women for whom there were indirect contraindications, the pill was not
recommended for as many as eight to nine women out of ten! These conclusions were widely propagated through the mass media and doctors in
practice, producing in the public an exceedingly hostile attitude toward
hormonal methods of contraception. In contrast with the supposed side
effects of the pill, induced abortion seemed relatively harmless.

Why did Soviet medicine take such a reactionary stance?

The first and most obvious reasons were the ignorance and lack of principle on the part of medical personnel, who clung to outmoded information and freely accepted any position presented as "anti-Western." In addition, leaders in the Soviet medical community, as were those in all other
areas of Soviet life, were extremely inert, highly unwilling to renounce
extant abortion services in favor of setting up something new; furthermore,
abortion clinics brought in quite a tidy sum to the coffers of the Ministry of

Health, and the doctors themselves were not averse to taking a share on the side.

There were also more general reasons. The authorities feared that the widespread availability of the birth control pill might lead to a considerable drop in the Soviet birthrate, which they wanted to keep high. The main worry was that any switch from an abortion strategy to one of true contraception would mean a substantial extension of individual rights, weakening state control over reproductive behavior and replacing it with conscious self-control. The doctor would become merely a consultant in this scenario; women themselves would make the decisions. That amount of potential autonomy went against the paramount principles of the Soviet regime and all its historical experience.

A few gynecologists, such as the Georgian Archil Khomasuridze,[14] and demographers such as Mikhail Bedny, Mark Tolts, and Larissa Remennick spoke out strongly against this reactionary strategy. In 1986, Larissa Remennick, formerly of the All-Union Oncological Center, published an article entitled "The Reproductive Behavior and Oncological Illnesses of Women," drawing on global statistics. She completely punctured the myth of the pill as cancer-promoting, noting that, statistically speaking, abortion was the riskiest form of birth control.[15]

Official Soviet medicine, however, did not pay any attention to such criticism, and word of it never reached the public inasmuch as demographers published their articles only in scientific periodicals with small circulation. In any case, why should people believe sociologists and demographers when doctors, including such specialists as gynecologists and endocrinologists, were assuring them of the very opposite?

In a 1987 interview with the weekly *Argumenty i fakty*, I argued that the USSR possessed an impoverished contraceptive culture and that we ought to alter our attitude toward hormonal contraception; the paper received many indignant letters, particularly from physicians, in response. This is how A. Sukharev, M.D., reacted to my cautious statement that *perhaps* we should acquaint senior high schoolers with the basic methods of contraception:

> The professor says he bases his argument on "objective reality"—i.e., on the fact that "many [it would be interesting to know exactly what percentage!] adolescents commence their sexual life without asking parental permission," and he appeals to a virtuous public to help the poor little children get their hands on condoms. (Hormonal methods are harmful, dear professor.) Why, honorable professor, do you raise such anomalies to the rank of a general law?[16]

A turning point in changing public opinion came, paradoxically enough, from a broadcast by the American television talk show host Phil Donahue. He had come to the Soviet Union in late 1986 or early 1987 (at an early stage of perestroika, literally on the eve of the proclamation of glasnost), and devoted one of his broadcasts to family matters. Soviet Central Television invited me to attend the broadcast as an expert. As they told me, "We don't know ourselves what's going to happen, but maybe you'll get a chance to say something." I went to the television studio fully determined to say nothing, but to listen and to watch.

At the start, people talked mainly in official, bureaucratic language, but gradually they came to life, warming to the subject and beginning to speak more frankly. Yet when Donahue asked a question about abortion and contraception, it was met by a long, deathly silence. One woman finally raised her hand and when the delighted Donahue went over to her, she attacked him angrily: "Why are you asking such trivial, unimportant, and dirty questions? Why aren't you asking about moral ideals and the upbringing of our children?" (The entire episode was edited before the tape was broadcast.)

Donahue was visibly taken aback, and I thought to myself that I had been invited there to say that we were really a backward country, but that we were starting to realize it. So that is what I did: I told him that in the USSR, one did not talk publicly on the subject, that the public was ignorant about contraception and therefore preferred abortion to birth control pills, that in any case contraceptives were in short supply, and so on. Of course, I could have said much more than I did. I had recently seen published figures on the numbers of "back alley" abortions, and I knew that American television was the best venue for informing the Soviet government of the facts. But I was afraid of going too far—after all, glasnost was only just beginning. Another Soviet participant, who worked at a pharmacy, immediately began to contradict me, saying that pharmacies had a good supply of every means of contraception and were well able to meet the demand!

Immediately after the broadcast had been recorded, I was apprehended in the lobby of Ostankino Television by a crowd of agitated women from Moscow, their eyes wide with astonishment and horror: "Why on earth do you think the pill is better than abortion? You're no physician, and everyone knows that the pill causes cancer and other problems." Without the worry of the American television camera, I was able to tell those poor women just what I thought of ignorant Soviet doctors and the Soviet Ministry of Health. I was prepared for all kinds of unpleasantness—after all, they were right: I wasn't a doctor—but there was no uproar, just great disbelief on their part.

But times were really changing. When Donahue's program was shown on the most popular channel of Soviet TV, almost everyone tuned in. For a few days I received largely unfavorable reactions: "Why is Kon poking his nose in where it's not wanted? What does he know about contraception?" But I did not have to stand up to the accusations alone. Progressive demographers joined in a counterattack. In early 1987, the mass-circulation women's magazine *Rabotnitsa* arranged a roundtable discussion on abortion and contraception. Conservative medics initially tried to defend their former positions, but Bedny and Tolts pinned them to the wall with incontrovertible facts. Meanwhile, the magazine's editorial board was ready with a huge stack of furious letters from their women readers. As a result, the deputy minister of health was forced to admit that the contraception situation was really scandalous. The editors not only published all this material but also sent it on to Raisa Gorbachev; rumor had it that Mikhail Gorbachev personally instructed the new minister of health, Yevgeny Chazov, to take urgent measures to protect the health of pregnant women.

The Ministry of Health subsequently shifted its ground substantially. The grandiose ten-year plan for health care, adopted in 1987, contained a special paragraph announcing a campaign to limit abortion and promote contraception; and this was widely reported in the press and on television.

Alas, these changes were more easily announced than accomplished. First, there was the glaring and chronic shortage of all contraceptives, especially the most up-to-date, which were not manufactured in the USSR and which the country had no funds to purchase abroad. In other words, people simply could not find and buy what they needed.

Furthermore, modern methods of contraception are complicated; they frequently require professional advice for selection and systematic medical supervision for best results. To introduce modern contraception to the former USSR, it would have been necessary to retrain practically all gynecologists. In the mid-1970s, nine out of ten women admitted choosing methods of contraception according to their availability rather than according to effectiveness or suitability.[17]

Finally, given the prevailing atmosphere of prudery, how could we quickly challenge the false stereotypes and prejudices that had taken shape over the past decades? Even as late as 1993, experts from the World Health Organization found that both doctors and women patients in St. Petersburg were convinced that hormonal contraceptives were terribly dangerous.[18] And only 11% of Russian gynecologists recognized the right of teenagers to confidentiality, a sine qua non of providing effective contraceptive service for teenagers.

It is hardly surprising that today, as at the end of the 1980s, induced abortion is still the principal form of birth control throughout the erstwhile Soviet Union.

The total annual number of induced abortions in the late 1980s, according to official statistics, amounted to six to seven million. That was virtually a fifth, perhaps even a fourth, of all abortions carried out in the world. If we add to that the "back alley abortions," the number of which amounted to 12% of the total according to officialdom but 50–70% of the official total according to independent experts, the aggregate number of abortions in the USSR came to 10–11 million a year. Even without these adjustments, the number of abortions per thousand women of reproductive age in 1985 surpassed by six to ten times the analogous figures for Western Europe.

In some areas the situation was even worse. The bare statistic of 770 abortions for every 100 births in rural areas of central Russia surely has no rival anywhere in the world, exceeding corresponding figures in the United Kingdom by 30 times and in Hungary by 12 times.

It is usually village women who resort to back alley abortions (medical assistance in the villages is worse and the fear of public shame is greater), as well as young women under 17. Such abortions, especially in the first pregnancy, are often accompanied by complications. Of the total number of deaths from abortions, one-quarter involve young women under 25. The most common cause of death from abortion is infection, followed by hemorrhage. Because of complications from abortion, about 20% of married couples are unable to have children, and having had their first abortion with little idea of the consequences, they may undergo lengthy and unsuccessful medical treatment in an attempt to have the child they decide they want when it is probably too late.[19]

In 1991, a group of Russian and Belgian researchers carried out a survey of the contraceptive behavior of Soviet women through the mass-circulation journal *Zdorovye* (*Health*). More than 8,000 women completed and returned the questionnaire. The sample was not representative: those who responded tended to be young (45% of respondents were under 25) and highly educated (35% had a university education). Moreover, *Zdorovye* subscribers are obviously more interested in and, consequently, more knowledgeable about such issues than most women—in recent years the journal regularly informed its readers on issues of contraception as well as other aspects of sex. Even so, the results of the survey present a fairly miserable picture.[20]

On the whole, the survey shows there have been marked changes in regard to contraception, although the level of information, like the contraceptive practice itself, leaves much to be desired, even for educated women. Unfortunately, we do not have any more fundamental or truly representative statistics. It would be desirable to know the opinion of men as well as women, and that of practicing physicians to learn to what extent they have overcome their former prejudices and convictions.

The largest-ever survey, conducted in 1990 by Goskomstat (the Central Statistical Committee of the USSR) and covering the entire former Soviet Union (93,000 married women of reproductive age were questioned), shows a pattern very similar to that of the *Zdorovye* survey. Contraception was "always" used by 21.7% , "sometimes" by 9.7%, and "never" by 56.8% of Russian women. Six percent said they had no knowledge of contraception. About two-thirds of Russian women knew about the pill, yet this method received one of the lowest ratings for perceived effectiveness, while condoms and withdrawal continued to be perceived as the most effective.[21]

The Russian Family Planning Association (RFPA), which was formed in 1991 with the ideological and financial support of IPPF, is today carrying out an intensive public information and educational campaign. Since 1993, RFPA has been publishing an international medical journal, *Planirovanie semyi* (*Family Planning*). It has also published Russian translations of some IPPF textbooks for social workers and of the few popular booklets for general audiences, including teenagers. The medicopedagogical center for family planning, mainly for teenagers, was organized in 1993 in one Moscow district. Several professional seminars for training social workers have been held in Moscow and other cities. In December 1994 the national conference on The Reproductive Health and Sexual Education of Youth was held in Moscow, together with the Commission on Women, Family, and Demographic Questions of the Russian presidency, and the Committee on Youth of the Russian State Duma, with the participation of the Ministry of Health and the Ministry of Education.

But RFPA is very poor, and its strategy is sometimes problematic. In the absence of trained psychologists and social workers, there is a real danger not just of the medicalization but of the *gynecologization* of sex education. Here are some statements by the chief of children's gynecology of St. Petersburg and the president of the Russian Federation's pediatric and adolescent gynecology, Professor Yury A. Gurkin:

The substance of sex education is the formation of the feminine personality traits—kindness, tolerance, cleanliness, the ability to keep house, compliance and so on. Still another task should be the cultivation of parental instinct. . . .

The sublimation of the sex drive is a must. . . .

Relatively greater demands from girls than from boys. . . .

Taking into account the biological differences of the female and male organisms presupposes certain limitations for the girls and women of reproductive age. The excess of the information will result in the syndrome of polycystic ovaries [sic]. . . .

The basic biological and social mission of woman is to be a wife, mother, educator, home keeper. . . .[22]

I don't think it needs commentary. . . . And Dr. Gurkin is a very nice fellow, an excellent doctor, and an enthusiast of sex education.

Both the health and psychological situation in Russia is constantly deteriorating.

According to Nikolai Vaganov, the Russian deputy minister of health, in an interview in 1993, the rate of maternal mortality in childbirth was 2.5 times higher in Russia than in Europe and continues to rise.[23] In the last three years the number of midwives has decreased to 20,000 nationwide. The incidence of anemia among pregnant women increased 4.5 times from 1985 to 1992. In some regions, the incidence of anemia is 30–40%, in others 50–60%. According to the official statistics, no more than 45%—and according to better scientific authorities, as few as 25–30%—of women have normal, complication-free pregnancies and deliveries. About 15% of married couples are infertile. Although the general number of induced abortions among women of fertile age is decreasing—in 1993 Russia had officially 2,970,000 abortions, 200,000 fewer than in 1992—these figures are unreliable and the relation between the number of abortions and the number of live births is deteriorating. In 1988, Russian women had 166 abortions for every 100 live births, and 225 in 1992. Only approximately 22% of women of childbearing age used contraception, the most widely used methods of which are outdated and primitive. Hormonal contraception was used by only 3% of women (in European countries the number was more than 20%), and hormonal contraceptives are not produced in Russia. According to the highly advertised presidential program "Children of Russia," thirty-five million hormonal contraceptive packs had to be bought abroad in 1993, but not a single one was really paid for by the state budget. Most of the available contraceptives are paid for by voluntary funds and international charity organizations (*Izvestiya*, December 9,

1994). And in the permanent mutual accusations between the health ministry and the International Fund for the protection of the health of mothers and children (the president of this fund is the former USSR deputy minister of health, Alexander Baranov), the overtones of the old bureaucratic feud and the competition for influence and money are clearly heard.

Here are some typical comments on the state of contraception in Moscow, as cited by Gaiges and Suvorova:

> A model, age 23: "Soviet condoms are low quality; they contain no glycerine, which is why they feel so awful. I always buy foreign makes."
>
> An engineer, age 24: "Soviet contraceptive devices harm women's health, so a man should use condoms. The trouble is that ours are so revolting and difficult to find that I often feel that the state is bent on pushing up the population numbers."
>
> A student, age 26: "My wife tried to use various imported devices, but couldn't get hold of them regularly. Then on her doctor's advice, she had a spiral [IUD] fitted; soon after, she got pregnant and had to have an abortion. Since condoms don't satisfy us, we now practice withdrawal."
>
> A student, age 17: "Foreign condoms give my partner and me pleasure. But Soviet condoms are only to prevent you getting pregnant. Even for that, however, they're of little use: they often tear and sometimes remain inside my partner."
>
> A technician, age 25: "Imported condoms are thoroughly reliable, but you can't use them once you're married—it's a sign of lack of trust in your spouse. Hormonal tablets are harmful to your future children, so they too are no good for preventing pregnancy. I usually use a syringe. I've had four abortions."
>
> A television executive, age 23: "After the birth of my daughter, I was terrified of getting pregnant again. . . . I tried hormonal tablets, but that only upset my cycle and I lost a lot of weight. . . . I went to a local clinic and had a Soviet-made spiral inserted. I reckon the gynecologist was cutting corners or something, for I was soon pregnant again. . . . After that I ran into a bit of luck: I purchased a Yugoslav spiral at the pharmacy and had it inserted once more—this time at a different district clinic. It helped me to become pregnant once more! This time I went through sheer hell: they put a mask over my face without an anesthetic; I

shouted, screamed, twisted my back. . . . I think it raised the doctor's blood pressure. Of course, it was all the usual Soviet circus show."[24]

The situation is especially difficult for teenagers. The Goskomstat survey from 1990 demonstrated that 30.5% of all girls under 15 had no knowledge at all about contraception; in 16- to 17-year-olds, the figure was 24.6%, and in 18- to 23-year-olds, it was 11%. Some 96.6% of young women aged 16–17 never used contraceptives. Most teenage sex—and the amount of teenage sexual activity is growing—still goes unprotected. A 1990 Soviet-German student survey (average age of respondents, 21) showed that 15% of female students had already had one abortion, and 6% more than one.[25] According to a recent Goskomstat survey, the number of teenage girls in Russia who had abortions in 1992 was 297,029 (16,320 of these were illegal).[26]

The government's decision to require women to pay for abortion, except in medical emergencies, is making the situation much worse. Even in 1992–93, in spite of the general availability of professional abortion services, 80% of women, according to the Juventa Reproduction Center in St. Petersburg, contact the abortion clinics only after they have already tried to do something, often dangerous, to themselves. And in 1994, according to Inga Grebesheva, the president of the Russian Planned Parenthood Association, an abortion in Moscow costs about 100,000 rubles, about five minimal monthly salaries).

Psychological factors are also important.

According to a 1993 report on teenagers, teens in Moscow and St. Petersburg are aware that undertaking abortion is undesirable; nevertheless, to the question "What should an unmarried teenage girl do if she becomes pregnant?" a quarter of the sample (20% of girls and nearly 29% of boys) answered, "Get an abortion." Eighty-one percent (in the oldest group 90%) know where to buy contraceptives, and more than half (in the oldest group 62%) believe doing so is not difficult. But only 54% (65 percent of 16- to 17-year-olds) have been instructed by someone in the use of contraception. In many cases, they had to obtain this information by themselves from television and magazines (51%) or from their school friends (22%). Parents were mentioned as sources of information by 12%, girl- or boyfriends by 9%, medical personnel by 7%, women's clinics by 4%, and school teachers by 3%.

It is no wonder, therefore, that the information teenagers do have is often haphazard, inadequate, and even blatantly wrong. All the St. Petersburg teenagers surveyed by Igor Lunin in 1993 knew something about condoms and were not embarrassed to discuss them. But 47% did not believe condoms were really effective for contraception, and only 18% of boys and 9% of girls knew that condoms were disposable. A sizable number (46% of boys and 40% of girls) believed a condom could be reused several times. Even among the "sexually experienced," every fourth boy and every fifth girl believed condoms could be used twice, provided they were given a "good wash." Not surprisingly, then, girls often discover they are pregnant too late, sometimes only in the seventh month of pregnancy. If such are the conditions in the two capital cities, where presumably people have the highest level of education and contraceptive culture (about 40% of the fathers and mothers of these teens have attended a university), what happens in the provincial towns and villages?

The problem also has its ideological parameters. Modern-day Russia is gradually opening up and becoming a pluralistic society. That means that conservative as well as liberal forces are operating openly and with increasing militancy. While liberal professionals, citing IPPF experience, appeal for campaigns against abortion through promotion of sex education and contraceptive culture, the conservative-religious forces harp on moral issues. The recently established Nadezhda (Hope) Charitable Fund takes the same antiabortion stance as the Western "pro-life" organizations.

Having fought the battle for banning abortion in the United States to something of a stalemate, American ultraconservatives are now transferring the struggle to Russia, where many people accept anything American uncritically, as a product of "Western civilization" and an embodiment of "universal values." As we have seen, a cultural basis for this point of view already exists in the form of traditional Russian conservatism.

It is unlikely that the ideas of the American antiabortionists will find much support in Russia, as the experience of total control over the individual is too fresh in the minds of most. In the VCIOM 1993 survey, only 16% said they would support the banning of abortion, while 60% said they would be opposed to this measure. Yet if future Russian sex education emphasizes biology and technology at the expense of moral and cultural issues, as has been the case in some Western countries, the popular mood may change.

For the present, the Russian Ministry of Education has in principle accepted a 12-hour program of sex education for teenagers in a course created by the Organon Laboratory, which has been used successfully in the

Netherlands. Should this project be financed by the United Nations (unfortunately, the European Community refused to do it and the Russian government has no money), the experiment, including the training of teachers, will begin in 1995 in eight schools in different regions.

This is better than nothing. But even if this project is completely successful, we have to ask whether just one type of course, designed only for adolescents, is enough for so large and heterogeneous a country as Russia as we face the twenty-first century.

## Chapter Eleven

# TEENAGERS AT RISK

*I would there were no age between ten and three-and-twenty,
or that youth would sleep out the rest; for there is nothing
in the between but getting wenches with child, wronging the
ancientry, stealing, fighting—"*

—William Shakespeare
*A Winter's Tale*, Act 3, Scene 3

Irina Pavlovna, a neighbor who shares my landing, recently obtained her degree and now teaches geography in secondary school. She is in charge of 8A. We had tea together one day last autumn and she was trembling like a leaf.

"My God, what a fool I am!" she suddenly blurted out. "Just imagine how stupid you have to be to take those cretins on an overnight field trip!"

"What happened?"

"You should have seen what they were up to at night! All of them screwing with one another. . . . Snot-nosed kids, fifteen-year-olds, for God's sake! The worst of it was they had no shame."

Thus commences Alexander Onezhsky's article "Lovers from Grade 8A: A Thousand and One Nights of Fifteen-year-olds: Depravity, or are they just plain different?" in *SPID-info* in April 1993. The journalist was a friend of the teacher and met her pupils, who confirmed her story. All the 15-year-olds had been having sex for some time—the girls had had as many as 7, 10, even 20 partners—and they discussed it all quite openly in class, even in the presence of a journalist they had only just met.

Such sensational articles regularly appear in the Russian press these days, especially in the "erotic" and the nationalistic papers. Invariably the stories report the extremes, though the erotic press seems to write of teenage sex with admiration, while the "red-brown" press writes of it with horror. For an expert in the field, the real question is whether the stories are true or not.[1]

Generally, Russian teenagers, like their parents, are definitely profamily. In a comparative study of senior formers from Moscow and Amsterdam[2]—1,162 Moscow senior high schoolers, 893 of the parents, and 681 of their teachers were questioned in spring 1991 about their general value orientations—"a happy family life" was ranked most important, mentioned by 73.5% of young Muscovites and by 67.8% of their Amsterdam coevals. But some 86% had no plans to marry soon; marriage, they considered, is a serious matter. Some 47.7% of Moscow teens believed they needed parental approval for marriage (only 31.8% of Amsterdam teens agreed), 45.5% wanted to register their marriages formally, and 26.7% (twice as many as in Amsterdam) wanted a church wedding.

Like their parents and teachers, Moscow teens believed the most important factors in a happy marriage are warm, sincere relationships and mutual understanding. But teens attributed much more importance to "sexual harmony" than did their educators, with 43% of teens selecting this point as opposed to 32.6% of their teachers and only 23.3% of their parents. And this value grew in importance with age: it was mentioned by 22.3% of 13- to 14-year- olds and by 57.5% of 17- to 18-year-olds. As early as 1991 Moscow teens were quite appreciative of the sexual aspects of marriage, more so than young Amsterdamers, only 29.4% of whom stressed that value.

What about sexuality as such, considered independently of marriage?

In late 1992 and early 1993, the first anonymous sociological survey was made of students in 16 secondary schools and 8 vocational-technical colleges in Moscow and St. Petersburg—a total of 1,615 12- to 17-year-olds.[3] The results showed that rumors of the impending end of the world owing to unbridled teenage sex were greatly exaggerated.

Interest in love and sex has always been a vital part of teenage life. Today, younger and younger teens are becoming both interested and active. Approximately half of teenagers "date" before they are 12. By age 16. only one in five had not had this pleasant experience; but it is much rarer to find more or less steady couples. During the secondary school years, some 60% of girls and 49% of boys were more or less "going steady" or dating regularly, but even among the 16- to 17-year-olds, over half had no permanent partner for dating at the time of the survey.

Of course, dating, even steadily, is one thing and sexual intimacy is another. All the same, we may note a certain dynamic here: 16-year-olds who had already made their sexual debut were overwhelmingly likely to have gone steady at some point; only 4% of teenagers who had begun their sex lives had never dated; among virgins, the figure was 24%. In the group of teens who had begun their sex lives but had not dated, boys outnumbered girls six to one.

Of all the teens surveyed, some 15% of girls and 22% of boys admitted to sexual experience; in that group, 34% of girls and 57% of boys had had sex before their fifteenth birthday, while 5% of girls and 20% of boys had had sex for the first time at age 12 or earlier. If we look at age groups, we find that 2% of teens under 14 had had sex, 13% of 14- to 15-year-olds, and 36% of 16- to 17-year-olds.

Similar data were obtained by Igor Lunin, who surveyed 370 tenth graders (185 girls and 185 boys, average age 15.9 years) in several St. Petersburg schools. Experience with intercourse was noted by 25% (32% of boys and 21% of girls), experience with oral sex was noted by 13 girls (36% of those sexually active) and 23 boys (42% of those sexually active), and experience with anal sex by 5 girls and 6 boys (some teens didn't answer these delicate questions). Three percent of sexually active girls had already been pregnant and 3% of boys said they had impregnated their partner. Two percent of girls and 3% of boys had contracted a sexually transmitted disease.

Do these numbers represent a lot of sexual activity or a little?

When we compare these data with earlier Soviet data, today's teens seem to be more sexually active, but the data are not completely comparable, since the earlier surveys used different samples and methodology, and no one younger than 18 was surveyed.

In the 1960s, Sergei Golod found that among the university students he surveyed, four out of five young men and one out of every two young women had had sexual experience; the figures were 88% and 45%, respectively, among manual workers. In 1965, 10% of young men and 2% of young women among sexually active university students had started their sex lives before they were 16, 42% and 13%, respectively, had first had sex between 16 and 18, while 33% and 50%, respectively, had first had sex between ages 19 and 21. In 1972, corresponding figures showed 12% and 4% before age 16; 38% and 21% between 16 and 18, and 38% and 54% between 19 and 21. A 1969 survey of Leningrad young professionals showed that 7% of men and only 1% of women had had their "first time" before 16, 22% and 8% between 16 and 18, and 30% and 40% between

19 and 21. A follow-up survey in 1989 demonstrated some changes: 11% of men and 1% of women before 16, 32% and 13% between 16 and 18, and 42% and 46% between 19 and 21.[4]

An earlier start to sex initiation in Russia, as everywhere else, can partly be attributed to acceleration of physical maturation. According to the findings of the Soviet physiologist V. G. Vlastovsky, in the 35 years between 1935 and 1970, the average age at menarche among Moscow girls fell from 15.1 to 13 years of age.[5] A corresponding drop in the age of physical maturation, including sexual maturation, of boys can be inferred.

If we compare contemporary Russian teenagers (the sample from the survey carried out in Moscow and St. Petersburg in 1992–93 was almost exclusively Russian in ethnic terms) with their Western European and American counterparts, their sexual activity is not excessive.[6]

It would seem therefore that the scandalous 15-year-olds of grade 8A with which we began this chapter are not particularly typical, statistically speaking.

The psychological problems of Russian teenagers are basically the same as teens elsewhere. A teenager typically encounters many bodily and psychosexual problems during puberty. Many boys are worried about lagging behind their contemporaries in height, weight, emergence of secondary sex characteristics (growth of beard, pubic hair, and penis and deepening of voice); they may also be self-conscious about the temporary growth of feminine-appearing breasts. Girls, on the other hand, are concerned about the size and shape of their developing breasts, and about becoming hirsute or gaining excessive weight, among other issues.

Teenage worries and doubts in regard to their bodies and external appearance are more or less universal, but in societies with a matter-of-fact attitude toward the body, young people can seek answers to their problems from parents, teachers, and books. Russian teenagers find this much more difficult to do.

I recall a holiday in a mountain resort community that was hosting a party of teenagers from a sports club; my attention was drawn to a 12-year-old boy taking a shower with his undershorts on. When I asked him what he was embarrassed about, he told me he had hair growing "down below." I said it was perfectly normal for boys his age—"You see, all of them are naked and not ashamed"—and he replied, "Yes, but the other boys are bigger, and I'm still little—though my mother did tell me something about it." It is interesting that it was the boy's mother and not his army officer father who had broken the ice on the subject—men are often embarrassed to discuss such matters with their sons.

Like their foreign peers, most Russian teenagers have their first sexual experience through masturbation. Although the subject is rarely mentioned in conversation, it is an open secret. I remember a clandestine ditty we sang in 1943 when I was a Young Pioneer: "The sun, fresh air, and onanism fortify the organism." Boys typically begin to masturbate at about 12 to 13; this reaches its peak at ages 15 to 16, when masturbation becomes a mass phenomenon. Girls start to masturbate somewhat later and do so less intensively than boys. According to V. V. Danilov's findings in 1982, 22% of girls had masturbated by the age of 13.5, 50% by 17.5, and 65% by 18.5.[7] Russian sexologists, like their Western colleagues, see nothing dangerous in juvenile masturbation. Among the patients of the sexologist Georgi Vasilchenko, the most frequent male masturbators were sexually healthy men, while men who had never masturbated had the higher percentage of impotence. And according to Abram Svyadoshch, women who had masturbated before beginning their sexual lives were three times less likely to be unable to reach orgasm than those who had never masturbated.[8]

Nevertheless, there is a very strong masturbation phobia among Russians. In a VCIOM survey of June 1993, "the behavior of people who masturbate" induced fiercer condemnation than either premarital sex or watching pornographic films. As many as 47% of men and 49% of women categorically condemned masturbation; only 20% of those surveyed saw "nothing reprehensible" in the practice. Although younger (ages 16 to 25) and more educated people were more tolerant (one-third condemned, and 30% were neutral), masturbation fears go deep into the Russian national consciousness.[9]

Here are some typical Russian responses to the issue:

A medical nurse, age 21: "Masturbation is sexual perversion and psychic deviance."
A female engineer, age 25: "It is a terrible illness occurring in childhood; children should be told how dangerous it is."

I am reminded of an incident that occurred in a summer camp for senior high schoolers. I was chatting with a tall, handsome, and intelligent 17-year-old, the secretary of the school Komsomol organization (a fact I mention as evidence of his good social adaptation and popularity among his peers). In his references to the future, I sensed a gloomy uncertainty about himself that contrasted markedly with his generally positive outlook. When I asked him whether he had any personal problems that I could help him with, he replied that no one could help him; in any case, he said, it was not my area of expertise (the lads knew I was a sociologist; no one had told them about my interest in sexology). I had no intention of dragging a confession out of him, although he clearly wanted to talk. The next time we met he mentioned that his memory was deteriorating, a complaint that became less murky when he came to admit that he was "losing a lot of albumen." So we had cleared up the main issue—or most of it; unfortunately, when I learned that he had begun to masturbate after older boys had masturbated him by force at age ten, I hurried to calm his fears instead of trying to understand his masturbatory fears and fantasies—I then asked him how his failure of memory was manifesting itself. It turned out that when he was 16, he had had difficulty with mathematics. I told him his case was very bad: if he had not realized by that age that mathematics was not a subject that requires good memory, then he was in fact suffering from the "overall degradation of mental faculties" he'd been warned of in the ridiculous brochures he'd been reading. At that he burst out laughing and ran off to play basketball. (Later I wrote an article for *Sovetskaya pedagogika* on teenage sexuality; the editorial board mulled it over for two long years before drastically curtailing the section on masturbation. "After all, we can't go around encouraging such things. . . . !")

It could have been worse. I know of a 19-year-old who could not rise to the occasion on his wedding night—he had had no previous sexual experience—and immediately blamed it on his accursed habit. Without saying a word to anyone, he departed for another city and pledged himself to total and lifelong abstinence. By the time his friends persuaded him to visit a sex consultant five years later, he was in a terrible state.

Such phobias are cultivated and utilized for political ends, even today. The conservative writer Nikolai Popov made no bones about it, writing in the weekly *Stolitsa* (*Capital*): "I know why it is that the death rate in Russia has overtaken the birth rate—it's all because of queers and masturbators. Give us our own kind any day."[10] Another Russian writer, Boris Kamov (despite his lack of medical education, the chief of the "nontraditional pediatric center" sponsored by the Russian Children's Fund) even made the "scientific discovery" that not only male impotence but most other diseases as well result precisely from the masturbation viciously propagated by corrupt Western and Russian sexologists. Kamov argued that the ancient Chinese philosophy that was absolutely opposed to masturbation had produced wonderful results: one of its adepts had lived nearly eight centuries. Thus had the founder of Moscow, Prince Yury Dolgorukii, followed these rules, he might still be alive. . . . This is not parody but a literal quotation from Kamov in a mass-circulation newspaper.[11]

But let us return to the teenagers. A first sexual experience by no means automatically signifies either passionate love or the start of a regular sex life. Early affairs are usually devoid of love and are often rather prosaic. Virtually a third of sexually active teenagers have never gone steady with a person of the opposite sex; almost half did not have a boyfriend or girlfriend at the time of the survey. Often the first episode of sexual intimacy takes place with a more or less chance acquaintance, if it is not in fact a first encounter with a total stranger. This is particularly true with boys, many of whom (41%) do not have a regular girlfriend. Sexually active girls are usually more discriminating: only 17% of them have never had a steady boyfriend. The proportion of sexually experienced boys is higher than that of sexually active girls in all age groups. The proportion is almost two to one (68% of boys and 38% of girls) among 16-year-olds.

There is nothing new or sensational in these findings. Every adult knows full well that sex and love are different things: over 90 years ago, Sigmund Freud analyzed the discontinuity between "tender" and "sensual" attraction in the teenage years, recognizing it as perfectly normal. Teenage sex is a kind of sociopsychological experimentation that teenagers carry out on themselves and, at the same time, on others, thereby testing their own capabilities and proving to themselves and others their own adulthood.

It is by no means a trivial question to ask what affects today's earlier (by average statistical indexes) sexual initiation and what impact it in turn has on other aspects of life. A comparison of virginal 16-year-olds with their more sexually active peers, taken from the 1992–93 Moscow/St. Petersburg survey, is illuminating. The difference between virgins and nonvirgins was considerable, both psychologically and statistically.

The survey's questionnaire contained a number of opportunities for self-description, and it discussed, among other topics, the place of risky behavior in teenage life. As many as 58% of sexually active teenagers—as opposed to 43% of virgins—agreed with the statement "I obtain genuine satisfaction from doing quite risky things." Sixty-five percent of the former as opposed to 44% of the latter averred that "I like constantly testing myself, doing something slightly risky." More than half of the sexually active teenagers—and fewer than a third of the virgins—agreed that "I often try to see how far I can go."

In other words, sex for teenagers is often something forbidden and risky. That is why it attracts at younger ages those who enjoy risk taking and testing themselves, and those who have a need for self-affirmation. At the same time, among sexually active youths one is more likely to

encounter boys and girls who are not fully autonomous, who are suscepti-
ble to dares and the contagious example of those around them. As many as
52% of them agreed that "Sometimes I allow others to talk me into doing
something I know I really shouldn't do." Some 10% fewer virgins agreed
with that statement.

A love of risk and a heightened dependence on the opinions of those
around one would seem to be contradictory traits. Yet such behaviors
depend on whom a person considers a model, on whose opinion prevails.
Thus, 43% of sexually experienced teenagers said they "sometimes do
something on purpose to shock their parents or other adults, just for fun."
The virgins acted thus more rarely: only 31% of them subjected their parents to shock tactics. However, dependence on the opinion of other teens
could become slavish dependence on one's peers. This is evident in more
than attitudes about sex. An adventurous turn of mind and a tendency
toward risk taking, together with a heightened dependence on those
around them, make many sexually active teenagers difficult for teachers
and parents.

It is not simply that teachers and parents invariably take a circumspect
attitude toward teenage sex, and even more so, toward teenage love, seeing dangers lurking in both. Judging by our 1993 findings, sexually active
teenagers did slightly less well in school than their peers: slightly more
than half of them received predominantly good and/or excellent grades,
whereas more than two- thirds of the virgins earned such grades. The sexually experienced were also more likely to violate school rules, finding
themselves two and a half times more likely to be removed from class
activities for disciplinary reasons (10% against 4%); only half of them had
not skipped class during the month previous to the survey, whereas only a
third of students with less sexual experience had done so. This is hardly
surprising, since the more sexually experienced students generally
reported valuing education less and were 10% less likely to be planning to
continue studies at the university level. However, there was no difference
in the way members of the two groups assessed the importance of marriage and family happiness; and success in a career was even more important to the sexually advanced than to the less experienced. Thus, in some
respects, the sexually advanced appeared to be more grown up than their
more complaisant peers.

An earlier initiation into sexuality is statistically related to earlier and
heavier smoking, drinking, and drug use. Nine out of ten sexually active
16-year-olds had already smoked their first cigarettes; in fact, three out of

four of them were now regular smokers. The respective figures for their virginal peers were 62% and 36%. Nine out of ten of those who had tried sex had also been drunk at least once (the figure was one in two for the sexually inexperienced); almost a third of sexually active teenagers had also tried drugs (the figure for drug use was five times higher among them than among their inexperienced peers).

The sexually active believed that their friends conducted themselves in the same way. To the question "Do many of your friends take drugs or drink alcohol?" 51% of the sexually active and only 25% of the sexually inexperienced students answered "the majority" or "practically all." It would seem that adult concern about the connection between early sexual activity and substance abuse is not groundless.

Unfavorable social circumstances, particularly family circumstances, often stand behind this sociopsychological syndrome. Among teenagers with early sexual experience, a little more than half grew up in one-parent families. The educational level and social status of their parents, particularly of their fathers, were somewhat lower than average. The percentage who had fathers without a regular job was almost three times greater among them (11% as opposed to 4% for virgins). These teens reported that it was less possible for them to have a frank talk about sexual problems with their parents. As many as 43% of virgins and only 35% of experienced 16-year-olds agreed in one way or another with the statement "I think I can talk to my parents about sex"; 45% of sexually advanced and 33% of their less adventurous peers, respectively, gave a categorical "no" to that statement.

It is scarcely worth mentioning the effectiveness of family sex education in Russia, since, to all intents and purposes, it does not exist. According to our findings, more than two-thirds of parents have never talked to their children about sex, while those who claim to have mentioned the subject have done so only once or twice. In addition, the children themselves are either unwilling to raise the subject or are very indirect when they do so. Over the year prior to the survey, 67% of girls and 77% of boys had never raised the issue at all. It is hardly surprising, then, that to the question "To what extent do your sexual principles and views on sexuality coincide with those of your parents?" over half of the teens replied that they did not know, while 38% of 16- to 17-year-olds were certain that their views sharply diverged from those of their parents.

The schools are as "guiltless" as the families on the subject of sexual enlightenment. A small number (17% ) of students in the two major capital cities obtained some information from minimal classroom instruction (one or two classes); the rest had no access to sex education.[12]

It is interesting to note the distinction made by teens in Lunin's survey in evaluating the "veracity" and "accessibility" of various sources of sex information. Teens tended to put high value on the veracity of information from parents (56%), considering it second only to that found in medical literature—which, however, was the least accessible. Friends were the most accessible source (named by 80% of respondents) but were considered the least reliable. After friends, the most accessible sources of information were videos (named by 72%), fiction (65%), and erotic magazines (53%). Teenagers did not give high marks to the reliability of this information, but most of them had little choice but to accept it when available.[13]

Given the long public conspiracy of silence, the peer group plays a decisive and overarching role in shaping the normative orientation of teenagers; it is their peers who frequently encourage teenagers to experiment with sexual initiation early. Although the Moscow/St. Petersburg 1993 survey showed that 44% of girls and 39% of boys claimed they did not know whether their views on sex coincides with those of their fellow students, 35% of girls and 45% of boys believed them to be identical or very similar. With increasing age, this perceived similarity of views increased from 35% among teens under age 14 to 60% among the 16- to 17-year-olds. This perceived coincidence was particularly great with the sexually active, 65% of whom believed that others feel very much as they do.

In responding to the direct question, the overwhelming majority of teens (78% of those under 14, and 86% of 16- to 17-year-olds) denied the existence of peer pressure toward an earlier start to their sex lives. All the same, such pressure does exist and is fairly strong. When asked "whether your friends would approve of or condemn persons your age for having sex," 11% of 16-year-old virgins said their friends would condemn them, 46% said they would neither condemn them nor support them, and 42% said they would be supportive. The figures were 4%, 30%, and 67%, respectively, among sexually experienced youngsters.

Teens are generally inclined to exaggerate the sexual experience of their friends and classmates. Although only 36% of the 16- to 17-year-olds in the 1993 adolescent survey reported having sexual experience themselves, when asked "Roughly how many of your friends have had sex?" 15% answered "about half," 16% "more than half," and about the same answered "practically all of them." This aberration was even more pronounced among the sexually experienced: fewer than 1% said that "none has had," 21% said "under half," 18% said "roughly half," 26% said "over whalf," and 33% said "practically all." Igor Lunin obtained an almost identical picture: almost 49% of his sample believed that the majority of teens their age already had had sexual experience.

So the teenagers themselves are just as unreliable "experts" in this delicate matter as their teachers and parents. A false assessment of the peer group "norm" encourages the teenager to engage in risky sexual and other experiments so as not to lag behind the others. Of course, teenagers everywhere worry about being sexually and socially backward, but this illusion looms larger when so little information is available.

Do teenagers possess moral convictions by which to measure their actions? They certainly do. But as with adults, and as at all times, those convictions are contradictory, and far from being consistently implemented in behavior. Some 41% of girls and 29% of boys claimed they accord considerable importance to religion; 46% of girls and 23% of boys asserted that premarital sex runs counter to their convictions. Yet among 16- to 17-year-olds, when the question changed from theory to practice, only 21% held this view, while 60% disagreed.

The attitudes and views of teenagers are frequently more radical than their behavior. Adults consider teenage sex dangerous behavior that deviates from the norm. Yet the teens themselves do not share this view; they think their sexual behavior is the norm. And if only a relatively few have any sexual experience, it clearly depends more on their life circumstances than on their moral principles.

Here we find big gender differences. As many as 46% of boys and 36% of girls fully agreed that "It is unrealistic to think that teenagers should refrain from sex"; 53% of boys and 36% of girls saw nothing wrong in premarital sexual relations as long as the young people love each other. "One should relate to sexual relations as an entirely normal and expected part of going steady," said 36% of boys and 21% of girls surveyed (56% and 37%, respectively, among the sexually experienced 16-year-olds).

Gender differences in attitudes reflect the traditional asymmetry of male and female sex roles, norms, and upbringing, as well as the fact that an unhappy and premature sexual initiation may have more serious consequences for girls than boys. For boys, sex means largely gratification; girls demand something more.

In response to the question "If you have never had sex or if you are consciously abstaining from it now, why are you doing so?" respondents selected answers from a prepared list of replies. The results are shown in Table 11.1.

**Table 11.1**

| Answers | Girls Responding (%) | Boys Responding (%) |
|---|---|---|
| It is against my religious principles | 9.9 | 5.4 |
| I don't find it particularly attractive | 20.0 | 9.3 |
| I'm afraid of the possibility of pregnancy | 31.5 | 17.4 |
| I dont want to catch AIDS of some other sexually transmitted disease | 40.9 | 30.7 |
| I haven't found a suitable partner | 13.5 | 26.0 |
| I haven't had the opportunity | 7.7 | 20.4 |
| It would make me feel uneasy | 14.7 | 7.9 |
| It seems morally wrong | 13.7 | 6.4 |
| I don't feel ready for it | 26.0 | 13.9 |
| I don't want to upset my parents | 15.9 | 7.7 |
| I don't want someone using me for his/her own pleasure | 25.7 | 8.1 |
| Other | 4.6 | 5.3 |
| No answer | 8.4 | 19.0 |

Their reasons appear to be rather pragmatic. Moral—"Why I shouldn't have sex"—and psychological—"Why I don't want to have sex"—considerations take a backseat to more practical concerns—"Why I'm afraid of having sex" and "What's stopping me?"

The first and strongest motive for abstinence for both sexes, and particularly pronounced with girls, is fear of contracting AIDS or other sexually transmitted diseases. Other motives vary among boys and girls. Girls are apprehensive about unwanted pregnancy, feel unprepared for sex, do not wish to become the object of sexual exploitation, or simply do not find sex sufficiently alluring. Boys are more likely to refer to the lack of a suitable partner, and then, in descending order, to unfavorable circumstances, lack of opportunity, and fear of impregnating their partner. Moral considerations, parental disapproval, and emotional discomfort are all mentioned twice as often by girls as by boys. More than twice as many boys as girls gave no answer to this question.

On the whole, today's teenagers are less afraid of sex than were teens of their parents' and grandparents' generations, although many of them know that early sexual experience is fraught with serious problems and dangers. However, they do not believe that early sexual experience is substantially likely to undermine their long-term chances of getting a good education, finding a successful professional career, or achieving future family happiness. This is particularly the case with older teens. There is no sense in trying to scare or threaten them; times are changing.

The type of sexual culture that has come to light in the 1993 adolescent survey is much like the situation that prevailed in the United States in the early 1970s. There an early start to sexual life also correlated with poor school performance, conflicts with parents, involvement in criminal groups, stealing, car theft, smoking, drinking, and drug use.[14] Yet sexual activity per se was not the cause of antisocial behavior. Behind the statistical correlations were the contours of a certain type of youth subculture wherein teenagers saw in early sexual activity, smoking, drinking, and experimenting with drugs the signs of growing up and acquiring independence of older people, primarily parents. But these phenomena are qualitatively different.

As soon as adult society stops stigmatizing teenage sexuality and begins to relate calmly to it, helping teenagers obtain the necessary knowledge for a safe and normal life, the link between early sexual experience and deviant conduct will weaken and perhaps even disappear altogether.

This is precisely what is happening today in Western Europe.[15] In comparison with 20 or 25 years ago, teenage sexuality is no longer a forbidden subject; it is no longer tied in with deviant behavior (the only exceptions are street gangs). The marked rapid fall in the age of sexual initiation typical of the previous two decades has practically come to an end, stabilizing, for about half of teenagers, at age 16. Today's youths are less dependent not only on their parents, who are compelled to recognize their sons' independence in the matter, but also on their own sexual impulses and peer pressure: the first sexual experience, with all its psychological import, has to some extent lost its significance as a symbolic frontier that, when crossed, turns a boy into a man. Inasmuch as sex has become more accessible, young men are aspiring not only and not so much to sex as to stable and psychologically intimate relationships. Thus, to a certain extent, there is a return to the values of romantic love.[16]

Similar, though less marked, changes are taking place among females. Girls now show more initiative and control over their sexual relations; at the same time, they often obtain less satisfaction from them. Differences in sexual behavior and attitudes of boys and girls, which sharply diminished during the previous period, remain roughly at that level. These shifts do not depend on the educational level of teenagers and are not the result of the AIDS epidemic, for which, alas, teenagers show little concern. It is simply that the "free sex" of the 1990s is engaged in less aggressively and more judiciously.

This has taken place, however, only where adult society possesses a fairly high and tolerant sexual culture. The United States has seen conservative forces in the late 1960s try to halt the sexual revolution through bans and threats, maintaining in particular that sex education was "a dirty Communist plot to undermine the spiritual health of American youth." Now American society is having to pay for its delay in enlightenment with teenage pregnancies, abortions, and sexual violence unprecedented in scope in the Western world.

What will happen in Russia depends on the Russians themselves. No one is capable of halting the processes of liberation and secularization of sexuality, despite certain temporary costs associated with them. But if the country continues the nonsensical Bolshevik-style sexophobia now camouflaged in religious-moral rhetoric, abandoning teenagers to their problems even as they are subjected to the burgeoning industries of pornography and primitive eroticism, the costs will be long-term and enormous.

That much is apparent already. The most worrying aspect of contemporary teenage sex is that it is often not voluntary. Every fourth girl and every tenth boy in our 1993 survey reported having experienced some sort of sexual coercion, with someone forcing them to go further than they had wanted. Fifty-eight percent of boys who answered thus also reported finding the experience sexually exciting and going along with what was wanted of them. Most of the girls, by contrast, said their reaction was negative: they had said nothing or had changed the subject, or gave an unequivocal "no" in response; as a result, two-thirds of them had been able to retain their virginity.

As is obvious, however, they are not always able to affect the outcome of such an encounter. In Igor Lunin's 1992 Petersburg pilot research, 25% of girls and 12% of boys said they had been victims of sexual harassment or violence; and 10% of boys and 1% of girls recognized that they themselves had compelled another to have sexual contact against their will. Forty-four percent of girls and 30% of boys said they personally knew other people who had been raped. For many, the very first sexual experience was associated with violence.

For many Russian teenagers, rape is a very normal occurrence:

Olga, Moscow: "This summer I went away to the countryside; that's where it all happened. I was raped. I didn't cry out while it was being done, though it was painful. The boy said that if I resisted he would call three of his friends. I suppose it's my own fault. I was wearing a tight mini-skirt and blouse, and lots of make-up; I wanted to look cool. Now I'm pregnant. I'm so sorry for my mother; she still doesn't know, though I'm already two months along. I won't have an abortion; I just can't bring myself to kill a living being inside me."

Larissa, age 14, Novosibirsk district: "My boyfriend called, as usual, to take me to the cinema. Afterwards he took me home. On the way a taxi drew up and three fellows jumped out: one of them gave some money to my boyfriend, right in front of me. Then two of them forced me into the car. All the while, my boyfriend stood by, smiling at me, holding the wad of ruble notes in his hand. I realized that he simply sold me."

Boy, age 17, Samara: "Our dormitory is co-ed, so you can imagine what goes on there in the evenings. Constant drinking and depravity. Many times older students have attempted to seduce me: at first they brought me the girls, then they openly tried to screw me. I came here to study, but this is practically impossible under such conditions."

In criminalized areas and social milieus that are becoming increasingly common in the devastated country, girls frequently have no choice: "You enter a store and a whole gang—about seven guys—between 14 and 19 descend on you; without ceremony they order you to follow them. And then they take turns. . . . "

Once a girl becomes "common property," there is no way back. This is what 15-year-old Masha had to say when asked if she had enjoyed it: "No, nor do I like it now." "But couldn't you refuse their humiliating proposal?" "It was impossible. Once you refuse it's worse. . . . You end up getting raped by several of them."

Sometimes the first episode is voluntary, but then the situation changes. A 15-year-old gave herself to a 19-year-old youth out of love, after which he "gave" her to all the other members of his group: "They dragged me with them. If I refused, they would take me by force. Then came the next step: the whole gang assembled for what they called 'a show.' I had no idea what it was then, but now I do: it's hell. The 'show' would take place in some cellar in a house out of town. I was taken there by force along with two other girls. They said, 'If you don't come, we'll kill you.'"

Journalistic descriptions of what happens in such gangs, as well as letters from the victims themselves, paint a pretty awful picture. Yet some youngsters do not believe the victims are innocent. Among Lunin's St. Petersburg tenth graders, 8% of girls and 19% of boys felt that "If a woman is raped, she must have given good cause for it"; 22% of girls and 26% of boys felt sure that "if someone resists, she cannot be raped," and more than half of teens agreed that "a woman who wears too short a skirt risks being raped."

Such are the fruits of Soviet education. Today's Russian teenagers find themselves at risk—to themselves and to those around them. But there is nothing sensational or extraordinary about their sexuality. The phenomena that look shocking and unacceptable to their parents and grandparents are in part simply the coming to light of what was earlier kept under wraps and in part the continuation and strengthening of some trends that were characteristic, although to a lesser extent, for their elders.

*Chapter Twelve*

# DANGEROUS SEX: RAPE, PROSTITUTION, AND SEXUALLY TRANSMITTED DISEASES

*More than once I've tried to figure out why our men find it shameful to give a young woman, say, 300 rubles for having a good time. Right away, they get indignant, claiming they can have it for free. What I'd like to do is to call upon all the girls in Kazan not to give themselves freely, to retain some sense of their own dignity!*
                    —Letter to the press from a female student at Kazan University

*I have a request of all girls. Don't ruin us boys!!! We don't want to go to jail for "rape"! These days it's terrible even to make a date: first you agree to fuck, then you report us to the police. What a nightmare! P.S. This is my second week in jail.*
                    —Roman, age 18, Sebastopol

This is what happened when 15-year-old Tania and 17-year-old Inna went to the cinema one evening:

Inna:     We went to the "Slava" Cinema and bought tickets for "The Curse of the Serpent." Some boys came and sat next to us, two about seventeen, one called Chek, the other Khaba, and two

210

about fourteen or fifteen, Bychok and Golova. . . . We watched the film together. Then they suggested we take a walk with them and stop on the way to take a look at their gym—a sort of basement where they do weight-lifting. Like fools, we agreed. Chek and Khaba seemed decent sorts, not louts. Bychok and Golova were just kids. . . . Then Khaba went off for a moment and came back with two bottles of wine, saying we had to toast the occasion of our meeting. . . . After that they took us into the basement. For some reason, they had no weights or dumbbells there. All they had was an old sofa in a tiny remote room with a steel door. They took Tania there, while Chek stopped me, saying, "It's like this, Inna: we didn't bring you here to show off our weights but to rape you."

Tania:     They sat me on the sofa, Bychok to my left, Golova to my right. Khaba stood in front of me, asking me whom I liked best. I realized something was wrong, yet I couldn't say anything. . . . Meanwhile, Khaba was telling me he fancied me. I said he was crazy, but he kept on saying he wanted me. Bychok muttered that I should do it with him. While that was going on, Golova, that little snot, was fumbling around under my coat. I put up a fight, though he was telling me to take my hands off him before he got nasty. . . . I was very upset, crying and begging them not to ruin my life; Khaba was telling me no one had ever gotten off scot-free before . . . I began to scream and beg, at which point Khaba told me he would leave me in one piece as long as I played ball. Despite my cries, he said they would take me by force. He counted to three and when I still resisted, he threatened to punch me in the face and kick me."[1]

Rape is not new. In the 1960s, rape constituted 90 to 95% of all Soviet sex offenses. That percentage remained the same in 1988.[2] But the absolute figures are rising. There has been a 60% increase since 1961, and since 1986 the increase has been 21.3%. While 17,658 rapes and attempted rapes were officially registered in the USSR in 1988, the number increased to 22,469 in 1990. According to official police statistics, the largest increase in registered cases of rape and attempted rape in Russia was in 1989 (14,597 cases, up 26.3% from the previous year). In the following two years, the number of cases of rape decreased somewhat, from 15,010 in 1990 to 13,653 in 1992. Yet in 1993, there was another increase:

14,414 rapes and attempted rapes were registered, a 5.7% increase. About a quarter of these crimes were committed by 14- to 17-year-olds and more than half by men between the ages of 18 and 29.[3]

When compared with American reports, these statistics seem insignificant: the United States has nearly 100,000 cases of rape and attempted rape reported each year—several times the frequency of rape in England, Germany, and France.[4] Alas, we have to remember the following:

First, the Russian Federation has seen a high rate of increase in sexual violence and rape in the last 30 years.

Second, rape statistics are unreliable everywhere. Russian criminal statistics are even less reliable than American or Western European figures. Most recorded rapes are those that place on the street and gang rapes, while date rape and marital rape remain largely unpunished and unrecorded in criminal statistics.

Third, the average age of sex offenders and rapists is dropping rapidly (this is also true of the age of the victims) and the abuse is becoming more vicious.

Fourth, in most cases, neither the victim nor the rapist receives any professional psychiatric or psychological counseling in Russia.

Fifth, whereas the rising number of rapes had been concealed from the public in Soviet times, those cases are widely and even sensationally exposed in the mass media today, which provokes a state of fear and panic in people. And the statistics themselves are becoming the subject of political manipulation.

As noted, the rapists are generally very young men. The most dangerous age is 16–17, yet the number of 14- and 15-year-old and even younger rapists is growing. In terms of their social backgrounds, about half of rapists in the early 1990s were laborers, 7% peasants, 15% students, 1.3% white-collar workers, and 24% without specific occupation. Every second registered rape was a gang rape; among minors, gang rapes accounted for 80% of the crimes. Every third rapist convicted already had a criminal record, and two-thirds of them were drunk at the time of the attack.

Among rape victims nine-tenths were women under the age of 25, of whom 46% were under 18; 70% had already had sexual experience; 55% had been drinking prior to the crime; 25% were "good-time girls" (prostitutes); 15% had been sexually assaulted on a previous occasion; 40% were raped in the victim's or rapist's home, which indicates acquaintance.[5] The number of victims who had known their assailants was 52% in 1983, but had grown to 73% by 1988.[6]

Russian public opinion is very divided on the issue of "date" or "acquaintance" rape. Women demand stronger punishment for all rapists, but men, bringing up other issues such as the controversial American cases involving Mike Tyson and William Kennedy Smith, strongly object to the very notion of "date rape," saying it gives women unlimited possibilities for blackmail; if a woman voluntarily goes to a man's apartment, she must be ready to take full responsibility for anything that may happen there. As Nikolai Popov writes in the popular weekly magazine *Stolitsa*: "If he beat her or robbed her—bring him to court; if he killed her—execute him! But don't transform a male into a law-abiding impotent. Every man is by nature an initiator of sex—that is, a rapist."[7]

The question is a difficult one. Every Russian girl or woman who takes part in a drunken party knows perfectly well what will probably happen afterward. A young man who does not make sexual advances in such a situation may lose his reputation for "manliness" not only among his pals but among the girls as well—and this is not an exclusively Russian phenomenon. Yet the idea that a woman has no right to change her mind is dangerous—as is the equation of sexual advance with rape.

According to some St. Petersburg sociological data, young women are often victims of sexual coercion. Marital rape is especially widespread in the working class and among student families. Some 38.5% of women surveyed complained about sexual harassment outside their families, mainly at work; about a quarter of them have been raped. About 7.5% of women report having been forced into their first sexual contact, and the researchers believe this is a gross underestimation.[8]

Communist and conservative lawyers and pundits explain the rise in sexual violence and rape by pointing to the overall decline in morals and especially to the liberalization of sexual morality. In fact, however, this phenomenon is part and parcel of the country's social situation and low sexual culture. The socioeconomic, political, and spiritual crises that the country is now experiencing invariably cause a rise in crime and violence. Sexual violence is just one manifestation.

Another aspect of the problem—well recognized in the West yet underestimated in Russia—is the prevalence of sexist psychology and the widespread cult of aggressive masculinity, which turns primarily to physical force when seeking a solution to any conflict. This is more or less a universal problem. Male sexuality often contains elements of real or conditional aggression: the man must "take" or "conquer" the woman; any resistance she offers only excites him. Fantasies of this kind are broadly represented in male, especially adolescent, erotic imagination. As Leo Tolstoy once put it, "When a sixteen-year-old boy reads about the rape of the heroine of a novel, it does not produce indignant emotions in him. He will not put himself in the role of the victim but will involuntarily take on the role of the seducer and enjoy a sense of sweet satisfaction."[9]

A few decades ago, when the USSR still had no erotic literature, a group of students was asked which artistic works most excited their erotic imagination. First prize went to the group rape scene in Mikhail Sholokhov's *And Quiet Flows the Don*. Yet it contains no sexual detail and is not remotely titillating.

The undermining of traditional gender stratification obscures and makes problematic the usual standards and regulations of gender relations. In men who are weak and uncertain of themselves, a loss of traditional gender privileges may evoke a protest that spills over specifically into sexual aggression and violence as the only possible means of affirming or proving to others—and even more important, to themselves—their own masculinity. This situation is very acute in Russia, as we have seen.

Typically, the psychological profiles of rapists obtained by the criminologist Yuri Antonyan and his colleagues through standard psychological tests are very similar to those that Western researchers provide. Antonyan finds that 61% of convicted rapists are psychologically healthy (16% are psychopaths, 9% are chronic alcoholics, and 7% are mentally retarded).[10] Their sex-role premises and their attitudes toward women are, however, unusual. They perceive women as representatives of a hostile, aggressive, and dominating force in relation to which they experience a sense of passivity and dependence. From a psychological point of view, sexual aggression and rape are often a manifestation of male "adolescent rebellion" against women in general. The rapist's priority is the humiliation and oppression of women, rather than the gratification of sexual needs. Most such men do not regard women as individuals, as potential sexual partners, or even as human beings. Instead, an individual woman is perceived as a member of the hated class of females in general. Such variables as age and attractiveness have no substantial importance for such a rapist.

Very often, a desire to settle a score with a dominant or cold mother underlies violent behavior. Rapists will say, "Mother never showed me any love; I felt that my grandmother loved me much more than my mother did"; "I was obedient, yet my mother punished me undeservedly; she hit me and never brought me presents, although she brought them for my brother"; "My mother and I never had a trusting relationship; she loved my sister more"; "My mother was very strict, and she never forgave me anything," and so on.[11]

Sexual violence, as we have already seen, is a normative element in many youth subcultures. And when rape takes place in this milieu, it is often difficult for the victim to find someone to complain to—the police do not want to investigate such cases, and conservative public opinion blames the victim.

Sexual violence frequently has its roots in authoritarian-style family upbringing, which reflects the overall style of human relations in Russian society as a whole. Family discipline, despite family-to-family differences, is everywhere closely associated with the general principles of social discipline. If society encourages the principle of the popular Soviet proverb "If I'm the boss, you're a fool; if you're the boss, I'm a fool," then children, who are always subordinate (although they also tend to be cunning, with an ability to exploit and deceive those in charge) are not trained to become autonomous or self-directed. Hence the love of firm discipline. What is more, children are the most accessible and defenseless victims of all adult frustrations and obsessions.

As in other countries, public statements and real educational practices in Russia are often at odds. Both Soviet pedagogical theory and the officially reported public opinion polls have always categorically opposed corporal punishment. When the 1992 VCIOM survey asked the question "Is corporal punishment of children permissible?" only 16% of Russian citizens said "yes" while 58% firmly answered "no." Russians seem to be more liberal than other nations of the former USSR: among Estonians 24% agreed with the idea of corporal punishment, among Latvians, 29% agreed, and among Uzbeks, 39%.

But everyday practices are different.

In the mid-1980s, the journalist Nikolai Filippov conducted an anonymous survey of 7,500 children between the ages of 9 and 15 in 15 cities.[12] He found that 60% of parents used corporal punishment in bringing up their children: 86% used flogging as punishment, 9% stood their children in the corner (some stood them on their knees on bricks, salt, or peas), and 5% hit them in the head or face. Sometimes the punishment for juvenile misdeeds was hard to distinguish from such brutality as stripping the child in front of others and administering a beating with a stick on his or her private parts.

According to Russian Children's Fund statistics, in 1989 more than

2,000 children in Russia tried to commit suicide because of abuse in the family.[13] Some 80 children are admitted to Moscow hospitals every year with serious injuries received from criminal parental actions. In the five years prior to 1992, the police uncovered over 1,500 case of infanticide by mothers. Because of the ongoing political disarray, current statistics are unavailable.

It is interesting that many children, both those who were beaten and those who were not, regard this kind of upbringing as normal and intend to use corporal punishment on their own children:

> Ten-year-old Kolya (boy): "What punishment is it without the strap?. . . . You must be firm with kids, not mollycoddle them."
> Nine-year-old Anya (girl), with a crafty smile: "Of course I'll hit my kids as Mother does me; they won't be any better than me."
> Eleven-year-old Vova (boy): "I get the strap every Monday, Wednesday, and Friday. I'll hit my child every day."
> Fourteen-year-old Roman (boy): "I don't often get hit, but when I do, it's good and hard. I will certainly beat my own son or daughter, though you should use only the strap so as not to break the child's spine."

And corporal punishment often has its sexual aspects, which the generations also pass along.

Discussion of incest, rape, and sexual abuse of children was absolutely taboo in the Soviet Union for many decades. There are no reliable statistics on these subjects at all, but it is certain that such cases were not at all unusual.

In a 1993 survey of adolescents, 6% of those younger than 14 and more than 27% of the 16- to 17-year-olds said they had experienced some sort of sexual pressure—someone pushed them to go further sexually than they themselves would have liked. The police statistics in this area are absolutely unreliable. Of the 333 persons (predominantly female, about half of them younger than 18) who called the St. Petersburg Help Center for Rape Victims in 1992, only 4 reported their cases to the police. In 1993, from 785 applicants, only 37 informed the police. The reasons for this widespread unwillingness to inform the authorities are as follows:

1. Fear of the psychological trauma of investigation and trial.
2. Fear of the loss of privacy, of the story getting out to schoolmates and acquaintances.

3. Doubts about the efficacy of legal help.
4. Fear for personal safety.

Unfortunately, all these fears are quite justified. Even when the victims are children, police are often unwilling to open a criminal investigation case or even to initiate a medical examination. In the present criminal situation where often even political assassinations go unprosecuted, who can bother with child abuse or rape?

And the consequences of rape are serious. In addition to rape trauma syndrome, 83 victims in the St. Petersburg group were impregnated and/or infected with a sexually transmitted disease. Almost all of them were anxious about the possibility of infection with the human immunovirus (HIV).

We do not know the abuser in most of these cases. Very often the culprit is an older adolescent. But parents and other family members are also possibilities.

A few years ago while on holiday in the Crimea, I was asked with some urgency to come to the Artek Pioneer Camp. The head of one of the Pioneer packs, an intelligent 45-year-old man, said something unusual had been going on; from his garbled explanation—he was too shy to call a spade a spade—I could not gather exactly what the problem was. Only when he let me read letters of explanation from the main character in the affair, a 14-year-old boy who had since returned home, did all become clear. The boy had initiated a diverse series of sexual games, forcing or persuading almost half his pack to join in. The boys who were on the losing side had to suck the penises and lick the feet of the winners, eat their feces, dance in threes in a circle with their penises tied together and sticks in their anuses, and so on. Sometimes this action was undertaken voluntarily, and sometimes not. The boys also went in pairs into the girls' dormitory, got into bed with a girl, and did anything that came into their heads. The girls squealed yet actually put up no resistance. Finally, someone made a complaint, following which the director received the letters of explanation that he showed me. In contrast with the adult's uncomfortable indirectness, the boy's explanation was perfectly clear.

Knowing something about adolescent sexuality, I was not particularly surprised at the games, but I assumed that the boy behind it all had learned them in an orphanage, where such things are common. "You're wrong," I was told and then was handed a second batch of letters. It turned out that the boy had learned all this behavior, and much more besides, first from his father, and then from his mother and elder sister, who practiced it, sometimes individually and sometimes as a group. Initiation was by force and was accompanied by beatings; then the boy became accustomed to it and began to obtain pleasure from it, which is how he happened to bring this experience into the camp. The camp director told me that now there were many such families, though he himself had never come across them earlier.

Child abuse in the family setting often leads to sexual violence. A *SPID-info* correspondent was told the following by 15-year-old Igor, who had been convicted under Article 117 of the criminal code—rape:

> It's a common story. My parents used to hit the bottle and occasionally gave me a drop when I was about 11. One time I woke up and felt someone kissing my prick. I found it was Auntie Galya, Dad's sister. I was dumb-founded.
>
> "What are you up to, Auntie Galya?" I asked. She was absolutely stewed. She said she wanted to make a man of me. Well, what could I do? At first, nothing came of it, but later, early in the morning, I managed to get it up. She was content, even praising me: "We'll make a decent man of you yet." And she invited me to come to visit her that evening.

The relationship with his aunt lasted a month before her partner returned. The nephew then got his walking papers; but what was he to do now that he had had a taste for it? A few days later he suggested to his friend Volodka that they might "try some girls." They looked around and found a young girl, Tania, following her home to an empty flat. But she told them she would not have sex without a condom.

> We didn't have a condom, but we decided to do it anyway. . . . Tania put up a struggle at first. But Volodka's a pretty tough cookie; he pinned her down and we got down to business. Then we discovered that Tania hadn't had it before; she screamed and swore at us until I shut her mouth for her. Anyway, we both gave her a good stuffing. Volodka warned her not to tell anyone or she'd be in big trouble. That evening, we were still feeling randy, so we grabbed another girl in a vacant lot by the student hostel and did her too.

The boys were arrested the next morning.[14]

In the reform schools or junior penal colonies, such boys are usually raped without pity themselves—after which they forfeit all human rights and become "degraded," required to submit to anything others demand of them. In a medicosociological investigation of 246 male convicts regis-tered by the camp's administration as having had homosexual contacts, one out of every two said he had already been raped in the preliminary confinement cell, 39% were raped on their way to the penal colony, and 11% in the camp itself.[15] Most of these men had had no previous homosexual experience, but after this tragic event they have practically no choice.

Here is a description of one such *opushchennyi* (degraded one) in the Moscow daily *Moskovksy komsomolets*:

> I was told he wouldn't speak to me. But he did. He was a short, pleasant-looking youth who looked no worse for the black overalls he wore and the short crew-cut that left him virtually bald. He had just turned sixteen. Eight months inside so far; three years total sentence. He was arrested for pick pocketing. He had no friends in the colony and was completely alone. It never dawned on anyone to share a cake sent from home or sweets brought by relatives. He would smoke a cigarette, but no one would ask him for a light. He was "degraded." His cellmates in the interrogation room picked on him. "There were five of them in the hut [camp jargon for the pretrial prison cell], three done for 117 [rape], and two adults. They closed the peephole in the door. After the third blow I passed out. Then it happened. . . . What could I do?"
>
> "How long were you there?"
>
> "Three and a half days."
>
> "But couldn't you call for help, ask to be taken to another cell?"
>
> "No. There's no point. The prison has its 'internal telephone.' The moment they sent me here, the word went round the prison yards. . . . "
>
> "How are you getting on now?"
>
> "OK at the moment. I still get dirty looks; no one says hello. Still, I haven't been beaten up again."
>
> "Have you told anyone about your troubles?"
>
> "No, the detachment chief said they know all about it. They knew from the hut who's next on the list, and they passed it on."

Usually the "degraded" feel themselves outcast in the fullest sense, and nobody can help them. Otherwise he will have the same fate. Now it is shown even in the movies such as *Bespredel* (*Without Limits*).

The rape of men and boys is a considerable problem in itself. According to a criminological text by Yuri Antonyan and Sofia Pozdnyakova, 36.3% of all women who were raped were underage at the time of the attack; the remainder were adult.[16] On the other hand, 80% of all raped men were underage; 35% of them were younger than 12 years of age at the time. Generally, these figures are similar to U.S. statistics: male victims are younger than females. Sometimes this is interpreted as proof of the particular dangers of homosexual violence against children and adolescents. But such conclusions are based mainly on criminal statistics. However awful their experience, men who have been raped usually prefer not to go to the police for fear of the publicity, which is worse for them than for women. After reporting such an experience, they fear, everyone will think they are homosexual. That is why criminal statistics cite such low figures for adult male rape. The "male rape" that it knows is predominantly what takes place in prisons, camps, and the army. Generally speaking, the term "homosexual rape" is very inaccurate in that it associates with individual sexual orientation what in most cases is determined by the circumstances and regulated by the rules of the particular subculture.[17]

It would, of course, be ridiculous to blame the spread of sexual violence in any of its forms simply on the Soviet regime; such violence exists everywhere. Yet the situation in the Soviet Union was influenced by something that did not exist anywhere else, at least not on so grand a scale—the system of prisons and camps through which millions of people passed. Certain problems could be traced as well to the armed forces.

Russian prison customs have always been extremely cruel. This cruelty, which often has sexual connotations, is not only condoned but is sometimes even initiated by the administrators. In October 1993, in the Far Eastern town Sovetskaya Gavan, a young man was falsely accused of the rape and murder of two adolescent girls. After heavy beating and torture by the police officers, he "acknowledged" committing the crime. But because investigators knew that he had an alibi, he was sent to another prison, where he was killed by criminals incarcerated there, rather than being sent to court. The newspaper *Izvestiya* (December 14, 1993) reported that he was found with a wire stuck into his penis and a stake in his anus. After the story ran, several senior officers of the Far Eastern police and the public prosecutor's officer were dismissed and were supposed to have been tried, but the trial never took place and the accused were set free.

I have already mentioned the category of the "degraded," whose position is even worse than that of the "*pidors*" (from the Russian for pederast) and "*vaflers*" (from *vaflya*, "wafer")—that is, the voluntarily "passive" homosexuals. To a certain extent the latter themselves choose their partners and patrons (performance of an active, "male" sexual role in a criminal environment is not stigmatized), while the former are at the mercy of everyone.[18] It is interesting that this division of homosexuals into "active" and "passive," depending on their preferred sexual positions, continues today in the Russian medical literature, and some Russian psychiatrists still associate "passivity" with "inborn" or "true" homosexuality and the "active role" with "acquired" homosexuality.

Prison and camp sexual symbolism, language, and rituals, closely connected with hierarchical relations of power, domination, and subordination, are more or less stable and universal. In the criminal community any rape—real or symbolic (such as is involved with the use of certain words or rituals)—is primarily a means of establishing or maintaining power relations. The victims, no matter how much they resist, forfeit their male dignity and prestige, while the violator enhances his. With any "change in power," the former bosses in their turn are abused and thereby sink irretrievably to the bottom of the hierarchy. Thus, such behavior is not at all a consequence of sexual orientation or even sexual deprivation but of social relationships of domination and subordination based on crude force and sanctifying the symbolic system, which is imposed on all newcomers and thus transmitted from generation to generation.

A similar, though slightly less vicious, system exists in women's camps, where the tough, mannish *kobly* ("male dogs," the Russian equivalent of "butches") who take on male names order about the *kovyryalki* ("picks," the Russian equivalent of "fems") dependent upon them. Their sexual roles are also irreversible. When male criminals somehow managed to break into a women's camp, their greatest glory was to rape a "butch," who was subsequently obliged by prison custom to commit suicide.

The actual state of affairs depended on the nature of the camp. In a "red" camp, where the administration holds power, prisoners could still find some defense. In a "black" camp, however, where criminals actually run the place themselves, vulnerable inmates are utterly defenseless. The prison or camp guards are practically impotent to change these relationships, even should they wish to do so; and they sometimes use them for their own ends.

An informer, a young man recruited by the KGB, said that when he would report to his superior on an act of rape that had either been committed or was being planned, the superior would say, "Sasha, what the hell does it matter? They're all the same to us, though we would, of course, like having more rape victims around since they come into contact with the administration quicker, and they work like packhorses, since there is nothing for them to do but drown themselves in hard work and seek our protection from the 'wolves.' So, sod the cocksuckers."[19] The threat of being "buggered" was always and still is frequently employed by interrogators and camp guards to obtain information they need from the prisoner or to recruit him.

Generally speaking, the mores of Soviet prisons and the rituals, language, and symbols common to them differ little from American or other penal institutions, yet Soviet prisons are far less comfortable than those in the West, so everything is even more vicious and terrifying.[20]

The view of the émigré authors Mikhail Stern and Mark Popovsky that homosexuality in Russia started exclusively with the Gulag, the national network of prison camps, is naive and ludicrous.[21] But the Gulag has no doubt been a breeding ground for all manner of violence, including sexual. And it was from the Gulag's criminal subculture, which permeated all facets of Soviet life, that certain particular habits have spread to the armed forces as well. For instance, there's the ritual of *dedovshchina*, or bullying— that is, the tyrannical power of "old sweats" over new recruits—which very frequently includes blatant or covert elements of sexual abuse. This was kept secret and categorically denied in the old days, but its existence has surfaced in recent times.[22]

Much is written and discussed about sexual violence in Russia today, especially when minors or children are involved, or when the violence is sadistic.[23] As a rule, however, the mass media only fan the flames of hatred for the perpetrators and demand stricter punishment for their crimes, saying nothing about psychological help for rape victims, much less the convicted rapists. They know nothing of the former and have no sympathy with the latter—"They ought to be executed, not mollycoddled" is the typical cry. Even the cruelest cases, for which capital punishment may be prescribed, are often reviewed by judges who have no special sexological expertise; it is sufficient that a psychiatrist, who may be—and often is—utterly illiterate sexologically, has pronounced the accused to be of sound mind.

Most cases of sexual psychopathology have little to do with the social system. But the way they are treated is very important. In the last 20 years, 80 serial killers have been examined by the Serbsky Psychiatric Institute in Moscow. One, a film mechanic, killed 14 women; another, an industrial worker and youth activist, killed 7 adolescents; a third, an emergency care physician, killed 7 women and 10 children; and so on. Most of these men have been sentenced and executed without undergoing a sexological examination. "Medical treatment of sexual perversion is unavailable in our country. We have a blind spot here," says Professor Boris Shostakovsky, the chief of the legal psychiatric examination services of the Serbsky Institute of Legal Psychiatry.[24]

Like sexual abuse, the existence of prostitution in the Soviet Union was officially denied for the most part up to the mid-1980s. Of course, a few "fallen women" with "heightened sexual appetites" had existed, but since the country officially had no poor people, prostitution did not, and could not, exist as a profession. A few legal experts and sociologists, particularly Georgians such as Professor Anzor Gabiani, had carried out research on the subject, but everything had been classified and printed under the "For Professional Use Only" rubric.[25]

The conspiracy of silence was broken when the newspaper *Moskovsky komsomolets* (November 18 and 21, 1986) published Yevgeny Dodolev's sensational piece, entitled *Interdevochka*, on the glamorous life led by prostitutes servicing foreign clients in exchange for foreign currency (*interdevochka*).[26]

According to Dodolev, one fair maiden, nicknamed "Flea," had amassed over a hundred thousand rubles—a lot of money at that time—during a five-year period. She had everything: a car, an apartment, luxurious furniture. Other articles, even more sensational, followed the first. And although they condemned prostitution on moral grounds, impoverished Soviet women living on meager wages and unable to purchase the expensive accoutrements of a fashionable life inevitably developed a burning envy of the *interdevochka* lifestyle.

An anonymous survey of senior high schoolers in Riga and Leningrad in 1989 found that prostitution for foreign currency had become one of the ten most prestigious professions. Another survey, carried out by *Literaturnaya gazeta* among Moscow schoolchildren and students at technical colleges, revealed that in a list of the most prestigious and lucrative positions, prostitutes shared ninth to eleventh places with managers and salespersons, ahead of journalists, diplomats, and taxi drivers, not to mention professors and academicians. One lady of the night told the journalist bluntly, "Tell me how much you can earn in a factory—a hundred rubles a month? And we make a hundred and fifty a day. On a good day we can even make a thousand!"

Of course, it soon came to light that the journalists, as always, had simplified matters. The *interdevochki*, or *putains*, working only for foreign currency were the elite, a tiny aristocracy; to get into their ranks required the right looks and measurements, the right qualifications, and, as everywhere, the right connections. Much more numerous were those prostitutes working for Soviet "wooden rubles" (as distinct from the gold of hard currency); those women risked far more, yet earned incomparably less. At the very bottom of the ladder were the down-and-outs who frequented railroad and subway stations, whom no one would envy. And of course, in addition to professional prostitutes there were also women who sold their bodies for extra income to buy new clothes or simply to supplement the family income.

No matter how Soviet journalists wrote about prostitution, their first articles on the subject were colored by envy on the one hand and hatred on the other; this was also characteristic of their readers, whose likely response to the article was to say things like "Those prostitutes should have gasoline poured over them and be set alight" or "I would exterminate the lot of them." As the Soviet economy slid toward ruin, the number of prostitutes—those forced into it and those who simply volunteered—continued to increase, and public attitudes toward them grew more accepting. Some sociological statistics began to be kept, though, sadly, not always reliable or allowing for real comparison (life is swiftly changing, so any comparison of statistics of the 1970s with those of the 1990s has only historical value today)—and often carrying strong official and police overtones. Thus, when some researchers say their figures prove that prostitutes come largely from poor, destitute, and underprivileged families, while others reject that idea out of hand, it is conceivable that both are right.

It is fairly safe to say that prostitutes enter the game early. Of 100 prostitutes in Moscow questioned by the police official Y. S. Zhikharev, 87% were under 25, and half were under 18. They were reasonably well educated (9.3% had a university education). More than half had no other job, but one in four was married and one in five had children. Seventy percent had become prostitutes while still minors (9.1% while under the age of 14, 36.4% between 14 and 15, and 21.2% at 16 to 17), and all had already had regular sexual contacts by then. Nine-tenths had started their sex lives voluntarily; for only 12% did that part of life commence with rape.[27]

According to Anatoly Dyachenko, another police sociologist, 79% of prostitutes were under 30. Almost one in five had started before the age of 18; one in seven had one or two under-age children who lived with their mother and witnessed her actions. Roughly half did not have another job; among those who did, the positions most frequently mentioned were sales assistant, hairdresser, waitress, nurse, nursery helper, and hotel staff. One in two had been in an alcoholic haze when arrested. One in ten had former convictions. One in seven suffered from venereal disease.

The more representative statistics collected by the USSR Ministry of the Interior Central Research Institute relating to 1987–88 show that age and other sociodemographic items differ with various categories of prostitute, and thus it is impossible to average them out.[28]

Child prostitution is a most serious and growing problem. For the adults who deal with it, child prostitution is a tragedy. The children themselves, however, accept it as a matter of course.

Fifteen-year-old Marina, who was interviewed by a correspondent from *SPID-info* (June 1991) in a hospital where she was being treated for gonorrhea, began her sex life at age 12, when she was raped: "We had been sitting with the boys in the garret, drinking and listening to music, and after that they gang-raped me." The boys, who had been 18-year-olds, were put in jail. It took Marina half a year to come to her senses, but she did recover. Now she has a "good boy"—a pimp—and she works at the railroad station:

> It is easy to find a client. You put on something bright, and stand still and smoke. Soldiers usually come—a lot of blacks [from the Caucasus, not Africa], but I don't like them; they are too cruel. The most profitable are old men and men from the North. They are generous. If you work alone, you have better luck with the soldiers. They don't cheat, and it's safe. . . . Also, after being abstinent so long, they finish fast. Yet they have little money. And if you are working with the boys, then they look for a client.
>
> Where does it all take place? In different places. The pensioners, who live near railway stations, rent us rooms, but that is only for the rich clients. Otherwise you can use deserted houses near the station, electrical trains that are sitting in the depots, the small baggage rooms, on the suitcases. And in summer, when it's warm and dark, the station passages . . . In every secluded corner where it's dark. The business is really fast . . . The cheapest is to take them into your mouth.

Male prostitution is also rapidly growing and expanding. A Moscow gay magazine called *RISK* published the following letter:

> I have a suggestion. Times are pretty tough right now. It's especially difficult for our newspapers and magazines. So why don't we organize some clandestine meeting places where people will pay for our services, and we can thereby help our publications to survive? It wouldn't be a bad thing for us either. Many are already fucking for either rubles or foreign currency. I'm quite prepared to make a fifty-fifty arrangement: half for me, half for the journal. I'm ready if you think it's OK.
>
> Zhenya, 25, Moscow

The magazine did not accept Zhenya's proposal. But there is plenty of private initiative. Not long ago, a ten-year-old boy from St. Petersburg, was found not only to be selling sexual services himself but other, younger children to adult customers. The police did not intervene.

As in the West, sexual services are often advertised as massage. In some newspapers, this is quite blatant: "Welcome, English-speaking guests of Russia! Two nice blondes will help you to organize your leisure. Russian compatriots are kindly asked not to bother." "Good-looking male, 39, height 161 cm., will perform cunnilingus for payment. Home visits possible." "Beautiful Russian women! You are awaited in the harems of the East! Travel to new places of residence for free!"[29]

Selling young Russian women abroad is now a big international trade. It began in the early 1980s. One enterprising businessman, Sergei, bold and arrogant on the eve of emigrating to the United States, told *SPID-info* of the way he sold five beautiful young virgins to an unnamed American pornographic film producer who needed "true and natural" scenes of defloration by a monster. For these "live" scenes Russian girls were used, while everything else was done by American actresses. At that time, the white slave trade was difficult and risky, so the group had to travel from Moscow to Budapest, then Vienna, and only after that to the United States.

Now everything is done openly. Sometimes the girls do not even know what they are getting into. They are promised prestigious work as models and when they discover themselves in a foreign bordello, it's too late: they have no money, no legal rights, they don't speak the language. For example, a group of young women from Saratov, some of them minors, were brought with false Georgian passports to Greece and then sold to bordellos for $5,000 to $7,000 apiece. The investigation began only when the mother of one of the girls became worried about her disappearance: her daughter had gone to Greece for a month and had not even sent a postcard! But to find such illegal immigrants is almost impossible—officially they do not exist.[30]

Soviet legal bodies traditionally did not accept the interpretation of "negative phenomena" as being socially determined, or caused by societal conditions; it was much less dangerous to explain such things by pointing to the proclivities of the individuals involved. Thus, criminologists would view prostitutes as sensualists working for money, in addition to which they were oversexed trollops who enjoyed sex. However, the notion of prostitutes possessing enhanced sexual drive is not reinforced by the evidence. According to Georgian data presented by Anzor Gabiani and Mikhail Manuilsky, no more than 20 to 30% obtained any sexual pleasure in their work. The most frequently cited motive for plying the trade was economic.

Whereas previously prostitution was more or less an individual enterprise, now it is increasingly tied to organized crime. Whole territories and spheres of influence are divided up by the local Mafia, and a prostitute who dares to violate the accepted order and refuses to pay for "protection" is likely to suffer unpleasant consequences, not excluding murder. An interesting new phenomenon is that pimps in Moscow are very often women.

Public health officials are particularly worried about the connection between prostitution and the spread of sexually transmitted diseases (STDs) and AIDS. In 1987, prostitutes made up two-thirds of people convicted of criminal responsibility for spreading STDs. At the same time, they remain mostly unconcerned. When a police official asked, "Are you afraid of getting AIDS?" a mere 42% answered in the affirmative.

Prostitution divides Russian public opinion as much as it does the experts. The question of legal responsibility for engaging in prostitution evokes especially heated arguments. Current legislation provides only for administrative police sanctions in the form of a warning or a small fine, neither of which is at all effective. Advocates of a tougher line maintain that prostitution is a moral blot on society, undermines the stability of marriage and the family, and encourages the spread of STDs and AIDS and the commission of a range of crimes, including—a favorite Soviet subject—"extraction of illegal income."

"Moderates" argue that the introduction of criminal responsibility (in the form of larger fines or prison sentences) would be woefully ineffective and only lead to arbitrary application of the law and false arrest; the emphasis, they say, should be on social and economic measures and education. Criminal charges should be reserved for actions that encourage the spread of prostitution, such as the recruiting of women for it, pimping, procuring, and maintaining "dens of vice" for personal profit.

The "radicals" consider all such measures quite useless and call for the legalization of prostitution, the licensing of prostitutes, and at the same time, regulation of sexual services for hygienic and health purposes—perhaps in private or state-owned bordellos.

As with the question of decriminalizing homosexuality, attitudes depend on one's background. In 1989, the police sociologist Anatoly Dyachenko questioned 154 employees of the internal affairs agencies (police officers) and 42 scholarly experts.[31] Advocates of stringent measures against prostitution predominated in the former; they proposed reinforcing administrative measures, increasing fines, stepping up arrests, nullifying residency permits, and expelling the miscreants from town. Many of them waxed nostalgic about the old (1961) Soviet law "On Stepping up the Campaign against People Avoiding Socially Useful Employment and Leading an Anti-Social Parasitical Lifestyle," which was applied to prostitutes (its most celebrated victim, however, was the future Nobel Prize winner, the poet Joseph Brodsky, who was sentenced because the authorities did not consider being a poet a formal and official job). As many as 72% of the police officials were in favor of making prostitution an outright criminal activity, as opposed to merely a local administrative one, while 77% wanted to extend some administrative discipline to the clients of prostitutes as well.

The lawyers, sociologists, and criminologists were much more liberal in their views: 83% were convinced that prostitution was inevitable, and 52% felt that prostitution did not automatically lead to further criminal activity, although just under half did see such a link. In response to the question whether they saw a need for criminal punishment—i.e., a high fine or prison term of some kind—for those engaged in prostitution, 83.3% saw no need; many were quite categorical in their views ("Good gracious, no!" or "I'm totally opposed!"). As many as 64.2% were also against making the clients of prostitutes criminally responsible.

In short, the debate about prostitution continues along the same lines as all other issues facing society: Will the state try to regulate everything (not very effectively, it must be said) or will people take responsibility for their actions themselves, including the inevitable moral and social costs?[32]

Yet all these discussions are more or less academic, and not only because of conservative public opinion. For public health as well as fiscal reasons, professional and organized prostitution would be much better and safer than what is available now. In my book *Tasting the Forbidden Fruit* (1992), I argued that it is precisely because our prostitutes are not professionals that Russian prostitution is more dangerous than in the West.

But who can control and regulate prostitution in a country that has neither a stable economy nor law and order? Only the Mafia. In Moscow, the police, whose chief is, most naturally, in favor of the repressive measures, from time to time conducts raids of some of the illegal but by no means clandestine dens of prostitution. But they are immediately reopened under new names. Yet the radical suggestions of legalizing prostitution and making "sexual workers" pay taxes are equally unrealistic. The idea of social regulation, and in a sense, socialization of sexual services seems rational but it goes contrary to the prevailing general policy of universal privatization. The prostitutes may be willing, in principle, to pay taxes in exchange for state protection and some medical help. But the Russian state, like its Soviet predecessor, wants to have everything for nothing. And it is physically unable to protect anybody. If presidents of the big banks and corporations are killed regularly in Moscow, who will protect poor, helpless prostitutes from their pimps, police bribery, and other dangers? It is much better for them to work without state intervention, relying only on themselves and on organized crime—even if it is dangerous for "all concerned". . . .

The spread of sexually transmitted diseases constitutes one of the greatest dangers of the liberalization of sexual morality in Russia, as everywhere and all at times. Throughout the Soviet regime, the customary hypocrisy prevailed, preventing an open discussion of such diseases, which were regarded as shameful, just as they had been in the last century. This prudery hampered health education, especially when the country was confronted by new infections.

Nonetheless, there was free state medicine, which combined treatment for STDs in specialized dermatological and venerealogical clinics with legal compulsion. All cases of STD had to be officially reported, treatment was paid for out of a special account, sources of infection were identified, and doctors, with police assistance, endeavored to follow the entire chain of dangerous contacts. Treatment was compulsory; refusing treatment and willful infection of another with a venereal disease were punishable under the Russian criminal code. Thus the state was able to confine the danger within certain limits.

The number of cases of syphilis and gonorrhea was even on the decline in the last days of the Soviet Union. According to official statistics, the USSR had 5.6 syphilis cases for every 100,000 people in 1987 (9.6 in 1985), which was less than half the rate in the United States, and 86 gonorrhea cases per 100,000 people (113 in 1985), which was one-sixth the U.S. rate. Even granting the unreliability of such statistics (which are nowhere quite reliable), these low rates of infection may be regarded as a significant achievement. True, in the early 1980s, doctors noted a substantial increase, especially among young people, in the so-called minor venereal diseases, such as chlamydia, nonspecific urethritis, genital warts, which often occur without causing symptoms and may, with promiscuous sexual contacts, form a flourishing "bouquet" that is then difficult to treat successfully. Soviet citizens had practically no knowledge of genital herpes until they came across it in their own doleful experience; nothing on the subject appeared in books, magazines, or newspapers, or was seen on television.

The demise of the Soviet system has adversely affected the epidemiological situation with regard to STDs. The exercise of greater sexual freedom, leading to multiple sexual affairs with different partners, is dangerous in itself, given the prevailing ignorance and lack of attention to elementary rules of public safety and hygiene. The state public health system is now debilitated and in some areas has collapsed outright because of the lack of funds, drugs, and equipment; private medicine in this area is less reliable, especially in the case of maladies requiring lengthy treatment and subsequent supervision, and it is not available to all. Public health supervision has now practically collapsed, and official statistics have become even less reliable.

Consequently, there has been an increase in the rates of STDs, particularly among young people. New cases of syphilis among 15- to 17-year-olds rose from 3.9% in 1990 to 6.2% in 1993. Statistics for STD infection are correlated with the age of first sexual intercourse (60% of STD-infected girls in Moscow began their sexual lives before 17 versus only 28% of a control group), and number of sexual partners (12.5 versus 2.3).[33]

There has been a continual rise in the incidence of syphilis in Moscow since 1988. By 1993, this growth reached near epidemic proportions. The number of newly infected in 1993 was twice as large as in 1992 and six times as large as in 1987. And medical authorities believe these figures represent less than half of the actual incidence.

The situation is more or less the same with gonorrhea, the rate of which has been growing gradually since 1991. Seventy percent of the highest-risk group are not homeless and poor people but tradespeople and other nouveaux riches. In the first nine months of 1993, almost 20,000 new cases of gonorrhea, including 103 children, were registered in Moscow, and this, authorities feel, represents only about one-third of the real numbers. The predominant majority of STD-infected children younger than 14 have been infected by sexual contact (*Sevodnyia*, December 13, 1993; April 19, 1994). Epidemiologists associate this increase primarily with the rise in increase in child and teenage prostitution involving girls as young as 10 to 12 and boys as young as 14.[34]

The chlamydia, which was for a long time underestimated by Soviet epidemiology—until 1993 it was not even included in epidemiological statistics for Moscow—is also growing, almost as fast as syphilis.

How widespread are STDs? In D. D. Isayev's 1993 telephone interview, 10.4% of men and 1.4% of women said they had had a STD once, and 5.6% of men and 1.4% of women reported they had had it more than once. These data may be unrepresentative, and they are much lower than U.S. figures (in the 1993 Chicago survey, 16.9% said they had had a STD). But the problem is that Russians are ill-prepared for the danger and very happy-go-lucky.

We have seen that Russian prostitutes do not seem overly concerned about STDs, and their clients are equally negligent. During random anonymous street interviews in different parts of Moscow in 1990, 150 men out of 280 approached said they paid for sexual services. Thirty-one percent did this for the first time before they were 18, and two-thirds of these even before the age of 16. They know it may be dangerous but 80% take no precautions.[35] What is to be done? Once again two basic strategies that have been advocated. One demands more stringent administrative measures—namely, a ban on private doctors treating STDs. Others say the solution should take into account the social and psychological realities.

According to Dr. Aishat Khazieva, from the Moscow Epidemiological Center,

> We should change our approach to the patient, give him or her the right to choose which doctor to go to; if he has money, he can go to a private doctor, if not, to state clinics. But the private doctor must inform the health authorities of cases of disease so that we can correctly evaluate the extent of the epidemic, forecast its likely development, and be prepared for any eventuality. For the moment a private venereologist has no legal right to treat such a patient. This is wrong. I would favor the principle of licensing such a practice: let qualified doctors enjoy the right of treating patients privately—providing they give us reliable statistics.

In April 1994, Moscow medical authorities took a compromise position: rather than taking the old (and compulsory) stationary cure in the hospitals, some people may receive outpatient treatment on a fee-for-services basis, in special STD dispensaries. But nobody holds out much hope about the efficacy of these measures. . . .

Probably the area in which all the contradictions of post-Soviet sexual culture are the most manifest is the attitude toward acquired immune deficiency syndrome (AIDS), caused by infection with the human immunovirus (HIV).

Because of the USSR's relative social and sexual isolation, HIV infection came much later to it than to the West, and much less virulently. Fate granted us several years' grace in which to prepare for the epidemic, but the entire period was utterly wasted.

First, the Soviet press in the 1980s, with the connivance of a number of official epidemiologists and managers at the Health Ministry, used the AIDS epidemic in the United States as fodder for a squalid, anti-U.S. propaganda campaign, claiming that HIV had been developed by the Pentagon for military purposes. At the same time, these authorities asserted that the Soviet Union had absolutely nothing to fear since the virus infected only homosexuals and drug addicts, against which the Russian criminal code was a powerful deterrent.

After the infection had nonetheless made its way into the USSR and the first AIDS sufferer had been diagnosed, the authorities began to establish a specialized diagnostic service; but they kept all the figures on the spread of the disease classified. The eminent late virologist Victor Zhdanov, who, in 1986, was the first to release reliable information about AIDS in the popular press, encountered some problems because of his audacity.

The authorities began to talk aloud and in public about AIDS in 1987, not so much because of awareness of the AIDS danger as the emergence of glasnost. However, all attention was focused on the so-called high-risk groups—prostitutes, drug addicts, and especially homosexuals—who found themselves painted in the blackest of tones. Ordinary, "sexually reliable" citizens were simply advised to adhere to the standards of monogamy and to be faithful to their marital vows. If any "slip" did occur—which should not happen—they were to use a condom, or, as Vadim Pokrovsky, the head of the first Soviet AIDS Diagnostics and Treatment Laboratory, put it delicately in a television interview, "Pardon me, a condom." That is how the wicked word first rang out on prudish Soviet television, a situation that made for entertainment rather than horror.

Those more inclined to decisive action knew what to do. On August 1, 1987, the newspaper *Komsomolskaya pravda* carried a letter, signed by 16 medical students, calling for the physical extermination of all prostitutes, drug addicts, and homosexuals. Not that the authorities agreed with them: Professor Valentin Pokrovsky, president of the Academy of Medical Sciences (and father of Vadim), said that the students were unworthy of a doctor's calling. But other people supported their views: said one letter to *Komsomolskaya pravda* (August 28, 1987), "I fully endorse the 16 medical students' view that AIDS is a cleansing agent for humanity that will rid society of drug addicts, homosexuals and prostitutes."

The first serious and fear-evoking publication on AIDS in the popular press was a series of interviews in July 1988 in the popular progressive weekly *Ogonyok*. Prepared by Alla Alova, the article was entitled "Life with AIDS: Are We Prepared?"

I was among those interviewed. In responding to the journalist's question, I said that I was extremely alarmed by the

> insistent talk about risk groups. By focusing on them we [are] somehow fencing ourselves off from the AIDS problem, as if to say, "AIDS is over there; it's their problem; it's on the other side of an impenetrable wall, and

all's well with us." But there is no wall; risk groups do not inhabit the moon; they are here, among us. And pardon me for saying so, but it is not only people in risk groups who engage in sex. Perfectly orderly people also do, and not only with their spouses, if only because not all have families. . . . The danger of contracting AIDS has long gone beyond the risk group "zone." The risk zone has become sexuality in general. Extramarital sex and premarital sex and even marital sex put everyone at risk.

But sex as such cannot be eradicated. Using the example of the U.S. Army's campaign against STDs, I discussed the advantages of "opportunist" tactics over "radical" demands that people refrain from sex altogether, and explained that effective use of condoms depends not only on their availability and quality but also on the public's overall sexual culture. These were quite elementary ideas, yet in this interview, the Soviet press was publishing them for the first time.

Most important, I attempted to warn people of the danger of AIDS phobia and moralizing:

> In the last century syphilis was no more dangerous than tuberculosis. But the attitude toward syphilis and TB victims was different. In the case of TB the infection produced fear, but the victims themselves evoked one's sympathy. In the case of venereal disease, inasmuch as it was connected with violation of religious and moral admonitions, the victim found himself faced with revulsion and horror as much at himself as at the disease. The end of the twentieth century has seemingly brought an entirely different attitude toward sex, and quite different moral criteria, yet in regard to AIDS sufferers people are again turning into merciless moralists and medieval inquisitors. . . . AIDS is a type of test for humankind to see how much humanity and common sense people have. . . . Generally speaking, if the morality of a particular society provides permission for people to discriminate according to one particular symptom, such as HIV infection, it also provides permission to discriminate as regards all other traits as well. Like a spark igniting parched grass, national and racial issues will join the conflagration . . . All society will become a ghetto system where people in each area hate the others.

Are you saying that what is immoral and inhumane is also unprofitable? asked the journalist.

> Exactly! The trouble is that we were taught for decades to abstract ourselves from the concept of humanity, to be able to counterpose dire historical necessity to moral impulses and use accusations of "slavering liberal-

ism" to repress feelings of pity and elementary human sympathy. We were well taught and much of it has stuck. Add to that the habit inculcated into our spirit by the quarter-of-a-century search for "enemies of the people," refined to the point where we were near automatons, acting reflexively so that we could transfer the battle against deficiencies from the deficiencies themselves to any scapegoat who happened to be around. The important thing was always to have a scapegoat. . . . So the AIDS epidemic is a test for our country that is much more severe and dangerous from a sociopsychological standpoint than for many other countries. It is hard to talk about it, but our people are very often aggressive, and it does not take much to turn that aggression in any direction.[36]

Nearly all educated people in Russia read that article. But the officials who held real power could not comprehend its meaning; for them it was just so many empty words whose very unusual nature merely shocked them. Even technical questions, such as that of providing condoms or disposable syringes, were beyond their ken. *Ogonyok* received a letter from Riga reporting on the complete absence of condoms there for a month. Alla Alova telephoned the head of the USSR Health Ministry Main Pharmacy Board. They had the following conversation:

You're interested in product No. 2? [The official could not call a condom a condom.] The makers of product No. 2 are the USSR Oil and Chemical Industry Ministry. We ordered 600 million items back in 1988. That was the public demand for product No. 2 for averting HIV infection."
"Excuse me, but how did you work out that demand?"
"Experts figured it out."
"What experts? From what institute?"
"I really can't say, I don't know . . . But anyway the Oil and Chemical Industry Ministry turned down the plan and reduced supplies for 1988 to 220 million on the excuse that they didn't have the necessary capacity. Of course 220 million does not solve the problem. But you'll have to address all your questions to the Oil and Chemical Ministry. We've enough trouble with them as it is. . . . "
"Perhaps we should purchase imported . . . products until our industry can cope with demand, in view of the anticipated AIDS epidemic?"
"No, we won't be buying any. We don't have enough foreign currency."
"Are you expecting higher quality in the next batch of condoms?"
"No, what for? Our products are now of reasonable quality. They are being manufactured on imported production lines so they are tough, they won't break. So in the sense of averting HIV infection, they are of high quality, no worse than imported ones. But in the sense of giving pleasure, pleasure to women, that shouldn't worry us now, should it? I'll tell you

what I think. condoms aren't responsible for the weather. There shouldn't be any chance affairs—that's the main thing. Then condoms won't be necessary. If a man sleeps only with his wife, why does he need condoms?"

"How about young people and all those who aren't yet married?"

"Well, those are chance affairs. . . ."

Since then, much water has flowed under the bridge. The major risk group in Russia has turned out to be *not* homosexuals, drug addicts, or prostitutes but newborn children infected in maternity homes owing to the negligence of medical staff and the lack of disposable syringes. After that, these children and their families became victims not only of the disease itself but also of AIDS phobia: medical personnel were scared of treating them, work mates did not want to work with members of their families, and the schools demanded their removal.

After the scandalous case of infection of a whole group of children, a certain number of disposable syringes was purchased or obtained through humanitarian aid. The quality of Russian condoms has improved considerably, and imported condoms are also on sale, but not always and not everywhere. Many pharmacies don't order them. Ordinarily, no instructions for use are given, and there is no systematic educational campaign.

However, there is not yet an AIDS epidemic in Russia. The World Health Organization estimates of 12,000 to 15,000 cases of HIV infection in Russia by 1993 have not materialized. At a news conference just before World AIDS Day on December 1, 1993, the health authorities announced that Russian production of 1.8 billion disposable syringes over the previous five years had helped stop HIV infection from spreading through medical treatment. From 1987 until April 1994, 740 cases of HIV among Russians were registered, plus 450 among foreigners (*Sevodnya*, April 21, 1994); 142 among the Russians were homosexuals and 286 were children, most of whom were infected in hospitals and maternity homes in 1989. Since that time, the main route of HIV transmission has been sexual contacts. Of 124 people who developed full-blown AIDS, approximately 100 have already died. HIV-infected foreign citizens have been deported from the country. On December 1, 1994, 831 HIV-positive Russian citizens were registered; the increase in the ten months of 1994 was 18%. Medical authorities do not expect a large increase in the number of cases in the near future.[37]

Yet the Soviet/Russian strategy of AIDS prevention is a good example of the effect of the command-administrative and medicobureaucratic mentality. All governmental funds have been concentrated in the hands of two epidemiologists, Professor Valentin Pokrovsky, the president of the Soviet (now Russian) Academy of Medical Sciences, and his son, Dr. Vadim

Pokrovsky, the head of the Russian AIDS Prevention Center. For mass anonymous testing, 748 diagnostic laboratories, 6 regional and 73 territorial centers, plus 128 consulting rooms have been organized. More HIV tests are done in Russia than in any other country—25 million a year! This service is extremely expensive, especially for a country in economic chaos. And independent experts are skeptical about the system's reliability. Some are afraid that the small number of registered HIV-infected people may be only a part—15 to 20%—of the real number.

Medical measures are supplemented by police-administrative measures. According to a new draft criminal code, conscious infection with a STD or HIV by a person who knew he or she was already infected constitutes a serious criminal offense (chapters 130 and 131). There was a battle over the new law on the curbing of HIV infection in Russia. The mass compulsory testing, which was advocated by the test-system producer's lobby, was too expensive. Then, despite massive protests and criticisms from many experts and social and professional organizations, including the World Health Organization (WHO), the Duma passed a federal law whereby all foreigners coming to Russia, even for a few days, are obliged to pass a HIV test. But who would visit Russia on such terms? After the President's veto, the law was changed. Now foreigners must present the certificate that they are HIV-negative only if they will stay for more than 3 months. Compulsory HIV testing for Russian citizens is limited to members of certain professions, the list of which has to be established by the government. Yet because Russia has never really ceased to be a police state, this law will inevitably produce large-scale police brutality and discrimination, and not only against gay men.

Also, billions more rubles will be wasted on testing, which even Pokrovsky father and son now declare unnecessary. And as usual, the authors of this law are unknown. General opinion in the country is that it was a joint effort of police authorities and a certain chemico-pharmaceutical lobby, having a vested interest in mass testing.

At the same time, very little has been done in terms of mass education. Sociologists and psychologists have never been consulted about developing an AIDS-prevention strategy. Medical doctors are largely ignorant of psychology, and they have no psychologists on their teams. The few published booklets and posters are primitive and do not take into account the specific mentality of the intended audience, whether teens, gay men, or women. Not a single Russian social worker has been professionally trained for work in the field of AIDS prevention. (However, it was very easy to obtain Western help for that purpose. One lecture and a ten-minute conversation at the University of California San Francisco's Center for AIDS Prevention (CAP) in 1991 was enough for me to obtain permission for Soviet citizens to take part in the CAP International Summer school, and this place was won by a St. Petersburg psychologist.) Dr. Vadim Pokrovsky is interested neither in social work nor in contacts with voluntary associations or the mass media. Even the papers he presented at international AIDS conferences are practically unknown in the country. Some other prominent members of the Russian epidemiological establishment, such as Professor Konstantin Borisenko in Moscow and Professor Aza Rakhmanova in St. Petersburg, are much more democratic and socially active, but their influence is limited.[38]

The conservatism and inefficiency of the official state medical service compelled Russian intellectuals to organize several voluntary, nonprofit organizations for AIDS prevention. The Ogonyok "Anti-SPID" Charity Fund, sponsored by the magazine *Ogonyok* and the "VID" television company, has collected more than $5 million since January 1990; the money is used for buying disposable syringes and for providing humanitarian aid to HIV-positive children. In addition, some funds go toward an effort to develop propaganda for AIDS prevention. In December 1993, the fund initiated the first international contest for AIDS-prevention videotapes, which are to be shown on Russian television.

The "AIDS Prevention Association," the first head of which was Dr. Vadim Pokrovsky, who was succeeded by the prominent television commentator Vladimir Pozner, publishes textbooks for medical institutions, doctors, and nurses, and popular booklets for laypeople, but is socially quite passive. At the beginning, the association launched a monthly newspaper, *SPID-info* (*AIDS info*). But in 1993 this extremely successful newspaper (circulation 4.5 million) broke away from the association and became a commercial newspaper, publishing interesting erotic and sexological material but almost nothing about AIDS. The AIDS Prevention Association itself seems nearly moribund.

*My i Vy* (We and You), a society of HIV-infected people and their friends, founded in 1992 with the financial help of some French and Belgian organizations, takes care of HIV-positive and AIDS sufferers, giving them psychological, social, and legal support. Crocus-Plus-ANTI-SPID ran an AIDS-hotline in Moscow, but it was closed in 1994. The Stop-SPID Association tries to educate Moscow teenagers, using the American peer education programs as a model. The AESOP Center (*An Effective Shield of Prevention*), initiated in 1993 by the American AIDS activist Kevin Gardner and sponsored by the Burroughs Wellcome Pharmaceutical Foundation and MacArthurs' Foundation, is trying to coordinate and expand these efforts; in 1994 the center received two substantial Western grants for its activities.

These organizations do more than the Russian government, but they are small, and their means lag behind their plans and ambitions. Most of their leaders and activists have no professional training, some of them dislike one another, and they often compete rather than cooperate. This is a typical post-Soviet situation: having liberated themselves from the bonds of enforced collectivism, Russians are both panic-stricken at the prospect of competition and exceedingly reluctant to cooperate with one another. Everyone pulls the blanket over to his own side of the bed.

What about the mass media and public opinion? Since the first wave of AIDS phobia passed, the general attitude has been one of indifference. In the survey conducted in Moscow in the spring of 1989, among 750 high school, and medical and technical college students aged 14 to 18, about two-thirds of the sample said the best solution for dealing with HIV-positive people would be some sort of quarantine; 49 to 57% felt compassion for such persons, with only 19 to 21% expressing negative attitudes toward them. But only 40% said that if their friends became HIV-positive, their attitudes toward them would not change.[39]

The real life of HIV victims is extremely difficult. Many of them complain of discrimination and isolation. At the same time, Russians are not very careful about AIDS. According to D. D. Isayev's 1993 St. Petersburg telephone poll, two-third of men and 56.6% of women surveyed said they are not worried about the possibility of being infected with HIV; only 28.5% of men and 16.6% of women said they changed their sexual behavior because of AIDS.

This is partly a manifestation of traditional Russian fatalism. On the other hand, people have other things than AIDS on their minds. At a time when people hear shooting in the streets and are reeling from rampant inflation, they are hardly likely to stop and think about what disease will threaten their lives in the future. Perhaps we are simply genetically impervious to AIDS? As the saying goes, what is food for the Russian is poison for the German. Wishful thinking. . . .

*Chapter Thirteen*

# COMING OUT INTO CHAOS

*Persecution and torment by no means require persecutors and tor-*
*mentors; all that is necessary is us ordinary folk confronted by some-*
*one who is not one of us: a Negro, a wild beast, a man from Mars, a*
*poet or phantom. Aliens are born to be persecuted.*

—Marina Tsvetayeva

I n 1989 I received the following letter:

I read your article in *Literaturnaya gazeta* and feel bound to write. Alas, I
belong to those whom you wrote about. . . . I can no longer keep my trou-
bles bottled up inside. I have to speak out, at least on paper. . . .

Yes, I am a "blue," and you are the first person to know. I am 23, an ex-
student, living with my parents. It all began when I was thirteen or fourteen. I tried to ward it off (by taking up various sports, every imaginable
kind of collecting, music, reading, etc.), but nothing helped. Everywhere I
met men I fancied (boys of my age and younger). Yet I never tried to fulfill
my desires. I was very ashamed. In my heart I hated myself, but there was
nothing I could do. It was beyond me. I forced myself to go out with girls
and fairly frequently I found myself in intimate situations, yet I never had
any desire. I was constantly forcing myself, and naturally, nothing good
came of it. Not a single girl could evoke in me such exquisite feelings as
when I accidentally brushed up against a man I liked. But let me repeat,
even now I have never had any sexual contact with young men. I simply

have no idea what to do. All my friends and relatives think me absolutely normal and have no inkling at all of my real state. But I can't go on living like this. For ten years I've been struggling with myself. I can't go on. The nights are the worst; it's a sheer nightmare.

I used to think how awful it would be to take one's own life, but now when I think of suicide I find I've no fear of death. I don't know if I'll have the courage. Please don't try to convince me, for God's sake, that this isn't the best way out. It is the only way. Over the past two or three years I've lost all interest in life. I move about, I talk, I do things, and all as in a trance.

The letter arrived after an interview with me appeared in the weekly *Literaturnaya gazeta* (March 29, 1989). I received many similar letters, each one representing a separate tragedy.

The following letter had prompted the newspaper's interest in the topic; and it took as long as nine months to publish the unusual interview:

Your newspaper deals with a variety of problems affecting different aspects of life in the country as a whole and individuals in particular. Yet there is one problem I wish to mention that our press passes over in embarrassed silence.

I am a woman, the mother of three children, and I find it incredibly difficult to write about it; but it's also hard to stay silent. You won't find counselors on such issues, there's no one with whom to share my problem or of whom to ask what I should do.

I want to tell you about my son, Igor. As a child he was no trouble at all. He grew up obedient and able. Maybe he was too meek and mild. Sensitive, responsive, mild-mannered—those became his main character traits as he grew older. He would take any hurt to heart (especially if it was not deserved); he could not abide any injustice, cruelty or violence. His friends and acquaintances were of the same nature.

He received top marks in school and served his time in the army. Then he entered college and got a first-class honors degree. He was always doing various voluntary jobs, always on the go. He was easy to get along with and people were drawn to him. Yet, to tell the truth, he had no really close friends. In his later years at college and when he started work at a research institute he would often get depressed and lonely. I began to tell him it was time to start a family, to bring home a wife. He would reply evasively that it was too early, that he wasn't ready for family life, that he wanted to devote himself to science.

He went on to postgraduate work and finished that too. Work on his dissertation was drawing to a close. He would disappear into his institute for days on end. Besides his principal work, he was also giving lectures and was constantly weighed down with volunteer work. He was accepted into the Communist Party. He had turned thirty almost without noticing it.

And then, all of a sudden, there came a bolt from the blue! I was summoned to the local internal affairs office; it was more like an interrogation, an information session to let me know who my son really was. It turned out that one of his acquaintances had ended up in the skin clinic with VD. And when they asked him about his contacts he named my son, telling them he and Igor had had a homosexual relationship.

Interrogation started; he was confronted with the facts. He could not bear it and wanted to put an end to it all, but he was saved. I wept, begged him not to kill himself, if only for his mother's sake. And he promised. Following the letter of the law, he was kicked out of the Party and fired from his job. At the end of the investigation he got a year's sentence.

When I went to the prosecutor and told him we would complain and submit an appeal, he told me to go on and do so if I had no shame. He added that such scum ought to be shot anyway.

I cannot say I have any sympathy with Igor's behavior. But I am his mother and I probably have even more pity for a child like him. After all, as he told me later, he just could not help himself. He could not do otherwise, not because he was perverted or tainted, but because that was his need. Even if he were to live on some deserted island, he could not become someone else. That's how he was.

He was released a year later. At present he is a manual laborer. he has remained just as kind and sensitive, never nasty to people. Yet somehow he is not the same person anymore. We, his nearest and dearest, as well as the neighbors, treat him differently. We try to pretend that nothing has happened, that everything is forgotten, that it's all water under the bridge. But he knows it isn't so.

Party officials find a way of bringing it up at their meetings, wondering how "such characters" had penetrated their ranks. What characters, I ask myself?

I would just like to know what it is—an illness? Or is it really a crime? I have searched high and low yet could find no literature on the subject. There must be a special attitude toward such people. Why is that so? Is there no other way? Why is science silent?[1]

But science, like society, had its mouth tightly shut. . . .

In regard to homosexuality in the Soviet Union, we may distinguish four key periods after 1933:

1. 1934–86: homosexuality is punished by prosecution, discrimination, and silence.

2. 1987–90: the start of open public discussions of the problem of homosexuality by professionals and journalists, from a scientific and humanitarian point of view.
3. 1990—May 1993: gay men and lesbians themselves take up the cudgels, putting human rights in the forefront of the struggle; there is exacerbation of conflict and sharp politicization of the issue.
4. June 1993-to present: partial decriminalization of homosexuality; the beginning of the conversion of the homosexual underground into a gay and lesbian community and "blue" subculture, with its own organizations, publications, and centers.

I have already discussed the first of these periods. The first antihomosexual campaign in the Soviet press was very short-lived. By the mid-1930s, a complete and utter silence on the subject had descended. Homosexuality was simply never mentioned; it had become an "unmentionable vice" in the full sense of the term. The conspiracy of silence even touched on such academic subjects as phallic cults and ancient Greek pederasty.[2]

The gloomy conspiracy of silence further intensified the psychological tragedy of Soviet "blues" (homosexuals and lesbians): they not only feared persecution and blackmail but could not even develop an adequate sense of self-awareness and so comprehend exactly who they were.[3]

Medicine offered little help. When the first sexopathological books began to come out in the 1970s, homosexuality was treated as a pernicious "sexual perversion," a disease that had to be treated.[4] Even the most liberal and enlightened Russian sexopathologists and psychiatrists, who support the decriminalization of homosexuality, regard it, with rare exception, as a disease and reproduce in their works the innumerable negative stereotypes prevalent in the mass consciousness. The latest medical reference book on sexopathology, published in 1990, defines homosexuality as "a pathological drive" and discusses it in a purely biological vein. In addition to biological causes, in the view of the authors, "a strong pathogenic factor encouraging the formation of homosexual attraction can be the inculcation by parents and teachers of a hostile attitude toward the opposite sex."[5]

The situation in regard to "blues," which was never good, had begun to deteriorate in the early 1980s, when a campaign was launched against them in educational literature. The first and at the time only teacher's manual on sex education, written by Antonina Khripkova and Dmitri Kolesov, defined homosexuality as a dangerous pathology and "a violation of normal principles of sexual relationships." It went on to say,

Homosexuality challenges both normal heterosexual relationships and society's cultural, moral attainments. It therefore merits condemnation both as a social phenomenon and as an individual's behavior and mental attitude. . . .

Treatment of homosexuality is vital in the sexual hygiene of boys, adolescents, and youths. It consists of alerting them to all those factors which can turn a boy, adolescent, or youth against the female sex, in controlling the nature of relationships with members of their own sex, in carefully selecting staff for educational institutions such as boarding schools.[6]

Thus, in the nation's only sex education guide, teachers as well as police and doctors were being put on their guard against homosexuality.

The AIDS epidemic made the position of gays still worse. When symptoms of the virus had just emerged in the United States, the initial information about it in the Soviet press was roughly as follows: a new and unknown disease has appeared in the USA; its victims are homosexuals, drug addicts, and Puerto Ricans. Brought up in the spirit of official internationalism, Soviet citizens were puzzled at the mention of Puerto Ricans. They could well understand God punishing homosexuals and drug addicts for their sins, but why Puerto Ricans? God surely wasn't a racist!

In 1986 Nikolai Burgasov, then USSR deputy health minister and chief doctor for hygiene, publicly announced, "We have no conditions in our country conducive to the spread of the disease: homosexuality is prosecuted by law as a grave sexual perversion (Russian Criminal Code Article 121), and we are constantly warning people of the dangers of drug abuse."[7]

Somewhat later, Alexander Potapov, then the Russian Federation minister and professor of psychiatry, ventured into print in *Literaturnaya gazeta*, answering questions on drug addicts; for some reason he linked them with homosexuals, adding, "My colleagues in Paris told me of an enraged crowd killing two homosexuals in a Paris park—right in front of the police." This representative of the most humane of professions gave no further commentary on this event, moving on to discuss what the authorities in Belgium were doing to confine the pornography business. He concluded by saying pensively, "You see how life forces one to act."[8] Nobody even remarked on the monstrosities he was mouthing. . . .

When AIDS did appear in the Soviet Union, heads of the state epidemiological program once again blamed homosexuals for everything, accusing them in public statements of being carriers of HIV infection and just about every other vice besides. Such were their sincere convictions, since the educational programs of the Soviet medical institutions had not discussed homosexuality. Even the liberal journal *Ogonyok*, in the first published profile of an AIDS victim, a gay engineer who had caught the virus in Africa, could not conceal its disgust and condemnation.

All the same, glasnost, plus the threat of AIDS, made possible for the first time more or less frank discussions of sexual orientation problems, initially in the scholarly and then in more popular literature—whether the authorities liked it or not.[9]

After 1987, the question of what exactly homosexuality was and how one should relate to "blues"—whether to regard them as sick, as criminals, or as victims of fate—began to be discussed extensively in the popular, especially youth, press (*Moskovsky komsomolets, Komsomolskaya pravda, Sobesednik, Molodoi kommunist, Literaturnaya gazeta, Ogonyok, Argumenty i fakty, SPID-info*, the teenage journal *Parus*, and some local newspapers), and on radio and television. Although discussion in these publications was extremely diverse in terms of orientation and level of sophistication, the very fact of it was of huge significance. For the first time, ordinary Soviet people began to learn—from journalistic articles and letters from gays, lesbians, and their parents—of the crippled destinies, the police brutality, the legal repressions, the tragic, inevitable loneliness of people doomed to live in constant fear and unable to meet people similar to themselves. Every article provoked a stream of contradictory reactions, which editors had no idea how to handle.

The question of the decriminalization of homosexuality has long been a subject for debate in professional circles. In 1973, a textbook on criminal law by Mikhail Shargorodsky and Pavel Osipov discussed the illogicality of Article 121 of the RSFSR criminal code:

> In the Soviet literature of jurisprudence, there has never been any attempt to articulate a sound scientific basis for the existence of criminal penalties for *muzhelozhstvo* [sex between men]. The only reason that is usually given—that the subject is morally depraved and has violated the rules of socialist morality—cannot be considered substantive, since negative personal traits cannot serve as grounds for criminal penalties and the amoral nature of an act is insufficient for declaring it criminal. . . . Serious doubts exist regarding the expediency of retaining criminal penalties for the unqualified act of *muzhelozhstvo*.[10]

This professional opinion was completely ignored. Professor Alexei Ignatov, now a leading legal expert on so-called sexual crimes, had raised the question with those in charge of the USSR Ministry for Internal Affairs back in 1979. I myself unsuccessfully tried to publish an article on the theme in the legal journal *Sovetskoye gosudarstvo i pravo* in 1982.[11]

Many arguments were advanced for decriminalization of homosexuality:

- From the legal point of view: Soviet legislation on the subject was not in accord with the standards and principles of international law; Soviet law lacked internal logic, since only male homosexuals were punished under Article 121; prosecution of homosexuality invited abuse and corruption on the part of the law enforcement agencies.
- From the humanitarian point of view: if an individual's sexual orientation is a matter of biology, not free choice, he should not be punished for pursuing it.
- From the scientific point of view: the criminalization of homosexuality went against the general views of contemporary science.
- From the medical and hygienic points of view: the criminalization of homosexuality made it particularly difficult to combat the spread of STDs.
- From the social point of view: criminalization causes social damage by alienating homosexuals from the larger society and forcing them into the squalid underworld.

Although such views never made their way into the press, the draft of the new Russian criminal code, prepared by a legal commission in the late 1980s, excluded Article 121. Yet as discussion and adoption of the new code was delayed, disputes on the subject spilled over into the popular press and onto television screens.

There were three major lines of thought on the subject:

1. Article 121 should be fully revoked; there should be no mention of sexual orientation in the Criminal Code, since children and adolescents, irrespective of their gender, as well as rape victims, are protected by other laws. This stand is taken by lawyers like Alexei Ignatov and Alexander M. Yakovlev, the psychoendocrinologist Aron Belkin, the present author, and some other scholars.
2. Criminal prosecution for homosexual contacts between consenting adults—Article 121.1—should be revoked, but the second part of Article 121, which refers to children and minors, should be retained. This was the view of many of the officials of the Ministry of Internal Affairs.[12]

3. Article 121 should remain as is. This was the demand of Communists, nationalists, and some religious organizations.

Since the late 1980s, according to official data, the number of men convicted under Article 121 has been steadily decreasing. In 1987, 831 men were sentenced under this law in the Soviet Union. In 1988, 800 were sentenced; in 1989, 538 were convicted; in 1990, 497; in 1991, 482; and for the first six months of 1992, 227, among whom only 10 were sentenced under 121.1 (figures are for Russia only).[13]

No matter how vociferous the legal debate, the position of sexual minorities depends not only on legislation but on public attitudes, which cannot be changed overnight. Homophobia, irrational fear of homosexuality, and hatred of gays constitute one of the main problems in present-day Russian sexual culture.

The term "homophobia" itself is inadequate, inasmuch as it is associated with individual psychopathology—with the individual's own repressed or latent homosexuality, with neuroses, sexual fears, and the like. But while homophobia *may* exist in many such individuals, an adverse attitude toward homosexuality is primarily the result of negative attitudes in the culture and public consciousness—prejudices and hostile stereotypes similar to racism, sexism or anti-Semitism—and we can come to understand it only in that sociopsychological context.[14] Individual predilections are derivative of cultural norms and social interests.

As cross-cultural research shows, the level of homophobia in a given society depends on a wide range of factors.

First, it depends on the overall level of a society's social and cultural tolerance. Intolerance of differences, typical of any authoritarian regime, is ill-suited to sexual or any other kind of pluralism. From the totalitarian standpoint, the homosexual is dangerous primarily because he is a dissident, because he differs from the rest. A society that tries to control the width of trouser legs and the length of hair cannot be sexually tolerant.

Second, homophobia is a function of sexual anxiety. The more antisexual the culture, the more sexual taboos and fears it will have. The former USSR in this respect was, as ever, an extreme case.

Third, homophobia is closely linked with sexism, and sexual and gender chauvinism. Its major function in social history has been to uphold the sanctity of the system of gender stratification based on male hegemony and domination. Obligatory, coercive heterosexuality is intended to safeguard the institution of marriage and patriarchal relations; under this system, women are second-class beings, their main—perhaps even sole—function is to produce children. In that ideology, a woman who works outside the home is just as much an instance of sexual perversion as the person involved in same-sex love. Moreover, the cult of aggressive masculinity is a means of maintaining hierarchical relations in male society itself; the gentle, nonaggressive male and the powerful, independent woman are both challenges to the dominant stereotypes. Even some sexually tolerant societies accord great importance to sexual positions: the one who is the inserter is worthy and normal, while the insertee is unworthy and dependent. Hatred of homosexuality is also a means of upholding male solidarity, particularly among adolescents, whom it helps to affirm their own problematic masculinity.

Fourth, much depends on the nature of the dominant traditional ideology, particularly the attitude of religion toward sex. Antisexual religions, such as Judaism and Christianity, are usually more intolerant of homosexuality than are more prosexual religions, such as the Tantra and Buddhism.

Fifth, the overall level of education, in particular the public's level of sexual culture, is extremely important. Education in itself does not obviate prejudices and stereotypes but, other things being equal, it does facilitate the fight against them. To understand Soviet and post-Soviet public consciousness on the subject of sexuality, one must imagine America before Kinsey or even before Freud.

Finally, there are situational, sociopolitical factors. Homophobia, like other social fears and forms of group hatred, is usually exacerbated at moments of social crisis, when an obvious foe or scapegoat is needed.

The level of toleration of homosexuality is historically changeable and varies from country to country. According to the American political scientist and social psychologist Ronald Inglehart, the Netherlands was the most tolerant country in 1980–82, with Denmark and West Germany following behind (22%, 34%, and 42% of those surveyed, respectively, agreed that "homosexuality is always wrong"), while Mexico and the United States were the most intolerant, as 73% and 65%, respectively, condemned homosexuality in all instances.[15] Young people (between 18 and 24) in all societies, however, were considerably more tolerant than their elders—twice as much so as those over 65. This may be due to their greater overall tolerance and level of education; also, they feel themselves more sexually confident and therefore can allow themselves more variation in behavior and attitudes than older people.

Soviet society was generally distinguished by extreme intolerance of dissident thinking and uncommon behavior, even when entirely innocent. And homosexuals are still the most stigmatized of all social groups, including even prostitutes and drug addicts (with whom homosexuals were frequently associated, owing to tendentious anti-AIDS propaganda). According to figures from the VCIOM survey of a representative sample of 2,600 undertaken in November 1989, the question "How ought we to treat homosexuals?" produced the following variety of answers: 33% were in favor of extermination; 30% of isolation; 10% of leaving them alone; and only 6% of proffering them any kind of help.[16]

Another sociological survey undertaken by the Moscow Youth Institute in July 1990 in 16 regions of Russia (a total of 1,500 people were involved, of whom 26% were under 30) discovered homosexuals to be once more the most hated group: 62% of those in the survey sharply condemned them, 20% were neutral, and 0.6% said they "like them very much," with 8% unable to answer.[17]

It is difficult for many people even to discuss these issues. In analyzing the results of a VCIOM 1989 public opinion survey, sociologists identified two extreme groups of respondents: the tolerant and the "rigid repressors." The groups differed in virtually everything, including attitudes toward homosexuals: the former favored social assistance to homosexuals and the latter were in favor of exterminating them. The only point on which the two groups agreed was that the problem of same-sex relationships should not be debated in the press.[18]

In 1990, the Russian Academy of Sciences Sociology Institute and the International Center for Human Values surveyed people in the European part of the USSR (a sample of 4,309 people) on their attitudes toward various ethnic, political, and social groups, including homosexuals. Evaluated on an 11-point scale, from "I do not like at all" to "I like very much," homosexuals now took third place in terms of hostility, after "neo-Nazis" and "Stalinists"; 68.7% of men and 69.4% of women took the most extreme negative position. In terms of age, the most intolerant were people between 41 and 50 (accounting for 75.2% of the extreme negative replies) and those aged 31 to 40 (72%). In this sample, education did not reduce homophobia but intensified it: people with a secondary professional training showed maximum hostility, with those with a university education in second place (70.4%).[19]

In 1992, an investigation involving scholars from the Political Science Department of Houston University—James Gibson and Raymond Duch—and covering the entire territory of the former USSR, produced similar results: homosexuals took second place in hostility after neo-fascists. Some

58.2% of men and 58.6% of women put them in the "don't like at all" category. True, the age dimensions of homophobia were slightly different here: people born between 1921 and 1960 were the most intolerant, while youth responses were 4 to 6% more tolerant.[20]

These evaluations were not reactions to individuals. Many respondents knew nothing about homosexuals and may possibly have heard about them for the first time only during the interview. Hostility toward gays and lesbians is a particular example of hostility toward all that is alien and unknown. All the same, that reasoning is hardly balm to those on the receiving end of hatred.

The Communist and chauvinist media, such as *Sovetskaya Rossiya, Den* (now called *Zavtra*), *Russkoye voskresenie, Nash sovremennik, Molodaya gvardiya,* and *Shchit i mech,* as well as the television program "600 Seconds," produced by Alexander Nevzorov, deliberately whip up homophobia and actively propagate it. The fascist press methodically and consistently lumps together Bolshevism, Zionism, democracy, and homosexuality. Thus the newspaper *Russkoye voskresenie* ran an article under the title "Let Us Defend Russian Orthodoxy Against the Yids" that said, "Both the Bolsheviks and democratic leaders are of foreign extraction. Both are sexual perverts. You will recall that the first decree issued by the Soviet government was to revoke punishment for homosexuality. Now it's the democrats who are after the same thing. (It was reintroduced by the Russian Orthodox Stalin [?!] and his Russian entourage in 1934)."[21]

So attitudes toward homosexuality constitute an acute political problem. Unfortunately, some eminent scholars do not take a consistent, clearcut position on the issue. Dr. Valentin Pokrovsky, the president of the Academy of Medical Sciences, who is in charge of the state program for AIDS prevention, may well have shown his distaste for medical students who would seek to exterminate AIDS sufferers (see Chapter 12), but not long after, in his capacity as a member of the Gorbachev Presidential Commission for Combating Pornography, he said in an interview with the newspaper *Megapolis-express,* that in his opinion, AIDS was "a moral sickness in society" and that demands to legalize homosexuality were absurd. When the interviewer mentioned that homosexuality was a disease, Pokrovsky replied, "That's exactly the point. There are people who are genetically predisposed to that kind of sexual contact. It is ridiculous to call that normal. It is even more so to regard as normal healthy people those who get mixed up in homosexual affairs and seduce young children through their sexual excess. It is not a disease, it's dissipation that must be combated, particularly through the courts."[22] The professor did not say exactly who—doctors or the police—should differentiate the sick from the dissolute, or exactly what criteria should be employed. Nor did he mention a "cure" for homosexuality.

The unholy alliance of ignorant medics and prejudiced police and legal experts deprived sexual minorities of human rights and all protection—medical, social, and legal. The repressive Soviet law on combating AIDS and the USSR Health Ministry's August 25, 1987, instructions on its application were formulated so vaguely that practically any citizen accused of homosexuality—by anyone, and even without evidence—might be liable to compulsory HIV testing and other offensive actions.

Nor were criminal sanctions the only problem. Until the end of 1991, gays and lesbians had no safe place to meet, no real way to encounter people of their own orientation in more or less decent conditions. Of course, big cities always have well-known places—certain squares, parks, public rest rooms, and the like—where gay men gather. Yet fear of exposure makes such sexual contacts impersonal, anonymous, and short-lived, stripped of human warmth and psychological intimacy. And such places are only for men. Lesbians do not meet in public parks or toilets, and hence are less visible and less liable to harassment, but it is more difficult for them to find lovers.

Extensive and anonymous sexual encounters sharply increase the risk of infection with HIV and other STDs. According to statistics from Ukrainian and Belorussian venereological centers, male homosexuals made up over 30% of all syphilis sufferers in the 1980s, while in Latvia they made up over half. Fearful of exposure, gay men have typically avoided doctors or gone to them too late. In Moscow, 84% of cases of late-stage hospitalization of syphilis sufferers were gays. It was even harder to locate the source of their infection. Professor Konstantin Borisenko, a Moscow venereologist and director general of the Association for the Prevention of Sexually Transmitted Disease, has reported that the source of syphilis infection among male homosexuals was identified in no more than 7.5 to 10% of the cases, while sources were identified in from 50 to 70% of the cases in the rest of the syphilitic population.[23] That is why Borisenko, in contrast to his senior colleague Valentin Pokrovsky, advocated the decriminalization of homosexuality, recognizing that until then, the epidemiological situation would be unlikely to improve.

Sexual contacts in public rest rooms are also dangerous in respects other than risk of disease. Organized bands of hooligans, sometimes operating with the unspoken support of the police, blackmail, rob, viciously attack, and even murder gay men. In doing so they hypocritically portray themselves as protectors of public morals, calling their actions *remont*, or "repair work"—that is, eliminating "vice" in their own way. Since gays are afraid of informing the police about such incidents, most crimes against them go unpunished, while police officers blame the victims for provoking crime. Time and again, cruel murder with robbery is depicted by the police as due to pathological "homosexual jealousy."

When most people speak of homosexuality in Russia, they are generally referring to male homosexuality; it is only recently that the popular press has begun to write about lesbians. However, their position is no better than that of gay men.[24] Although it is true that lesbian relationships did not fall under the rubric of any criminal code statute, and close relations between women are less likely to set tongues wagging, a young woman who becomes aware of her psychosexual differences will find it more difficult than a young man to find a soulmate. Public attitudes toward lesbians are just as obdurate as those toward gay men: ridicule, persecution, expulsion from university, termination of employment, compulsory psychiatric treatment, threats to remove custody of children were the lot of many lesbians.

A 23-year-old lesbian writes:

> How did it all begin? Well, I probably had these feelings all along. As a child I hung around with the boys, played ice hockey, soccer, and soldiers; later I fell in love with my girlfriends and other young women. How I suffered and tormented myself—but there was no one I could talk to. I often had adventurous or erotic dreams where I was fighting for and protecting the lady of my heart's desire. I used to think it was something infantile, something romantic that would pass. But it didn't. The most difficult thing of all was to admit it to myself. In my eagerness to convince myself of the opposite, I tried meeting men. I even had sexual intercourse and experienced orgasm. Yet I didn't get that spiritual uplift, that excitement I felt when alongside a woman. After such affairs I felt ashamed, and simply hated myself as if I were a common prostitute. So I stopped those experiments.

The situation is particularly difficult for lesbian mothers. The notion that gays and lesbians would and can be good and healthy parents would seem absolutely monstrous to the vast majority of Russians—which is the same reaction most would have to the idea of same-sex marriage.

Until the late 1980s, Soviet gays, with rare exception, were victims who could only complain about their fate and futilely bemoan their humiliation. In 1984, some 30 young people in Leningrad, led by Alexander Zaremba, a young philologist who had recently moved there from Kiev, set up a "Gay

Laboratory." They established contact with a Finnish gay and lesbian association, dispatched information to the West about the woeful state of Soviet gays, and started, to the extent that circumstances allowed, to provide information on AIDS prevention for homosexuals, which the Soviet medical community had completely failed to do. It did not take long, however, before the group caught the eye of the KGB and found itself on the receiving end of political and ideological accusations, threats, and repression, as a result of which group members were forced to emigrate or hold their peace.

During the initial years of glasnost, only "experts" on the subject spoke of the problems of sexual minorities in estranged if sympathetic tones. But gradually gays and lesbians themselves broke through to the press, the victims gaining the courage to fight for themselves. International gay and lesbian organizations and publications offered considerable help to Russian gays and lesbians in their emerging self-awareness.

The first international conference on "The Status of Sexual Minorities and Changing Attitudes Toward Homosexuality in 20th Century Europe" to be held anywhere in the Soviet Union took place in Tallinn at the end of May 1990. Held on the premises of the History Institute of the Estonian Academy of Sciences, it was organized with the support of international gay organizations. The conference was very successful and encouraged increased self-awareness and elucidation of the social and psychological identity of Soviet gays and lesbians.[25] Many foreign scholars such as Jeffrey Weeks and Gert Hekma took part. The first comparative questionnaire survey into the status and problems of sexual minorities in Finland and Estonia was initiated within the framework of the Soviet-Finnish program for studying social minorities; it had its base in Tallinn under the leadership of the demographer Teet Veispak. The questionnaire was later extended to Russia, but no results have been published.

In late 1989, Moscow witnessed the establishment of the first Sexual Minorities Association (later the Union of Lesbians and Homosexuals). According to the program announced at a press conference in February 1990, it was "primarily a human rights organization with the main purpose of obtaining the complete equality of people of different sexual orientations." It saw its prime objectives as campaigning for the revocation of Article 121, changing public attitudes (or, rather, prejudices) toward members of sexual minorities by employing all the opportunities presented by the official mass media and pressing for the social rehabilitation of AIDS sufferers. The group began to publish a newspaper, *Tema* (*The Theme*). It also considered it important to study homosexual problems, to campaign for safe sex, to gather all available information on gay persecution, and to offer assistance to people in their search for friends and soulmates. There were no formal requirements for membership, and no membership lists, and anyone over 18 could join.

*SPID-info* published the association's appeal to the USSR president and supreme soviets of the USSR and union republics, which they simply discovered in their editorial mail. Signed, pseudonymously, by V. Ortanov, K. Yevgeniev, and A. Zubov, the appeal requested the removal of discriminatory statutes (referring to article 121.1) from the criminal code and the declaration of an amnesty for those convicted under it. At the same time, the authors of the appeal declared their "resolute condemnation of any attempts to seduce minors and use violence, in any form and in regard to persons of any age, and regardless of who actually makes such attempts." They went on to say, "We do not attempt to convert anyone to our belief, but we are what nature made us. Help us to stop being afraid. We are part of your life and your spirituality, whether you or we like it or not."[26]

Unfortunately, the political climate of Soviet society and the impossibility of having a constructive dialogue with the authorities encouraged a situation where all democratic movements immediately began to splinter into factions of "radicals" and "moderates" who refused to work with one another. Gays and lesbians were no different in this respect. Immediately after the publication of *Tema's* second trial issue, a split emerged in the association, which then actually ceased to exist; in its place appeared the Moscow Union of Lesbians and Homosexuals (MULH), headed by Yevgenia Debryanskaya and the 24-year-old student Roman Kalinin, who became the sole editor and publisher of *Tema*. The paper was officially registered by the Moscow City Council (Mossovet) in October 1990.

The establishment of the Sexual Minorities Association had opened up new opportunities to gays and lesbians. It was an event triumphantly acclaimed in the West. The fact that a few courageous people had "come out," demanding civil rights in place of compassion and condescension, was an important moral victory. The International Gay and Lesbian Human Rights Commission (IGLHRC) was founded in 1991, with the American Julie Dorf as executive director. The question now was how to continue the struggle.

MULH decided to operate through street meetings and protest demonstrations, employing trenchant political slogans aimed more at the Western press than at Soviet citizens. It was a tactic that found favor with radical American gay activists. Kalinin was particularly well received in the United States, where he was cordially welcomed by the mayor of San Francisco; in fact, the day of his arrival in the city was proclaimed "Roman Kalinin Day," and Kalinin was awarded an honorary certificate and given promises to flood the USSR with free condoms.[27]

Funds collected in the United States enabled the International *Tema* Organization to hold international symposia on gay and lesbian rights and the fight against AIDS in both Leningrad and Moscow in the summer of 1991. Plenary sessions took place in large conference halls. The first gay and lesbian film festival was a part of the conference, which was very successful. Apart from the plenary sessions devoted mainly to political issues, the organizers arranged several symposia at which specific questions concerning sexual minorities were debated, including psychological health and culture, AIDS prevention, and so on. At the last moment, the participants sensibly decided against holding a gay parade with the slogan "Turn Red Squares into Pink Triangles" in Moscow's Red Square,[28] confining themselves instead to a more modest protest meeting near the Moscow City Council accompanied by free distribution of condoms.

Despite the discretion in this particular case, the common features of post—Soviet politics—extremism, lack of political experience, and an unwillingness to deal with reality—soon began to manifest themselves in the activity of Kalinin and his group. Demands by the Libertarian Party, of which MULH was a part, to legalize homosexuality, prostitution, and drugs were understandable; but when lumped together without any detailed argument—the press was given only the bare slogans—they served only to reinforce the stereotype that homosexuality, prostitution, and drug addiction were one and the same thing and that "such people" should be given no quarter.

In autumn 1990, the Communist and nationalist press whipped up a dreadful scandal regarding an alleged interview with Kalinin published in the Moscow district paper *Karetny ryad*. The article said that the Sexual Minorities Association was not protecting the rights of gays and lesbians only, but also the rights of pedophiles, necrophiles, and those favoring bestiality as well. "I don't go in for children myself," Kalinin was quoted as saying, "but our Association's position is clear: the statute on seduction of minors should be removed from the Criminal Code. We are against forced abuse, but if sexual contact takes place by mutual consent, it's normal at any age and in any combination of sexes. . . . Where do you get hold of kids? There are channels: a child costs between 3,000 and 5,000 [rubles]. A pedophile gets a fantastic thrill; after all, a child has a wonderful body and mind, completely unsullied."

"But bodies for necrophiles?"

"No problem there, either; some necrophiles work in morgues, or the ambulance services, or cemeteries. Others come to an arrangement with them."[29]

It is not so important that Kalinin's words may have been blown out of proportion or that Kalinin and his friends were having fun at the expense of a young and inexperienced journalist. TASS and the rest of the official Party and conservative press—*Sovetskaya Rossiya*, *Pravda*, *Semya*, and many other periodicals—as well as the television program "600 Seconds," at once seized upon the sensational piece published in the hitherto obscure *Karetny ryad*. It provided the perfect pretext for a propaganda campaign against the democratic Mossovet, which was roundly condemned for encouraging sexual perversion and pornography. Protest meetings were even held at a number of factories far from Moscow, and there were resolutions, ultimately tabled, demanding immediate new elections for the Moscow City Council, and, at the very least, an absolute ban on *Tema* and the Sexual Minorities Association. Parents were alarmed. They were already scared of letting their children out of doors because of crime; they didn't want to see someone openly defending pedophilia and trade in children!

The democratic press justly assessed the statements from TASS and similar mass media as deliberate political provocation, and a newspaper war broke out. The Moscow City Council took *Karetny ryad* to court on the charge that neither the *Tema* program submitted to the council for registration nor the previously published issues had contained anything like the alleged Kalinin interview, and the gay and lesbian association as such had never been registered at all. The court ruled that the Mossovet claims were justified and compelled *Karetny ryad* to print an apology. *Pravda*, frightened off by the subsequent court case, apologized, too, but repeated its attacks on *Tema* and sexual minorities.[30] Mossovet was able to safeguard its honor. But the damage done by the scandal to the reputation of gays and lesbians was not lessened thereby.

During the press war, both sides tried above all to distance themselves from the unpopular "sexual minorities." The Communist press blamed Mossovet for giving them succor, while Mossovet remonstrated that it was the Communist and conservative press that was giving free advertising to homosexuality by kicking up such a fuss. Only one influential mass-circulation weekly, *Argumenty i fakty*, would publish an article I wrote at the time defending the political correctness and necessity of the legal existence of gay and lesbian associations, despite the possibility of extremist outbursts by their leaders, who were generally typical of Soviet political activists.[31] But what good could a single article do in the face of a propaganda campaign directed at people who were already sufficiently alarmed?

In April 1991, Kalinin's political activism took another step when it was announced that he would be a candidate for the Russian presidency. However, he was not eligible to do so, since he did not meet the age requirement, and he was forced to extricate himself from a situation that soon proved embarrassing. The other leaders of the gay movement (Vladislav Ortanov, Olga Zhuk, and Alexander Kukharsky) were annoyed by Kalinin's antics, which conservative local authorities used as an excuse for refusing to register other, more constructive gay and lesbian organizations and publications.

After the collapse of the August 1991 coup attempt, the social situation of sexual minorities greatly improved. Following the dissolution of the Soviet Union, some republics (Ukraine, Estonia, Latvia, Moldova, and Armenia) revoked their antihomosexual legislation. Under strong pressure from Western public opinion, Russian President Boris Yeltsin also followed this line, and Article 121.1 was annulled by presidential decree, signed April 29 and published May 27, 1993. Now Article 121 (*Muzhelozhstvo*) reads: "Sexual relations between men committed with the use of physical force or in relation to a minor or through taking advantage of the victim's dependent position shall be punishable by incarceration for a term of up to seven years."

Thus, sex between consenting adults has finally been decriminalized. Yet the change is neither radical nor final. The new criminal code has to be passed by the Parliament (Duma). In the last draft of the new criminal code, which was presented to the Duma by the Ministry of Justice and the president's legal office in the middle of 1994, there is an Article 142 on "Forced *muzhelozhstvo*": *muzhelozhstvo* accomplished by the use of physical force, or threat to use force, against the victim or his people, or by using the victim's state of helplessness, is punishable by the deprivation of freedom for from 3 to 6 years; if such actions are done more than once, or in a group, or to a minor, the punishment is from 4 to 10 years; and if the victim is under 14 or if the actions resulted in his death or a heavy detriment to his health, or in HIV infection, the punishment will be from 8 to 15 years. *Muzhelozhstvo* is also mentioned in Article 144, on "Compulsion of a Person to Sexual Intercourse." An earlier version, formulated by Alexei Ignatov, which did not mention sexual orientation at all, had mysteriously disappeared at the last moment, and the working group as a whole was not informed about this change. Given the strength of antidemocratic forces in the Duma, all sorts of political games can be expected. And many legal issues, such as the age of consent, have yet to be resolved.

Despite formal repeal of Article 121.1, neither legal nor prison authorities are in any hurry to release victims of the repressive law. When a delegation from IGLHRC attempted to collect information on the prisoners and their possible release, many officials were unwilling to help. Sometimes it was largely a matter of bureaucracy and the absence of clear instructions. Russian bureaucracies have never been efficient; as one official told the delegation: "We have a thousand inmates here. Do you want me to look through everybody's file?" Yet in some cases, open animosity was expressed: "I don't care what law has been repealed. Those prisoners are still in here, and they will stay here, " or "They chose this life for themselves, they don't deny that they are this way, so why should we try to protect them?"[32] In addition, Russian prison and camp officials are now in a quandary as to what to do with voluntary sexual contacts between inmates. Should they be punished, as before, or should the situation just be ignored?

Nobody can tell how many gay men and lesbians exist in Russia. Even in the West, statistics on the subject are extremely contradictory; perhaps the question itself is scientifically invalid.[33] Russian gay activists, like their Western counterparts, claim that every tenth male is gay; the most stable gay newspaper, edited by Dmitri Lychev, is even named *1/10*. In a journalistic, statistically unreliable questionnaire survey on AIDS and safe-sex attitudes among teenagers conducted in the popular journal *Zdorovye* (*Health*) in February 1990, 4% of boys said they were homosexual and 0.7% of girls declared themselves as lesbians.[34] In a telephone interview conducted by D. D. Isayev in St. Petersburg in 1993, among 155 men surveyed, 2.9% admitted to having had homosexual contacts "often," and another 2.9% "rarely," while 94.2% said they had "never" had homosexual contacts. Of the 280 women surveyed, the respective figures were 1.9%, 1.9%, and 96.2%. But it must be repeated that these statistics are not in any way representative.

Still, both the social and cultural situation of gay men and lesbians in Russia has substantially improved in the last few years. The conspiracy of silence does not exist anymore. Homosexuality has become a popular and even fashionable topic for the newspapers and art.

There are now many independent political and cultural organizations for gay men and lesbians, some of them formally registered, some not. In 1991, the *Osvobozhdenie* (Liberation) Union was founded in Moscow by Yevgenia Debryanskaya and Roman Kalinin to take the place of MULH. The ARGO-RISK Association (ARGO—*Assotsiatsiya za ravnopravie gomosexualistov*, the Association for Homosexual Equal Rights) was officially registered in Moscow in 1992; its leader is Vladislav Ortanov, who holds a doctorate in biochemistry. MOLLI (*Moskovskoye obyedinenie lesbijskoi literatury i iskusstva*—The Moscow Union of Lesbian Literature and Art) was founded

in 1991 by Mila Ugolkova and Lyubov Zinovieva for humanitarian and cultural activity. In St. Petersburg, the two main organizations are the
Tchaikovsky Cultural Initiative and Sexual Minorities' Defense Fund, set up
by Olga Zhuk (after an initial refusal, city authorities permitted the group to
use Tchaikovsky's name) and the *Krylya* (Wings) Homosexual Defense Association, whose president is Alexander Kukharsky, professor of physics.
*Krylya* was initially called *Nevskie berega* (Neva Shores), then *Nevskaya perspektiva* (Neva Perspective), but the city fathers, who thought these names
were "advocating the homosexualization of the district," forced the change.
Similar associations have arisen in a number of former Soviet republics
(Ukraine, Belarus, Latvia, Estonia) and Russian cities (Nizhny Tagil, Bar-
naul, Kaluga, Murmansk, Rostov, Omsk, Tomsk, to name a few).

In August 1993, 27 regional gay and lesbian organizations formally
established a national union, *Rossiyskaya assotsiatsiya lesbiyanok, geev i
biseksualov "Treugolnik"* (The Russian Lesbian, Gay and Bisexual Association
"Triangle"). Like most organizations—and people—in Russia, the Triangle
has ambitious plans but no money. Thus far, they have managed only to
publish a small information bulletin, "The Triangle." As is the case with all
other post-Soviet organizations, gay and lesbian groups suffer the inability
to cooperate with one another. Their leaders accuse each other of grievous
sins and each desires complete independence.

Approximately half a dozen gay newspapers are published in Russia.
Kalinin's *Tema*, which had published a total of 13 issues, ceased publication
in 1993; according to Kalinin, it had "fulfilled its historic mission." Kalinin
himself is now more involved in gay commercial activities. Seven issues of
RISK (*Ravnopravie-Iskrennost-Svoboda-Kompromiss*, or "Equality-Sincerity-
Freedom- Compromise"), edited by Vladislav Ortanov, with a circulation of
5,000, were published between 1992 and 1994. In 1994, Ortanov published also the first issue of an illustrated erotic gay journal, *ARGO*. The gay
newspaper published most regularly—ten issues since November 1991 (up
to mid-1994); largest circulation a print run of 50,000 copies—is *1/10*,
edited by Dmitri Lychev; in 1994, the first international edition, in English,
was published. Other gay newspapers and illustrated magazines (*Ty*, [You]
and *Gay, Slavyane*) are rather ephemeral, often publishing one issue and
then disappearing because of financial and other difficulties.

The gay newspapers and magazines cover virtually the same issues as
those in the West—information about gay and lesbian life, erotic photos
(taken mainly from Western journals), translated and original articles, personal dating service ads, medical and other advice (on how to deal with
gay-bashing, for example), advertisements for condoms and other sexual

aids—but they are, of course, poorer. Material of interest to women, as well as erotica for them, is in substantially shorter supply than material for men. Much appears primitive, but the overall intellectual and artistic level of the publications is rising steadily, which is especially impressive when one considers how difficult and costly it is to publish at all.

Letters and ads vividly show that the lifestyles of and problems facing Russian gays are just as multifarious as in the West. A typical personal ad reads, "Social, easygoing, intelligent young man, 22/180/58, seeks tall, sports-loving, educated gay friend with decent statistics and 22–28 cm size penis." Many young men frankly seek rich patrons. On the other hand, there are also quite a few ads stressing the need for love and friendship.

*RISK* (1992, no. 2–3) opened a discussion on the issue of having a permanent partner. Nineteen-year-old Igor writes:

> In my view all this talk about constancy is just a load of rubbish. . . . To sleep all the time with the same person is boring: it's hardly conceivable! I'm not a monster, thank God, and can find any number of fellows I want: different bodies, different lips, different penises—a new thrill every time. Maybe in a score or more years, when I won't need any of this, I'll have to tie myself down with someone permanent, but for the time being—you can keep it, thank you very much.

Alongside Igor's note is a letter from 27-year-old Dmitri:

> I don't understand what a "permanent partner" is. Since he walked into my life a year ago, my life has gained a purpose and fullness. I want him constantly, all the time, but that isn't the point: for some time now sex has been secondary: we haven't anywhere to live anyway, so we spend most of our time walking the streets and drinking tea with his or my friends whom we've known together for some time. . . . You could probably call us permanent partners, but he is no "partner" to me; he is the man I love. And that's forever.

By contrast with ethnic minorities, gays and lesbians cannot proclaim their sovereignty and set up their own independent state (the most popular post-Soviet idea!); their emancipation and sociocultural integration are two sides of the same coin. This will be a long and difficult process. Sexual minorities can be liberated only by concerted effort from all democratic forces. Political happenings and street confrontation are fine for a community of contented, benevolent people with full bellies, but in Russia, such actions may only provoke general irritation and intensify the tensions of daily life.

Another formidable task is educating the ignorant public about sexual minorities. This will be possible only though the actions of the mainstream mass media, science, and the arts. The development of a true gay subculture is also vital if the homosexual ghetto is to become a normal gay and lesbian community, with its own publications, clubs, counseling centers, and so on, as is the case in the West.

All this can be accomplished only through cooperation and dialogue with the heterosexual majority—political action alone is inadequate.

Recent progress in this direction is undeniable. In June 1994, in the framework of the government-sponsored international conference in Moscow, "The Family on the Eve of the Third Millennium," a roundtable on "Same-Sex Marriages: Moral and Legal Issues" was organized, and the recommendation to legalize such unions was taken without contradiction. Not that anybody will do so in the foreseeable future.

Formerly suppressed and forbidden "gay sensibilities" and eroticism are gradually being recognized and integrated into the elite culture. The most popular theater director in Moscow is the openly gay Roman Viktyuk, and his theater, where some performances have marked homoerotic overtones, is always full, although the audience is not even predominantly gay. In St. Petersburg, the eminent classical dancer Valery Mikhailovsky recently established a first-rate all-male ballet company, and the prominent choreographer Boris Eifman staged a very successful piece about the life of Tchaikovsky in his Modern Ballet Theater. The problems of gay and lesbian life are often discussed on television and in the mainstream newspapers. A shockingly revealing interview with Boris Moiseev, an openly gay popular dancer, was recently published. Moiseev spoke frankly about his sexual experiences with former Komsomol bosses. Foreign films with homosexual allusions, and even some completely dedicated to this topic, are shown openly in the cinemas and sometimes even on television.

Mikhail Kuzmin's classic homoerotic poetry and his famous novel, *Kryla*, as well as novels by Jean Genet, James Baldwin, and Truman Capote have been published. A two-volume collection of the works of the Russian gay writer, actor, and theater director Evgenii Kharitonov (1941–81) was published for the first time in 1993.

Nor is only gay high culture available. There are now (mid-1994) four gay discos in Moscow and two in St. Petersburg. Moscow gays can meet one another in The Underground, a popular gay bar, or in The Elf, a cafe club. But who can afford such luxuries? Only the very rich, foreigners, and male prostitutes.

These are the impressions of one visitor to a gay restaurant in Moscow:

The street-sex heritage in cooperation with a specifically male mentality—all men are sexy animals—transforms many victims of passion into a commodity of this market. Men buy others and sell themselves here, entering into contracts, constantly haggling. Using the only currency it has—the body—poor but attractive youth pays for the merriment and satiety of rich but-no-longer-fresh old age.[35]

Furthermore, these places exist in an atmosphere of threat and danger. Gay bashing and discrimination are still the norm, especially in the provinces.

All gay newspapers and organizations engage in some anti-AIDS propaganda, but the sexual behavior of many gay men is still risky. In 1993, D. D. Isayev surveyed 290 St. Petersburg gay men aged 16 to 40 on the premises of gay organizations and gay discos and at gay beaches. Some 40.5% had had more than 20 male partners, and 27.5% among them had had more than 50; 47% had no permanent partner, and 14% preferred anonymous and short-term contacts. Only 12% had sex exclusively with their permanent partner. Twenty-six percent combined permanent partnership with occasional short-term contacts. Only 19% had had heterosexual contact before their first homosexual experiences, but parallel homo- and heterosexual contact is widespread (52%).

This type of sexual behavior is epidemiologically dangerous. Although 47% of the gay men surveyed were worried about possible AIDS infection (16% more than among straight men), 33% had never used condoms and 24% did so only rarely. Another 33% thought it was enough to use condoms in casual contacts and for anal sex. Like the majority of St. Petersburg males, only 12.5% used condoms regularly. Nineteen percent of the gay men had had a venereal disease, and 2% had had more than one.[36]

It is extremely difficult to organize counseling services for gay men. Official medicine has a negative attitude toward them, and gay and lesbian organizations have neither the money nor the professional qualifications to provide such services.[37]

Like almost everything else in contemporary Russia, the advances in gay and lesbian social and legal situations are extremely tentative. Many things that are possible in the capital are still absolutely impossible in the provinces. Political opposition to the legalization of homosexuality is very strong. In a television interview in June 1993, ex-Vice President Alexander Rutskoy was asked about his attitude toward sexual minorities; with a squeamish gesture of pushing away, he said, "In a civilized society there should be no sexual minorities."

The former Komsomol activist Valery Skurlatov, who initiated the campaign for "moral purification" in the 1960s, is now chairman of the extreme nationalist *Vozrozhdenie* (Renewal) Union. At a press conference in August 1993, he said that "70% of the men in Yeltsin's cabinet are homosexuals" who posed a danger to state security because of their "hostility toward healthy citizens" and "their links to foreign homosexuals." He proposed forming a parliamentary commission to investigate the sexual preferences of government officials. "Russians have never stood for homosexuality," Skurlatov said. "We have decided to campaign actively to bring the truth about homosexuality in the government to the people."[38]

Concern about AIDS is very often used as a pretext for antigay campaigns. For example, in November 1993, the Moscow newspaper *Kommersant-Daily*, representing "the new Russians" (i.e., the new Russian capitalists), published an article with the headline "AIDS epidemic among homosexuals has begun in Moscow. " This sensationalist story was presented as an interview with Dr. Vadim Pokrovsky, the epidemiologist, who was quoted as saying there was already a real AIDS epidemic among gay men in Moscow. To a professional, the statistics purporting to document this claim look strange; they could not have been compiled by a professional. Yet the article was supplemented by a commentary from Vladimir Pron, the chief of the Moscow police's vice squad division:

> Society wanted depravity, and now it has it. At present, the militia has no right to control homosexuals in any way. The article punishing homosexuality was deleted from the Criminal Code, and now only violence against minors can be punished. Even if we know about a "blue" den, we have no right to raid it because these dens have become, as a rule, legal clubs.[39]

The militant homophobia of Pron's department and that of the newspaper that published the interview is well known. But I have seen no disclaimer of this provocative publication from Pokrovsky. Only *I/lO* published a rebuttal to this nonsense.

Antigay articles are often published in the Russian government newspaper *Rossiyskie vesti* (*Russian News*). A typical example is an article entitled "Pathology should not take hold of the masses," by the Moscow psychiatrist Mikhail Buyanov (during perestroika he became a vocal critic of the former Soviet "repressive psychiatry"), which was full of open hatred toward homosexuals and their "sympathizers" and demanded strong, repressive measures against them. Like other "patriots," Buyanov claims that homosexuality was always alien to Russia and that its "popularity" now is the result of Western, primarily American and British, ideological expansionism.[40]

The democratic *Komsomolskaya pravda* published a long article by Dr. B. Irzak in July 1993. The article's subtitle was "What should the majority do when homosexuality becomes fashionable?" Unlike Buyanov, Irzak supports decriminalization of homosexuality and is in principle against society's interference in private life. But he is worried about the growing "normalization" and popularization of same-sex love: "As a biological phenomenon, homosexuality is in need of research, and as a social phenomenon, it needs strict control."[41] Even some liberal Russian intellectuals opposed to fascism and anti-Semitism, such as the famous actor and film director Rolan Bykov, sometimes talk publicly about the existence and danger of a "homosexual conspiracy."

On the one hand, such statements may be interpreted as a natural reaction to the excessive, noisy, and sometimes aggressive publicity of the homosexual lifestyle in the Russian mass media; Russians are unaccustomed to this. For a strongly normativist psychiatry, a pluralistic attitude to sexual orientation is also intellectually unacceptable. On the other hand, these statements are clearly a part of a large-scale ideological campaign, which may have tragic social consequences. It is not by chance that the current wave of antihomosexuality had its start with the repeal of Article 121.1.

While gay activists claim to be involved in big political issues and continue to quarrel among themselves, prominent Russian "blue" artists and intellectuals with few exceptions are in no hurry to come out publicly—partly because they are afraid to do so,[42] partly because they prefer privacy to exhibitionism, and partly because they, like the majority of the Russian people, are generally disillusioned with politics.

The idea of a separate "gay identity " is unacceptable to many Russian intellectuals. They are deeply shocked by the fast commercialization and vulgarization of the gay lifestyle, including sexuality. The new gay discos are already monopolized by the nouveaux riches on one side, and the male prostitutes on the other. This style of life is expensive, dangerous, aesthetically unpleasing, and vulgar. And Russian gay politics is no better than any other kind of post-Soviet politics.

"Those creepy activists actually go and talk about their sexuality all over the place. And they do it only for the attention they get from the West; activism occurs here because Westerners put Russians up to it. My good friends know I'm gay, but it's my private business. I'm not interested in telling everyone that I like to sleep with men," said one gay Russian man to the American journalist Andrew Solomon. Added another: "I don't want to be part of any subculture. I know that's the fashion in the West, but though I may choose to *sleep* mainly with gay men, that doesn't mean I want to *socialize* primarily with them."[43]

Such attitudes are fairly typical. But if there is no gay community, who will defend gays' and lesbians' human rights, which are by no means guaranteed in Russia? And who will give them professional social and psychological advice and help them deal with stressful situations? Homophobic old-style psychiatrists or equally ignorant, self-educated "gay doctors"?

According to VCIOM 1994 survey replicating one of 1989, in the last five years people became more tolerant of almost all stigmatized groups, including gays. The number of people wanting "to liquidate" homosexuals dropped from 27% in 1989 to 18% in 1994, and of those wishing "to isolate" them from 32% to 23%. The number of those wishing to "help," on the contrary, rose from 6% to 8%, and those wishing to "leave them by themselves" from 12% to 29% (the figures for 1989 are only Russian and not the whole of USSR, as at page 248). It is an important change. But is it stable?

Gays and lesbians are now finally coming out in Russia as a social and cultural minority, but they still lack a clear self-image. And it is very dangerous to come out into a ruined and chaotic world, where everything is disconnected and everyone is looking not for friends but enemies. If the country takes a radical turn to communism or fascism, gays and lesbians and their "sympathizers," along with Jewish intellectuals, will be the first candidates for murder and the concentration camps.

Once again, this a social, not a sexual problem. . . .

*Conclusion*

# SEXUALITY AS A MIRROR OF RUSSIAN REVOLUTION

*He who has hail raining down on his head thinks that the whole world is engulfed in storms and tempests.*

—Michel de Montaigne

We have discussed the basic traits of the history as well as the present state of Russian sexual culture. We are now left with two questions: Are the processes involved as dramatic as they seem? And is it possible to consider these dramatic processes as a model and reflection of Russian social-political development?

The Russian eros, with all its contradictions, has always been and still remains an integral part of Russian social, cultural, and political life. The dramatic gap between "top" and "bottom," "high" and "low," spirituality and carnality, word and deed; the drive toward anarchy on the one hand and strict external controls on the other; the difficulties of the processes of individualization and the formation of a high erotic culture—all are intrinsically tied to the fundamental features of Russian history, particularly the gap between the masses and the elite that is much greater than in the West.

My book is entitled *The Sexual Revolution in Russia*, but "revolution" is perhaps the wrong word. What we really see is the unfolding not of a single dramatic transformation but of a long series of interrelated—albeit discontinuous, contradictory, and unfinished—social and cultural processes that have been only loosely associated with specific political events.

The early-twentieth-century cultural revolution of the "Silver Age," which was closely related to the urbanization and industrialization of Russia, was the first serious blow to traditional forms of social control and the symbolic opposition of "sex" and "culture" among the intellectual elite. But it was a relatively isolated cultural phenomenon, far from the everyday lives of the working and middle classes, and it evoked strong criticism from both the right and the left.

The October Revolution of 1917 saw a complete breakdown in the old normative culture and the institutional order that included family, marriage, and gender stratification. This revolution seemed extremely radical, and it evoked jubilant celebration from one side and terrified indignation from the other. In reality, however, this "transformation" proved superficial, involving only a small segment of the population. And to a certain degree, it was more verbal than substantial. "Freedom from" was not transformed into and supplemented by "freedom for." In spite of the blatant radicalism of leftist-anarchist phraseology and some changes in their sexual behavior, the fundamental unconscious values, attitudes, and stereotypes that informed the actions of young people during the 1920s remained substantially similar to those of young people in the pre-Revolutionary period. The 1920s saw the same primitive sexism, the same irrational sexual fears, the same intolerance, the same lack of erotic sophistication. For the Bolsheviks as a ruling party, it was easy first to suppress and then to exterminate the feeble shoots of sexual—as well as any other kind of—individual freedom, and then to restore and even strengthen the other side of traditional Russian life—i.e., external regimentation.

Stalinist sexophobia was an important element of the "cultural revolution," rather, the counterrevolution of the early 1930s, aimed at liquidating social and cultural diversity and at establishing total control over the personality. But instead it had a boomerang effect. The elimination of erotic culture and the degradation of the elite to the level of the masses produced not so much a desexualization of public and private life as its impoverishment, primitivization, and vulgarization. Sexuality, driven underground and degraded to the level of a simple "sex instinct," became more and more wild, and potentially aggressive.

At the beginning, the Communist regime was able to use sexuality in the interests of the state, transforming suppressed sexuality into the cult of the leader and into hatred for "enemies of the people," but later the repression turned against the regime itself. Just as had been forecast by Yevgenii Zamiatin and George Orwell, first in the official propaganda and then in the mass consciousness, sex—of any kind!—became a sign of social protest and a refuge for individuals from the totalitarian state. Forbidden erotica became a strong anti-Soviet and anti-Communist symbol, pressing the people to make their choice—and whatever their public declarations may have been, their practical choices were invariably against the regime.

The gradual liberalization and transformation of the Soviet regime from totalitarian to authoritarian caused its sexual policy to shift from one of brutal suppression to one of awkward taming. But Soviet sexual liberalism, advocating the medicalization and pedagogization of sexuality, failed as completely as political and economic reforms. Communist liberalism had no clear social goals; it strove not to lift but merely to soften state control, and it naively looked for implementation of its principles to the same state and Party authorities who had vested interests in maintaining the status quo. As in other spheres of social life, Party bureaucrats were unwilling to sacrifice a part of their power to save the whole. Thus, the time when liberal reforms might have worked was irrevocably squandered.

The breakdown of the Soviet regime brought the Russian people their long-desired sexual liberation. But, as has been the case with the economy and politics, sexual freedom was immediately transformed into anomie and anarchy. The birth of sophisticated sexual-erotic culture is a long and painful process. Instead of sexuality becoming individualized—more private and intimate—it is being deromanticized, commercialized, and trivialized. This wild, uncivilized sex, like the wild and criminal primitive accumulation of capital, produces growing frustration and irritation among people of the older generation, and "an end to sexual anarchy" becomes the rallying cry of conservative forces who seek to create moral panic and increase social tension.

Most of the brazen erotica and pornography in Russia now carries the label "Made in the USA," and even though this label is often fake, it is associated in the mass consciousness with American influence. This Americanization of Russian sexual culture, coupled with its commercialization and vulgarization, is a dangerous social phenomenon, engendering and provoking strong anti-Western and especially anti-American feelings even among liberal intellectuals. It also allows Russian nationalists and fascists to pose as the saviors of traditional Russian cultural values and spirituality.

Not all these complaints, however, should be taken at face value. Judging by professional surveys, we note that the mass media grossly exaggerate negative changes in sexual behavior and underestimate their heterogeneity. Many things that seem to be brand-new have really been in existence for a long time, albeit under cover. And every transitional period is accompanied by anomie and social disorganization, which are difficult to endure but should not produce panic. The main questions are, Do we know where we are going? and What do we really want?

The Russian anti-Communist revolution is deeply ambivalent. As directed against the authoritarian regime, it is democratic and liberal. But it is also conservative, because for many people its aim is simply a return to the pre—1917 social order and the restoration of traditional moral and religious values. Not surprisingly, the people behind these opposite convictions also have very different ideas about sexuality.

However peculiar and even exotic Soviet and post-Soviet life may seem to Western eyes, its fundamental problems, including shifts in sexual values, are largely the same as those found in the West. The "World Sexual Revolution," the beginning of which was heralded by *Time* magazine in 1964 and the end ("the revolution is over") in 1984, was really only one step in the long process of secularization and individualization. Its costs, emphasized by conservative critics, were very similar to what is now going on in Russia. Does "the end of the revolution" mean that everything has come full circle, returning to the status quo ante? By no means. The sexual revolution of the 1960s accomplished its destructive tasks and opened the door for the quieter, more difficult, lengthier, and ultimately more constructive process of formation of new sexual-erotic norms and values. According to the sociologist Ira L. Reiss, the United States is still experiencing the labor pains of sexual pluralism as a necessary aspect of the democratic way of life.[1]

What about contemporary Russia?

A look at the post-Soviet sexual scene evokes contradictory feelings. The first thought might be, "How awful! Those poor people. . . . " But the second thought is likely to be, "Why is everything so sensationalized and exaggerated, as if the Apocalypse has come? Many Western countries, even those without such terrible economic and social turmoil, have the same or similar problems, and life still goes on." Both these reactions may be justifiable, and much depends on whether you look at the Russian situation from within or from without, and whether your perspective is short- or long-term.

Historically speaking, the current Russian sexual scene has much in common with previous critical points that produced similar states of moral panic in Russia: the beginning of the twentieth century, just prior to and just after the 1905 revolution, and the 1920s, which followed the October Revolution. In all these cases, the attitudinal changes have been faster and more radical than those of real sexual behavior, and conservative ideology was prone to emphasize the negative consequences of social change at the expense of positive ones.

For members of the older generation, such a critical stance is natural. But we must interpret the current cultural situation not only in the light of our ideal values but also in a very specific historical perspective.

Yes, it's very bad that, instead of systematic scientific sex education, Russia now has cheap, commercial erotica. But even that is better than the crazy Communist sexophobia, which made sexuality—every sort of sexuality—into an unmentionable vice.

Yes, the level of contraceptive culture in Russia is extremely low. Yet only a few years ago, the situation was much worse, and people did not even know how much they were risking and losing because of their ignorance.

We worry about social, political, and sexual discrimination against and abuse of Russian women; but ten years ago this situation was considered absolutely normal, and the word "sexism" didn't exist, not even in the professional sociological language.

We complain about strong homophobia and gay bashing; but until June 1993, homosexuality was a criminal offense in Russia, and any form of coming out for gays and lesbians would have been the near equivalent of suicide.

Even such new and dangerous trends as the growth of sexual violence and the spread of STDs are fundamentally by-products of the individual's newly acquired freedom from the bureaucratic state, police, and medical control. All civilized industrial countries have had to pay the same or similar prices for such a transition.

The comparison of Russia with the West should also be more specific and intellectually sophisticated. Absolutely all the developmental problems of Russian sexual culture—whether gender equality, the relation of love and sex, child abuse, prostitution, pornography, or AIDS prevention—are in reality global, rather than local, issues and are common to other nations as well. The general trends in these developments are basically the same in Russia as elsewhere.

Russian sexual culture generally lags about 25 years behind that of the West. But "the West" is too broad an abstraction. The United States has wonderful achievements in sex research. But in such fundamental social dimensions as sexual tolerance, sex education, and contraceptive culture, the contrast between the Netherlands and the United States may be greater than that between the United States and Russia.

The contrasts and similarities between Russia and Western countries may also differ markedly depending on the specific dimension. Russia leads the industrial world in the number of induced abortions and trails in the complete absence of any sex education. Yet in many other sociosexual issues, there may be more similarities with, than differences from, the West. Russia seems to lead Western Europe but trails the United States in rape and STD statistics, even without taking AIDS into account. Russian attitudes to pre- and extramarital sex, according to public opinion polls, are quite similar to American. The level of homophobia also seems to be more or less the same in both counties.

But most tentative quantitative generalizations are statistically unreliable and often intellectually misleading because of scarcity of data and methodological flaws in analysis. That is why I have tried to resist the temptation of direct comparisons. To know something more or less for certain, we need well-organized international surveys, using the same questionnaire, similar samples, and so on. At present, such research seems impossible for financial reasons. For assessing qualitative differences in sexual values, notions of romantic love, patterns of courtship, and criteria of marital satisfaction, even very sophisticated questionnaire research will prove inadequate.

Russia now has a choice: to move forward, to the twenty-first century, or backward, to the nineteenth century or even to the preindustrial society that preceded it. Some people hanker after the latter, since the country at present faces a no-win situation, combining all the minuses of various social systems without any of their merits.

If democratic and economic reform programs fail, Russia will have an openly "red-brown" fascist government, or at best, an extremely conservative, ultranationalistic one. Despite whatever economic and political concessions it will have to make to the West, its ideology will be strongly anti-democratic, anti-Western, and anti-American. Sexophobia, along with anti-Semitism, will be a very powerful propaganda weapon again, and it will find understanding and support among some Western conservatives. The immediate practical results of this new reaction may be terrible.

I must confess I'm pessimistic about the near future. Russian anticommunist revolution is justly defined as a *criminal revolution*. Both President Yeltsin and his government are extremely unpopular. Nominally democratic institutions are helpless before the wave of corruption and crime. In a recent express TV public opinion poll in Moscow, 95% of respondents said they believe that the real power in the country belongs to the Mafia. People are disillusioned and afraid of the future.[2] In such a climate, the turn to some sort of authoritarianism seems almost inevitable.

In the long run, however, there is no going back. The roads in that direction are closed.

Like many other aspects of Soviet/Russian life, sexophobia has been the offspring of the marginal, déclassé lumpen proletariat, ex-peasants who did not really belong to town or countryside. This segment of the population is gradually disappearing from the historical stage. In 1990 the number of native urbanites (those born in the cities) among 60-year-old Russians did not exceed 15 to 17%, while such people represented about 40% of the population among 40-year-olds, and more than 50% of the 20-year-olds. Although these first-generation urbanites still bear the marks of the past, they are already different from their fathers and grandfathers. Some 70% of all children in Russia are now born and brought up in towns. By the year 2000, fewer than half of 40-year-olds, but 63% of 30-year-olds and 70% of 20-year-olds will have been born in cities.[2] In the years 2000–2010, urbanites will become the majority. This process is irrevocable.

Urban culture requires pluralism by its very nature. In the United States, the most virulent opponents of sexual tolerance are from rural communities and small towns. Childhood and adolescent socialization is a better predictor of sexual conservatism than social status, individual psychological traits like an authoritarian personality, or even individual sexual experiences.[3]

Russia's current sexual attitudes and practices are already highly diversified according to age; gender; education; regional, ethnic, and social background; generational cohort; and religious affiliation. In the near future, this heterogeneity will probably increase and may produce more cultural conflicts. Yet in the long run, it is the younger, urban, better-educated people who will certainly have the upper hand in defining what is right and what is wrong. Any attempt by the state, church, or local community to forcibly limit sexual freedom is not only doomed to failure but will be terribly detrimental to the authority of the institution involved.

Precisely because of this new freedom, Russia badly needs a sophisticated sexual-erotic culture. It cannot be imported but must be created. Western experience, whether in sex research, sexual education, or erotic art, can make important contributions to Russian sexual culture. But Western sexual culture and experience are also heterogeneous. At present, Russia is taking from the West mainly what is bad, cheap, or easily attainable. If this trend continues, future generations will pay an enormous price.

Yet it is not only Russians who have something to learn.

For Western, especially American, conservatives, the Soviet sexual experiment offers an instructive lesson: although it may be possible to block the development and spread of sexual-erotic culture, subordinating sexual behavior to arbitrary authoritarian standards is not effective. Irrational bans engender not chastity but hypocrisy and blind revolt, as well as the most dangerous consequences of uncivilized sex—abortions, teenage pregnancies, sexual violence, and sexually transmitted disease—which parents and educators want to avoid at all costs.

To Western sexual radicals, including some American feminists, the Soviet experience may teach the lesson that not everything in human relationships will submit to radical change; and fast changes sometimes produce unforeseen and even boomerang effects. Human nature and historical traditions, given all their plasticity, should be taken seriously.

It is easy and legitimate to replace the biological term "sex" with the sociological term "gender," and thus to make people more sensitive to the idea that gender differences and stratification are historical social constructions and not innate biological givens. But if sex dimorphism is largely ignored by social scientists afraid to appear "politically incorrect," who will discuss and interpret the relationships between sex and gender, and the practical implications of sex differences? I am drawn to the diverting pluralism of postmodern philosophy, where everything seems flexible and possible. But do we expect a postmodern Brave New World to be fundamentally sexless (a very Soviet idea) or to be composed of "different but equal" ghettos of gender, race, and ethnicity (a very post-Soviet idea)?

Alas, humans rarely seem to learn from history. As the Russian proverb says, "Everyone understands according to his own sins."

# ACKNOWLEDGMENTS

This book would have been impossible to write without the help of many Western, particularly American, colleagues and institutions.

I would not have been able to engage in this work had it not been for the assistance of the American Sociological Association, which during the 1960s and 1970s generously sent me scholarly books and periodicals that were absent in Soviet libraries.

Although, first, Soviet restrictions and then lack of money prevented me from attending its annual conventions, except for two occasions, in 1979 and 1988, membership in the International Academy of Sex Research ensured professional contacts with the world's leading scholars, many of whom also helped with advice and literature.

Frequent, albeit short, lecture visits after 1986 to various American and European universities and research centers, including the Kinsey Institute, have broadened my scientific and general outlook. Acquaintance with Western lifestyles was important not simply in itself; it forced me to question and helped me to recognize the peculiarities of Soviet life, some of which I had previously accepted as natural and normal. Book knowledge is insufficient for this kind of perspective.

My main debt of gratitude is to the Russian Research Center of Harvard University. The grant I obtained to study there in 1991/1992 presented me with an opportunity to work in peace, to read a host of books and periodicals unavailable in Moscow, and to discuss problems of mutual interest with colleagues in various fields. A short-term grant at the Kennan Institute for Advanced Russian Studies at the Woodrow Wilson International Center, which allowed me access to the Library of Congress and the technical facilities of the institute, was very important. I also appreciate the hospitality of and the technical assistance provided by the Russell Sage Foundation in New York City and by the Sociology Department of Wellesley College, where I taught in spring 1993.

It is a pleasure to express my gratitude to my friend and colleague James Riordan for the English translation of the manuscript, as well as for valuable advice and moral support. My Russian colleagues Yuri Levada,

Valery Chervyakov, Vladimir Shapiro, Igor Lunin, and Dmitri Isayev have permitted me to quote from their unpublished research data, and Laura Engelstein of Princeton University helped me overcome my doubts about using personal recollections in a book like this. Arthur J. Rosenthal and Beth Anderson of the Free Press and Alexia Dorszynski labored heroically to make the book more dynamic and accessible to a wider audience.

My last word of gratitude is for John H. Gagnon. By inviting me to the Prague session of the International Academy of Sex Research in 1979 and by making himself available for subsequent numerous and lengthy theoretical discussions, he brought me into the "squalid" business of sex research. It made my life in the former Soviet Union much more difficult, but I know it was the right choice.

# APPENDIX

## List of the Soviet and Russian Sexual Surveys Referred to in the Text

Because not a single Soviet/Russian sexual survey was ever published in the normal scientific way, with all tables, questionnaires, and methodological discussions, I had to use not only published papers and summaries but also, with the kind permission of the authors, some of the unpublished data, raw tables, and so on. Below is a short description of the most important recent surveys referred to in the text. The responsibility for any possible errors or misinterpretation of these data is exclusively mine.

### 1. VCIOM 1992 Survey

Vsesoyuznyi (since 1992—Vserossiiskii) Tsentr izucheniya obshchestvennovo mnenia (All-Union [since 1992—All-Russia] Center for Public Opinion Research) (VCIOM), Director, Professor Yuri Levada. Poll "Culture," June 1992.

Representative sample, about 3,500 persons, in three different areas: Slav (Russia and Ukraine); Baltic (Estonia and Lithuania); Asiatic (Uzbekistan and Tadzhikistan). In the Slav area the population was surveyed without regard to ethnic origins or "nationality" (that is, not only ethnic Russians but also Tatars, Jews, Germans, and others were questioned), while in the other two regions only members of indigenous nationalities were surveyed (that is, in Estonia, Estonians but not Russians). Questionnaires were completed by the respondents in the presence of a professional interviewer. Among many other questions, some were related to sexuality: Are people happy in love and family life; what are their family values, their attitudes to premarital and extramarital sex, conjugal fidelity, erotica, sex education, and so on.

### 2. VCIOM 1993 Survey

Poll "The Fact," June 1993.

Representative sample for the Russian Federation, 1,665 persons (746 men and 909 women), aged from 16 to 84 (16–25, 285; 24–40, 546; 40–55, 383; 55–84, 461), from 13 different regions. Education: university,

235; high (secondary) school, 803; fewer than 9 years of secondary school, 616. Occupation: nonworking pensioners, 409; manual workers, 330; professionals, 284; technicians, 136; other employees, 120; students, 87. Place of residence: capitals and regional cities, 604; towns, 614; villages, 344. All procedures are standard ones normally used in public opinion polls.

Some of the questions concerned attitudes toward the following aspects of sexual behavior (5-point scales, from "It deserves censure" to "I don't see anything wrong in it"): masturbation, premarital sex, frequent change of sexual partners, marital infidelity, viewing of pornographic films, group sex, homosexual contacts, induced abortions, and so on. There were also a few questions about personal sexual experience, such as age at the first sexual contact, number of lifetime sexual partners, and present sexual activities. About 40% did not answer these personal questions.

## 3. Adolescent Sexuality Survey 1993

Done by Vladimir Shapiro and Valery Chervyakov, Institute of Sociology, Russian Academy of Sciences, with Igor Kon as a consultant and Maria Gerasimova as the field research organizer. An adapted version of the American sociologist Stan Weed's questionnaire was used. Time of data collection: end of 1992 to beginning of 1993. Sample: 1,615 students (50.4% boys, 49.6% girls) from 16 high (secondary) schools and 8 vocational schools in Moscow and St. Petersburg, aged from 12 to 17 years (7th to 11th grades). The questionnaire contained 135 questions about aspects of sexual experience and attitudes: dating, going steady, age at and the motives for the first sexual intercourse, sources of sexual information, communication with parents and peers, moral and religious values, involvement in deviant behavior, and some personal psychological characteristics. The schools were selected to represent different social strata of the city population. Questionnaires were completed in the classrooms, anonymously, voluntarily, and individually, in the presence of a professional interviewer. The permission of the school administration was obtained, but nobody had access to this confidential information. There were no refusals from students to take part in the research, but some respondents didn't answer certain questions. Detailed statistical analysis is in progress. General popular overview of the results: Igor Kon, Valery Chervyakov, and Vladimir Shapiro, "Podrostki i seks: Utrata illuzii," *Ogonyok*, no. 2 (1994), 22–25.

## 4. Igor Lunin 1993 survey

Adolescent sexual attitudes, representations, and practice questionnaire survey, by Dr. Igor Lunin, St. Petersburg Crisis Prevention Service for Children and Adolescents, May—September 1993. Sample: 370 (185 boys and 185 girls), high (secondary) school tenth graders and vocational school students from three socially and economically different districts of St. Petersburg. The average age: 15.9 years. An anonymous questionnaire was preliminarily reviewed in teenage discussion groups. Participation, on the school premises, was individual and voluntary. Questions concerned sexual values and behavior, main sources of sexual and contraceptive information and the evaluation of its availability and reliability, sexual harassment, violence, and rape experience, attitudes to condoms and to different forms of sex education. A detailed statistical analysis is in progress. I. I. Lunin, "Seksualnoe prosveshchenie kak faktor profilaktiki seksualnykh posyagatelstv," *Problemy planirovaniya semyi v Rossii. Pervaya natsionalnaya konferentsia Rossiiskoi Assotsiatsii "Planirovanie semyi"* (Moscow, 1994), pp. 96–105. See also Igor Lunin, Thomas L. Hall, Jeffrey S. Mandel, Julia Kay, and Norman Hearst, *Adolescent Sexuality in St. Petersburg: Russia in the Era of AIDS* (in press).

## 5. D. D. Isayev 1993 Telephone Survey

Done by Dmitri D. Isayev, M.D., in St. Petersburg, September—December 1993. Sample: 435 people, 16 to 55 years old; 155 men (average age, 35.4 years; 67.5% were married), and 280 women (average age, 37.3 years; 67% were married). Questions about personal sexual experience and attitudes, number of partners, safe-sex practices, and AIDS-prevention measures.

## 6. Olga Loseva 1991 Survey

The Moscow venereologist Olga Loseva's unpublished dissertation (1991) summarized 15 years of research of sexual behavior and sexual values of syphilitics. She collected data on 3,273 heterosexual men and women at a venereological clinic in Moscow (300 medical histories and about 3,000 questionnaires: 1,782 from the patients and 1,191 from the control group, persons without sexually transmitted diseases), plus 120 teenage girls' questionnaires. Sociologically, the samples were not representative, but a comparison of three control groups, divided by five-year intervals, is informative for the shifts in sexual attitudes and practices. In my book, only data about control groups are used.

O. K. Loseva, "Seksualnoe povedenie bolnykh sifilisom (epidemiologicheskie i mediko-sotsialnye problemy)," Avtoreferat dissertatsii na soiskanie uchenoi stepeni doktora meditsinskikh nauk (Moscow: Tsentralnyi nauchno-issledovatelskii kozhno-venerologicheskii institut, 1991); O. K. Loseva, T. V. Chistyakova, A. V. Libin, and E. V. Livin, "Seksualnoe povedenie podrostkov, bolnykh sifilisom," *Vestnik dermatologii i venerologii*, no. 2 (1991), 45–49. K. K. Borisenko, O. K. Loseva, "Zabolevaemost molodyozhi boleznyaimi, peredavaemymi polovym putyom," *Planirovanie semyi* 4 (1994), 20–22; O. K. Loseva, "Sotsialno-meditsinskie aspekty boleznei, peredavaemykh polovym putom, u detei i podroskov," Rossiyskaya assotsiatsyia "Planirovanie semyi," Pervaya natsyonalnaya konferentsya *"Problemy Planirovania Semyi v Rossii" (materialy konferetnsii. 7–9 dekabrya 1993, Moskva* (Moscow: "Kvartet," 1994), pp. 89–96.

# NOTES

## NOTES TO INTRODUCTION

1. Eve Levin, *Sex and Society in the World of the Orthodox Slavs, 900–1700* (Ithaca, N.Y.: Cornell University Press, 1989).
2. Laura Engelstein, *The Keys to Happiness: Sex and the Search for Modernity in Fin-de-Siècle Russia* (Ithaca, N.Y.: Cornell University Press, 1992).
3. There are, to my knowledge, only four book-length essays on Soviet sexual culture. Joseph McGabe, *Sex Life in Russia* (Girard, Kans.: Halderman-Julius, 1948), says that "Soviet Russia is a Puritan Commonwealth in comparison with Tsarist Russia, but this change has been effected neither on religious nor moral grounds . . . Russia is working out the sex problems, but it has been delayed by prolonged and terrible distractions" (pp. 31, 32); Dr. Mikhail Stern and Dr. August Stern, *Sex in the Soviet Union* (London: W.H. Allen, 1981), written by an émigré gynecologist from the provincial Ukrainian town of Vinnitsa and his son, contains interesting personal reminiscences and some impressionistic evidence of poor sexual culture but no sociological analysis. Sexologically, both doctors are also very naive. A book by the émigré writer Mark Popovsky, *Trety Lishny: On, Ona i Sovetsky Rezhim* (*The Superfluous Third, He, She, and the Soviet Regime*) (London: Overseas Publications, 1985), p. 457, is much better. He collected a good deal of factual material, including historically informative statistics, and a small questionnaire administered to a group of former Soviet citizens living in the United States. He gives a vivid and generally accurate picture of the deformation of human relationships under inhuman living conditions. Unfortunately, Popovsky's analysis of the material is much weaker than his description. Clearly, the Bolsheviks are the villains of the piece. But are they simply perpetuating pre-Revolutionary peasant barbarity or doing something new? The last journalistic book, Adrian Gaiges and Tatyana Suvorova, *Lyubov—vne plana (Sex and Perestroika)* [Love Is Outside the Plan: Sex and Perestroika] (Moscow: "Sobesednik," 1990) (a German edition was published in 1989), is presented by the authors as a "journalistic research," but it is really a mixture of quotations from people in the street and equally subjective statistics. "The leading Soviet sexologist, Professor Igor Kon," is respectfully quoted and praised (I gave them an interview), but all Soviet professional publications about sexual behavior are ignored. Two young journalists have just discovered in Papua New Guinea an unknown, exotic, illiterate, and sexually ignorant tribe and hurry to present it urbi et orbi . . .

4. *Sex and Russian Society*, edited by Igor Kon and James Riordan (Bloomington: Indiana University Press, 1993).
5. Friedrich Engels, "*Kniga otkroveniya*," Karl Marx and Friedrich Engels, *Sochineniya*, Izd. 2, vol. 21 (Moscow: Politizdat, 1962), p. 8.

## NOTES TO CHAPTER ONE: SEX IN "HOLY RUSSIA"

1. Adam Oleary, *Opisanie puteshestviya v Moskoviyu i cherez Moskoviyu v Persiyu i obratno* (St. Petersburg, 1906), p. 187. There is also an English-language translation: Adam Olearius, *The Travels of Olearius in Seventeenth-Century Russia*, ed. by H. Baran (Stanford, Calif.: Stanford University Press, 1967).
2. The eminent Russian lexicographer Vladimir Dal' completed his compilation of *Russkie zavetnye poslovitsy i pogovorki* (*Russian Secret Proverbs and Sayings*) in 1852; the book was first published in the Hague in 1972. [Claude Carey, *Les proverbes erotiques russes. Etudes de proverbes recueillis et non-publiés par Dal' et Simoni* (The Hague: Mouton, 1972)]. Alexander Afanasiev (1826–71) had to send his celebrated collection of Russian erotic folktales *Russkie zavetnye skazki* (*Russian Secret Folk Tales*), to Geneva for publication; it is regularly reprinted in the West. Yet the book represents only a tiny fraction of Afanasiev's collection, which includes, incidentally, some of Dal''s material. When Dal' gave Afanasiev the texts for approximately 1,000 folktales in 1856, he wrote, "I have many such [tales] in my collection that cannot be printed— a great pity, since they are very amusing." Quoted in Leonid Bessmertnykh, "Netsenzurnye syuzhety. Ob izdaniyakh A. N. Afanasieva," *Eros. Nauchno-publitsistichesky i illyustrirovanny zhurnal*, no. 1 (Moscow, 1991), 16. The extensive manuscript by Afanasiev, *Narodnye russkie skazki. Ne dlya pechati. Iz sobraniya A.N. Afanasieva, 1857–1862* (Russian Folktales. Not for Publication. From the A.N. Afanasiev Collection, 1857–1862), is preserved in the Manuscript Department of Pushkin House (Russian Literature Institute of the Russian Academy of Sciences).

   Authoritative research into Russian swear words by the eminent Moscow linguist Boris Uspensky was published in 1983 and 1987 in the Hungarian journal *Studia Slavica Hungarica*, unknown to the general Soviet reader. B.A. Uspensky, "Mifologichesky aspekt russkoi ekspressivnoi frazeologii. Stati pervaya i vtoraya," *Studia Slavica Hungarica* 29 (1983), 33–69; vol. 33 (1987), 33–76.

   The only album-monograph of Russian erotic art ever issued is *Eroticism in Russian Art*, published in London. Alex Flegon, *Eroticism in Russian Art* (London: Flegon Press, 1976).

   The first historical monographs on Russian sexuality, by the American historians Eve Levin and Laura Engelstein, were published in the United States in 1989 and 1992: Eve Levin, *Sex and Society in the World of the Orthodox Slavs, 900–1700* (Ithaca: Cornell University Press, 1989); Laura Engelstein, *The Keys to Happiness: Sex and the Search for Modernity in Fin-de-Siecle Russia* (Ithaca: Cornell University Press, 1992).

The most complete surveys of the history of homosexuality in Russia and of its reflection in Russian literature are those by the American scholars Simon Karlinsky, Vladimir Kozlovsky, and Alexander Poznansky. Simon Karlinsky. "Russia's Gay Literature and History (11th—20th centuries)," *Gay Sunshine* 29/30 (Summer/Fall 1976), 1–7. S. Karlinsky, "Russia's Gay Literature and Culture. The Impact of the October Revolution," M. L. Duberman et al., eds., *Hidden from History: Reclaiming the Gay and Lesbian Past* (New York: NAL Books, 1990), pp. 347–63. V. Kozlovsky, *Argo russkoi gomoseksualnoi subkultury* (Benson, Vt.: Chalidze, 1986). Alexander Poznansky, "Tchaikovsky's Suicide: Myth and Reality," *19th Century Music* 11, no. 3 (Spring 1988), 199–220; Alexander Poznansky, *Tchaikovsky: The Quest for the Inner Man* (New York: Schirmer, 1991); Alexander Poznansky, *Samoubiystvo Tchaikovskovo: Mif i realnost* (Moscow: Glagol, 1993).

3. See Igor Kon, "O russkom sekse," *Stolitsa*, 11 and 12 (1991), 111–19, 122–24; of particular interest was a special issue of the periodical *Literaturnoye obozrenie*, no. 11 (1991), devoted to the erotic tradition in Russian literature.

4. V. O. Klyuchevsky, *Kurs russkoi istorii, Sochineniya v 8 tomakh*, vol. 1 (Moscow: Gosudarstvennoye izdatelstvo politicheskoi literatury, 1987), p. 31.

5. The most important sources consulted on ancient Slav paganism and early Christian attitudes to sexuality are N. M. Galkovsky, *Borba khristianstva s ostatkami yazychestva v Drevnei Rusi* (Kharkov, 1916); V. F. Mansikka, *Die Religion der Ostslawen* (Helsinki, 1922) (Folklore Fellows Communications, no. 43); D. Zelenin, *Russiche (Ostlsawische) Volkskunde* (Berlin-Leipzig, 1927); N. M. Matorin, *Zhenskoe bozhestvo v pravoslavnom kulte* (Moscow, 1931); B. A. Romanov, *Lyudi i nravy Drevnei Rusi, Istoriko-bytovye ocherki* (Leningrad: Nauka, 1966); B. A. Rybakov, *Yazychestvo drevnikh slavyan* (Moscow: Nauka, 1981); B. A. Uspensky, "Mifologichesky aspekt russkoi ekspressivnoi frazeologii," Stati pervaya i vtoraya, *Studia Slavica Hungarica* 29 (1983), 33–69; vol. 33 (1987), 33–76; Eve Levin, *Sex and Society in the World of the Orthodox Slavs: 900–1700* (Ithaca, N.Y.: Cornell University Press, 1989); A. L. Toporkov, "Materialy po slavyanskomu yazychestvu (kult materi-syroi zemli v der. Prisno)," in D. S. Likhachev, ed., *Drevnerusskaya literatura. Istochnikovedenie. Sbornik nauchnykh trudov* (Leningrad: Nauka, 1984), pp. 222–23; A. L. Toporkov, "Maloizvestnye istochniki po slavyanskoi etnoseksologii (konets XIX—nachalo XX v.)," in A. K. Baiburin and I. S. Kon, eds., *Etnicheskie stereotipy muzhskovo i zhenskovo povedenia* (St. Petersburg: Nauka, 1991), pp. 307–18; Joanna Hubbs, *Mother Russia: The Feminine Myth in Russian Culture* (Bloomington: Indiana University Press, 1988); N. L. Pushkaryova, *Zhenshchiny Drevnei Rusi* (Moscow: Mysl, 1989).

Judging by the extant historical ethnographic data, we note that attitudes toward sexuality in ancient Rus were just as contradictory as they were in the rest of Europe. Like other cultures, Slav paganism considered sexuality as having a cosmic source: in Russian songs, the female silver birch interlaced tenderly and passionately with the mighty male oak, and Mother Earth became fecund from celestial rain. There were innumerable orgiastic festivals at which men and women bathed naked together, the men symbolically fertilizing the earth, the women seeking rain by lifting up their skirts and showing their genitals to the heavens. As late as the nineteenth century, in some parts of Ukraine, the custom of rolling in pairs over the sown soil was still in existence, as a substitute for the ritual copulation in the fields during sowing.

The typical ancient Russian phallic symbol—an animal, usually the lion, with either a long tail or sexual organ—is seen even in ornamental church architecture (as, for example, at the Temple of the Protector on the Nerl and the Cathedral of St. Dmitri in Vladimir).

The history and semantics of Russian curse words give some understanding of pre-Christian sexual symbolism. Foul and offensive language, so-called invective lexis, is very ancient. In the archaic consciousness, there are two extreme categories: the sacred, invested with divine grace and perceived as something honorable and precious, and the demonic. The concepts of sacred and demonic are also interpreted as clean and unclean: thus, "dirty" = low = base = obscene. Since both gods and demons represented some dangers, people endeavored to keep their distance in everyday life, to avoid summoning them up or uttering their names in vain. Invective lexis violates these bans, and the power offending is directly proportional to the significance of the ban being violated. (See V. I. Zhelvis, "Invektiva: opyt tematicheskoi i funktsionalnoi klassifikatsii," in A. K. Baiburin, ed., *Etnicheskie stereotipy povedeniya* [Leningrad: Nauka, 1985], pp. 296–320).

We may distinguish certain large areas among "sexual" insults:

1. Expressions that send the person being insulted into the area of the female genitalia, reproductive organs, or nether regions ("Go to cunt"), which is nothing less than a death wish, since the female genitals simultaneously represent both birth and death.
2. Expressions that hint at someone having possessed the insulted one's mother (*"Yob tvoyu mat"* [Fuck your mother]).
3. Expressions that accuse the insulted one of committing incest with his mother (seen widely in English-language insults as "motherfucker").
4. Expressions that refer to the male genitals ("Poshol na khui" [Go to prick]), thus putting the insulted one in a female sexual position, which is equivalent to depriving him of his virility and dignity. (See Igor Kon, *Vvedenie v seksologiyu* [Moscow: Meditsina, 1988), pp. 101–2.

For a more theoretical discussion of this issue, see Daniel Rancour-Laferriere, *Signs of the Flesh* (Berlin and New York: Mouton de Gruyter, 1985).

The Russian language is particularly rich in "maternal " expressions, which may be found in Hungarian, Romanian, Norwegian, Chinese, Swahili, and many other languages as well. Nonetheless, these expressions may have different meanings. Sometimes the implied subject of the "shameful" action is the speaker himself, who is thereby maintaining that " I am your father" or "I could be your father" and thus consigning the insulted to a lower social and age category. One Chinese term of abuse, as M. V. Kryukov has informed me, literally means "You are my son." In Russian, the pronoun "I" is hardly ever used in this context, while phrases involving "mother" are employed for designating a past event and in the imperative mood and the infinitive. Even without identifying the subject, however, this form of abuse is very sharp, casting doubt on the morals of the insulted one's mother, and consequently, on the insulted's origins.

According to another interpretation that crops up in the notes of the sixteenth-century German diplomat Baron Sigizmund von Herberstein, the subject and actor of the shameful action is a dog; this is connected with widespread expressions of the "son of a bitch" or "dog's blood" type in many languages. (See A. V. Isachenko, "Un juron russe du XVIᵉ siècle," *Lingua viget. Commentationes slavicae in honorem V. Kiparsky* [Helsinki, 1964], pp. 68–70.) When we consider that in the sixteenth century, the dog was regarded as an unclean animal, such an insult was very strong.

Even in ancient Rus, swear words were regarded as blasphemy that offended the Mother of God, the mythological "Mother Earth," and the mother of the person swearing. Yet these expressions themselves were of sacred origin and had at one time been associated with ritual functions.

In the view of Boris Uspensky, at the deepest, most basic level, "maternal" expressions are coupled with the myth of the sacred marriage of Heaven and Earth, through which Earth became fertile. The connection between swear words and fertility is evident in the ritual wedding and agrarian uses of foul language, as well as its association with thunder. At that level, it did not possess any blasphemous meaning but was a magical formula, a sacred oath (such formulas also exist in Buddhism). At another, more superficial level, the subject in question is the dog as opponent to the Thunderer and the demonic source. Swear words here acquire a blasphemous character, expressing the notion of a dog fouling the earth—all the fault of the person with whom one is conversing. At the next, even more superficial language, a woman becomes the object of implied action, while the dog remains the subject. Such swear words are readdressed directly to the mother of one's conversant, and here they begin to take on a direct, offensive tone, as is the expression "Son of a bitch." Finally, at the most superficial, genteel level, the speaker himself is the subject of the action, while the object is the conversant's mother. Swearing thus becomes an indicator of dissipation, doubtful origin, and so on.

The most colorful of Russian obscene words, however, were by no means always intended as insults. According to the observations of Russian ethnographers in the nineteenth century, obscene language caused offense only if it was uttered harshly, with obvious intention to offend, whereas when used in jocular male conversation, it served as an amicable greeting or merely as a sort of conversational "seasoning" unaccompanied by sexual innuendo; this was often misunderstood by foreigners, which is why many of them thought Russians nothing short of sex maniacs.

6. B. N. Mironov, *Istoria v tsifrakh. Matematika v istoricheskikh issledovaniyakh* (Leningrad: Nauka, 1991), pp. 19–20.

   Russian wedding ceremonies widely included the custom of *posad* (seating), whereby the bride was to sit in a special sacred place—something she would not dare to do if she had already lost her virginity. In some places, if on her wedding night the bride was found not to be intact, the offending bride, her parents, or the matchmaker had to wear a horse collar around the neck as a sign of shame, the collar being a symbol at once of the female genitals and of a "sinner" belonging to the world of animals, ignorant of cultural prohibitions. (See A. K. Baiburin and G. A. Levinton, "K opisaniu organizatsii prostranstva v vostochno-slavyanskoi svadbe," K. V. Chistov and T. A. Bernshtam, eds., *Russky narodny svadebny obryad* (Leningrad: Nauka, 1978), pp. 94–95.

7. See Levin, *Sex and Society*, pp. 197–203. 290–92, and Simon Karlinsky, "Russia's Gay Literature and History, 11th—20th Centuries," *Gay Sunshine* 29/30 (Summer/Fall 1976).

8. See Lloyd E. Berry and Robert O. Crummy, eds., *Rude and Barbarous Kingdom* (Madison: University of Wisconsin Press, 1968).

9. J. Krizhanitch, *Russkoye gosudarstvo v polovine XVII veka*, vol. 2 (Moscow, 1866), pp. 17–18.

10. See T. A. Bernshtam, "Devushka-nevesta i predbrachnaya obryadnost v Pomorie v XIX—nachale XX," *Russky narodny svadebny obryad. Issledovaniya i materialy* (Leningrad: Nauka, 1978), pp. 49–71; T. A. Bernshtam, "Traditsionny prazdnichny kalendar v Pomorie vo vtoroi polovine XIX-nachale XX vv," *Etnograficheskie issledovaniya Severo-Zapada SSSR* (Leningrad: Nauka, 1977), pp. 88–115. See also V. Y. Propp, *Russkie agrarnye prazdniki* (Leningrad: Nauka, 1963); G. A. Nosova, *Yazychestvo v pravoslavii* (Moscow: Nauka, 1975).

    By the way, the Russian word "*devushka*" (maiden) is often translated in English as "girl." For Americans, that sounds strange; they want to translate it as "young woman." But in Russia, every young female, from age 14–15 to 20–25, is a *devushka*. She is never addressed as "*zhenshchina*" (woman). *Zhenshchina* generally means a married or at least sexually experienced female.

11. See D. Zelenin, *Russische (Ostslawische) Volkskunde* (Berlin-Leipzig, 1927), pp. 338–41.

12. Bernshtam, "Devushka-nevesta." Descriptions of such counternormative customs in ethnographic literature are exceedingly contradictory. One correspondent of the ethnographic office of Prince V. N. Tenishev in the 1890s wrote that although the custom no longer prevailed, in the Poshekhonsky region in Yaroslavl province, "folks say that in the old days, in some remote places of the region, for instance, in Podorvanovskaya district, there were "extinguishings" [*gaski*] . . . at village gatherings. Young people who had remained alone

put out the lights of their torches and engaged in group sex. Nowadays only the word *gaski* remains here and there." Quoted from M. M. Gromyko, *Traditionnye normy povedeniya i formy obshcheniya russkikh krestyan XIX v.* (Moscow: Nauka, 1986), p. 231. Yet another correspondent thought that everything was really kept under control by the parents.

13. Similar attitudes existed in Vladimirski province and western Siberia as well. See B. M. Firsov and I. G. Kiselyova, eds., *Byt velikorusskikh krestyan-zemlepashtsev. Opisanie materialov etnograficheskovo byuro knyazia V. N. Tenisheva (na primere Vladimirskoi gubernii)* (St. Petersburg: Izdatelstvo Evropeiskovo Doma, 1993); T. A. Bernshtam, *Molodyozh v obryadovoi zhizni russkoi obshchiny XIX-nachala XX v. Polovozrastnoi aspekt traditsionnoi kultury* (Leningrad: Nauka, 1988), pp. 51, 109. N. A. Minenko, *Russkaya krestyanskaya semya v Zapadnoi Sibiri (XVIII-pervaya polovina XIX v.)* (Novosibirsk: Nauka, 1979), p. 217.

14. B. N. Mironov, "Traditsionnoye demograficheskoye povedenie krestyan v XIX-nachale XX v.," A. G. Vishnevsky, ed., *Brachnost, rozhdaemost, smertnost v Rossii i v SSSR. Sbornik statei* (Moscow: Statistika, 1977), pp. 83–104.

15. Mikhail Bakhtin, *Rabelais and His World*, translated by Helen Iswolsky (Boston: MIT Press, 1968), p. 7.

16. See Y. Lotman and B. Uspensky, "Novye aspekty izucheniya kultury drevnei Rusi," *Voprosy literatury* no. 3 (1977), 159–61. Compare with D. S. Likhachev, A. M. Panchenko, and N. V. Ponyrko, *Smekh v Drevnei Rusi* (Moscow: Nauka, 1984); A. Y. Gurevich, *Problemy srednevekovoi kultury* (Moscow: Iskusstvo, 1981).

17. Quoted from Lotman and Uspensky, "Novye aspekty."

18. According to the eminent Russian historian Nikolai Kostomarov, in the sixteenth and seventeenth centuries Russians married very early; sometimes the groom was as young as 12. N. I. Kostomarov, *Ocherk domashnei zhizni i nravov velikorusskovo naroda v XVI i XVII stoletiyakh* (St. Petersburg, 1887), p. 226. However, both the church and the state objected to too early marriages: in 1410, Metropolitan Fotij forbade girls to marry earlier than age 12; in 1714 Peter I forbade gentlemen to marry younger than age 20 and gentlewomen to marry before age 17. In 1775, Catherine II forbade the gentry to marry before 15 for men and 13 for women; anyone violating that order would have the marriage dissolved, while the priest performing the ceremony would be deprived of his position. By the mid-nineteenth century, men were permitted to wed only after their eighteenth birthday, women after their sixteenth. B. A. Romanov, *Lyudi i nravy Drevnei Rusi*, p. 188. A. Tereshenko, *Byt russkovo naroda* (St. Petersburg: 1848), pp. 37–38. On the other hand, postponing marriage was not recommended either. In 1607 Czar Vasily Shuisky instructed that a "maiden [should not be kept housebound] after 18; a widow without a husband for more than two years and an unmarried man beyond 20 should not be given freedom to be unmarried." V. N. Tatishchev, *Istoriya Rossiyskaya* (Leningrad: Nauka, 1968), p. 374.

Still, early marriage was universally alive in the late nineteenth and early twentieth centuries, albeit in a hidden form in many regions. Fathers arranged matches for their children between the ages of 12 and 15, betrothed them at 14 or 16, and married them off between 16 and 17. In southern and western Russia, weddings for 12–14 children were sometimes arranged with all the ceremony except the wedding night, the children living at home separately with their parents until they came of age. In the Far North, grandmothers in the middle of the last century recalled how they had scurried home for their dolls the day after their wedding. See T. A. Bernshtam, *Molodyozh v obryadovoi zhizni russkoi obshchiny*, pp. 48–49. The family, the village community, and the young people themselves had an interest in early marriage. A young man, irrespective of his age, was taken seriously within the village only once he had married; before that, he had no influence within the family and could not vote in the village assembly. Bachelors were neither liked nor respected: "Bachelors are dolts," "A bachelor is only half a man" were typical peasant sayings. The status of old maids was even worse. Mironov, "Traditsionnoye demografich-eskoye povedenie krestyan v XIX-nachale XX v.," p. 86.

19. Andrei Bolotov, *Zhizn i priklyucheniya Andreya Bolotova, opisannye samim dlya svoikh potomkov, 1738–1793* (Moscow-Leningrad: Academy, 1931), p. 251.

20. Ibid., pp. 276–77. For an interesting work on the evolving concept of love in Russian culture, see A. G. Vishnevsky, "Strast i supruzhestvo," *Sotsiologicheskie issledovaniya*, no. 2 (1986), 108–21.

21. G. R. Derzhavin, *Izbrannaya proza* (Moscow: Sovetskaya Rossiya, 1984), p. 80.

22. Bolotov, *Zhizn i priklyucheniya*, pp. 306–7.

23. Ibid., p. 310.

24. Quoted from Mironov, "Traditsionnoye demograficheskoe povedenie," p. 94.

25. Bolotov, *Zhizn i priklyucheniya*, p. 645. A century later we find the same attitude from Pozdnyshev, the main character in Tolstoy's *Kreutzer Sonata*, who beats his wife for her excessive suffering on the occasion of the death of their children:

If she were a complete animal, she would not have suffered such torment; if she were a complete human being, she would have had faith in God, and she would have spoken and thought as the religious old wives do— God giveth and taketh away; He is omnipotent. . . . She would have thought that life and death of all people, including children, are beyond man's power to control, and only in the hands of God; then she would not have suffered for having no power to avert the children's illness and death and she would not have done so. L. N. Tolstoy, "The Kreuzer Sonata," *Sobranie sochineniy v 22 tomakh*, vol. 12 (Moscow: Khudozhestvennaya lit-eratura, 1982), p. 160. For more detail, see A. G. Vishnevsky, "Mesto istoricheskovo znaniya v izuchenii prokreativnovo povedeniya v SSSR," *Vtoroi sovetsko-frantsuzsky demografichesky seminar, Suzdal, 15–19 September 1986* (Moscow, 1986). If that is how a gentleman felt, then what chance did the peasantry have?

26. O. P. Semyonova-Tyan-Shanskaya, "Zhizn 'Ivana'," *Zapiski Imperatorskovo Rossiyskovo Geograficheskovo obshchestva po otdeleniyu etnografii*, vol. 39 (St. Petersburg, 1914), p. 59.

27. G. I. Uspensky, "Vlast zemli," *Sobranie sochineniy v 9 tomakh*, vol. 5 (Moscow: Gosudarstvennoye izdatelstvo khudozhestvennoi literatury, 1956), p. 186.

28. A. G. Vishnevsky, "Rannie etapy stanovleniya novovo tipa rozhdaemosti v Rossii," A. G. Vishnevsky, ed., *Brachnost, rozhdaemost, smertnost v Rossii i v SSSR. Sbornik statei* (Moscow: Statistika, 1977), pp. 1–5—34.

29. A. F. Koni, "Samoubiystvo v zakone i zhizni." *Sobranie sochineniy v 8 tomakh*, vol. 4 (Moscow: Yurdicheskaya literatura, 1976), p. 465.

## NOTES TO CHAPTER TWO: THE RUSSIAN EROS

1. "*Mat* is a shadow image of the Russian language as a whole. From a semantic point of view, what interests us is the means of communication, via *mat*, of everyday meanings that transcend the limits of direct abuse and of sex. In *mat* a particular form of expressive, substandard language—one that is essentially neutral vis-à-vis the communicated referential meaning. *Mat* is a potentially limitless quantity of expressions. *Mat* takes over from the standard language the latter's word-derivational mechanisms, applies a versatile system of interpretations, and uses certain special mechanisms in the sphere of syntax and poetics.

This contrast generated in *mat* an aesthetic function: the "acquisition of reality" through the transcendence of the limits of the basic obscene lexicon. This function raises *mat* to a special genre of folk art, in which millions of Russians are, more or less effectively, proficient." Felix Dreizin and Tom Priestly, "A Systematic Approach to Russian Obscene Language," *Russian Linguistics* 6 (1982), 233–34.

Without *mat*, a considerable part of Russian literature is incomprehensible. See Daniel Rancour-Laferriere, "The Boys of Ibansk: A Freudian Look at Some Recent Russian Satire," *Psychoanalytic Review* 72, no. 4 (Winter 1985), 639–56.

For Russian *chastushki*, see Nikolai Starshinov, "Razreshite vas poteshit," A. Shchuplov and A. Ilyushin, eds., *Tri veka poezii russkovo Erosa. Publikatsii i issledovaniya* (Moscow: Izdatelsky tsentr teatra "Pyat vecherov," 1992), pp. 131–57; V. Kabronsky, *Nepodtsenzurnaya russkaya chastushka* (New York: Russica, 1978). The well-known Russian actor and film producer Rolan Bykov reports that when filmmaker Andrei Tarkovsky was making a film on the life of Russian medieval master painter Andrei Rublyov, he strove for historical accuracy and was eager to use genuine songs that the *skomoroki* (jesters) of Rublyov's time had sung. It was extremely difficult to find the texts, which had been classified as secret, but when he did so, he was unable to use them because they were too "filthy."

2. See Alex Flegon, *Eroticism in Russian Art* (London: Flegon Press, 1976).

3. For a theoretical discussion, see Leo Steinberg, *The Sexuality of Christ in Renaissance Art and in Modern Oblivion* (New York: Pantheon, 1983); Arnold I. Davidson, "Sex and the Emergence of Sexuality," *Critical Inquiry* 14 (Autumn 1987), 16–41; Peter Brown, *The Body and Society: Men, Women and Sexual Renunciation in Early Christianity* (New York: Columbia University Press, 1988); Sander L. Gilman, *Sexuality: An Illustrated History* (New York: Wiley, 1989).

4. Although it is true that some seventeenth-century churches (for example, the holy Trinity Church in Nikitniki and the Ascension Church in Tutayev) have retained frescoes that quite realistically portray seminude bodies in such subjects as Bathsheba bathing, Susannah and the Elders, and the baptism of Jesus, this was at variance with strict Byzantine canon and an exception to the general rule.

5. The table legs, for example, were tapered in the shape of male sex organs. The furniture is today kept in the Hermitage Museum in St. Petersburg.

6. A. S. Pushkin, "Evgenii Onegin," chap. 1, stanza 9 (omitted from the final version of the novel), *Sobranie sochineniy v 10 tomakh*, vol. 14, p. 453.

7. Quoted from *A.S. Pushkin v vospominaniyakh sovremennikov*, vol. 2 (Moscow: Pravda, 1985), p. 193.

8. Alexander Ilyushin, "Ivan Barkov i drugie," *Tri veka poezii russkovo Erosa* (Moscow: Izdatelskii Tsentr Teatra Pyat vecherv, 1992), pp. 6–7. See also Andrei Zorin, "Barkov i barkoviana. Predvaritelnye zamechaniya," *Literaturnoye obozrenie*, no. 11 (1991), 18–21.

9. Ilyushin, "Ivan Barkov i drugie," *Tri veka poezii russkovo Erosa*, p. 8.

10. N. P. Ogaryov, *Izbrannye proizvedeniya v 2 tomakh*, vol. 2 (Moscow, 1956), p. 476.

11. Pushkin's fine, mischievous, though not licentious fairy tale in verse, *Tsar Nikita and His Forty Daughters*, tells the story of the czar who had 40 daughters from different mothers—"forty beautiful girls, forty heavenly angels" with every imaginable skill. The only trouble was that the princesses lacked one small detail to their perfection, so the czar sends his courtier Faddei to a wizard for the objects that "the princesses lack between their legs." The wizard gives the courier a casket with strict instructions not to open it, but tormented by curiosity, he does so and lets out the 40 "missing jigsaw pieces," which fly up and settle in the branches of a nearby tree. After desperate attempts to call them back, the courier sits astride the open casket and begins to display his own wares. At once the hungry orifices fly back at him; he catches every one and locks them back in the casket. In most multivolume collections of Pushkin's works, this tale was given only in a small extract form, ending with the following significant verse: "How might one explain,/Without making plain,/The devout nonsense/Of an over-zealous censor?"

12. See G. S. Novopolin, *Pornografichesky element v russkoi literature* (St. Petersburg, 1909).

13. Quoted from André Maurois, *Literaturnye portrety*. Translated from the French (Moscow: Progress, 1970), p. 190. See also Alec Craig, "Censorship of Sexual Literature," *The Encyclopedia of Sexual Behaviour*, vol. 1 (New York: Hawthorne, 1961), pp. 235–47.

14. A. S. Pushkin, Letter to S. A. Sobolevsky, second half of February 1828, *Sobranie sochineniy v 10 tomakh*, vol. 9, p. 273.

15. James H. Billington, *The Icon and the Axe: An Interpretative History of Russian Culture* (New York: Vintage, 1970), p. 349.

16. Ibid., p. 350. This style of life was imposed on women too. Irrespective of her own individual temperament, "a decent woman" was not supposed to display sensuality, but had to be embarrassed by it, even after marriage. This reserved attitude estranged her husband sexually, encouraging him to seek satisfaction on the side. Man and wife, without wishing to, imposed on each other the same deliberate lack of sexual satisfaction based on conventions and silence.

17. Vissarion Belinsky (1811–48) harbored the notion that nature had put the "curse of ugliness" upon his face, and because of this, no self-respecting woman could ever love him. V. G. Belinsky, *Polnoye sobranie sochineniy*, vol. 11 (Moscow: Gosudarstvennoe izdatelstvo khydozhestvennoi literatury, 1956), p. 390. The only emotional outlet for him was to engage in passionate, unconsciously homoerotic friendships whose pivot was endless intimate outpourings. "I no longer love Botkin as I used to, I am simply in love with him and recently made him a formal declaration," writes Belinsky to his friend Mikhail Bakunin (ibid., p. 190).

In the correspondence between Belinsky and Bakunin, the men are literally competing with each other in shameful self-exposure. Bakunin had only to confess that as a youth he had masturbated for Belinsky to write that he had sinned even more deeply: "I only took it up when you stopped—at nineteen. . . . At first I resorted to this means of pleasure through my shyness with women and inability to enjoy any success with them; I simply carried on because I had begun. Sometimes lustful pictures came into my head—which made my head and bosom ache, produced fire and feverish trembling throughout my body: sometimes I'd hold back, and sometimes I'd finish a vile dream with an even more vile reality." Letter from Belinsky to M. A. Bakunin, Nov. 15–20, 1837. This excerpt was deleted in all editions of Belinsky's letters. Quoted from V. Sazhin, "Ruka pobeditelya. Vybrannye mesta iz perepiski V. Belinskovo i M. Bakunina," *Literaturnoye obozrenie*, no. 11 (1991), 39.

Despite the constant "need for talking" about himself, Belinsky circumspectly concealed these experiences from other friends. "St[ankevich], talking of his exploits in this area, once asked me whether I practiced this noble and free art; I blushed scarlet, made a pious and innocent grimace, and said I certainly did not." (Ibid.) On the other hand, when he and Bakunin confessed their "vile weakness" to each other, their friendship was expected to become everlasting (though it didn't). It is typical that these outpourings of the soul stopped the moment Belinsky married. (See Lidia Ginzburg, *O psikhologich-eskoi proze* [Leningrad: Sovetsky pisatel, 1971); I. S. Kon, *Druzhba. Etikop-sikhologichesky ocherk*, 3d ed. (Moscow: Politizdat, 1989).

The problem of the relationship between love and friendship, which he portrayed in exclusively elevated terms, and vulgar sexuality, which appalled him, occupied a prominent place in the diaries of the 20-year-old Nikolai Chernyshevsky (1828–89), later to become an influential literary critic: "I know that I am also easily attracted to men, though I have never had occasion to be attracted to girls or even women generally (I say that in the decent sense since I feel uneasy because of my physical mood, it is sex rather than a person, and that makes me ashamed." (N. G. Chernyshevsky, "Dnevniki," *Polnoye sobranie sochineniy*, vol. 1 [Moscow: Gosudarstvennoe izdatelstvo khudozh-estvennoi literatury, 1939], pp. 35–36. "How many secret abominations, which no one would suspect, for example, I cause myself by examining the children and my sisters and so on while they're sleeping." (Ibid., p. 38.)

On August 11, 1848, Chernyshevsky recounts, he and his closest friend, Vasily Lobodovsky both "said, each adjusting his own trousers, how awful this thing is we've been given." "I woke up . . . in the night, as before I felt like going to lie beside . . . a woman, as I had done before." (Ibid., p. 83.) "At night the devil again made me go to Maria and Anna and feel them and put my . . . to the naked parts of their legs. . . . When I do so, my heart was beating fast, yet when I was lying next to them nothing happened." (Ibid., p. 91)

18. Richard Stites, *The Women's Liberation Movement in Russia: Feminism, Nihilism and Bolshevism, 1860–1930* (Princeton: Princeton University Press, 1978), p. 229.

19. Peter Gay, *The Bourgeois Experience: Victoria to Freud*, vol. 1, *Education of the Senses* (New York: Oxford University Press, 1984), p. 391.

20. Billington, *The Icon and the Axe*, p. 432.

21. In further exposition of this issue, I draw from the excellent monograph by Peter Ulf Møller, *Postlude to the Kreutzer Sonata: Tolstoy and the Debate on Sexual Morality in Russian Literature in the 1880s* (Leiden-New York: E.J. Brill, 1988).

22. L. N. Tolstoy, Letter to L. E. Obolenski, *Polnoye sobranie sochineniy v 90 tomakh*, vol. 65 (Moscow-Leningrad, 1957), p. 61.

23. L. N. Tolstoy, *Kreutzerova sonata* (Moscow: Khudozhestvennaya literatura, 1982), p. 151.

24. Ibid., "Posleslovie k Kreutzerovoi sonate," *Sobranie sochineniy v 22 tomakh*, vol. 12 pp. 201, 206.

25. Ibid., p. 206.

26. Tolstoy's American translator, Isabel Hapgood, not only refused to translate it but publicly explained her motives for refusing: "After making allowance for the ordinary freedom of speech, which has greater latitude in Russia [as else-where in Europe] than is customary in America, I find the language of *The Kreutzer Sonata* to be too excessive in its candor." (Cited by Møller, *Postlude to*

*the Kreutzer Sonata*, p. 103.) The United States Postmaster General officially termed the book "indecent," which, naturally, increased its popularity. Col. Robert G. Ingersoll's reaction was typical: "Although I disagree nearly with every sentence in this book, regard the story as brutal and absurd, the view of life presented as cruel, vile, and false, yet I recognize the right of Count Tolstoy to express his opinion on all subjects, and the right of men and women of America to read it for themselves" (ibid., p. 105). In France, Emil Zola said the author must have gone "off his head," while the German psychiatrist H. Beck called the story "an expression of a highly gifted psychopath's religious and sexual insanity" (ibid., pp. 109, 115).

Opinions were just as vociferous in Russia. Tolstoy received a huge number of letters, with those from women usually being supportive of his views while men's were mainly critical toward his asceticism. One such letter preserved in the Tolstoy archives says, "After having read your *Sonata*, I advise you in all charity to seek psychiatric assistance, as psychiatrists are the only people who can cure abnormal disposition of the brain" (ibid., p. 120).

Three strands were apparent in the public disputes over the story. The democrats of the 1860s welcomed Tolstoy's debunking of bourgeois and religious marriage, but saw the way out not in renunciation of carnal love but in viewing the wife as an equal being, which would sanctify and ennoble animal feelings. The conservatives, for their part, also welcomed Tolstoy's work, but as a protest against hedonism and the premature involvement of young people in sexual pleasures. Finally, the reactionary clergy regarded Tolstoy's views as sheer heresy, undermining the very foundation of Christian morality and marriage.

27. Chekhov's attitude to *The Kreutzer Sonata* was interesting. His first reaction was strong and mainly positive: the boldness of the work far outweighed its shortcoming, in his view, although he said in a letter in February 1890 that Tolstoy's views "on syphilis, orphanages, women's disgust at intercourse and so on are not only disputable, they indirectly show the man as being ignorant, not having bothered during his long life to read two or three little books written by the experts." A. P. Chekhov, "Pismo A.N. Pleshcheyevu, 15 February 1890," *Polnoye sobranie sochineniy i pisem v 30 tomakh. Pisma*, vol. 4 (Moscow: Nauka, 1976), p. 18. Yet after reading Tolstoy's "Postscript," Chekhov's attitude sharply changed and he became more critical. "To hell with the philosophy of these great people!" he wrote to a friend in September 1891. "All great sages are despotic, like generals, and ignorant and indelicate, like generals, because they are so sure of their being beyond reproach. Diogenes spat into his beard, knowing that nothing would happen to him for what he wrote; Tolstoy calls doctors scoundrels and plays havoc with great issues because he is just the same Diogenes whom you cannot take down to the local nick or curse in the papers." "Pismo A.S. Suvorinu, 8 September 1891." *Polnoye sobranie sochineniy i pisem v 30 tomakh. Pisma*, vol. 4 (Moscow: Nauka, 1976), p. 270.

28. In a long article entitled "The Meaning of Love," published in 1892, Solovyov defended love from abstract and rigid moralism, although, in his view, "the external communion, worldly and particularly physiological, has no definite relationship to love. It can exist without love, and love without it. It is necessary for love as its ultimate realization only, and not as its invariable condition and independent goal. If this realization is set as an end in itself before love's ideal, it destroys love." Moreover, "for man as an *animal*, the unrestrained satisfaction of his sexual need through a certain physiological action is completely natural, but man as a moral being finds this action at variance with his superior nature and is *ashamed* of it." Vladimir Solovyov, "Smysl lyubvi," *Sochineniya v 2-kh tomakh*, vol. 2 (Moscow: Mysl, 1988), pp. 518, 526.

29. V. Rozanov, *Opavshie listya. Korob pervy* (St. Petersburg, 1913), p. 322. Reprinted in V. V. Rozanov, *Tom 2. Uedinyonnoe* (Moscow: Pravda, 1990), p. 366.

30. "Metafizika pola i lyubvi," *Pereval*, no. 5 (1907) Reprinted in N. A. Berdyaev, *Eros i Lichnost* (Moscow:Prometei, 1990), pp. 18–19.

31. Engelstein, *The Keys to Happiness: Sex and the Search for Modernity in Fin-de Siècle Russia* (Ithaca and London: Cornell University Press, 1992), p. 394.

32. K. Balmont, "O Lyubvi," (1908), reprinted in *Russky Eros ili filosofia lyubvi v Rossii*, V. P. Shestakov, ed. (Moscow: Progress, 1991), p. 99.

33. Quoted from K. Mochulsky, *Valery Brusov* (Paris: YMCA Press, 1962), p. 93.

34. Ibid., p. 59.

35. See John E. Bowlt, "Through the Glass Darkly: Images of Decadence in Early Twentieth Century Russian Art," *Journal of Contemporary History* 17 (1982), 101.

36. Engelstein, *The Keys to Happiness*, p. 301. In this highly subjective book, the talented writer attempted to give a theoretical basis to his coming to terms with his uncertain masculinity and his rejected Jewishness. Soon after publication, the author committed suicide. Some saw in his work the first serious discussion of the problem of sex differences, especially androgyny; others interpreted it as representing the author's strong antifeminist principles; still others wallowed in his anti-Semitism. Weininger had a considerable impact on Zinaida Gippius. On the other hand, Andrei Bely regarded Weininger's book as "no more than the precious psychological document of a youthful genius. And the document itself gives us only a hint that Weininger had personal scores to settle with a woman." Andrei Bely, "Weininger o pole i kharaktere," A. Bely. *Arabeski* (Moscow:Musaget, 1911), p. 290. Rozanov, with typical penetrating clarity, actually revealed the nature of those "scores": "You can hear Weininger's cry on every page: 'I love men!'" V. Rozanov, "Opavshie listya. Korob pervy," V. V. Rozanov, Tom 2, *Uyedinenennoye* (Moscow: Pravda, 1990), p. 289.

37. Sergei Makovsky, *Portrety sovremennikov* (New York: Izdatelstvo imeni Chekhova, 1955), p. 201.

38. M. Kuzmin, "Krylya," Alexander Shchuplov, ed., *Eros. Russia. Serebryany vek* (Moscow: Serebryany Bor, 1992), p. 158.

39. Andrei Bely was embarrassed by its theme and regarded some scenes as "sickening." Zinaida Gippius felt the theme was acceptable but was treated too tendentiously and with "painful exhibitionism." See Engelstein, *The Keys to Happiness*, pp. 391–92. On the other hand, Alexander Blok, who usually avoided all talk of sex, noted in his diary, "I read Kuzmin's *Wings*—tremendous." Alexander Blok, *Zapisnye knizhki, 1901–1920* (Moscow: Khudozhestvennaya literatura, 1965), p. 85. Although in a published review Blok found "parts where the author descends to crude barbarity and which the guardians of journalistic orality have seized upon with gusto," this barbarity ". . . completely drowns in the transparent and crystal moisture of art. . . . Kuzmin's name, which is presently surrounded by some coarse, barbaric-trivial rumor, is for us enchanting." Alexander Blok, "O drame (1907)," *Sobranie sochineniy v 8 tomakh*, vol. 5 (Moscow-Leningrad: Gosudarstvennoe izdatelstvo khudozhestvennoi literatury, 1962), p. 183.

40. G. S. Novopolin, *Pornograficheskmy element v russkoi literature* (St. Petersburg: 1909), chap. 10.

41. A. F. Koni, "Pismo N.V. Sultanovu, 18 April 1908," *Sobranie sochineniy v 8 tomakh*, vol. 8 (Moscow: Yuridicheskaya literatura, 1969), p. 259.

42. For the 17-year-old Pavel Rybakov, the main character in Leonid Andreyev's short story "In the Fog" (1902), although his mustache had not yet grown, the word "woman" "was the most incomprehensible, the most fantastic and terrible word." Having lost his virginity at 15 and then caught the "shameful disease" from a prostitute, he considers himself morally and physically sullied. Erotic fantasies mingle with plans to kill himself. He has no one with whom he can speak frankly; his father feels that something is bothering him, but he does not know how to approach his son. When he finds Pavel's pornographic drawings, he feels hurt and only intensifies the boy's alarm. As he wanders aimlessly around the city, Pavel makes the acquaintance of a pitiful prostitute, with whom he has a glass of tea; then he insults her. The woman slaps his face and a dreadful fight ensues, as a result of which Pavel murders her with a kitchen knife, and then stabs himself.

Like much of the work of Leonid Andreyev, the story is melodramatic. But his moral pathos is obvious: Andreyev does not incite sexual depravity but condemns bourgeois hypocrisy, which keeps silent on vitally important problems for young people, leaving them morally defenseless. Chekhov, who did not like naturalism and was aesthetically demanding, admired this story, especially the scene in which the young man is having a conversation with his father: "It gets full marks from me," said Chekhov. A. P. Chekhov, "Pismo L.N. Andreyevu, 2 January 1903," *Polnoye sobranie sochineniy i pisem v 30 tomakh. Pisma*, vol. 11 (Moscow: Nauka, 1982), p. 112. But the conservative critic N. E. Burenin branded Andreyev an "erotomane" and his story a harmful, pornographic work. Countess Sofia Tolstaya shared that view: "One must not read, not buy up, not glorify the work of the Andreyevs, and the whole of Russian society should rise up in disgust against the filth which this squalid magazine is circulating in Russia in thousands of copies." Zinaida Gippius also reproached Andreyev for savoring painful experiences (Engelstein, *The Keys to Happiness*, p. 374).

43. A. B. Goldenweizer, *Vblizi Tolstovo*, vol. 1 (Moscow: 1922), p. 303–4.

44. Quoted from A. I. Kuprin, *Sobranie sochineniy v 6 tomakh*, vol. 5 (Moscow: Gosudarstvennoe izdatelstvo khudozhestvennoi literatury, 1958), pp. 749–50.

45. Engelstein, *The Keys to Happiness*, p.374.

46. Here are the feelings of Artsybashev's character Captain Zarudin, the professional Don Juan and sadist:

And a hint of gloating began to mingle unconsciously and subtly with the sweet languid feeling of voluptuous anticipation—this proud, intelligent, pure and well-read girl would soon be lying beneath him like all the rest of them; and he would be doing with her exactly what he wanted, as with all the others. The acute, cruel thought began vaguely to present him with preciously humiliating, voluptuous scenes in which Lida's naked body, disheveled hair and intelligent eyes interlaced with some sort of wild Bacchanalia of voluptuous cruelty. Suddenly he saw her clearly on the floor, he could hear the whistle of the whip, he saw the pinkish weal on the naked, tender, submissive body, and trembling, he reeled back from dealing the blows with blood rushing to his head. M. Artsybashev, *Sanin* (Letchworth, Bradda Books, 1969), p. 25.

The youthful student Yuri Svarozhich is cut from a different pattern. Yet he has only to be left alone with an attractive woman and

his head would suddenly spin. He would cast a furtive glance at the high breasts barely hidden by the flimsy Ukrainian blouse, and her round sloping shoulders. The thought that she could actually be in his arms with no one to hear was so strong and unexpected that for a brief moment it all went blank before his eyes. But in a flash he managed to control himself because he was sincerely and invincibly convinced that it was disgusting to rape a woman, and absolutely unthinkable for him, Yuri Svarozhich, [even though] he was dying to do just that (ibid., p. 45).

Sanin's main character says that a scoundrel

is a person completely sincere and natural. . . . He does what is perfectly natural for a man. He sees something that does not belong to him, but which is good, so he takes it; he sees a beautiful woman who does not succumb to his charms, so he takes her by force or deceit. And that is utterly natural insofar as the need for and understanding of enjoyment is precisely one of the few traits by which a natural man differs from an animal (ibid., p. 36).

So he himself virtually goes out and acts accordingly.

Artsybashev's women are merely overcome by force. Lida "unwillingly and submissively, like a slave, gives in to his rough caresses" (ibid., p. 52). Karsavina loves Yuri, yet gives herself to Sanin:

She had neither the will nor the strength to come to her senses. . . . She put up no resistance when he started kissing her again, and almost unconsciously accepted the burning novel delight. . . . At times she felt she could see, hear, and feel nothing, yet she took each of his movements, every abuse of her submissive body, as something exceedingly acute, with mixed feelings of humiliation and insistent curiosity. . . . The secret carnal curiosity seemed to want to know what more he could do to her, this remote and yet close, this hateful and this strong man" (ibid., p. 279).

It is worth mentioning that all the women in the novel are virginal, innocent, and all the men, even the idealist Svarozhich, already possess sexual experience.

47. Kornei Chukovsky, "Nat Pinkerton" (1908), *Sobranie sochineniy v 6 tomakh*, vol. 6 (Moscow: Khudozhestvennaya literatura, 1969), p. 147.

## NOTES TO CHAPTER THREE: THE "SEX QUESTION" ON THE EVE OF THE OCTOBER REVOLUTION

1. Laura Engelstein, *The Keys to Happiness: Sex and the Search for Modernity in Fin-de Siècle Russia* (Ithaca and London: Cornell University Press, 1992), pp. 3–4.

2. See Eve Levin, *Sex and Society in the World of the Orthodox Slavs, 900–1700* (Ithaca, N.Y.: Cornell University Press, 1989), pp. 175–79.

3. At the end of the nineteenth century, it was noted that "of all the methods used to terminate pregnancy, the most popular is the mechanical: raising weights, jumping down from a table or a bench, binding the stomach tightly or kneading it, shaking the whole body, etc." A. O. Afinogenov, Zhizn zhenskovo naseleniya Ryazanskovo uyezda v period detorodnoi deyatelnosti zhenshchin i polozhenie dela akusherskoi pomoshchi etomy naseleniyu (St. Petersburg, 1903), p. 57. Quoted from A. G. Vishnevsky, "Rannie etapy stanovleniya novovo tipa rozhdaemosti v Rossii," in A. G. Vishnevsky, ed., *Brachnost, rozhdaemost, smertnost v Rossii i v SSSR. Sbornik statei* (Moscow: Statistika, 1977), p. 127.

4. V. A. Milyutin, in 1847, wrote in *Sovremennik*, the most progressive periodical of the day, "There have been of late . . . methods recommended for counter-

acting population growth. . . . Some are incredibly ridiculous . . . for example, the proposal to satisfy sensual inclinations by using a certain method that prevents childbirth, or one doctor's suggestion to extract the fetus before birth with a special instrument fitted ad hoc. Other methods may not be so objectionable, but they are extremely odd." V. Milyutin, *Izbrannye proizvedeniya* (Moscow, 1946), p. 93.

5. For a general overview of this issue, see Engelstein, *The Keys to Happiness*, chap. 9.

6. A. G. Boryakovsky, "O vrede sredstv, prepyatstvuyushchikh zachatiyu," *Vrach*, no. 32 (1893), 886, 887. Quoted from Vishnevsky, *Rannie etapy*, p. 128.

7. *Obshchestvo russkikh vrachei v pamyat N.I. Pirogova. Dvenadtsaty Pirogovsky syezd*. Vyp. 2 (St. Petersburg, 1913), p. 88.

8. Engelstein, *The Keys to Happiness*, p. 85.

9. For a history of prostitution in czarist Russia, see G. M. G(ertsenshtein), "Prostitution," *Entsiklopedichesky slovar Brokhausa i Efrona*, vol. 25A (St. Petersburg, 1898), pp. 479–86; V. O. Deryuzhinsky *Politseiskoye pravo* (St. Petersburg, 1903); B. I. Bentovin, *Torguyushchie telom. Ocherki sovremennoi prostitutsii*, 2d ed. (St. Petersburg, 1909); V. M. Bronner and A. I. Yelistratov, *Prostitutsiya v Rossii* (Moscow, 1927); Richard Stites, "Prostitute and Society in Pre-Revolutionary Russia," *Jahrbuch für Geschichte Osteuropas* 31 (1983), 348–64; Laurie Bernstein, "Yellow Tickets and State-licensed Brothels: The Tsarist Government and the Regulation of Urban Prostitution," Susan Gross Solomon and John F. Hutchinson, eds., *Health and Society in Prerevolutionary Russia* (Bloomington: Indiana University Press, 1990), pp. 45–54; Laura Engelstein, *The Keys to Happiness*, chap. 2.

10. *Statistika Rossiyskoi Imperii. XIII. Prostitutsiya v Rossiyskoi imperii po obsledovaniyu na 1 avgusta 1889 goda* (St. Petersburg, 1890), p. xxxvi. Quoted from B. F. Kalachev, "Vzglyad na problemu cherez . . . stoletie," *Prostitutsiya i prestupnost* (Moscow: Yuridicheskaya literatura, 1991), p. 39.

11. For the more sensitive young men this experience was quite harrowing. This is how Alexander Kuprin described sexual initiation in his novel *Yama* (*The Pit*):

He always remembered that evening with horror, disgust and vagueness as if it were some drunken dream. With difficulty he recalled how for Dutch courage he had drunk real bedbug-smelling rum while in the carriage, he remembered feeling confused from this drink, going into a large hall where chandeliers and wall lamps shone like fiery cartwheels, where women floated about in fantastic pink, blue and violet blobs and the white of necks, bosoms and arms shone with a blindingly-heady, triumphant gleam. One of his companions whispered something into the ear of one of those fantastic figures, and she trotted up to Kolya and said, "Listen here, you nice little cadet, your companions tell me you're still innocent. . . . Come . . . I'll teach you everything."

Then followed something that was so hard and painful to recall that halfway through his memories Kolya got so tired he turned his thoughts by strength of will to something else. All he remembered vaguely were the revolving and dancing circles from the lamplight, the insistent kisses, embarrassing touching of bodies and then a sudden sharp pain from which he felt like dying of pleasure at the same time as screaming from terror, and then he himself was surprised to see his pale, shaking hands fumbling in vain to do up his clothes. A. I. Kuprin, "Yama," *Sobranie sochineniy v 6 tomakh*, vol. 5 (Moscow: Gosudarstvennoe izdatelstvo khudozhestvennoi literatury, 1958), pp. 251–52.

Even sadder are the reminiscences of the same experience by Tolstoy's Pozdnyshev:

I remember it, right away, right there, without leaving the room, I just felt so dreadfully miserable that I felt like crying, crying for my lost innocence, for my eternally ruined relations with women. Oh yes, natural, simple relations with women had been destroyed forever and ever. From then on I never had any pure relations with women, nor could I have. L. N. Tolstoy, "The Kreutzer Sonata," *Sobranie sochineniy v 22 tomakh*, vol. 12, p. 135.

The interesting thing is that these dear boys feel sorry only for their own loss of innocence; they give no thought to the prostitute.

12. Simon-André Tissot's famous book, *Masturbation, or a Discourse on Illness Deriving from Self-Abuse*, originally published in French in 1758—the author believed that masturbation was the root of practically all disease and vice—was translated into Russian and republished several times, forming for decades the "authoritative" basis of near hysteria on the subject. See Engelstein, *The Keys to Happiness*, pp. 225–48.

13. M. A. Chlenov, "Polovaya perepis moskovskovo studenchestva," *Russky vrach*, no 3 (1907): 1072–11. It was also published in book form: M. A. Chlenov, *Polovaya perepis moskovskovo studenchestva i yeyo obshchestvennoe znachenie* (Moscow, 1909). Another questionnaire compiled by a commission headed by D. N. Zhbankov and V. I. Yakovenko and intended for circulation among students at Moscow women's colleges was confiscated by the police. Of the 6,000 questionnaires, only 324 completed copies were saved; their results were published only after the October Revolution. (D. N. Zhbankov, "O polovoi zhizni uchashchikhsya zhenshchin," *Vrachebnoe delo* 10, no. 12 (1922), 225.

14. Quotes from Engelstein, *Keys to Happiness*, pp. 250–52.

15. On the history of homosexuality in Russia, see Simon Karlinsky, "Russia's Gay Literature and History (11th—12th Centuries)," *Gay Sunshine* 29/30 (Summer/Fall 1976). For information on literature about homosexuality in the USSR, see Daniel Healey, *A Social History of Homosexuality in Soviet Russia,*

*1917–1939* (unpublished manuscript). Engelstein's *Keys to Happiness* also has important information about lesbianism and medical theories of homosexuality.

16. For example, Nikolai I's education minister, Count Sergei Uvarov (1786–1856), arranged for his handsome but not particularly intelligent lover Prince Mikhail Dondukov-Korsakov to take up the prized appointment of deputy president of the Imperial Academy of Sciences and rector of St. Petersburg University, which gave rise to several witty epigrams that played on the "arsehole" theme, including one from Pushkin:

> In the Academy of Sciences, look
> There sits Prince Dunduk.
> It's said he doesn't deserve
> To plan such an honored role,
> How does he have the nerve?
> Because of his big . . .

(A. S. Pushkin, "V akademii nauk," *Sobranie sochineniy v 10 tomakh*, vol. 2 [Moscow: Gosudarstvennoye izdatelstvo khudozhestvenoi literatury, 1959], p. 451.)

When it was a matter of friends rather than enemies, however, Pushkin's attitude to that phenomenon was ironical-cum-playful; he saw nothing shameful in it, as witnessed by his letter and verse greeting to Philippe Vigel, whose weakness for young boys was well known. The poet sympathizes with Vigel's boredom in Kishinev and recommends "three sweet beaus" of whom "I reckon the youngest would suit you best: N.B., he is sleeping in the same room as his brother Mikhail and they shag like a rattlesnake—from which you can draw important conclusions; I present them for your experience and prudence." Pushkin ends with the following verse:

> I'll gladly serve you true
> By verse or prose or soul
> But Vigel, spare my hole!

(A. S. Pushkin, Letter to F. F. Vigel, 22 October—4 November 1823, *Sobranie sochineniy v 10 tomakh*, vol. 9, pp. 75–77.

17. Homosexual relations in the military schools are described in fullest detail in the long anonymous poem "The Adventures of a Page," written in the first person and ascribed to A. F. Shenin. The lyrical hero of the poem is seduced immediately on entering the Page Corps (i.e., around age 18) by an older companion, after which he develops a taste for the practices and starts to go the rounds, including consorting with his superiors; then he dresses in female clothing and carves out for himself a glittering career that continues right up to the time he leaves the corps. The poem also describes erotic whipping experiences in detail. All this is strongly reminiscent of the custom and habits

of the English public schools of the nineteenth century. And it was practically unpublished.

After yet another scandal featuring Shenin, when he was dismissed from the service and for some time deported from St. Petersburg in 1846, the story in the capital was that "the war minister had summoned Rostovtsev and conveyed His Majesty's order to prosecute pederasty severely in educational institutions. Prince Chernyshov is said to have added, "Yakov Ivanovich, as you know, this has a harmful effect on the boys' health," to which Rostovtsev replied, "Pray, permit me to disagree, Your Grace; I can tell you frankly that when I was in the Page Corps there were many who did it: I was coupled with Traskin [later a stout general notorious for his ugliness] and it had not effect on our health!" Prince Chernyshov burst out laughing. (*Eros russe. Russky erot ne dlya dam* [Oakland, Calif.: Scythian Books, 1988], p. 59.)

18. For the most substantive analysis of the history of Russian law on these issues, see V. D. Nabokov, "Plotskie prestupleniya, po proektu ugolovnovo ulozheniya," *Vestnik prava* 1902, Nos. 9–10. This long article is also published in Nabokov's book *Sbornik statei po ugolovnomu pravu* (St. Petersburg, 1904). The section on homosexuality is also published in German translation in the periodical *Jahrbuch für sexuelle Zwischenstufen* 56, no. 2 (1903), 1159–71. See also Engelstein, *Keys to Happiness*, chap. 2.

## NOTES TO CHAPTER FOUR:
## THE SOVIET SEXUAL EXPERIMENT

1. I rely in the following section particularly on these studies: Sheila Fitzpatrick, "Sex and Revolution: An Examination of Literary and Statistical Data on the Mores of Soviet Students in the 1920s," *Journal of Modern History* (June 1978), 252–78; Sergei Golod, "Izuchenie polovoi morali v 20-e gody," *Sotsiologicheskie issledovaniya*, no. 2 (1986), 152–55; Richard Stites, *The Women's Liberation Movement in Russia: Feminism, Nihilism and Bolshevism, 1860–1930* (Princeton, N.J.: Princeton University Press, 1978); Eric Naiman, "The Case of Chubarov Alley: Collective Rape, Utopian Desire and the Mentality of NEP," *Russian History/Histoire Russe* 17, no. 1 (Spring 1990), 1–30; Wendy Goldman, "Women, Abortion and the State, 1917–36," and Elizabeth Waters, "The Female Form in Soviet Political Iconography, 1917–32," in Barbara Evans Clemens, Barbara Alpern Engel, and Christine D. Worabec, eds., *Russia's Women: Accommodation, Resistance, Transformation* (Berkeley: University of California Press, 1991). The following collections contain valuable documents and articles: Abbott Gleason, Peter Kenez, and Richard Stites, eds., *Bolshevik Culture: Experiment and Order in the Russian Revolution* (Bloomington: Indiana University Press, 1985); Joachim S. Hohmann, ed., *Sexualforschung und -politik in der Sowjetunion seit 1917* (Frankfurt am Main: Peter Lang, 19).

2. Karl Marx, "Svyatoye semeistvo," Karl Marx and Friedrich Engels, *Sochineniya*, 2d ed, vol. 2 (Moscow: Politizdat, 1956), p. 24.

3. Karl Marx and Friedrich Engels, *Iz rannikh proizvedeniy* (Moscow: Politizdat, 1956), p. 587.

4. Karl Marx, letter to Jenny Marx, June 21, 1856, in Marx and Engels, *Sochineniya*, 2d ed, vol. 2, pp. 434, 435.

5. Friedrich Engels, "Kniga otkroveniya," in Marx and Engels, *Sochineniya*, 2d ed, vol. 21, p. 6.

6. Friedrich Engels, "Proiskhozhdenie semyi, chastnoi sobstvennosti i gosudarstva," in ibid., p. 85.

7. Clara Zetkin, "Iz zapisnoi knizhki," *Vospominaniya o Lenine*, vol. 5 (Moscow: Politizdat, 1979), p. 435.

8. In this section I have widely relied on works by Susan Gross Solomon, "Social Hygiene in Soviet Medical Education, 1922–30," *Journal of the History of Medicine and Allied Sciences* 45, no. 4 (October 1990), 607–43; and "The Demographic Argument in Soviet Debates over the Legalization of Abortion in the 1920's," *Cahiers du Monde Russe et Soviétique*, no. 7 (1992).

9. A. M. Kollontay, "Dorogu krylatomu Erosu! Pismo k trudyashcheisya molodyozhi," *Molodaya gvardiya* 3, no. 10 (1923), 111–13.

10. Aron Zalkind, *Revolutsia i molodyozh* (Leningrad, 1924).

11. Instead of Lenin, it was done by Nikolai Bukharin. He said about Zalkind's commandments, "Nonsense and philistine scum, which want to climb into all pockets," *Pravda*, February 12, 1925.

12. Zetkin, "Iz zapisnoi knizhki," p. 436.

13. Ibid.

14. Ibid., p. 437.

15. Ibid., p. 435.

16. See Mikhail Zolotonosov, "Masturbatsiya. 'Erogennye zony' sovetskoi kultury 1920–1930-kh godov," *Literaturnoye obozrenie*, no. 11 (1991), 93–99.

17. S. R. Ravich, "Borba s prostitutsiei v Petrograde," *Kommunistka*, no. 1 (1920), 23. Quoted from Golod, "Izuchenie polovoi morali v 20-e gody," p. 155.

18. A. M. Kollontay, *Lyubov pchol trudovykh: Iz serii rasskazov "Revolyutsiya chuvstv i revolyutsiya nravov"* (Moscow- Petrograd, 1923), pp. 43–44.

19. B. N. Mironov, *Istoria v tsifrakh* (Leningrad: Nauka, 1991), p. 133.

20. See more about that in Richard Stites, *The Women's Liberation Movement in Russia*, chap. 11.

21. V. I. Lenin, "Rabochij klass i neomaltuzianstvo," *Polnoye sobranie sochineniy*, vol. 23 (Moscow: Politizdat, 1964), p. 257.

22. Goldman, "Women, Abortion and the State," p. 248.

23. Solomon, "The Demographic Argument."

24. Goldman, "Women, Abortion and the State."

25. M. A. Vein, "Osnovnye faktory, vliyayushchie na rost i rasprostranenie venericheskikh boleznei," *Venerologiya i dermatologiya*, no. 6 (1925), 133–35.

26. I. Gelman (1923) and G. Batkis (1925) surveyed, respectively, over 1,500 (1,214 men and 338 women), and over 600 Moscow students (341 men and 270 women). V. Klyachkin (1925) did the same among students in Omsk

(616 men and 274 women), and D. Lass (1928) followed suit with a survey of students in Odessa (1,801 men and 527 women). M. Barash (1925) examined the sex lives of 1,450 Moscow workers, S. Burshtyn (1925) surveyed 4,600 army personnel and students, S. Golosovker (1925 and 1927) studied 550 women and more than 2,000 men in Kazan, N. Khrapkovskaya and D. Konchilovich (1929) studied 3,350 workers in Saratov, and Z. Gurevich and F. Grosser (1930) surveyed 1,500 Kharkovites. The list is almost endless. Special studies were made of school children, prostitutes, venereal disease sufferers, and so on.

27. Some of these figures are really impressive. Some 47% of male workers and 67% off female workers in Petrograd had begun their sexual lives before age 18 (*Trud, zdorovje i byt leningradskoi rabochey molodyozhi*, vyp. 1 [Leningrad, 1925], p. 23). Almost 88% of male and more than half of female students surveyed by Gelman in 1922 had had short-term sexual affairs (I. Gelman, *Polovaya zhizn sovremennoi molodyozhi* [Moscow, 1923], pp. 65–71). In 1928, 78% of male and 68% of female delegates to a youth conference said that they had their first sexual experience before age 18 (V. Ketlinskaya and Vl. Slepkov, *Zhizn bez kontrolya* [Moscow, 1929]). Komsomol activists were also sexually more active.

28. Golod, "Izuchenie polovoi morali v 20-e gody."

29. Fitzpatrick, "Sex and Revolution," p. 271.

30. Ibid., p. 275.

31. Ibid., p. 277.

## NOTES TO CHAPTER FIVE: SEXOPHOBIA IN ACTION

1. Quoted from Mikhail Zolotonosov, "Masturbatsiya," *Literaturnoe obozrenie*, no. 11 (1991), 98.

2. Eric Naiman, "The Case of Chubarov Alley," *Russian History/Histoire Russe* 17, no. 1 (Spring 1990), 8.

3. Ibid.

4. I. Ilf, "Zapisnye knizhki (1925–1937)," Ilya Ilf and Yevgeny Petrov, *Sobranie sochineniy v 5 tomakh* (Moscow: Gosudarstvennoye izdatelstvo khudozhestvennoi literatury, 1961), p. 178, 251.

5. Ilf and Petrov, "Savanarylo," *Sobranie sochineniy*, vol. 3 (Moscow, 1961), pp. 188–89.

6. Wilhelm Reich, *The Sexual Revolution* (New York: Orgone Institute Press, 1935), p. 186.

7. M. A. Sereisky, "Gomoseksualism," *Bolshaya Sovetskaya Entsiklopediya*, vol. 17 (Moscow: Sovietskaya Entsiklopediya, 1930), p. 593.

8. Ibid.

9. For detailed information on the lives of Soviet gays, see S. Karlinsky, "Russia's Gay Literature and Culture: The Impact of the October Revolution," N. L. Duberman et al., eds., *Hidden from History: Reclaiming the Gay and Lesbian Past*

(New York: NAL, 1990). Vladimir Kozlovsky's *Argo russkoi gomoseksualnoi sub-kultury* (Benson, Vt.: Chalidze, 1986) is much broader in scope than its title suggests; it contains figures and documents about all aspects of homosexual lifestyles and their reflection in literature, diaries, and so on. See also Joachim S. Hohmann, "Zur rechtlichen und sozialen Problem der Homosexualität," in *Sexualforschung und -politik in der Sowjetunion seit 1917* (Frankfurt: Peter Lang, 1990); Siegfried Tornow, "Rückschritt gleich Fortschritt. Geschichte der Schwulen in Sowjet-Russland," *Siegessäule*, no. 6 (1987).

10. The report on Krylenko's speech is published in *Sovetskaya yustitsiya*, no. 7 (1936) and reproduced in Kozlovsky's book.

11. *Bolshaya Sovetskaya Entsiklopediya*, 2d ed., vol. 12 (Moscow: 1952), p. 35.

12. See Alla Bossart, "Sergei-Iosif: apokrify," *Ogonyok*, no. 31 (1991), 15.

13. In 1907, Gorky writing to another eminent Russian writer, Leonid Andreyev, who shared his homophobia, about the contemporary Russian avant-garde, said, "All this is a product of old slaves, people who *are bound* to confound freedom with pederasty; for example, for them "human freedom" is oddly mixed up with a shift from one watering hole to another, and is sometimes even reduced to freedom of the penis and nothing more." *Gorky i Leonid Andreyev. Neizdannaya perepiska, Literaturnoye nasledstvo*, vol. 72 (Moscow, 1965), p. 288.

14. A. M. Gorky, "Predislovie," in S. Zweig, *Smyatenie chuvstv, Iz zapisok starovo cheloveka* (Leningrad, 1927).

15. A. M. Gorky, "Proletarsky gumanizm," *Sobranie sochineniy v 30 tomakh*, vol. 27 (Moscow: Khydozhestvennaya literatura, 1953), p. 238.

16. For statistics on changes in birthrates and abortion, see A. G. Vishnevsky and A. G. Volkov, *Vosproizvodstvo naseleniya SSSR* (Moscow: Statistika, 1983); Wendy Goldman, "Women, Abortion and the State, 1917–1936," in B. E. Clemens et al., eds., *Russia's Women* (Berkeley: University of California Press, 1991); Susan Gross Solomon, "The Demographic Argument in Soviet Debates over the Legalization of Abortion in the 1920s," *Cahiers du Monde Russe et Soviétique*, no. 1 (1992). See also A. G. Vishnevsky, "Evolyutsiya semyi v SSSR i printsipy semeinoi politiki," A. G. Vishnevsky, ed., *Semya i semeinaya politika* (Moscow: Institut sotsialno-ekonomicheskikh problem narodonaseleniya AN SSSR i Gomkomtrud SSSR, 1991).

17. Anton Makarenko, *Kniga dlya roditelei* (Moscow: Uchpedgiz, 1954), p. 233.

18. Ibid., p. 256.

19. Prof. I. A. Aryamov, "Znachenie sokhraneniya polovoi energii dlya molodezhi," *Komsomolskaya pravda* (Feb. 7, 1926), 5. Quoted in Eric Naiman, "The Case of Chubarov Alley," p. 18.

20. Ibid. Aryamov's interpretation of Pushkin's legendarily prodigious output during the autumn of 1830 at Boldino was that he was cut off from his beloved by an outbreak of cholera. Pushkin, said Aryamov, burned with desire. He quotes Valery Briusov's essay on Pushkin, "Tormented by the passionate desire to see his betrothed, in receipt of foolish, alarming letters from her, with no

one around him with whom he might share his thoughts, virtually deprived of books, the poet devoted himself to poetic creativity with unusual fervor. In this period he wrote *The Covetous Knight*, 'Mozart and Salieri,' and 'The Stone Guest' and nearly finished *Eugene Onegin*; he also wrote 'The Little House in Kolomna,' 'Feast in a Time of Plague,' and many lyric poems." But Briusov's interpretation is not materialistic enough for Aryamov: "Thus does Briusov describe the surge in Pushkin's creative work, but he does not understand its causes. For us, this productive upsurge in Pushkin's work is completely clear: his strong sexual drive, not finding an outlet, was transformed into the highest of cerebral processes, the creative work."

21. Andrei Platonov, "Antisexsus," *Novy mir*, no. 9 (1989), 170.
22. George Orwell, *1984* p. 109.
23. Yuri Borev, *Staliniada* (Moscow: Iskusstvo, 1990), pp. 84, 153–54.
24. Quoted from Zolotonosov, "Masturbatsiya," p. 99.
25. Richard Stites, *Revolutionary Dreams, Utopian Vision and Experimental Life in the Russian Revolution* (New York: Oxford University Press, 1989).
26. Ibid., p. 215.
27. For the history of psychoanalysis in Russia, see Alexander Etkind, *Eros nevozmozhnovo. Istoria psikhoanaliza v Rossii* (St. Petersburg: Meduza, 1993).
28. Vladimir Shlapentokh, *Private and Public Life of the Soviet People: Changing Values in Post-Stalin Russia* (New York: Oxford University Press, 1989).
29. Mark Popovsky, *Trety lishny: On, Ona i Sovetsky Rezhim* (London: Overseas Publications, 1983), p. 119. Nor is this only history. The following letter was published in a Russian newspaper in 1992: "My wife and I live with my parents and my mother has a very nice habit of bursting into our room just when we are *doing* it. If the door is locked or barricaded by a chair, she will knock until she turns blue. And at night she tries to see what these smart children are up to. We are now used to it and don't jump off each other when she comes in. But at the beginning we were really nervous." And this couple at least had a room to themselves. Many young couples have absolutely no privacy.
30. Ibid., p. 129.
31. See I. P. Ilina, "Vliyanie voin na brachnost sovetskikh zhenshchin," A. G. Vishnevsky, ed., *Brachnost, rozhdaemost, i smertnost v SSSR* (Moscow: Statistika, 1977), pp. 50–61; A. Y. Kvasha, "Demograficheskoye ekho voiny," in Y. A. Polyakov, ed., *Problemy istoricheskoi demografii SSSR* (Kiev: Naukova dumka, 1988), pp. 18–26.

## NOTES TO CHAPTER SIX:
## FROM SUPPRESSION TO DOMESTICATION

1. I remember well an incident involving foreign books. during the relatively liberal 1960s, I was a consultant to scientific libraries in Leningrad, giving advice on stocking their philosophy, history, and sociology collections so as to spend scarce foreign currency that had been allocated for the purchase of important

books as rationally and economically as possible. In one of the catalogues, I came upon an inexpensive and, judging by its description, an informative book on sex crimes by the American psychiatrist Frank Caprio, so I recommended it to the Public Library. A year of two later—the normal passage of time for the ordering and receiving of foreign books—I received a phone call from the agitated censor, Vladimir Tupitsyn, an intelligent man with whom I had enjoyed good personal relations. The conversation went something like this: "Igor Semyonovich, was it you who ordered the Caprio book?" "Yes, what about it?" "It's a dreadful scandal. I've just had a call from Moscow, from the infuriated boss at Glavlit [Central Censorship Bureau] saying the book is pornography and cannot b kept even in a special library; they want the book destroyed and are demanding your blood. Write a note of explanation." "I haven't seen the book, but judging by the catalogue description, it isn't pornography." "All right, I'll try to convince them the book was sent here temporarily, on my personal responsibility, and we'll look at it together." When the book arrive, al became clear. As advertised, it was a popularly written book based on medical case histories. But the author had quoted sex offenders, who had naturally spoken in the vernacular, rather than Latin; they had called a spade a spade. Some woman or other in Glavlit had read through it, was horrified, and had informed her superiors; hence the commotion. Tupitsyn and I wrote an explanation that calmed down the Moscow bosses, and the book stayed in the public library's special custody section. However, if Tupitsyn had telephoned the Party regional committee instead of me, the people there would have been happy to extend the scandal, and I would have been in hot water, perhaps even lost my job.

2. Actually, Freud's works were never on the official list of banned books; it was librarians who took the initiative in restricting access in this case.

3. This practice came to an end only in 1987, after I had poked fun at it in an article in *Kommunist*, the theoretical journal of the Party Central Committee. Before the era of perestroika and glasnost, nothing of this kind could have been printed; the existence of censorship and its procedures were just as secret as was sex. And censorship could not be criticized in the press. So when I refer later in this book to the crass ignorance of Soviet doctors and educators in sexual matters, do not judge them too harshly; not only were they taught nothing, but regardless of how much they might have wanted to learn, their opportunities for self-enlightenment were restricted.

4. See S. I. Golod, "Sexual Behavior of Contemporary Youth," in Igor Kon and James Riordan, eds., *Sex and Russian Society* (Bloomington: Indiana University Press, 1993); S. I. Golod, *Stabilnost semyi: sotsiologichesky i demografichesky aspekty* (Leningrad: Nauka, 1984); A. G. Kharchev and S. I. Golod, "Molodyozh i brak," *Chelovek i obshchestvo*, vyp. 6 (Leningrad: Izdatelstvo Leningradskovo universiteta, 1969), pp. 125–42.

5. For a comparative analysis of the Soviet and U.S. family, see David H. Olson and Mikhail S. Matskovsky, "Soviet and American Families: A Comparative

Overview," in James W. Maddock, ed., *Families Before and After Perestroika: Russian and U.S. Perspectives* (New York: Guilford Press, 1994).

6. *Demografichesky entsiklopedichesky slovar* (Moscow: Sovetskaya entsiklopedia, 1985), p. 359.

7. M. Sonin, "Demograficheskie aspekty sluzhby braka," *Molodaya semya* (Moscow: Statistika, 1977), pp. 73–87.

8. Sometime in the 1950s I heard an apt joke: God gave man three virtues—intelligence, honesty, and Party membership—but only on the condition that they never coincided in the same person. There were no exceptions to this rule. And when today many of my peers (as well as people much younger) who are making new "democratic" careers for themselves assert that they have always been honest, only there were some things of which they were not aware . . . I cannot help wondering at the gullibility of those voting for them. After all, these candidates are either lying through their teeth or are hopelessly stupid. The latter is probably worse. As we Russians say, the drunk can sleep it off, the fool never.

9. See V. V. Nagayev, *Sotsialno-gigienichesky i psikhologichesky analiz formirovaniya polovovo povedeniya molodyozhi, problemy yevo korrektsii i psikhogigenicheskovo vospitaniya. Avtoreferat dissertatsii na soiskanie uchonoi stepeni doktora meditsinskikh nauk* (Moscow: Vsesoyuzny nauchno-issledovatelsky institut sotsialnoi gigieny i organizatsii zdravookhraneniya im. N.A. Semashko, 1987), p. 8.

10. M. Popovsky, *Trety lishny: On, Ona i Sovetsky Rezhim* (London: Overseas Publications, 1983), pp. 220–21.

11. V. N. Kolbanovsky, "Vstupitelnaya statya. Polovaya lyubov kak obshchestvennaya problema," in Rudolf Neubert, *Novaya kniga o supruzhestve. Problema braka v nastoyashchem i budushchem*, trans. from German (Moscow: Progress, 1969), pp. 20, 22–23.

12. The English translation of this document appears in Alexander Yanov, *The New Russian Right* (Berkeley: University of California Press, 1978), pp. 170–72. See also Walter Laqueur, *Black Hundred: The Rise of the Extreme Right in Russia* (New York: HarperCollins, 1993).

13. A. G. Khripkova and D. V. Kolesov, *Devochka—podrostok—devushka* (Moscow: Prosveshchenie, 1981), pp. 73, 84, 87.

14. A. G. Khripkova and D. V. Kolesov, *Malchik—podrostok—yunosha* (Moscow: Prosveshchenie, 1982), pp. 19, 75, 76.

15. I. F. Yunda and L. I. Yunda, *Sotsialno-psikhologicheskie i mediko-biologicheskie osnovy semeinoi zhizni* (Kiev: Vysha shkola, 1990), pp. 138, 147, 160, 224, 225.

## NOTES TO CHAPTER SEVEN: THE BEAST HAS BROKEN LOOSE

1. My personal experience may best illustrate the situation.

In January 1987, the moment Alexander Yakovlev, the main architect of perestroika, became a Politburo member, I sent him a note proposing the creation of a social (i.e., free of charge!) interdepartmental problem council on matters of sexology and sexual enlightenment. Yakovlev's personal adviser, an educated psychologist, fully concurred with my suggestions and the Central Committee Scientific Section was instructed to draw up the appropriate documents. The officials, however, did not want to do this—not because they were against it but simply because they had enough on their hands as it was; so they even failed to ask the various departments (Health Ministry, Education and Internal Affairs Ministries, Academy of Sciences, Academy of Medical Sciences, Academy of Pedagogical Sciences) for the necessary forms without which nothing could commence. So the initiative died an early death. My innumerable forays into the press were just as fruitless.

2. Jeffrey Weeks, *Sexuality and Its Discontents: Meanings, Myths and Modern Sexualities* (London: Routledge and Kegan Paul, 1985), p. 45. See also Stan Cohen, *Folk Devils and Moral Panics* (London: McGibbon and Kee, 1972).

3. For a general discussion, see Igor S. Kon, "Identity Crisis and Post-Communist Psycyhology," *Symbolic Interaction* vol. 16, no. 4 (1993), 395–410.

4. Prokuratura Soyuza SSR, *Prokuroram respublik, krayev, oblastei. Informatsionnoye pismo*, April 17, 1989, "O praktike primeneniya ugolovnovo zakonodatelstva ob otvetstvennosti za rasprostranenie pornograficheskikh predmetov i proizvedeniy, propagandiruyushchikh kult nasiliya i zhestokosti."

5. *Ogonyok*, no. 3, (January 1990), 18.

6. Lynne Attwood, "Sex and the Cinema," in Igor Kon and James Riordan, eds., *Sex and Russian Society* (Bloomington: Indiana University Press, 1993), p. 64.

7. Ibid., p. 85.

8. Victor Yerofeyev, "Vystuplenie na besede 'Erotika i literatura'," *Inostrannaya literatura*, no. 9 (1991), 226.

9. Ibid., p. 227. According to Article 246 of the new draft Criminal Code, distribution, advertising, and selling of pornographic mateirals is punishable only when minors are involved. Adults have freedom of choice.

## NOTES TO CHAPTER EIGHT: SEXLESS SEXISM

1. In the interests of justice, I must add that in *A Dictionary of the Social Sciences*, edited by Julius Gould and William L. Kolb, compiled under the auspices of UNESCO (Glencoe, N.Y.: Free Press, 1964), and in the 17-volume *International Encyclopedia of the Social Sciences*, edited by David L. Sills (New York: Free Press, 1968), such articles were also absent. Only "sexual behavior" was covered, although "sex differences" and "sex roles" were discussed in other articles. The picture is radically different in *The Encyclopedia of Sociology*, edited by Edgar F. Borgatta and Marie L. Borgatta (New York: Macmillan, 1992), which has articles on "gender," "sex differences," "femininity," and "feminist theory."

2. See V. A. Geodakyan, *Evolyutsionnaya logika differentsiatsii polov v filogeneze i*

*ontogeneze. Avtoreferat na soiskanie uchenoi stepeni doktora biologischeskikh nauk* (Moscow: Institut biologii razvitiya imeni N. K. Koltsova, 1987).

3. V. A. Geodakyan, "Teoriya differentsiatsii polov v problemakh cheloveka," in I. T. Frolov, ed., *Chelovek v sisteme nauk* (Moscow: Nauka, 1989), p. 188.

4. V. P. Bagrunov, *Polovye razlichiya v vidovoi i individualnoi izmenchivosti psikhiki cheloveka. Avtoreferat dissertatsii na soiskanie uchenoi stepeni kandidata psikhologicheskikh nauk* (Leningrad: Leningradskii Universitet, 1981), p. 15.

5. Lynn Attwood, *The New Soviet Man and Woman: Sex-Role Socialization in the USSR* (Bloomington: Indiana University Press, 1990), p. 94. This is the only Western book on this important topic, and it contains much useful information. Unfortunately, the author makes no attempt to compare Soviet ideological stereotypes with the real practices of sex/gender socialization. The book is not really a picture of "sex-role socialization in the USSR" but only of *some* Soviet ideas about it. Attwood's simple ideological contrasting of "Western" and "Soviet" theories and opinions as if they were uniform is often misleading. And I was surprised to find that in the chapter on "The Work of I. S. Kon," my ideas were presented and discussed on the basis of my newspaper articles, instead of my professional books and writings.

6. Ibid., p. 157.

7. According to Bakhtin, the grotesque body of medieval carnival culture is "a body in the act of becoming. It is never finished, never completed; it is continually built [and] created, and it builds and creates other bodies. . . . This is why attention is focused on those parts of the grotesque body that grow beyond the body itself, transgressing its limits, the parts in which it conceives a new, second body: the bowels and the phallus. . . . The body that is featured in all the expressions of the unofficial speech of the people is the body that is fertilized and fertilizes, that gives birth and is born, devours and is devoured, drinks, defecates, is sick and dies. In every language there are a great number of expressions related to the genitals, the anus and buttocks, the belly, the mouth and nose. But there are few expressions for other parts of the body: arms and legs, face and eyes." (Mikhail Bakhtin, *Rabelais and His World*, trans. by Helen Iswolsky [Cambridge, Mass.: MIT Press, 1968], pp. 317, 319.)

On the other hand, the new bodily canon, which emerged at the beginning of modern time, "presents an entirely finished, completed, strictly limited body, which is shown from the outside as something individual. That which protrudes, bulges, sprouts, or branches off (when the body transgresses its limits and a new one begins) is eliminated, hidden, or moderated. All orifices of the body are closed. . . . The verbal norms of official and literary language, determined by the canon, prohibit all that is linked with fecundity, pregnancy, childbirth. There is a sharp line of division between familiar speech and 'correct' language" (ibid., p. 320). Unfortunately, I could not consult the volume *Sexuality and the Body in Russian Culture*, edited by Jane T. Costlow, Stephanie Sandler, and Judith Vowles (Stanford, Calif.: Stanford University Press, 1993).

8. L. V. Zharov, *Chelovecheskaya telesnost: filosofsky analiz* (Rostov: Izdatelstvo Rostovskovo universiteta, 1988).

9. I realized how important verbal uninhibitedness and a fairly rich erotic vocabulary were when I began to receive "erotic stories" from a hack writer (I could not call his work "literature") in the late 1980s, as Russians finally began to talk about sex out loud. This man believed his stories were needed for, among other things, the sexual education of adolescents. But how plainly can one describe sexual actions without resorting to "vulgar" language? The author regarded the common word *huey* (prick) as improper, so in some places he used the academic-sounding "penis" or "male sex organ" and in others, the children's word *piska* (willy). The literary effect was strange. When the author describes a group of students sunbathing on a hot Black Sea beach with their "male sex organs" standing at attention, he is simply uproarious. In another story, he describes a threatened gang rape, which the ingenious young heroine manages to turn into a sexual orgy by suggesting that the boys first demonstrate their physical prowess as they stand in line, so that she can rate them. And in this context, the use of the childhood diminutive, the innocent, nearly sexless *piska*, which carries a feminine gender—to describe the most massive and terrifying of these organs, he merely drops the diminutive ending and invents the masculine-sounding *pis* (pisser)—seems not so much ridiculous as obscene, standing in sharp contrast to the extremely unchildlike situation. The counternormative *huey* would have been far more resonant in this context. Incidentally, in both literary and colloquial Russian, the words *samets* (male) and *samka* (female) are used only to designate animals and never (with the exception of biological literature) to refer to human beings. To call a man (*muzhchina*) a male or a woman (*zhenshchina*) a female is the equivalent of calling the person in question a sexy animal—an insult. This linguistic differentiation of biological and human—i.e., cultural—sex is much older than the Soviet regime and is indicative of certain cultural anxieties.

10. Sometimes wearing a uniform does not in fact deindividualize a person, but actually accentuates his or her individuality. At the best Soviet Young Pioneer camps, such as Artek and Orlyonok, boys and girls alike wore the same uniform: shorts, shirt, and tie. It was very attractive. When the children wore their street clothes, differences in their social and economic circumstances were the most noticeable: some dressed well, others poorly. When the children were in uniform, on the other hand, these differences disappeared immediately. In fact, the uniformity of their dress accentuated the individuality of their faces. Before the children changed into uniforms, one would notice the boy in a red shirt or the girl in a colorful skirt. Once they were all wearing the same outfit, one would remember their names and faces. This was all to the good, and it is a pity we have renounced all uniforms in the name of individuality—although, to be fair, poverty has something to do with the situation as well.

11. I vividly recall my impressions on visiting France for the first time in 1966. My colleagues and I dropped in on a cozy student dance hall on the rue

d'Uchette and were amazed to see one young man wearing a suit and bow tie and a girl just as elegantly dressed dancing right next to another pair, both of whom were wearing threadbare jeans. Neither couple seemed at all put out by the appearance of the other. That situation would have been impossible in Russia: the presence of someone incorrectly dressed would have been a case for the police or some other third party to sit in judgment. In France, no one in charge seemed to care.

A second memorable impression was made by the miniskirt. As I took a good look at the shapely legs exposed by the skirts, I constantly expected to see something shocking so that I could go home with a clear conscience and say that this new fashion was rather pathetic. But I saw nothing ugly or shocking. Then I began to look at the faces and figures as well as the legs of the women, and I noticed that the shortest skirts were primarily worn by young girls. This was not surprising; after all, they had the legs worth showing off. Older women and those with less attractive legs tended to wear slightly longer skirts despite the prevailing fashion. It was not long before the miniskirt made its appearance in the USSR. And many women, young and old, of every shape and size, began to wear the short skirts, even those who would have looked more attractive in a longer skirt.

12. Mark Popovsky, *Trety Lishny: On, Ona i Sovetsky Rezhim* (London: Overseas Publications, 1983), p. 404.

13. See Vasily Belov, "Privychnoe delo," *Za tremya volokami* (Moscow: Sovetsky pisatel, 1968), p. 27.

14. The urgency of the request was due to the fact that the journal was then without an editor-in-chief and therefore the editorial board was more willing to take a chance. As it turned out, they were absolutely right about the urgency; when a new editor-in-chief was appointed, he was frightened of his own shadow, and I could not publish another article there.

15. Let me reassure the reader, who will certainly think I suffer from delusions of grandeur, claiming to have "discovered" sexuality and the body, and now gender as well. It was Soviet life that was actually suffering delusions—if not outright schizophrenia!

16. See, for example, T. I. Yufereva, "Obrazy muzhchin i zhenshchin v soznanii podroskov," *Voprosy psikhologii*, no. 3 (1985); T. I. Yufereva, "Formirovanie psikhologicheskovo pola," *Formirovanie lichnosti v perekhodnyi period ot podroskovogo k yunosheskomu vozrastu* (Moscow: Pedagogika, 1987), pp. 137–46; V. S. Ageev, "Psikhologicheskie i sotsialnye funktsii polorolevykh stereotipov," *Voprosy psykhologii*, no. 2 (1987), 152–58; V. Y. Kagan, "Stereotipy muzhestvennosti—zhenstvennosti i 'obraz Ya' u podroskov," *Voprosy psikhologii* 4, no. 3 (1989), 53–62.

17. See I. S. Kon, *Rebyonok i obshchestvo (Istoriko-etnograficheskaya perspektiva)* (*The Child and Society: A Historical-Ethnographic Perspective*) (Moscow: Nauka, Glavnaya redaktsia vostochnoi literatury, 1988); *Etnografia detstva* (*Ethnography of Childhood*), ed. I. S. Kon et al. (Moscow: Nauka, Glavnaya redaktsia vos-

tochnoi literatury, 1883–1992 [This was a series of essays on traditional socialization of children and adolescents among different peoples of Asia, Australia, and Oceania. Four volumes were published from 1983 to 1992]; *Etnicheskie stereotipy muzhskovo i zhenskovo povedeniya* (*Ethnic Stereotypes of Male and Female Behavior*), ed. A.K . Baiburin and I. S. Kon (St. Petersburg: Nauka, 1992).

18. See V. V. Ivanov and V. N. Toporov, *Slavyanskie yazykovye modeliruyuschchie semioticheskie sistemy* (Moscow: Nauka, 1965).

19. See Tatyana Mamonova, ed., *Women and Russia: Feminist Writings from the Soviet Union* (Boston: Beacon Press, 1984).

20. See O. A. Voronina, "Zhenshchina v 'muzhskom obshchestve,'" *Sotsiologicheskie issledovaniya*, no. 2 (1988), 104–10; N. Zakharova, A. Posadskaya, and N. Rimashevskaya, "Kak my reshaem zhenskii vopros," *Kommunist*, no. 4 (1989), 56–65.

21. Y. Ryurikov, "Po zakonu Tezeya. Muzhchina i zhenshchina v nachale biarkhata," *Novy mir*, no. 7 (1986), 186, 188.

22. For more details, see chaps. 2 and 6 in *Families Before and After Perestroika: Russian and US Perspectives*, ed. James W. Maddock, M. Janice Hogan, Anatolyi I. Antonov, and Mikhail S. Matskovsky (New York: Guilford Press, 1994).

23. *Vestnik statistiki*, no. 1 (1988) 62.

24. *Izvestiya*, Dec. 2, 1993.

25. *Canada and the World: An International Perspective on Canada and Canadians* (Canada: Angus Reid Group, 1992), pp. 154, 138.

26. See *Sotsialno-kulturnyi oblik sovetskikh natsii. Po resultatam etnosotsiologicheskovo issledovaniya*, ed. by Yu. V. Arutyunyan and Yu. V. Bromley (Moscow: Nauka, 1986).

27. Y. V. Gruzdeva and E. S. Chertikhina, "Polozhenie zhenshchin v obshchestve: konflikt rolei," *Obshchestvo v raznykh izmereniyakh. Sotsiologi otvechayut na voprosy* (Moscow: Moskovksy rabochy, 1990), p. 157.

28. *Vestnik statistiki*, no. 1 (1988), 62. Of course, this uneven distribution will be familiar to many women in other countries as well. The American sociologist Arlie Hochschild's studies showed that American women work a virtual "second shift" in the home after a full day's work outside it. Hochschild: *The Second Shift* (New York, 1989).

29. *Narodnoye khozyaistvo SSSR v 1987. Statistichesky yezhegodnik* (Moscow: Statistika, 1988), pp. 384–85.

30. See S. I. Golod, *Stabilnost semyi: sotsiologichesky i demografichesky aspekty* (Leningrad: Nauka, 1984) p. 71.

31. Landon Pearson, *Children of Glasnost: Growing Up Soviet* (Toronto: Lester and Orpen Dennis, 1990), p. 129.

32. See Igor Kon, "Ravenstvo? Odinakovost?" *Razreshite poznakomitsya* (Moscow: Izvestiya, 1978), pp. 51–59.

33. See Igor S. Kon, "Das Verhältnis der Geschlechter in der UdSSR in einer Zeit des Wandels: Wissenschaftliche Aspekte und soziale Entwicklungen," *Inter-*

*disziplinäre Aspekte der Geschlechterverhältnisse in einer sich wandelnden Zeit*, K. F. Wessel and H. A. G. Bosinski, eds. (Bielefeld, Germany: Kleine Verlag, 1992), pp. 165–72.

34. See V. I. Perevedentsev, *Sotsialnaya zrelost vypusknika shkoly* (Moscow: Znanie, 1985); *Polozhenie detei v Rossii 1992. Sotsialnyi portret*, ed. by A. A. Likhanov and E. M. Rybinsky (Moscow: Dom, 1993).

35. For a general overview of these data, see I. S. Kon, *Psikhologiya rannei yunosti* (Moscow: Prosveshchenie, 1989), pp. 114–19.

36. See T. B. Shchepanskaya, "Zhenshchina, gruppa, simvol (na materialakh molodyozhnoi subkultury), *Etnicheskie stereotipy muzhskovo i zhenskovo povedeniya* (St. Petersburg: Nauka, 1991), pp. 17–29; T. B. Shchepanskaya, *Simvolika molodyozhnoi subkultury* (St. Petersburg: Nauka, 1993).

37. *Domostroi (House Manager)*, a very influential Russian book, written in the mid-sixteenth century by the monk Silvester, was a normative prescription for family life. Before 1989, *Domostroi* was usually mentioned as a negative example of patriarchy and male dominance; one of its rules was "A wife should be afraid of her husband." Now it is often used as a positive example of strong family ties and the values of stability and chastity. Both these interpretations are fundamentally ahistorical.

38. Du Plessix Gray, *Soviet Women: Walking the Tightrope* (New York: Doubleday, 1989), p. 178.

39. Ibid., p. 97.

40. Ludmila Chubarova, "Okhotnik i dich. Intervyu s Efraimom Seveloi, " *SPID-info*, no. 8 (1991), 24. It is interesting to note that for all Sevela's agitation about women using vibrators—and despite the fact that he had at this point lived in the United States for 17 years—he does not appear to know what voltage is used.

41. "Ot redatktsii. Nash feminizm," *Vse lyudi syostry*, Bulletin 1–2 (St. Petersburg, 1993), p. 4.

42. Russian conservatism is sometimes extremely radical. Russian women are suffering from unemployment. Yet in the *Semya (Family)* weekly (1993, no. 3), it was said that "the current [high rate of] unemployment among women may even have the progressive effect of strengthening the family" and that "the air smells this spring of the liberation of women from social work."

43. V. Arkhangelsky, "Reproduktivnoe povedenie i tsennostnye orientatsii gorodskovo naseleniya," *Gorodskaya i selskaya semya* (Moscow: Nauka, 1992), pp. 42–43. See also *Russkie. Etnosotsiologicheskie ocherki*, ed. by Yu. V. Arutyunyan (Moscow: Nauka, 1992), pp. 167–68.

44. V.A. Sysenko, *Ustoichivost braka. Problemy, faktory, usloviya* (Moscow: Nauka, 1992), pp. 76–77.

45. Monika Jaeckel, "Das Beziehungsklima zwischen Frauen und Männern. Ergebnisse einer international Untersuchung von Geschlechterbeziehungen in Ost und West," *DJI [Deutsches Jugendinstitut] Bulletin* 30 (Summer 1994), 10–14.

## NOTES TO CHAPTER 9: SEX, LOVE, AND MARRIAGE

1. Francine du Plessix Gray, *Soviet Women: Walking the Tightrope* (New York: Doubleday, 1989), p. 54.
2. See, for example, S. N. Ikonnikova and V. T. Lisovsky, *Molodyozh o sebe, o svoikh sverstnikakh* (Leningrad: Lenizdat, 1969); I. S. Kon, *Druzhba: Etiko-psikhologicheskii ocherk*, 3d ed. (Moscow: Politizdat, 1989).
3. W. R. Jankowiak and E. F. Fischer, "A Cross-cultural perspective on romantic love," *Ethnology* (April 1992), 149–55. See also E. Hatfield and R. L. Rapson, "Historical and Cross-cultural Perspectives on Passionate Love and Sexual Desire," *Annual Review of Sex Research* 4 (1993), 67–98.
4. Quoted from V. L. Yanin, "Kompleks berestyanykh gramot. Nos. 519–521 iz Novgoroda," *Obshchestvo i gosudarstvo feodalnoi Rossii* (Moscow: Nauka, 1975), pp. 36–37.
5. In his story "Tyomny sluchai" (A Gloomy Incident), the nineteenth-century writer Gleb Uspensky described the passionate and tragic love of a young village trader: "For pity's sake! Did I love her? Even now I would wither and die without her, but I could not put into words what I felt at the very start. And who wouldn't have loved her? She was simply a splendid angel, there are no other words to describe her." G. I. Uspensky, "Iz derevenskovo dnevnika" *Sobranie sochineniy v 9 tomakh,* vol. 4 (Moscow: Gosudarstvennoye izdatelstvo khudozhestvennoi literatury, 1956), p. 130. The young couple had loved each other from early childhood, had stolen their first kiss at nine or ten, then married. But later, after they neglected and then lost their child, the husband took to drink and beat his wife to death—in short, "a gloomy incident."
6. A. P. Chekhov, "Ariadna," *Polnoye sobranie sochineniy i pisem v 30 tomakh. Sochineniya*, vol. 9 (Moscow: Nauka, 1977), p. 117.
7. V. P. Astafiev, *Zhizn prozhit* (Moscow: Sovetsky pisatel, 1986), pp. 121–22.
8. V. N. Sherdakov, "Razmyshlenia o lyubvi i nravstvennom dolge," *Eticheskaya mysl, 1988*. Nauchno-publitsisticheskie chtenia (Moscow: Politizdat, 1988), p. 185.
9. Y. N. Davydov, "Tsennosti semyi i romantichesky kult 'strasti'," *Eticheskaya mysl, 1988*, p. 156.
10. Ibid., p. 164.
11. Ibid., p. 176.
12. See *Naselenie SSSR 1987. Statisticheskiy sbornik* (Moscow: Finansy i Statistika, 1988), p. 175.
13. This contradiction is not specifically Russian. A 1989 Gallup poll in the United States found that most married individuals were "satisfied" with their marriage. Yet although 85% of couples reported that they were "very satisfied" with their marriage, 40% considered leaving their partner. David H. Olson and Mikhail S. Matskovsky, "Soviet and American Families: A Comparative Overview," *Families Before and After Perestroika: Russian and U.S. Perspectives*, ed. James W. Maddock et al. (New York: Guilford Press, 1994), pp. 22–23.

14. *Russkie. Etnosotsiologicheskie ocherki*, ed. Yu. V. Arutyunyan et al. (Moscow: Nauka, 1992), pp. 163–66.

15. Kurt Shtarke and Vladimir Lisovsky, "Lyubov. Erotika. Sex. Opyt sravnitelnogo issledovania (Rossia—Germania)," *Molodyozh. Tsyfry. Fakty. Mnenia* (St. Petersburg, 1993), pp. 1, 147–52. K. Starke, A. Ph. Visser, "Sexuality and Contraception in Russian Students: A Comparison with Students from East and West Germany," *International Journal of Health Sciences* 4, no. 3 (1993), 111–19.

16. S. S. Sprecher, A. Aron, E. Hatfield, A. Cortese, E. Potapova, A. Levitskaya, *Love: American Style, Russian Style, and Japanese Style*. Paper presented at the Sixth International Conference on Personal Relationships (Orono, Maine: July 1992). (Quoted with permission.)

17. S. I. Golod, *Stabilnost semyi* (Leningrad: Nauka, 1984), p. 21.

18. John W. Smith, "The Sexual Revolution (The Polls—A Report)," *Public Opinion Quarterly* 54, no. 3 (Fall 1990), 415–21.

19. Questions about sexual techniques are especially delicate. Only 4.4% of Olga Loseva's male respondents (1991) admitted engaging in anal and 8% engaging in oral intercourse in the marriage bed (in extramarital contacts both figures were slightly higher). D. D. Isayev's (1993) figures are much higher. Oral sex experience was admitted by 49% of men, of whom 44.2% practiced it "often," and 53% of women (43.4% did it "often"). Anal intercourse was practiced by 20% of men (14.4% did it "often" and 5.8% "rarely") and by 15% of women (10.% often, 4.4% rarely). Group sex experience was had by 16% of men (12.5% "often") and 6% of women (5.1% "often").

20. Kurt Shtarke and Vladimir Lisovksy, "Lyubov. Erotika. Sex. Opyt sravnitelnovo issledovania." K. Starke, A. Ph. Visser, "Sexuality and Contraception in Russian Students," pp. 111–19.

21. O. K. Loseva, *Seksualnoe povedenie bolnykh sifilisom: epidemiologicheskie i mediko-sotsialnye problemy* (*Sexual Behavior of Syphilis Patients: Epidemiological and Medical-Social Problems*). Avtoreferat doktorskoi dissertatsii (Moscow: Tsentralny Nauchno-Issledovatelskij Kozhno-venerologicheskij Institut, 1991).

22. A. Spira and N. Bajos, *Les Comportements sexuals en France* (Paris: La Documentation française, 1993).

23. S. I. Golod, *Budushchaya semya: kakova ona?* (Moscow: Znanie, 1990), p. 20.

24. Golod, *Stabilnost semyi*, p. 71.

25. Golod, *Lichnaya zhizn, lyubov, otnosheniya polov* (Leningrad: Znanie, 1990), p. 30.

26. Z. A. Rozhanovskaya, *Profilaktika sexualnykh narusheniy u zhenshchin* (Kharkov, 1977).

27. The psychological tension between "love" and "sex" is reflected even in the Russian language itself. Expressions such as "to make love" or *"faire l'amour"* are easily translatable (*zanimatsya liubovyu*) but are never used in colloquial Russian. The subtitle of Alex Comfort's famous book, *The Joy of Sex—A*

*Gourmet Guide to Lovemaking*—was translated into Russian in 1991 as *Kniga o premudrostyakh lyubvi*) (*a book of wisdom about love*). "Love" in Russian is something you feel, not something you do. You "make" sex, you don't "make" love. The most widespread colloquial Russian verb for sexual intercourse today is *trakhatsya*, which has no romantic connotations; the literal meaning of the verb *trakhat* is "to beat (someone)." One can also use such words and expressions as the archaic *soitie* (coitus), or "intimacy" or "to sleep together." The words *yebat, yebatsya, yeblya* (to fuck, fucking) are much more offensive in Russian than their English equivalents; they are considered "nonnormative" and unprintable.

28. Lev Shcheglov, "Medical Sexology," *Sex and Russian Society*, ed. by Igor Kon and James Riordan (Bloomington: Indiana University Press, 1993), pp. 156–57.

29. Mikhail Armalinsky, *Dobrovolnye priznaniya—vynuzhdennaya perepiska* (Minneapolis: M.I.P., 1991), p. 300.

30. Adrian Gaiges and Tatyana Suvorova, *Lyubov vne plana* (Moscow: Sobesednik, 1990), pp. 90–97.

31. Pauline G. Boss and Tatyana A. Gurko, "The Relationships of Men and Women in Marriage," *Families Before and After Perestroika: Russian and U.S. Perspectives*, ed. by James W. Maddock et al. (New York: Guilford, 1994), p. 58.

32. Sergei I. Golod, "Adultery: Facts and Considerations," *Sexual Cultures in Europe*, June 24–26, 1992, Forum on Sexuality (Amsterdam: SISWO, 1992), pp. 42–51.

33. See Tom W. Smith, "The Sexual Revolution," pp. 415–21; Ulrich Clement, "Surveys of Heterosexual Behavior," *Annual Review of Sex Research* 1 (1990), 45–74; John H. Gagnon, "The Explicit and Implicit Use of the Scripting Perspective in Sex Research," *Annual Review of Sex Research* 1 (1990), 1–44.

34. June M. Reinisch with Ruth Beasley, *The Kinsey Institute New Report on Sex* (New York: St. Martin's Press, 1990), pp. 2, 21.

35. Samuel S. Janus and Cynthia L. Janus, *The Janus Report on Sexual Behavior* (New York: Wiley, 1993), p. 97. About the methodological shortcomings of this study, see Clive M. Davis, "A Reader's Guide to *The Janus Report*," *Journal of Sex Research* 30, no. 4 (November 1993), 336–38.

36. Edward O. Laumann, John H. Gagnon, Robert T. Michael, and Stuart Michaels, *The Social Organization or Sexuality: Sexual Practices in the United States* (Chicago: University of Chicago Press, 1994); Robert T. Michael, John H. Gagnon, Edward O. Laumann, and Gina Kolata, *Sex in America: A Definitive Report* (Boston: Little, Brown, 1994). Unfortunately, the original book being unavailable in Moscow, I had to use its summary: Joanie M. Schroff with Betsy Wagner, "Sex in America," *U.S. News and World Report*, October 17, 1994, pp. 74–81.

37. John O. G. Billy, Koray Tanfer, William R. Grady, and Daniel H. Klepinger, "The Sexual Behavior of Men in the United States," *Family Planning Perspectives* 25, no. 2 (March/April 1993), 52–60.

38. See Spira and Bajos, *Les Comportements sexuels en France*.

# NOTES TO CHAPTER 10: ABORTION OR CONTRACEPTION?

1. The principal source of information for this chapter are demographers. See Larissa I. Remennick, "Birth Control Patterns in the USSR," in Igor Kon and James Riordan, eds., *Sex and Russian Society* (Bloomington: Indiana University Press, 1993); Andrei A. Popov, "Family Planning and Induced Abortion in the USSR: Basic Health and Demographic Characteristics," *Studies in Family Planning* 22, no. 6 (November/December 1991), 368–77; Andrei A. Popov, "Induced Abortions in the USSR at the end of the 1980s: The Basis for the National Model of Family Planning." Paper presented and distributed at the Population Association of America Annual Meeting (Denver, Colorado), April 30—May 2, 1992; A. A. Popov, A. Ph. Visser, E. Ketting, "Contraceptive Knowledge, Attitudes, and Practice in Russia During the 1980s," *Studies in Family Planning* 24, no. 4 (1993), 227–35.

2. Figures for 1936–38 were collected by Y. A. Sadvokasova. See Y. A. Sadvokasova, *Sotsialno-gigienicheskie aspekty regulirovaniya razmerov semyi* (Moscow: Meditsina, 1969).

3. Popov, "Family Planning," p. 369.

4. See *Detnost semyi: vchera, sevodnya, zavtra* (Moscow: Mysl, 1986); S. I. Golod, *Stabilnost semyi* (Leningrad: Nauka, 1984).

5. Popov, "Family Planning," p. 373.

6. I. A. Belova and L. Y. Darsky, *Statistika mneniy v izuchenii rozhdayemosti* (Moscow: Statistika, 1972).

7. Y. F. Achildieva and O. K. Loseva, "Analiz nekotorykh aspektov zavisimosti mezhdu kontraseptivnym povedeniem i udovletvorennostyu brakom," *Planirovanie semyi i natsionalnye traditsii* (Tbilisi, 1988).

8. A. A. Popov, *Mediko-demograficheskie faktory regulirovaniya rozhdeniy.* Avtoref, kand. diss. (Moscow, 1986).

9. See I. V. Dzarasova and V. M. Medkov, "Reproduktivnoye povedenie semyi," in A. I. Antonov, ed., *Semya i deti* (Moscow: Izdatelstvo MGU, 1982), p. 16.

10. Y. B. Babin, "Kontratseptivnoye povedenie suprugov v gorodskikh semyakh," *Detnost semyi*, pp. 146–56.

11. Golod, *Stabilnost semyi*, p. 110.

12. M. S. Tolts, Y. Y. Oberg, and O. A. Shishko, "Nachalnye etapy realizatsii reproduktivnoi funktsii zhenshchin," *Zdravookhranenie Rossiyskoi Federatsii*, no. 7 (1984), 13–15.

13. A. Gaiges and T. Suvorova, *Lyubov vne plana* (Moscow: Sobesednik, 1990), pp. 49–57. Here is a longer, but not atypical, story:

How does the path to Calvary begin for a simple mortal? With an examination, of course. For syphilis, AIDS, etc. You wait one and a half hours in a queue by each office. And since the laboratories are shut weekends, you have to get time off from work. I asked for time off once, twice, three times . . . My boss was beginning to lose patience.

Finally, all the analyses were completed. Off I went to the hospital, to the department which is known by one and all as "the abortary. . . . "

In the hospital cloakroom I found myself standing next to a good dozen young women. By their dull gaze, taciturn nod and a certain doomed meekness about their movements I guessed they were my companions-in-misery.

"Right, my beauties, are you ready?" an orderly asked with a smirk. . . .

I don't know, perhaps I didn't breathe very deeply and couldn't totally switch off, but I soon felt a sharp pain. Perhaps it was simply the "laughing gas" that made me imagine things.

"Hold on, don't moan, don't moan, darling," shouted the nurse, while the doctor . . . began to ask questions. All the time making unpleasant hints: "Who made you pregnant? Your husband? An unlikely story! I bet he thinks the same. . . . "

"How dare you!" I exclaimed.

"I do dare," said the doctor with a laugh. "I've seen too many of you here. Right, done, off you go!"

The nurse helped me to my feet, and I left the operating theater. My companions were lying there, right in the corridor, two to a bed, top to toe. One got up for me to lie down. . . .

We stayed like that lying in pairs along the corridor until evening: nobody took any interest in how we were feeling, no one asked if we were OK. There was just a nurse shouting, "Who needs a sickness certificate?"

A few days later I realized it was too soon to celebrate. The most terrible discovery was still ahead. When my three days' rest had elapsed, my temperature remained high and, what is more—Oh God, no!—the feeling of sickness returned and my husband had to call an ambulance. Imagine my amazement mingled with fear when, upon examining me, the clinic head pronounced sentence:

"You had twins; we removed one fetus, the other is still there. Go to the operating theater."

14. See A. G. Khomasuridze, "Osnovnye rezultaty i puti razvitiya gormonalnoi kontratsepsii," *Mediko-sotsialnye aspekty rozhdayemosti. Sbornik nauchnykh trudov* (Tbilisi, 1985).

15. L. I. Remennick, "Reproduktivnoye povedenie i onkologicheskie zabolevaniya u zhenshchin," in A. I. Antonov, ed., *Detnost semyi*, pp. 168–69. Remennick emphasized that "out of the entire arsenal of available means for constraining childbirth, the optimal, both from a position of the family's and society's reproductive interests, and from the viewpoint of minimizing oncological risk is likely to be oral contraceptive preparations taken in brief series (one to two a year) alternating with other effective methods, such as the IUD. Comparing the risk that always accompanies any intervention in a person's physiology of reproduction and sexual function, the greatest evil is undoubtedly abortion."

16. Some of this debate will sound familiar to Americans, who are having similar disputes over the idea of distributing condoms to sexually active high school students.
17. See V. K. Ovcharov, L. I. Kirilenko, and I. A. Allenova, "Sotsialno-gigienich-eskie predposylki optimizatsii planirovaniya semyi v razlichnykh rayonakh SSSR," *Sovremennye metody profilaktiki iskusstvennovo aborta i regulyatsii repro-duktivnoi funktsii zhenshchiny* (Moscow: Vsesoyuzny nauchno-issledovatselky institut sotsialnoi gigieny i obshchestvennovo zdorovya, 1987); A. A. Avdeyev, "Sotsialnye problemy planirovaniya semyi," *Sotsialny potentsial semyi* (Moscow: Institut sotsiologicheskikh issledovaniy AN SSSR, 1988).
18. Svetlana Tutorskaya, "Kak byt nelyubimoi," *Izvestiya,* March 24, 1994; A. Ph. Visser, N. Bruyniks, and L. Remennick, "Family Planning in Russia: Experi-ence and Attitudes of Gynecologists," *Advances in Contraception* 9 (1993), 93–1-4; A. Ph. Visser, L. Remennick, and N. Bruyniks, "Contraception in Rus-sia, Attitude, Knowledge, and Practice of Doctors," *Planned Parenthood in Europe* 22, no. 2 (1993), 26–28.
19. Inga Grebesheva, "Abortion and the Problems of Family Planning in Russia," *Planned Parenthood in Europe* 21, no. 2 (May 1992), 8.
20. Phillippe Lehert, Irina Pavlenko, Larissa Remennick, and Adrian Visser, "Con-traception in the Former USSR: Recent Survey Results on Women's Behavior and Attitudes," *Planned Parenthood in Europe* 21, no. 2 (May 1992), 9–11. The majority of women responding to the questionnaire had experienced induced abortion. 41% had had one or two abortions, and 19% had had three or more. The frequency of abortion is related to the number of unwanted preg-nancies resulting from failing contraception. About two-thirds of respondents had had one unwanted pregnancy, and 30% had experienced this more than twice. The first unwanted pregnancy was carried to term in 42% of the cases, which meant that more than half of the women chose an abortion. The sec-ond unwanted pregnancy resulted in abortion even more frequently—73% of the time.

**CONTRACEPTIVE METHODS USED DURING THE PREVIOUS FIVE YEARS**

|  | Always (%) | Sometimes (%) | Not Used (%) |
|---|---|---|---|
| Condom | 18 | 51 | 31 |
| Coitus interruptus | 14 | 46 | 40 |
| IUD | 37 | 11 | 52 |
| Rhythm | 17 | 31 | 52 |
| Vaginal douche | 10 | 29 | 61 |
| Pill | 10 | 19 | 71 |
| Chemical spermicide | 2 | 14 | 84 |
| Chemical spermicide and condom | 1 | 4 | 95 |
| Diaphram | 0 | 1 | 99 |

Most of the women indicated they had used some form of contraception during the previous five years; only 18% did not use any contraception. Most likely not to use contraception were women between 15 and 20 years of age (40%), unmarried women (29%), poorly educated women (24%), and those living in the countryside (22%).

What is quite obvious is the lack of use of more modern forms of contraception, which tended to be popular largely with women under 25 and with better-educated women. All the rest commonly employed more traditional methods, which are less reliable but more accessible.

The method of contraception most preferred was the IUD; half of the women mentioned IUD as the method they most favored and 25% gave it as their second choice. The pill was less popular; 18% mentioned it as their first preference, with 25% giving it as a second choice. The condom took third place, and traditional methods were preferred by only a small proportion of women.

In answering the question "Which is more dangerous: regular use of contraception or abortion?" 89% judged abortion to be more dangerous. But 13% of women between 45 and 50 believed contraception was more dangerous than abortion. In rating various contraceptives from the viewpoint of their convenience, reliability, and safety from a health perspective, women put the IUD at the top; the condom was considered to be safer but less reliable and especially less convenient. The attitude toward the pill was not positive. Respondents judged it negatively in terms of convenience and safety, and its reliability was perceived to be less than that of the condom and the IUD. Even the rhythm method was judged more positively than oral contraceptives. This is an evident consequence of the long propaganda campaign against hormonal forms of contraception.

What are the sources of contraception information? Although almost half of the women had asked them for advice, their doctors had been the main source of information for no more than 12%. The most regular sources of information were books and journals (45%) and friends (37%). Parents were mentioned by 4% of those surveyed, and partners by only 1%.

As many as 76% of the women expressed the view that both partners should take responsibility for averting pregnancy, although only 59% described their partner as actively involved. Twenty-six percent of respondents described their partners as indifferent and 11% as passive, and 3% indicated that their partner was opposed to contraception. When asked who buys condoms, 52% replied that they did; 48% said it was their partner. Discussion about contraception with partners was always possible for 54% of the respondents, but 35% said it was possible only sometimes, and 8% said it was never possible. About 90% of the women believed that the responsibility for preventing sexually transmitted diseases should be shared by both partners.

21. Goskomstat SSSR, "Ispolzovanie kontratseptsii v SSSR," *Vestnik statistiki*, no. 3 (1991), 60, quoted in Andrei A. Popov, Adrian Ph. Visser, and Evert Ketting, "Contraceptive Knowledge, Attitudes, and Practice in Russia during the 1980s," *Studies in Family Planning* 24, no. 4 (July/August 1993), 227–35. Very

often these practices continued even after women emigrated. According to Israeli data for 1988, the general rate of applications for a legal abortion for USSR-born Israeli women was 26% higher than that of the total for all Israeli women and 29% higher after age adjustment. (Eltan F. Sabatello, "Soviet Immigration in Israel: Consequences for Family Planning and Abortion Services", *Planned Parenthood in Europe* 20, no. 2 (September 1991), 9–11.

22. Yu. A. Gurkin, "Elementy, sostavlyayushchie programmu podgotovki devochki k materinstvu," Rossiyskaya assotsiatsyia "Planirovanie semyi," Pervaya Natsyonalnaya konferentsya *"Problemy Planirovania Semyi v Rossii" (materialy konferentsii). 7–9 dekabrya 1993, Moskva* (Moscow" "Kvartet," 1994), pp. 79–85.

23. N. N. Vaganov, interview, *Planirovanie semyi*, no. 3 (1993), Moscow: "TIMO-TEK," pp. 1–5.

24. A. Gaiges and T. Suvorova, *Lyubov vne plana*, pp. 56–57.

25. K. Starke and A. Ph. Visser, "Sexuality and Contracetion in Russian Students: A Comparison with Students from East and West Germany," *International Journal of Health Sciences* 4, no. 3 (1993), 111–19.

26. Goskomstat, *Statistical Data on Maternal Deaths and Death Related to Abortions in the Russian Federation 1993*.

## NOTES TO CHAPTER 11: TEENAGERS AT RISK

1. Unfortunately, some representatives of medical establishments often popularize wrong and unreliable data. Dr. Nikolai Chaika, the chief of the Department of Information of St. Petersburg Pasteur Institute, told several international conferences on AIDS that "during the last 25 years the age of the first sexual intercourse decreased from 20 (men) and 22 (women) years to 14 and 15" (N. Chaika, Y. Brodyanski et al., "Low Level of AIDS Knowledge in the USSR and Some Approaches to Mass Education," *Third International Symposium on AIDS Information and Education*, Feb. 3–7, 1991, Manila, Philippines). These fantastic conclusions are based on the incorrect interpretation from the nonprofessional survey in the popular magazine *Zdorovje (Health)* in February 1990 pretending to have 500,000 respondents (N. Chaika, "Navstrechu sobsvennoi pogibeli," *Zdorovje*, no. 3 (1991). Professor Aza Rakhmanova, the St. Petersburg chief epidemiologist, said that "according to anonymous research, 90% of our high school graduates already have sexual experience. Aza Rakhmanova, "Dlya menya eta statya davno otmenena . . . ," *Ty*, no. 2 (1993), 4.

   More reliable figures from a gynecological survey indicate that 25% of urban school girls between 15 and 18 years have sexual contacts, whereas at vocational schools, 65% of girls and 85% of boys begin sexual life before the age of 18. N. Komyssova, "Family Planning in the Russian Federation," *Planned Parenthood in Europe* 21, no. 2 (1992), 7.

2. V. S. Sobkin and P. S. Pisarsky, *Zhiznennye tsennosti i otnoshenie k obrazovaniu: Kross-kulturnyi analiz Moskva—Amsterdam* (Moscow: Tsentr sotsiologii RAO, 1994), pp. 32–36.

3. The research was designed by V. D. Shapiro and V. V. Chervyakov; Igor Kon was the consultant and M. Gerasimova the field director. The adopted questionnaire of the American sociologist Stan Weed was used. See Igor Kon, V. D., Shapiro, and V. V. Chervyakov, "Podrostki i seks: utrata illyusiy" ("Teenagers and Sex: Lost Illusions"), *Ogonyok*, no. 2 (1993), 22–25; I. S. Kon, "Podrostki i seks," *Planirovanie semyi* 4 (1994), 15–18.

4. Sergei Golod, *Lichnaya zhizn, lyubov, otnosheniya polov* (Leningrad: Znanie, 1990), p. 23. According to an anonymous questionnaire in 1988 among 600 female students from seven senior schools and three professional schools in Moscow, 9.1% of secondary school students and 42% of professional school students had already had coital experience. The average age of sexual initiation was 16.4 years (because of the large number of professional school students). Among 14- to 15-year-old females, 3.2% had been sexually active; among 16- to 17-year-olds, 13.4%; and among 18- to 19-year-olds, 58.3%. E. I. Sotnikova and S. G. Perminova, "Reproduktivnoe povedenie i kontratseptsia u podroskov," Rossiyskaya assotsiatsyia "Planirovanie semyi," Pervaya Natsyonalnaya konferentsya *"Problemy Planirovania Semyi v Rossii" (materialy konferentsii). 7–9 dekabrya 1993, Moskva* (Moscow: "Kvartet," 1994), pp. 143–50.

5. See V. G. Vlastovsky, *Akseleratsiya rosta i razvitiya detei* (Moscow: Izdatelstvo Moskovkovo Universiteta, 1976).

6. In 1990 40% of 16- to 17-year-old West German males and 34% of females had had coital experience. Gunter Schmidt, Dietrich Klusmann, Uta Zeitzschel, and Carmen Lange, "Changes in Adolescents' Sexuality Between 1970 and 1990 in West Germany," *Archives of Sexual Behavior* 23, no. 5 (1994),489–513. Among their East German coevals, the corresponding figures were 47% and 59% for 16-year-olds and 52% and 58% for 17-year-olds (females here were ahead of males). Konrad Weller and Kurt Starke, "Veränderungen 1970–1990 (DDR)," G. Schmidt, ed., *Jugendsexualität, Sozialer Wandel, Gruppenunterschiede, Konflikfelder* (Stuttgart: Enke Verlag, 1993), p. 62.

   According to the latest available U.S. data, the median age for first intercourse was 16.6 years for boys and 17.4 years for girls; by age 16, 42% of American teens had this experience. *Sex and America's Teenagers*, Alan Guttmacher Institute, 1994. According to the 1994 national telephone survey by the Roper Starch Worldwide, of 503 American teens, from 9th to 12th grade, 36% had sexual intercourse, 26% had oral sex, 15% had mutual masturbation, and so on. Forty percent of sexually active students had their first intercourse at age 14 or earlier. Eight in 10 abstinent teens cited fear of sexually transmitted diseases, AIDS, and pregnancy among the reasons they remained virgins. Only 40% cited religion. *Teens Talk about Sex: Adolescent Sexuality in the 90s* (New York: SIECUS, 1994).

7. V. V. Danilov, *Polovoye vospitanie starsheklassnikov* (Krivoi Rog, 1982). Cited in D. N. Isayev and V. Y. Kagan, *Psikhogigiena pola u detei* (Leningrad: Meditsina, 1986), p. 137.

8. G. S. Vasilchenko, ed.,*Obshchaya seksopatologiya* (Moscow: Meditsina, 1977),

p. 203. A. M. Svyadoshch, *Zhenskaya seksopatologiya* (Leningrad: Meditsina, 1974).

9. In this particular case, Russian and American attitudes seem to be most different. According to *The Janus Report,* by contrast, 66% of American men and 67% of women agreed that "masturbation is a natural part of life and continues on in marriage"; only 5% of men and 11% of women said they had never masturbated; 81% of men and 72% of women continued this practice into adulthood. S. S. Janus and C. L. Janus, *The Janus Report on Sexual Behavior* (New York: Wiley, 1993), pp. 30–32, 76. According to the Chicago survey, 60% of adult American men and 40% of women masturbated in the past year. Among couples living together, that increased to 85% of men and 45% of women. Joanie M. Schroff with Betsy Wagner, "Sex in America," *U.S. News and World Report,* October 17, 1994, pp. 74–81.

10. Nikolai Popov, "Smeshali, vypili, pogovorili . . . ," *Stolitsa,* no. 40 (1993), 33.

11. Boris Kamov, "Seksualnaya katastrofa," *Sovershenno sekretno,* no. 2 (1994), 22–24.

12. Since school education in Russia is still secular and the church has no right to meddle in education, it is interesting to note that one St. Petersburg school banned the questionnaire, referring to the "Russian Orthodox leanings" of the school. They also commented on the Jewish names of the researchers; anti-Semitism is very strong in the country generally, and especially strong in the St. Petersburg area, and it is expressed quite openly.

   Russian teens strongly distrust their school teachers. When asked about the necessity of special school classes on sexual issues, a positive answer was given in 1993 by 71% of Moscow teachers, 69% of parents, and only 21% of adolescents. And 83% of teachers also believed that a person teaching such a course should be an "outsider." O. G. Butorina, "Interview," *Planirovanie semyi* 4 (1994), 5.

13. This picture is not very different from what is typical for some Western European countries. Answering the questionnaire of the Organon Laboratory and the popular French journal *20 ans,* one in four of 10,600 girls aged from 13 to 25 years said her sexual information was "insufficient." As main sources of sexual education, doctors were mentioned by 17%, mothers by 40%, journals by 67%, and friends by 73%. M. Bonierbale, "Adolescence, urgence de vivre," *Sexologies* 3, no. 11 (March 1994), 17. But even in the conservative United States, according to a recent Roper Starch Worldwide report, three quarters of the teen ssomehow discussed sexual issues with their parents, and 72% ahd some, even if inadequate, school classes. *Teens Talk about Sex.*

14. See P. Y. Miller and W. Simon, "The Development of Sexuality in Adolescence," in Joseph Adelson, ed., *Handbook of Adolescent Psychology* (New York: Wiley, 1980).

15. See, for example, G. Schmidt, D. Klusmann, and Uta Zeitzschell, "Veränderungen der Jugensexualität zwischen 1970 und 1990," *Zeitschrift für Sexualforschung* 3, no. 5 (September 1992), 191–218; G. M. Breakwell and C. R. Fife-

Schaw, "Sexual Activities and Preferences in a UK Sample of 16–20 Year Olds," *Archives of Sexual Behavior* 21, no. 3 (1992); J. Bancroft and J. M. Reinisch, eds., *Adolescence and Puberty* (New York: Oxford University Press, 1990).

16. The most interesting illustration of this trend may be found in West German research on youth sexuality for the last 20 years. Gunter Schmidt has summarized his main findings in the following 12 points:

1. The beginning and the extent of adolescent sexual experience in the last 20 years has changed only insignificantly, but the extent of parental acceptance of adolescent sexuality has very much increased.

2. The changed attitudes of parents to their children's sexuality leads to some sort of "familization" of adolescent sexuality—that is, youth sexuality has become a legitimate subject of intrafamily communication, and it is developing in the family.

3. Adults' and society's liberal attitude toward adolescent sexuality helps boys and girls to take more responsibility for their sexual behavior.

4. For boys, sexuality today is less stringent and impulsive than it was 20 years earlier.

5. Boys' "transitory" homosexual behavior is gradually disappearing, with reports of homosexual contacts between boys 16–17 years old in the last 20 years dropping from 18% to 2% of respondents.

6. Boys are relating sexuality much more closely to love, relationships, and fidelity than they were 20 years ago.

7. The classical puberty of bourgeois adolescents described by novelists and psychologists of the early twentieth century no longer exists.

8. Girls are now taking more control in heterosexual situations and demanding more autonomy in relationships.

9. Girls experience sexuality now as less lustful, exciting, and gratifying than before.

10. The differences between West and East German youth now are similar to the differences between 1990 and 1970 West German adolescents.

11. Sociohistorically, the observed changes of adolescent sexuality in the direction of romanticizing men and self-determining women have been coming for a long time.

12. The moving force of the contemporary changes in adolescent sexuality is the change in cultural notions of gender. See Gunter Schmidt, "Jugendsexualität in den Neunziger Jahren: Eine Synopse in zwölf Thesen," in Gunter Schmidt, ed., *Jugendsexualität. Sozialer Wandel, Gruppenunterschiede, Konfliktfelder* (Stuttgart: Ferdinand Enke Verlag, 1993), pp. 1–11. Some of Schmidt's theses, like the disappearance of transitory adolescent homosexuality, may be overgeneralizations—415 boys and girls from Hamburg and Frankfurt may not be representative of the whole of West Germany—or fail to take into account important individual and cultural differences, but his general reasoning seems enlightening.

# NOTES TO CHAPTER 12: DANGEROUS SEX: RAPE, PROSTITUTION, AND SEXUALLY TRANSMITTED DISEASES

1. Vitaly Yeromin, "Podval," *Ogonyok*, no. 8 (1989), 22.
2. See *Kriminologiya* (Moscow: Izdatelstvo uridicheskoi literatury, 1968), p. 418; Y. M. Antonyan, V. P. Golubev, and Y. N. Kudryakov, *Iznasilovanie: prichiny i preduprezhdenie* (Moscow: Vsesoyuzny nauchno-issledovatelsky institut Ministerstva vnutrennikh del SSSR, 1990), p. 8.
3. *Prestupnost i pravonarusheniya* (Moscow: Ministerstvo vnutrennikh del Rossiyskoi Federatsii, Ministerstvo yustitsii Rossiyskoi Federatsii, Statisticheskii Komitet Sodruzhestva nezavisimykh gosudarstv, 1993).
4. Ann W. Burgess, ed., *Rape and Sexual Assault*, vol. 2 (New York: Garland, 1988). For the methodological controversy about rape statistics and definition, see "Symposium," *Journal of Sex Research* 31, no. 2 (1994), 143–53. According to the most recent U.S. sexual survey, 22% of women said they have been forced to perform a sexual act, and 96% knew the person who forced them; in 46% of the cases it was someone she loved; in 22% it was someone she knew well; in 19% it was an acquaintance; in 9%, a spouse; and in only 4%, a stranger. Joanie M. Schroff with Betsy Wagner, "Sex in America," *U.S. News and World Report,* October 17, 1994, pp. 74–81. Certainly, sexual coercion and rape are not synonymous.
5. A. J. Dyachenko and I. Y. Koloskova, "Kharakteristika iznasilovania: statisticheskij analiz," *Problemy sotsialnovo kontrolya za prostitutsiej, spidom i pornografiej* (Moscow: Akademia MVD RF, 1993), pp. 44–58; V. N. Kudryavtsev, ed., *Kurs sovetskoi kriminologii. Preduprezhdenie prestupnosti* (Moscow: Yurizdat, 1986), pp. 187–88.
6. Quoted from Antonyan et al., *Iznasilovanie: prichiny i preduprezhdenie*, p. 11.
7. Nikolai Popov, "Smeshali, bypili, pogovorili . . . ," *Stolitsa*, no. 40 (1993), 36. This is a really difficult issue. So-called token resistance to sexual intercourse, when women (and sometimes men) "say no to sex even when they mean yes and that their protests are not to be taken seriously," is one of the most widespread sexual miscommunications. In recent comparative research on U.S., Russian, and Japanese students, it was found that Russians had the highest level of it. Fifty-nine percent of Russian women, against 38% of Americans and 37% of Japanese, said they had at least once said no to sex although they "had every intention of and [were] willing to engage in sexual intercourse"; 30% did it two or three times, and 12% reported four or five times. S. Sprecher, E. Hatfield, A. Cortese, E. Potapova, and A. Levitskaya, "Token Resistance to Sexual Intercourse and Consent to Unwanted Sexual Intercourse: College Students' Dating Experiences in Three Countries," *Journal of Sex Research* 42, no. 2 (1994), 125–32. It seems that some part of the males' complaints are justified.
8. Yelena Zabadykina, "Zhenshchiny v sovremennoi Rossii (na primere Sankt-Peterburga)," *Vse lyudi—syostry*, Bulletin No. 1–2 (1993), p. 71.

9. L. N. Tolstoy, "Dnevniki," *Sobranie sochineniy v 20 tomakh*, vol. 19 (Moscow: Khudozhestvennaya literatura, 1965), p. 59.

10. Antonyan et al., *Iznasilovanie: prichiny i preduprezhdenie*, p. 52.

11. Ibid.

12. See N. Filippov, "Ustydimsya, vzroslye," *Semya* no. 3 (1988), 4; N. Filippov, , "Otkuda v nikh eti geny zla?" *Semya*, no. 24 (1988), 4.

13. T. Y. Sofronova, I. S. Demyanenko, and Y. I. Tsymbal, "Problema zhestokovo obrashcheniya s detmi v sovremennom obshchestve," *Aktualnye problemy sovremennovo detstva (sbornik nauchnykh trudov)* (Moscow: Nauchno-issledova-telsky institut detstva Rossiyskovo detskovo fonda, 1992), pp. 26–29.

14. Alexander Nevsky, "Po 117-oi," *SPID-info*, no. 1 (1992), 24.

15. M. T. Shakirov, *Zabolevania, peredayaemye polovym putem, u muzhchin-gomosek-sualistov*. Avtoreferat dissertatsii na soiskanie uchenoi stepeni doktora med-itsinskikh nauk. Moscow, 1991, p. 16.

16. Y. M. Antonyan and S. P. Pozdnyakova, *Seksualnye prestupleniya lits s psikhich-eskimi anomaliyami i ikh preduprezhdenie. Uchebnoye posobie* (Moscow: VNII MVD SSSR, 1991), Pp. 12–13.

17. Not a few sadists can be found in the police force as well. The following story was reported in November 1993 in *SPID-info*.

I've been carrying grief from this very sad incident in my life for more than two months. And it all started out incredibly well. My friend and I were out celebrating an anniversary, having a drink or two. Then we decided to go dancing int he park. I was feeling quite free and easy, which is probably what caught the duty policeman's eye. After following me around for a bit, they pushed me into their van and drove off. Arriving at the station, I found myself in the company of other young people. It soon became clear that they wanted money if we wished to get away by mid-night and without being charged. It was then that I noticed a sergeant standing on the other side of the desk, watching me. I made a gesture to show I wanted a word with him. With a knowing smile (he was about two or three years older than I), he led me out of the waiting room and, with the same smile, heard me out: I had no cash on me. His response at first stunned me. What he meant was that all he could do to help was "to assess my 'peep-hole'." I returned to the stinking pit. You know, I could have just sat around 'til morning, and to hell with it. But there was one problem I had to think of : my mother was very sick and my being away from her for long was bound to upset her. Once more I summoned the sergeant (all the while he was standing by, smiling, keeping an eye on our menagerie) and tried my best to convince him of my plight. He said it all depended on me. That came as a terrible shock. I had hoped for a miracle (that's how naive I was). Taking me by the arm, he led me through some door or other . . . I later hated myself for being so weak.

I found myself in some sort of classroom with desks and a blackboard.

He suggested I go over to a desk and kneel upon it. I was shaking all over. He took off his jacket and unbuttoned his trousers, letting them fall to the floor; he then took off his shorts. Holding his tool in his hand, he sat at the desk. With his free hand he grabbed hold of the back of my head and told me "to suck his cock good and proper." I almost vomited there and then. The whole procedure lasted quite a long time. I was all wet from the heat. The sergeant seemed to be having a great time, judging by his sighing and constant jerking. After he came, I was just about to leave the room when I was stopped by the policeman's sudden movement to block my way; grabbing me by the trousers he told me to undress. Placing me across the desk, he then pulled my buttocks apart and inserted his tool. The pain was almost unbearable. I could hardly breathe, what with his whole weight lying on top of me. I was only half conscious. Then, swinging me over on to my back and supporting my hips with his hands, he again thrust his tool into me with great enthusiasm. My legs were in such an awkward position that all I could do was to put them on his shoulders. I just felt like a slut. . . .

The sergeant was in ecstasy; for a full five minutes more he just lay on top of me, dribbling on my neck.

When I got home and calmed my mother, I took a good look at myself. My violated asshole still hurt, but there were no serious consequences. . . .

I now live like a monk. I rarely go out, never think of going to dances, cannot bring myself to look at girls. . . . I used to get an erection in the mornings, not anymore. . . .

I should probably go to the doctor. I have a feeling that something is happening with my mind. . . .

What is interesting about this case is that in the accompanying commentary by a professor of psychiatry, which the newspaper published, medical expert expressed some surprise about the victim's "strong emotional reaction"; in the psychiatrist's opinion, men are generally less sensitive to the experience of rape than women.

18. Accurate statistics on Russian prison sexuality and homosexuality don't exist. But research has begun (D. D. Isayev's personal communication). The best qualitative description of this specific world and its language is given by the Russian-American journalist Vladimir Kozlovsky in his book *Argo russkoi gomoseksualnoi subkultury* (New York: Chalidze Press, 1986). See also Lev Samoilov, *Perevernuty mir* (St. Petersburg: FARN, 1993); L. Nikitsky, "Bespredel," *Ogonyok*, no. 32 (1989), 27–29.
19. Alexander Ekshtein, "Dnevnik stukacha," *Ogonyok*, no. 35 (1990), 29.
20. See, for example, Robert N. Boyd, *Sex Behind Bars* (San Francisco: Gay Sunshine Press, 1989), Anthony M. Scacco, Jr., ed., *Male Rape* (New York: AMS Press, 1982); Wayne S. Wooden and Jay Parker, *Men Behind Bars: Sexual Exploitation in Prison* (New York: Plenum, 1982); Stephen Donaldson, "Pris-

ons, Jails, and Reformatories," *Encyclopedia of Homosexuality*, vol. 2, ed. Wayne Dynes (New York: Garland, 1990), pp. 1035–48.

21. Says Stern, "My experience as a prisoner allows me to state unhesitatingly that the principal factor in the increase of homosexuality in the Soviet Union is the prison system. It is particularly in the camps that people learn to be homosexual and when they leave, they remain so." (Dr. Mikhail Stern and Dr. August Stern, *Sex in the Soviet Union* [London: W. H. Allen, 1981], p. 178) According to Mark Popovsky, "the same-sex love was almost universally produced by Soviet camp life, by camp prohibitions against normal life." (Mark Popovsky, *Tretij lishnij* [London: Overseas Publications, 1985], p. 399) Note that both Stern and Popovsky are medical doctors; such was Soviet medical education!

22. Now there is talk not only about violence but also about sexual deprivation in the military forces. In the first ever small and unrepresentative survey of 360 soldiers, officers, and cadets in Moscow (1993)—earlier such research would have been unthinkable—the military sociologist Yevgeny Kashchenko found that all cadets, every other soldier, and 65% of officers thought about women every day; 70% believes themselves sexually deprived; and 30% thought they did not get the kind of sex they needed. Every second soldier dreamed of love, yet 20% were ready to accept any sex, with or without love (all the officers older than 50 categorically opposed such laxity). For most of the soldiers and cadets the most widespread means of sexual release was masturbation (half of them masturbated once a week, and 49% did so 2–3 or more per week). Most of the military men were sexually ignorant. Some of them confused erection with ejaculation, had no idea about female physiology, and so on. E. A. Kashchenko, *Seksualnaya kultura voennosluzhashchikh. Sotsialno-filosofsky analiz. Avtoreferat kandidatskoi dissertatsii.* Moscow: Gumanitarnaya Akademia vooruzhonnykh sil Rossijskoi Federatsii, 1993. Russian military authorities are even thinking now about the introduction of elementary sex education courses in army units, instead of old-style ideological indoctrination. Dr. Kashchenko's dissertation was written at the philosophy chair of the Russian Humanitarian (earlier it was called Political) Military Academy, which was a citadel of the dogmatic, even by Soviet standards, Marxism-Leninism. Tempora mutantur!

23. In October 1992, the trial and execution of 56-year-old Andrei Chikatilo, the "Rostov serial killer," was a national sensation. From 1978 through 1990, Chikatilo, who was university-educated, married, and the father of two children, sadistically killed, raped, and mutilated some 52 children, adolescents, and women, eating parts of the their bodies. Two journalists have written a book about him entitled *Comrade Killer.*

His early childhood coincided with World War II, and he was deeply impressed by the sight of mutilated corpses. He was impotent for most of his marital life. Both his gender identity and his sexual orientation were problematic. During his childhood, and later, in the army and in prison, he was sexually approached by both boys and men, who apparently considered him not as a male but a female. "Finally, I don't know myself to which sex I do belong.

Such a bifurcation," he said. M. Krivich and O. Olgin, "Intervjiu s chelovekom iz kletki," *Moskovskie Novosti*, no. 48, Nov. 29, 1992, p. 21.

24. B. Shostakovsky, "Nuzhen li manyaku vrach?" *Ogonyok*, no. 37 (1993), 26.

25. See, for example, A. A. Gabiani and M. A. Manuilsky, "Tsena 'lyubvi' (obsledoanie prostitutok v Gruzii)," *Sotsiologicheskie issledovania*, no. 6 (1987).

26. For a survey of the Soviet press on prostitution, see A. P. Dyachenko, *Prostitutsiya i prestupnost* (Moscow: Yuridicheskaya literatura, 1991), pp. 71–98.

27. Y. S. Zhikharev, "Na grebne 'seksualnoi' volny," *Prostitutsiya i prestupnost,* pp. 240–44.

28. V. V. Dyukov, "Grimasy rynka 'svobodnoi lyubvi'," *Prostitutsiya i prestupnost,* pp. 118–62.

29. Fyodor Podkolodny, "Zametki na poliakh chastnykh ob'iavlenii: gazeta devchatam zhit pomogaet," *SPID-info*, April 4, 1993, pp. 5–6.

30. Andrei Martyniuk and Leonid Belaga, "Priglashenie v rabstvo, *SPID-info*, July 7, 1993, pp. 24–25.

31. See A. P. Dyachenko, "Voprosy, kotorye zhdut resheniya," *Prostitutsiya i prestupnost,* pp. 162–79.

32. See, for example, *Problemy sotsialnovo kontrolya za prostitutsiei, SPIDom i pornografiej* (Moscow: Akademia MVD RF, 1993). According to the draft of the new criminal code (1994), prostitution per se is not a criminal offence but the compulsory drawing of somebody into prostitution, as well as the organization or maintenance of dens, is to be punishable by heavy fines or imprisonment (articles 244 and 245).

33. K. K. Borisenko and O. K. Loseva, "Zabolevaemost molodyozhi boleznyaimi, peredavaemymi polovym putyom," Planirovanie semyi 4 (1994), 20–22. O. K. Loseva, "Sotsialno-meditsinskie aspekty boleznei, peredavaemykh polovym putyom, u detei i podroskov," Rossiyskkay assotsiatsyia "Planirovanie semyi," Pervaya Natsyonalnaya konferentsya *"Problemy Planirovanie semyi v Rossii" (materialy konferentsii), 7–9 dekabrya 1993, Moskva* (Moscow: "Kvartet," 1994), pp. 89–96.

34. Victor Ilyin, "Vam ne khvatalo ulichnoi nimfetki?" *Venera-press* 9, no. 4 (1992), 2.

35. A. P. Dyachenko, "Seksualnaya kommertsaia: prostitutki i ikh klienty," *Problemy sotsialnovo kontrolya za prostitutsiej, spidom i pornografiej* (Moscow: Adademia MVD RF, 1993), pp. 25–43. These data are surely not statistically valid.

36. Alla Alova, "Zhizn so SPID-om: gotovy li my?" *Ogonyok*, no. 28 (1988), pp, 12–15.

37. Lidya Ivchenko, "Prosveshchennost—poka samoe nadyozhnoe sredstvo borby so SPIDom," *Izvestiya*, Dec. 3, 1993; Hester Abrams, "Health Chiefs Say Russia Keeping AIDS at Bay," *Moscow Tribune*, Dec. 1, 1993; *Izvestiya*, December 1, 1994.

38. Since 1992, Professor Aza Rakhmanova has published a popular scientific quarterly, *SPID, Seks, zdorovie (Aids, Sex, Health)*, which is the best anti-AIDS magazine in Russia; 200,000 copies were sold in 1993. Dr. Rakhmanova has

good contacts in both the St. Petersburg medical community and in various
voluntary organizations, including those serving gays and lesbians.

39. N. A. Chaika, "Navstrechu sobstvennoi pogibeli," *Zdorovje*, no. 3 (1991). The
best general overview of the AIDS prevention situation in Russia is Christo-
pher Williams's "Sex Education and the AIDS Epidemic in the Former Soviet
Union," *Sociology of Health and Illness* 16, no. 1 (1994), 81–102.

## NOTES TO CHAPTER 13: COMING OUT INTO CHAOS

1. "Spravedliva li kara?" *Literaturnaya gazeta*, no. 13 (March 29, 1989).
2. In 1974, I published an article on "The Concept of Friendship in Ancient
Greece" in a scientific journal, *Vestnik drevnei istorii (Ancient History Review)*. I.
S. Kon, "Ponyatie druzhby v Drevnei Gretsii," *Vestnik drevnei istorii*, no. 3
(1974). Of course, the entire editorial board knew full well what Greek pederasty was. Yet two of the women members demanded that there be no mention whatsoever of either the word "pederasty" or the word "homoerotic."
Finally, on the advice of the editor-in-chief, Professor Sergei Utchenko, who
had warmly supported the article, we employed the euphemistic "those specific relationships." It was quite out of the question to speak about "it" in the
popular press even employing veiled terminology. For example, in my interdisciplinary research into friendship, I was really interested in friendship as a
social institution and form of personal relationship, not as a euphemism for
designating forbidden same-sex love. I could not openly discuss the problem
of the homoerotic aspects of same-sex friendship. Thus following the tried
and tested Soviet formula of "Evil to him who evil thinks," I had to leave readers to flounder in riddles. See I. S. Kon, *Druzhba: Etiko-psikhologichesky ocherk*,
3d ed. (Moscow: Politizdat, 1989).
3. Given the scarcity of available information, it is hardly surprising that Soviet
"blues" eagerly seized on every crumb of more or less reliable information
about themselves. With enormous difficulty and risk to themselves, they
sought out the works of Freud and other pertinent foreign literature. When
the first short article on adolescent homosexuality came out in an esoteric
psychiatric collection that had a minuscule circulation (200 copies) (I. S. Kon,
"Psikhologiya podrostkovoi i yunosheskoi gomoseksualnosti," *Diagnostika,
lechenie i profilaktika polovykh rasstroistv [Sbornik trudov]* [Moscow: Moskovsky
Nauchno-issledovatelsky institut psikhiatrii, 1978]), it was immediately
reproduced and circulated. In the French weekly *Gai Pied Hebdo*, I read an
interview with Basil, a 50-year-old St. Petersburger, who tells how hard it was
for him to understand himself and what he felt: "Finally, in 1980, I got hold of
the banned manuscript *Introduction to Sexology* by Igor Kon; it was a revelation! Thanks to that book, I was freed of my prejudices and now, I always
defend gays openly." ("Vous avez quelque chose à dire?" *Gai Pied Hebdo*, October 10, 1991, p. 57.
4. See, for example, G. S. Vasilchenko, ed., *Obshchaya seksopatologiya* (Moscow:

Meditsina, 1977); G. S. Vasilchenko, ed., *Chastnaya seksopatologiya* (Moscow: Meditsina, 1988).

5. G. S. Vasilchenko, ed., *Seksopatologiya*. Spravochnik (Moscow: Meditsina, 1990), pp. 429–36. I should emphasize that Professor Vasilchenko is a most educated and liberal Russian sexopathologist of the older generation who invariably upheld the idea of decriminalizing homosexuality, in contrast to most other Soviet psychiatrists.

6. A. G. Khripkova and D. V. Kolesov, *Malchik—podrostok—yunosha* (Moscow: Prosveshchenie, 1982), pp. 96–100.

7. N. P. Burgasov, "Vystuplenie na kruglom stole: SPID: bolshe voprosov, chem otvetov," *Literaturnaya gazeta*, no. 7 (May 1986), 15.

8. Antonina Galeyeva, "Interview s Ministrom zdravookhraneniya RSFSR A. I. Potopovym," *Literaturnaya gazeta*, no. 7 (August 20, 1986), ll.

9. A handbook on children's sexual psychohygiene contained a section on the "Formation of Sexual Orientation" with information on adolescent and youth homosexuality; this time it was presented as an aspect of normal psychosexual development rather than a "sexual perversion." (D. N. Isayev, V. Y. Kagan, and I. S. Kon, "Formirovanie seksualnoi orientatsii, " D. N. Isayev and V. Y. Kagan, *Psikhohygiene pola u detei. Rukovodstvo dlya vrachei* (Leningrad: Meditsina, 1986), pp. 47–65).

After a number of difficulties , my *Introduction to Sexology* was published in 1988 (see Chapter 6); the chapter on sexual orientation set out contemporary theories on homosexuality, citing historical-anthropological and psychological as well as biological-medical data, and demonstrating, among other things, the harmful and unjust nature of discrimination against homosexuals. The book nonetheless skirted specific issues on the position of homosexuals in the Soviet Union, as well as all legal problems. It left open the question of whether homosexuality was a lifestyle or a disease. Without such gaps and compromises the book would not have seen the light of day. I was able to fill in the gaps only in a new, more popular book *Vkus zapretnovo* ploda (*Tasting Forbidden Fruit*), which was published in 1992.

In the 1989 edition of my book *The Psychology of Early Youth,* which was intended for a wide audience of teachers and parents and was widely available (over 800,000 copies sold), I was able to include a few pages about homosexuality in adolescence and youth, considering it as an aspect or version of normal psychosexual development, rather than a disease or the result of adults' "perverting" adolescents. The book emphasized that "intimate erotic experiences of adolescents and youths are practically beyond the sphere of pedagogical control" and that any tactless intervention by adults may cause the adolescent irreparable harm: "Human problems invariably lie behind sexual problems." (I. S. Kon, *Psikhologiya rannei yunosti. Kniga dlya uchitelya* (Moscow: Prosveshchenie, 1989), pp. 223–28.) That topic had been absolutely impossible to discuss in the three previous editions of the textbook, going back to 1979.

10. M. Shargorodsky and P. Osipov, *Kurs sovetskovo ugolovnovo prava*, part 3 (Leningrad: Izdatelstvo LGU, 1973), p. 656.

11. Knowing full well that my doing so would have no effect other than to cause difficulties for me, I had not intended to become involved in this issue. But at a meeting of sexologists from socialist countries in Leipzig in 1981, Siegfried Schnabl, the eminent sexologist from the German Democratic Republic, suddenly asked which national legal codes had antihomosexual legislation and why. It turned out that only the USSR did so (no Romanian scholars were in attendance). I was abashed and uncomfortable at learning this and the moment I returned I decided against all common sense to tell my superiors and colleagues about the discussion and ask what they thought. Professor Vasilchenko told me that they had tried to raise the issue, but the bigwigs in the Health Ministry had always been against it. And the legal experts said they did not have enough information. Professor Mikhail Piskotin, then the editor of the legal journal *Sovetskoye gosudarstvo i pravo* (*Soviet State and the Law*) suggested that I write an article about it. When I protested that they were unlikely to print it, he said it would at least give them food for thought. I plunged into a study of legislation of other countries and wrote what I considered to be a well-documented article, which was warmly supported by the medical professors Georgi Vasilchenko and Dmitri N. Isayev. But the powerful lawyers took fright and dispatched the article to the administrative department of the Party Central Committee, where they were told the time was "inopportune," so the trail went cold.

12. See, for example, the remarks by the Moscow police officer V. Kachanov in the weekly *Argumenty i fakty*, no. 9 (1990) and my article "Zakon i polovye prestupleniya," no. 12 (1990).

13. Masha Gessen, *The Rights of Lesbians and Gay Men in the Russian Federation: An International Gay and Lesbian Human Rights Commission Report by Masha Gessen. Foreword by Larissa Bogoraz* (San Francisco: IGLHRC, 1994).

14. For more detail, see Gregory M. Herek, "Stigma, Prejudice and Violence against Lesbians and Gay Men," in John C. Gonsiorek and James D. Weinrich, eds., *Homosexuality: Research Implications for Public Policy* (Newbury Park: Sage, 1991), pp. 60–80. G. M. Herek and E. K. Glunt, "Interpersonal Contact and Heterosexuals' Attitudes Toward Gay Men: Results from a National Survey," *Journal of Sex Research* 30, no. 3 (August 1993), 239–44; E. D. Riggle and A. L. Ellis, "Political Tolerance of Homosexuals: The Role of Group Attitudes and Legal Principles," *Journal of Homosexuality* 26, no. 4 (1994), 135–48.

15. Ronald Inglehart, *Culture Shift in Advanced Industrial Society* (Princeton, N.J.: Princeton University Press, 1990), pp. 194–95. For U.S. statistics, see Tom W. Smith, "The Sexual Revolution (The Polls—A Report)," *Public Opinion Quarterly* 54, no. 3 (Fall 1990), 415–21.

16. The degree of homophobia very much depends on the educational level (38% of those with incomplete secondary education favored extermination and 22% of those with college education were in favor) and on age (the most

intolerant were people over 50); it is practically unconnected with gender. Old-age pensioners, housewives, and military personnel exhibit maximum homophobia, while "cooperators" (i.e., small-scale entrepreneurs) were at the other end of the scale (0% for extermination and 25% for help), with scientists, writers, and artists scoring 20% for "extermination" and 34% for "isolation." There is no marked correlation between homophobia and property ownership, although there is with possession of a domestic library: people with a substantial domestic library are much more liberal than those without one. Regionally, homophobia was the strongest in Uzbekistan (54% for extermination), followed by Georgia and Armenia (43% for extermination), with Moscow and Lithuania being the most liberal (26% for extermination). Much depends also on the size of the local community: Muscovites are more tolerant than villagers or residents of remote towns.

17. S. I. Rylyova, "Plyuralizatsia tsennestnovo soznanyia molodyozhi," *Tsennosti sotsialnykh grupp i krizis obshchestva* (Moscow: Institut filosofii, 1991), p. 76

18. L. D. Gudkov, "Fenomen 'prostoty'. O natsionalnom samoosoznanii russkikh," *Chelovek*, no. 1 (1991), 20.

19. Cited with the kind permission of the International Center for Human Values. I'm afraid that in 1994 "Nazis" would be more favorably evaluated.

20. See James L. Gibson and Raymond M. Duch, "Postmaterialism and the Emerging Soviet Democracy." Paper presented at the 1991 Annual Meeting of the American Political Science Association, Washington, D.C.

21. Quoted from Mark Deutsch, "Uzelki na 'Pamyat'," *Ogonyok*, no. 51 (1991), 8.

22. Vladislav Likholitov, "Obnazhonnaya natura—sevodnya i yezhednevno. Interview s Valentinom Pokrovskim," *Megapolis-express*, no. 6 (February 7, 1991), 14. For a response to this publication, see Igor Kon, "Seksmeny: i ne pozor, i ne bolezn," *Megapolis-express*, no. 24 (June 13, 1991), 7.

23. All figures are taken from K. K. Borisenko, *Zabolevaniya, peredavayemye polovym putyom u muzhchin-gomoseksualistov (diagnostika, taktika vedeniya, lechnie). Metodicheskie rekomendatsii* (Moscow, 1990).

24. For more information about the situation of lesbians in the former USSR, see Olga Zhuk, "Lesbijskaya subkultura. Istoricheskie korni lesbiyanstva v byvshem SSR," *Gay, slavyane*, no. 1 (1993), 16–20; M. Gessen, *The Rights of Lesbians and Gay Men* . . . .

25. See Teet Veispak and Udo Parikes, eds., "Sexual Minorities and Society: The Changing Attitudes Toward Homosexuality in 20th Century Europe." Papers presented at the International Conference in Tallinn, May 28–30, 1990 (Tallinn: Institute of History, 1991). See also J. Riordan, "Coming Out: The Gay Community in the USSR," *Slovo* 1, no. 1 (May 1990), 51–65; D. Healey, "The Russian Revolution and the Decriminalization of Homosexuality." Paper presented at the Study Group on the Russian Revolution, April 2–4, 1992.

26. *SPID-info*, no. 12 (1990).

27. See *Ogonyok*, no. 12 (1991), 23.

28. I had to explain to them that Red Square is not a Communist symbol but an

old Russian name (*krasnaya* = both "red" and "beautiful" in Russian). Traditionally, the "red corner," the place where the icons usually stand, is the most honored place in the Russian home. Thus slogans of this type would sound blatantly provocative and offensive to the Russian ear.

29. "Seks-menshchinstva i Mossovet: lyubov i soglasie," *Semya*, no. 47 (1990), 2.

30. V. Andreyev, "Vozvrashchayas k 'Teme'," *Pravda*, May 5, 1991.

31. Igor Kon, "Levshu ne pereuchish," *Argumenty i fakty*, no. 51 (1990).

32. M. Gessen, *The Rights of Lesbians and Gay Men . . .*, pp. 24–33.

33. For a general overview of this problem and its methodological difficulties, see Milton Diamond, "Homosexuality and Bisexuality in Different Populations," *Archives of Sexual Behavior* 22, no. 4 (August 1993), 291–310.

34. V. V. Pokrovsky and G. I. Makarova, "Otsenka otnosheniia podroskov k probleme SPID," *Sovetskoe zdravookhranenie*, no. 6 (1991).

35. Sergei Paramonov, "Noch otrazenij," *Ty*, no. 2 (1993), 60.

36. D. D. Isayev, personal communication. Preliminary data from this survey, based on a sample of 160 gay men, were published in D. D. Isayev, "Survey of the Sexual Behavior of Gay Men in Russia," *ILGA Bulletin*, no. 3 (June–August 1993), 12.

37. The Raduga (Rainbow) Charity Fund was registered in Moscow in July 1992 as "an independent non-profit organization for affirming human values, implementing and protecting the civil, social, and cultural rights and liberties of the individual, according to the principles of charity and toleration, and proffering psychological, medical, legal, and financial help to homosexuals." The fund was associated with the Medicine and Reproduction Treatment and Diagnostic Center, which has been giving medical and psychological aid "to people of a homosexual orientation" since 1990. But Raduga was short-lived, and its ambitious plans have never materialized.

A special telephone hotline for gay men, "Crocus Anti-SPID," was established in Moscow in 1992, sponsored by the Russian-USA company Crocus International; half of the questions people typically asked were related to AIDS, and another half were mainly psychological. The questions were answered by psychologically trained volunteers, yet in 1994 it was closed for lack of money.

Professional consulting services for gays and lesbians were established in St. Petersburg by the psychiatrist Dmitri Isayev, supported jointly by the Bekhterev Psychoneurological Institute, St. Petersburg AIDS-prevention Center and by the Tchaikovsky Foundation. Dr. Isayev not only does an important psychotherapeutic work but also helps young gays to be released from the draft before induction.

According to Russian legislation, homosexuals may be released from military service after a clinical-medical examination. Quite the opposite of the U.S. situation, gay men see this not as discrimination but as a privilege. But to use this privilege may be risky; the disgraceful and dangerous diagnosis, written on one's medical card, goes down with one forever. Because of that, young gay men often preferred to hide their inclinations, despite the difficulties of military service. Now, at least in St. Petersburg, the situation is improving. Army draft officials, when they have to discharge a young man, are no longer interested in him, and they are under no obligation to send his file to his local psychiatry institution, which would stigmatize and victimize him forever. Dr. Isayev, as an established medical expert, may discharge the young man on the basis of psychological testing, without the compulsory two months of intense examination in an overcrowded psychiatric hospital.

38. David Filipov, "From Graft to Gays: Nationalists Alter Attack," *Moscow Times*, August 28, 1993.

39. Mikhail Kirtser, "V Moskve nachalas epidemiia SPIDa sredi gomoseksualistov," *Kommersant-Daily*, no. 221 (November 17, 1993).

40. Mikhail Buyanov, "Patologia ne dolzhna ovladevat massami," *Rossiiskie vesti*, March 17, 1994.

41. B. Irzak, "Zholty, krasny, goluboy—vybirai sebe lyuboi?" *Komsomolskaya pravda*, July 11, 1993.

42. Western mass media often do not understand the Russian situation and the consequences of their sensationalist approach. In 1992, a journalist for Pilot Productions, an Australian-British-Hungarian television company, interviewed two gay men at a Moscow "blue" beach, promising them that the interview would never be shown in Russia or any other ex-Soviet country. Yet in January 1993, this interview was shown on Moscow Ostankino television as part of a program on homosexuality in Russia. The very next day, when one of the gay men who had been interviewed went to his office, he was greeted with "Hello, we saw you on television yesterday." He quit his job that day. The other man had to do the same and was unable to find a new one for five months. His neighbors became openly curious about him and worst of all his much-loved 16-year-old son ceased speaking to him. (*Treugolnik*, no. 4 [January 1994]). The Western correspondents surely know something about privacy. Or was it just that they did not care about these Russians?

43. Andrew Solomon, "Young Russia's Defiant Decadence," *New York Times Magazine*, July 18, 1993, p. 22.

## NOTES TO CONCLUSION

1. Ira L. Reiss, with Harriet M. Reiss, *The End of Shame: Shaping Our Next Sexual Revolution* (Buffalo, N.Y.: Prometheus, 1990).

2. About the moral situation in contemporary Russia, see Igor Kon, "The Moral Culture," in Dmitri Shalin, ed., *Russian Culture at the Crossroads: Paradoxes of Postcommunist Consciousness* (Denver: Westview, 1995), in press.

3. A. G. Vishnevsky, "Na polputi k gorodskomy obshchestvu," *Chelovek*, no.1 (1992), 5–20.

4. See M. Wood and M. Hughes, "The Moral Basis of Moral Reform: Status Discontent versus Culture and Socialization as Explanation of Anti-Pornography Social Movement Adherence," *American Sociological Review* 49, no. 1 (1989), 71–75. Compare with Louis A. Zurcher, Jr., and R. G. Kirkpatrick, *Citizens for Decency: Anti-pornography Crusades as Status Defense* (Austin: University of Texas Press, 1976).

# INDEX